SHATEL
TOM'S TAKE ON 20 UNFORGETTABLE YEARS OF SPORTS
Omaha World-Herald

SHATEL
TOM'S TAKE ON 20 UNFORGETTABLE YEARS OF SPORTS
BY TOM SHATEL

EDITOR
Dan Sullivan

DESIGNER
Christine Zueck

EXECUTIVE EDITOR
Mike Reilly

PRESIDENT AND PUBLISHER
Terry Kroeger

All rights reserved. No part of this book may be reproduced, stored in a retrieval system, or transmitted in any form or by any means, electronic, mechanical, photocopying, recording or otherwise, without prior consent of the publisher, Omaha World-Herald Co. Copyright 2011

Omaha World-Herald Co.
1314 Douglas St.
Omaha, NE 68102

First paperback edition
ISBN: 978-0-615-51155-9
Printed by
Walsworth Publishing Co.
Marceline, MO

ON THE PREVIOUS PAGE:
"Not the victory but the action; Not the goal but the game; In the deed the glory."

The words of Hartley Burr Alexander, a University of Nebraska philosophy professor, were penned nearly 90 years ago for the opening of Memorial Stadium. First engraved on the southwest corner of the original stadium, the inspiring words were added to the facade facing 10th Street.

II • 20 YEARS WITH TOM SHATEL

FOREWORD

IT MAY SEEM odd for a former football coach and a current athletic director to write a foreword for a book written by a sportswriter. Sometimes it is assumed that there is a natural suspicion on the part of coaches and athletic directors of those who are in the media. Having said that, I realize that we do need each other. The media keep the fans informed and interested and, even though at times it may be a little uncomfortable for those of us in coaching, we benefit greatly from the coverage that we receive. On the other hand, sportswriters and other media types have a difficult time getting their message out if they don't have access to the coaches and players.

Tom Shatel joined The Omaha World-Herald in September 1991. Nineteen ninety-one was not my favorite year, not because Tom had joined The World-Herald, but rather because we had a disappointing football season the year before. We ended up 9-3 in 1990 but lost to Colorado, a team that eventually tied for the national championship, and then lost to Oklahoma after Mickey Joseph, our quarterback, was severely injured. We then lost in the Citrus Bowl to Georgia Tech, the team that tied Colorado for the national championship. So our three losses were to very good teams, but I did not feel that we played up to our full potential that year, and 1991 eventually proved to be one of those watershed seasons where major changes were made and the results of those changes proved to be very positive. We started our Unity Council, gave players a stronger voice in setting team policy and goals, and team chemistry began to improve noticeably.

My first impressions of Tom Shatel were mixed. Tom obviously had talent as a writer but had come from a newspaper in Kansas City, where he covered professional and college sports. Metropolitan reporters are often more caustic and opinionated than media types in smaller towns. It struck me that Tom had strong views and was at times fairly critical of what we did in the football program (probably with some reason), so I was a little wary when Tom and I first interacted. As time went on, however, things changed. We both aged, which usually makes people a little more understanding, and Tom eventually married – something that surprised me as I thought he was a confirmed bachelor. Marriage has a way of making us realize that we don't have all the answers and often leads to a more understanding view of human foibles – including losing football games. As the years have gone by, I believe that Tom and I have developed a good relationship. He doesn't always write what I would prefer, but I do know that he will try to be fair, will do his homework and will have a reasonable perspective. His job is to attract readers and sell newspapers and this does not always coincide with the best interests of the Athletic Department but, as I said earlier, we do need each other, and I have a healthy respect for what Tom does.

The job of a sportswriter has gotten more difficult over the years. The Internet has exploded, and bloggers have sprung up all over the place. The problem with Internet postings is that there does not have to be a single kernel of truth in what is written in them. As a result, there are many rumors and false reports that are spread across cyberspace, and often readers of these blogs attribute some truth to

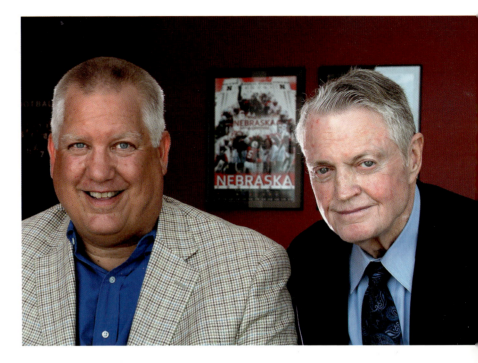

them, as readers are conditioned to believe that what is seen in print is factual. Sportswriters and others in the media often feel pressure to write columns that may be influenced to some degree by what others are writing in their blogs. I'm not saying they buy the Internet columns hook, line and sinker, but I'm sure they are at times influenced by persistent online rumors that fans are reading and talking about. The amount of instant communication has become almost overwhelming when one thinks of the recruiting services, television reports and Internet gossip. We are all engulfed by the flood of information and have a hard time sorting out what is legitimate and what is largely fiction.

I believe that as time has gone on, I have realized that being a writer and having to produce something of interest on a regular basis is more difficult than it looks (kind of like coaching). The desire for information about Nebraska athletics, particularly Nebraska football, seems to be almost insatiable in Nebraska, and to write clearly, accurately and with a flair for what people want to read is a difficult assignment day in and day out, week in and week out, in season and out of season. Tom is one of those writers who do this on a consistent basis.

Tom has interesting insights historically in his book about events that occurred over the past 20 years. I'm sure that the reader will find it interesting to take a trip back in time and to reflect with Tom on events that he has covered.

— **TOM OSBORNE**

TABLE OF CONTENTS

Year	Highlights	Page
1991	RALLYING PAST OU | NU VOLLEYBALL ROLLS ON | JIM HENDRY DEPARTS	2
1992	LANCER MANIA | OLYMPICS | CREIGHTON SOCCER SUCCESS | DEVANEY RETIRES	12
1993	RACERS WIN IT ALL | THE VOICE OF OMAHA | WILD GAME WITH WILDCATS	28
1994	ORANGE BOWL LOSS | NU BASKETBALL TOURNEY TITLE | FRAZIER'S RECOVERY	40
1995	OSBORNE WINS HIS FIRST | CWS STAR POWER | NU VOLLEYBALL CROWN	58
1996	HUSKERS ROUT FLORIDA | BROOK BERRINGER'S DEATH | BIRTH OF UNO HOCKEY	76
1997	DEVANEY'S DEATH | OSBORNE'S RETIREMENT | BIG 12 FOOTBALL CROWN	94
1998	NATIONAL CHAMPIONS AGAIN | SLUGFEST AT CWS | HAYDEN FRY'S RETIREMENT	112
1999	JAYS BACK IN NCAA | BIG 12 BASEBALL TITLE | OSBORNE TO HALL OF FAME	128
2000	NEE'S EXIT | THE RED SEA SWAMPS SOUTH BEND | NU VOLLEYBALL TITLE	144
2001	NEBRASKA TO THE CWS | HUSKER MAGIC BEATS OU | CROUCH'S HEISMAN	158
2002	RED FACES AT ROSE BOWL | TERRELL TAYLOR'S SHOT | STEVE PEDERSON HIRING	172
2003	BO REVIVES BLACKSHIRTS | SOLICH FIRING | DOWNTOWN ARENA OPENS	186
2004	LAMBASTED IN LUBBOCK | BOWL STREAK ENDS | TURNER GILL LEAVES NEBRASKA	198
2005	ANOTHER TITLE FOR JAYS | JOBA BEATS MIAMI | STREAK ENDS AT KU	210
2006	TOUGH LOSS TO LONGHORNS | ZAC TAYLOR HONORED | NU VOLLEYBALL TITLE	224
2007	COTTON BOWL FRUSTRATION | ALTMAN TURNAROUND | OSBORNE RETURNS	236
2008	MICHAEL PHELPS IN OMAHA | BO'S IN CHARGE | ALEX HENERY'S BIG KICK	248
2009	TIGERS WIN CWS | SUH'S HUSKER LEGACY | UNO HIRES TREV ALBERTS	260
2010	NU'S BEST BASKETBALL SEASON | HUSKERS TO BIG TEN | ROSENBLATT'S FINALE	270
2011	MAVS' DIVISION I MOVE | NEW BALLPARKS OPEN | OSBORNE'S NEW LEGACY	282

INTRODUCTION

MY NAME'S TOM. I'm from Omaha, Nebraska.

There's something I never thought I would ever say, or type. Certainly not 20 years ago, when I arrived at The World-Herald with a dream and an attitude, but no clue as to what I was getting myself into.

Twenty years? Nebraska had lost to Georgia Tech in the Citrus Bowl, and Tom Osborne stood at a crossroads. Creighton had just played in the College World Series. Ak-Sar-Ben was in full gallop. As I drove into downtown Omaha in my maroon Honda Accord, I asked myself, "Where's downtown?"

I pulled up next to a small brown building that looked like a post office. On the side were the words "World-Herald." I thought, "You've got to be kidding me." My next thought: "I don't think I'll be spending the rest of my life here."

Many of you appeared to agree and were even eager to help in my career advancement. If I had a dollar for every time a reader said or wrote, "Why don't you go back to Missouri?" I'd have a condo on a golf course at the Lake of the Ozarks.

It's been 20 years. And I'm still here. Here at home.

For some, home is wherever they currently happen to be standing. When someone asked where I was from, I'd always say Kansas City. That's where I lived the longest, from 1970 to 1989. But my time in Omaha has eclipsed that now. I'm an Omahan, and a Nebraskan, though I probably have known that for a long time.

How long? The revelation may have come to me somewhere during my countless drives to Lincoln and Memorial Stadium, which was always my favorite place to spend a college football weekend when I covered the Big Eight. Or on a lazy autumn afternoon, sitting in the stands at Caniglia Field watching UNO football practice.

Talking to Bruce Rasmussen. Watching thousands pile into Ak-Sar-Ben Coliseum on a winter night and turn an Omaha Lancers game into a big deal. Going to the Bird Cage at Creighton Prep. Going to any high school football game on a Friday night. Playing golf at Miracle Hill. Walking up and down 13th Street during the College World Series.

Maybe it was when I married a Valley girl and became the official luckiest guy in the world. Or during the birth of my three beautiful girls. My four girls are from Nebraska. I must be, too.

Being recognized on the street or while standing in line for a hot dog at the Devaney Center. That still blows me away, that people know me. Do the sports columnists in St. Louis or Los Angeles get recognized at the store? I don't know. But there's a small-town feel to the city of Omaha, and the entire state of Nebraska, that absolutely appeals to me. That surprised the heck out of me. I didn't see that one coming.

I've learned a lot about myself in 20 years in Omaha and Nebraska. Since I was 13, I wanted to be Oscar Madison. I wanted to be a sports columnist. I used to read columns in the Sporting News, then practice typing them. I read all the big city papers every day at the journalism school library at Mizzou. I wanted to be those guys. I wanted to be the columnist at the Washington Post or L.A. Times or Kansas City Star, where my hero, Joe McGuff, wrote so eloquently. But even more than writing, McGuff was Kansas City. He helped bring the Royals to town. He got things done. I wanted to do that.

I've found what I wanted here, at home, in Omaha and in Nebraska. Some say I've had an impact here. I don't know about that. But I've enjoyed chronicling the transformation of this city as a sports town, and sports player, and it's been cool that many things I wrote about and pushed for years ago have come to fruition.

This book is about that transformation. It's about the history that has happened here, over and over, and keeps happening. Think about it. We've seen Nebraska football rise to unprecedented heights — three national titles in four years — and fall down and climb up again. We've seen Creighton basketball's greatest run. We've seen majestic icons like Ak-Sar-Ben and Rosenblatt Stadium go away and shiny new icons appear. UNO became a hockey school, but lost football and wrestling. And now we're a regular on the Olympic swimming circuit and in the NCAA hoops rotation.

Has there ever been a 20-year period of sports like this in Nebraska? I don't know. I just got here 20 years ago.

But this book is also about the transformation of a sportswriter, too. When I began, back in the stone age of 1991 and 1992, Rush Limbaugh was just warming up. All media started getting loud, to draw attention. I fell into that trap. Several of my column subjects paid the price. Yes, I'm talking about you, Mike Grant. You, too, Scott Frost.

Funny how things go. The world today is a meaner place. Sports media and sports have become screamers. Following sports has gotten personal. But somewhere along the way, I made a U-turn. Somewhere, I discovered that's not who I am, not who I want to be. Somehow, I figured out that I wanted to also give coaches and players a break, write perspective, talk about the characters and have some fun. These are games, right?

It's been said that I became "soft" about the time I became a husband and a father. There might be some truth to that. But I'm going to give Omaha, and Nebraska, most of the credit. This is an old-school world we live in here. I've always said Nebraska football was like a show on "TV Land," something from the past – hidden, almost in a bubble, away from the cold, cruel sports world. There's perspective here. There are morals. Omaha, and Nebraska, have completely rubbed off on me.

It may have actually hit me a few years ago, when I took an L.A. Times columnist to task for calling Nebraskans a bunch of hicks. Once upon a time, I wanted to be that big-city smart-aleck. Now here I was, writing about being proud to be a hick. A lot can happen in 20 years. Now, when they ask me where I grew up, I say, "Omaha, Nebraska."

Tom Shatel

TIE GAME WITH THE BUFFS | NU BIG EIGHT FOOTBALL TITLE | NU BIG EIGHT VOLLEYBALL TITLE

1991

> "I remember being here, at least 20 years ago, talking to Cip (Joe Cipriano) about a cigarette tax (to build an arena). It was an original thought. So original that you joked about it. Now, I'm walking out and seeing this building, built on this joke."
>
> — AL MCGUIRE, FORMER MARQUETTE COACH, TALKING ABOUT THE DEVANEY CENTER

Ground Rules for Column: There Are None

There are no rules. Except to have fun. Remember, this isn't Operation Desert Storm. These are just games. Remember that. And remember that we will hardly agree on anything. But we will have something in common: the feeling of anticipation this time of year, the feeling of excitement on Saturday mornings. Memorial Stadium, that beautiful, old palace, still is my favorite college stadium. I can recite (with eyes closed) the engraved words on the one corner that send chills down my spine: "Not the victory but the action; not the goal but the game; in the deed the glory." Certainly, words for Husker fans to live by in recent years. This must be the good life.

— **FIRST COLUMN, SEPT. 1, 1991**

Every rivalry has its stereotypes. Iowa graduates the lawyers and doctors; Iowa State, the engineers and aggies. This is the corporation vs. the small company, the government taking on the farmer. Iowa was going to Rose Bowls before Iowa State reached 15,000 students. So Iowa has been The School while Iowa Staters have had The Complex, even though in the late '70s a Des Moines Register poll showed more Iowa State fans in the state. "Take the feelings Nebraskans have for Oklahoma and double or triple that here for Iowa," said Matt Rehberg, an ISU defensive tackle from Millard South High School. "They are the rich kids who get all the breaks, and we are struggling just to get to the top."

One loudmouth acquaintance in Colorado asked me, "Why did you move to Omaha?" Easy. Give me Nebraska, where honest, hard-working and genuine people live a simple life and support a single cause. Nebraska football, win or lose, is the lifeblood of an honorable people. It was there before Bill McCartney rejuvenated Colorado, and it will be there after McCartney leaves. That's the thing he can't copy from his Big Red blueprint. The longevity. The support. And the special bond between a program and people that will transcend the 20th century and this "rivalry."

2 • 20 YEARS WITH TOM SHATEL

CREIGHTON BASEBALL COACH JIM HENDRY'S DEPARTURE | CHANGING COLLEGE FOOTBALL SCENE

Rodie, the mascot of the Omaha Racers, took desperate measures to wake a slumbering crowd at Ak-Sar-Ben. Taking hold of one of the large plastic trash containers in the walkways, Rodie began pounding the trash can up and down in order to revive a clapping chant. Needless to say, it didn't work. If the Racers die in Omaha, that will be the lasting image: a blue and white horse with kneepads and sneakers pounding a trash can to no avail.

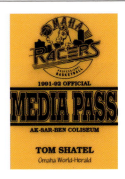

Sitting in the empty bleachers at Ownby Stadium in Dallas after a recent practice, SMU graduate assistant Turner Gill's mind was stuck on the present, which included feeding his wife and new daughter and beating Texas Tech. In that order. But if you prod long enough, the words spill out of the articulate Gill. Remember, Gill is a quarterback second and a Tom Osborne disciple first.

"People are saying to win the big ballgame you have to throw," Gill said. "I don't believe it because I played there and we were able to win running. You say we weren't able to win the big ballgame against Miami or whatever, but it wasn't because we didn't throw the football. We could run against anybody. Why change to be changing? "Just because Nebraska is going to throw the football doesn't mean a national championship. A lot of people forget about what has happened over the last 20 years. You want to take that and just throw it away, I guess. I would hate to see the fans there go through a losing season, how they would react. They would really stop and appreciate what has happened." Gill is intrigued by SMU's run-and-shoot offense. "It's something that is completely opposite as far as what I played in at Nebraska," Gill said. "We're throwing first, running second. Hopefully, down the road, I'd like to be a head football coach and I can see both sides and put my own thing together." Intriguing. But the vision is blurry. "I have got to get a full-time assistant's job first," Gill said, laughing.

Eric Piatkowski's biggest critic — Eric Piatkowski — was reviewing his latest stat line when, suddenly, it hit him like a ton of . . . boards. Twenty-three points. Two 3-pointers. Seven of nine free throws. Two assists. One block. One steal and . . . "FIFTEEN REBOUNDS?!" Piatkowski said. "Ooooh. I like that." Around the Nee-braska locker room, after the Eastern Washington game, not everyone was buying it. "You had 15 rebounds?" cried center Derrick Chandler. "They must have been getting my stats mixed up."

NOVEMBER 4, 1991 • NEBRASKA FOOTBALL

A Waiting Game in Boulder

BOULDER, COLO.

WAITING. THAT'S ALL you or Nebraska kicker Byron Bennett could do in the frost-freezer known as Folsom Field.

Waiting for Nebraska to find a way to lose. After all, it was the fourth quarter. The Huskers were down 19-12. Then they tied it.

Waiting for Bennett's frigid foot to win it. Colorado Coach Bill McCartney literally froze Bennett with three consecutive timeouts with four seconds left and Bennett facing a game-winning 41-yard field goal. They blocked it.

The 19-19 tie was a small victory, really. Yet so big for answering the doubting Thomases out there — this one included — who kept waiting for you-know-what. That fourth-quarter choke thing.

And now we are waiting. Presumably, if the Huskers win their last three, they will stay ranked above Colorado. Presumably, then, they will go to the Orange Bowl for the first time since 1988.

We'll just have to wait.

Nebraska's 19-19 tie with Colorado in Boulder left the two teams tied for the Big Eight lead.

2011 INSIGHT *I had covered the Colorado-Nebraska rivalry from afar, from Kansas City, the previous five years before this game. I had found it kind of amusing. Once I got inside it, it was pretty intense. I remember all the Nebraska jokes on Denver radio on this trip and thinking they were pretty sophomoric. Something like a foot of snow fell in Boulder before this game, and the Huskers barely made it there. I wrote a column defending Nebraskans the night before the game. When I made it back to Omaha, I remember someone mentioning that column on a sports talk show, and someone saying, "This Missouri guy might be all right."*

NOVEMBER 30, 1991 • NEBRASKA FOOTBALL

Nebraska tight end Johnny Mitchell caught seven passes for 137 yards in the Huskers' 19-14 win over Oklahoma.

Gibbs Helps NU Wake Up

IT WAS RAINING cats and demons. The Huskers were down, 14-3, and the outlook was as bleak as the weather. This wasn't just a rerun. This was an ugly rerun.

And, sure, you had seen it before. Felt it before. When Oklahoma got up two touchdowns early and Nebraska could do no right, the air was sucked right out of depressed Memorial Stadium.

You knew how this script ended but, with the prospect of a Gator Bowl date with Virginia staring at Nebraska, this was somehow worse. Losing like this on the national tube — before the national dart-throwers — was all the Oklahoma, Colorado, Miami, Florida State and Georgia Tech losses put together.

And then it happened. Gary Gibbs to the rescue.

You don't normally expect an Oklahoma head coach to post bail for a Nebraska team. But when Gibbs had the choice to open the second half, he elected to kick off rather than taking the ball — and the wind for the fourth quarter — and to try to bury the Huskers while the burying was good.

Nebraska woke up. Nebraska got emotional. Nebraska got efficient. All in the second half. All before a national audience.

There had been comebacks this year to beat Kansas State and Kansas and tie Colorado. But this was different. This was for the Orange Bowl.

Mission accomplished, 19-14. And Nebraska has a wondrous second half — in which it shoved the ball and a reputation down its demons' throats — to thank for it.

Not to mention Gibbs.

"That turned out to be a big mistake," said Husker left guard Erik Wiegert. "That was the turning point. We couldn't believe it. We got all fired up. We were going to make them pay for it."

20 YEARS WITH TOM SHATEL • 5

DECEMBER 2, 1991 • NEBRASKA VOLLEYBALL

Terry Pettit, here with Nancy Meendering, coached the Huskers to 694 volleyball victories and a national championship in 1995 before retiring in 1999.

This Big Red Keeps Rolling

HO-HUM, ANOTHER Big Eight championship. The Nebraska dynasty rolls on, but one question still lingers. Can the coach win the Big One?

Just kidding, Terry.

No, we're not talking about you, Tom Osborne. We're talking about the other Big Red machine, the one that rolls quietly through the fall months, methodically in the autumn shadow of football. Yes, volleyball.

Perhaps you already know Terry Pettit, the creator and keeper of Nebraska's volleyball tradition. And perhaps some introductions are in order. Last week, as the 15th-year Nebraska volleyball coach spoke at the weekly Extra Point luncheon, he was introduced as "Gary."

Pettit, smooth and charismatic, took it in stride and asked the crowd, "If I understand this right, I talk about next week's opponent and you complain about the defense, right?"

Like all NU coaches, Pettit understands his role as a supplement to Nebraska's football mentality. But few have perfected the role like Pettit.

Last weekend was another example. While the state was celebrating Nebraska's return to the Orange Bowl, Pettit and his team were in Omaha's Civic Auditorium, polishing off another Big Eight tournament in straight games. The 15-8, 15-7, 15-4 victory over Colorado gave Nebraska its 15th conference tournament title in 16 years.

And it didn't really matter. Like the postseason men's basketball tournament, it's just a device to settle the automatic bid for the NCAA tournament. That matters.

Pettit won't say it, but the Huskers have nothing left to prove in the Big Eight. They are a national team now.

"It's a reflection of what has happened in the last 15 years in college sports," Pettit said. "The success and growth of the NCAA basketball tournament changed the emphasis of doing well at the conference level to doing well nationally. That has filtered into other sports."

This month the game is volleyball. The sights are set for the top, and the stakes are high: national exposure to continue bringing in the top players and feeding the monster. Funny, but Pettit says his "biggest asset is Nebraska football" because of the automatic identity it brings with recruits.

Gary, er, Terry, and his girls have become a pretty valuable asset themselves.

DECEMBER 18, 1991 • CREIGHTON BASEBALL

Jim Hendry, now the general manager of the Chicago Cubs, led Creighton in 1991 to its only College World Series appearance.

Hendry Made the Easy Choice

TEARS WELLED IN Jim Hendry's blue eyes. His smooth voice cracked. Begrudgingly and painfully, before a press conference that included Hendry's own players, a Creighton University era came to an end.

This, understand, was a no-brainer. After seven years and one College World Series appearance, Hendry is leaving his Creighton baseball program for the perfect job with the Florida Marlins.

Perfect because Hendry knows his superiors. Perfect because they are going to let Hendry move from scouting to player personnel to instructing, if he so chooses. Perfect for a 35-year-old south Floridian who always dreamed of wearing a big-league uniform, even if it includes a tie.

But never before has such a no-brainer been so hard to execute. We can only guess how much Hendry tossed and turned, hemmed and hawed, before deciding for sure. He said, "I want the people of Omaha to know that in no way was I looking to leave Creighton after our success."

There was no job or amount of money, he said, that Creighton could have offered to change his mind.

"I would have been insulted if they had," Hendry said. "If I was meant to be the A.D., I would have gotten the job already.

"Ten years from now, you can always go back and be a college athletic director. But you can't get a baseball job like this. So, I'll make my best run."

The hardest easy run ever made.

2011 INSIGHT *I never got to cover Jim Hendry and Creighton. I missed that fairy tale by three months. But in the few months that I came to know Hendry before he left, I understood what the fuss was all about. Nobody knew it at the time, but this was a historic moment for Creighton baseball, because it's never been the same since Hendry left.*

20 YEARS WITH TOM SHATEL • 7

DECEMBER 29, 1991 • NEBRASKA FOOTBALL

Even After 19 Years, Osborne Wonders if Job Safe

THE HEAD COACH sat stewing in his hotel suite last Jan. 1, devastated by his team's performance in that day's bowl game. He was embarrassed. Angry. He contemplated quitting.

"It went through my mind," he said. "Here you are . . . (working hard), and people don't realize that to maintain a program at this level is not as easy as you think."

The speaker was not your favorite (?) football coach, Dr. Tom Osborne. The man on the brink of chucking it was none other than University of Miami Coach Dennis Erickson.

Surprised? Don't be. Though Osborne and Erickson seem worlds apart, they have more in common than meets the critic's eye.

Osborne is the unassuming legend-at-large in Nebraska. Erickson is the hottest college coaching commodity at the hottest college program. Osborne has labored over 19 seasons without a national title. Erickson fell into one his first year at Miami.

The connection? The sighs of relief.

Osborne and Erickson are enjoying the sweet fruits of victory and contentment. After one year of heavy criticism and soul-searching, they meet in the Orange Bowl to top a year when coaching became fun again. For now.

Osborne and Erickson come out of 1991 leaning in different directions. Erickson is a candidate for every job in the NFL except Commissioner Paul Tagliabue's, yet he insisted again that he has learned to handle the pressure and never wants to leave Miami. Period.

Osborne, meanwhile, revealed that he turned down a college feeler last week — reportedly Minnesota — but hinted that, should he tire of the criticism, he might look harder next time.

"I'm a native Nebraskan," Osborne said. "I like the state. (But) I don't think the situation is such that it's overly comfortable. In athletics you never say never. But I do plan to keep my commitments."

The discussion came up in the wake of Erickson being pestered by rumors of his leaving Miami. Osborne said he hadn't heard about an NFL opening since the mid-1980s, when Houston and Seattle contacted him.

In fact, Osborne, who checked out a Colorado offer amid criticism in 1978, said in the last 10 years he has told Ohio State, USC, Arkansas, LSU and Auburn: Thanks, but no thanks.

But after getting hammered at home and abroad like never before, Osborne said for the first time he wondered whether even he was safe.

"I got a call last week from a school that was pretty persistent," Osborne said. "As I told them, the biggest problem I have is I told the players I recruited that I would try to be there.

"The only reason that would change is if the situation became intolerable or people didn't want me around. The last year or so was the first time there had been some talk in that direction."

Osborne said one thing that has kept him at Nebraska is trying to maintain a loyalty he didn't see elsewhere in the country. Yet you have to believe Osborne has a pretty huge comfort zone after 30 seasons in Lincoln.

"I don't perceive it that way," Osborne said. "In coaching you are never more than one year from being fired. Maybe I have more security than I think."

Osborne seemingly picked himself off the ground this year. He opened up his offense. He helped create a players' unity council, some gripes were aired, and a feeling of togetherness — unlike that of recent years — came over the team. And he is back in the Orange Bowl, playing the game every coach wants to play: against the No. 1 team in the country.

He called this year's team the most enjoyable one he had coached.

Yet he knows the four-game bowl losing

Tom Osborne had lost four straight bowl games as he looked ahead to the 1992 Orange Bowl against Miami. The bowl losing streak eventually reached seven before ending with a 24-17 victory over the Hurricanes in the 1995 Orange Bowl.

streak is becoming an albatross. And it wouldn't be a Tom Osborne press conference if a national news media type didn't ask whether he craves a national championship.

Without hesitation, Osborne said he has had a "couple of teams" that were worthy of national championships and, frankly, that meant as much to him as "getting the trophy."

"I've been at it 19 years, and I haven't brought the trophy home," Osborne said. "Some people would like somebody else to try it, and some would like to go along with me a little longer. Some people look at Bobby Bowden because he's beaten us a couple times, but he hasn't brought home the trophy, and he's had good teams.

"If we beat Miami, we would not win it, but we would be at that level. As far as I'm concerned, that's what it's all about."

Next year, Bob Devaney will step down as athletic director. Will Osborne quit coaching? He said that he had no plans "at this time" to become A.D. and still wants to coach another "five or six years."

But will it be at Nebraska? More than likely, yes. Is Osborne pulling your chain, or is a man who has won the right way for 19 years tired of the criticism? He shouldn't be above getting it. But he also should have the right to walk away should he so choose.

That's the point Osborne seemed to bring up. "It's been an enjoyable year," Osborne said. He quickly added, "Last year drilled some things in my head about how things really are. You can go along for years getting lulled to sleep. My eyes are wide open now."

That's coaching. Whether you're fishing in the Platte River or Biscayne Bay, it goes with the territory.

"It's part of the profession," Osborne said. "You take a battering. All you can do is have your own philosophy and do things the right way. Every coach has to count the cost and wonder if the battering is worth it."

Osborne diagrams a play for quarterback Keithen McCant, left, and running back Derek Brown.

2011 INSIGHT *A generation of Nebraskans knows Tom Osborne as an icon, our all-knowing Yoda. They might be interested in this column. In 1991, Osborne was the guy who couldn't win a bowl game, couldn't beat Miami or Florida State. He hadn't even beaten Colorado since 1988. Plus, his team had quit on him the year before. Osborne turned down Ohio State and USC? My, how history – and this book – would have been different.*

TOM'S TAKE — REFLECTIONS ON

Big Eight Is Getting Squeezed in the New Bowl Alliance

PLAIN AND SIMPLE, it's a whole new bowl game. There was a time the Big Eight runner-up could lose the Oklahoma-Nebraska game and still get some prime time on Jan. 1 in the Fiesta, Sugar or Cotton Bowl. Those days are gone.

This year, if nothing else, has shown us that the Big Eight no longer carries that automatic clout. OK, there was that dreaded Colorado-Nebraska tie. The Big Eight has had two teams playing on Jan. 1 every year since 1983. A freak year, you say.

Maybe. But fans of the Big Eight football axis no longer have that Jan. 1 safety net to fall back on.

The new Bowl Alliance Committee, also known as the Big Squeeze, includes the Orange, Cotton, Sugar and Fiesta Bowls. That's eight spots for five conferences — Big Eight, Big East, SEC, SWC and ACC — and Notre Dame. That's six teams going into eight spots. And that's two spots left for five runners-up.

"It's a concern to us, naturally," Nebraska coach Tom Osborne said. "The alliance and TV sets are going to control a lot of where you go."

How many years can Osborne or Oklahoma's Gary Gibbs go without a Jan. 1 date and not feel some heat?

"We have something of a mind-set regarding New Year's Day bowls," said OU Athletic Director Donnie Duncan. "There are a number of bowls that offer the same things that are not on that day."

In other words, coaches and A.D.s everywhere — not just Big Eight — soon will be asking their fans to throw away years of mind-set. The brainwashing will begin next year. Repeat after me: Jacksonville is wonderful this time of year. Jacksonville is . . . .

— NOVEMBER 20, 1991

> "As far as the fans, supporters, alumni, etc., Texas is the game that is the most important."
>
> — FORMER OKLAHOMA COACH BUD WILKINSON

10 • 20 YEARS WITH TOM SHATEL

THE CHANGING SPORTS LANDSCAPE 1991

Conference Ties Are Settled, but It's Only Temporary

THE WATERS ARE calm now. There has been no talk of conference-hopping since the summer of 1990, when Arkansas fled to the Southeastern Conference. The Big Ten can't expand to a 12th team for at least two more years.

But it doesn't take Bob Dylan to figure out that the times are a changin'.

There is talk that Oklahoma could be the next addition to the SEC conglomerate. Or to the Southwest Conference, which would make more sense because the Sooners recruit Texas and favor the SWC revenue-sharing policy over the Big Eight policies that feel about as comfortable as a noose around OU's neck.

All heck could break loose in 1995 when the College Football Association television deal expires and the SEC, as expected, cuts its own conference TV deal. Schools like Texas, Texas A&M and Oklahoma want to make sure they aren't out on the street carrying excess baggage like TCU and Iowa State.

While Texas, OU and A&M are heavily involved in behind-the-scenes talk, Nebraska's name never comes up. Are the Huskers asleep at the wheel?

No. Dual legends Bob Devaney and Tom Osborne may not be involved in backroom dealings, but they are leery of what is going on around them.

"I have no idea what Oklahoma's plans are," Osborne said. "It's all speculation. But I think a lot of people are uneasy."

Osborne said he can see "four or five major (TV) conferences" when the CFA package expires in 1995. But will OU and Nebraska be together in that? Only OU knows.

"The problem is, nobody will come out and tell you what they are thinking," Osborne said. "Nobody seems to look at loyalties anymore. It's just kind of discouraging."

— DECEMBER 6, 1991

> "Oklahoma talks big about what they could do outside the Big Eight, but they're still here."
>
> — NEBRASKA ATHLETIC DIRECTOR BOB DEVANEY

Nebraska Athletic Director Bob Devaney, shown with men's gymnastics coach Francis Allen, was cautiously navigating the shifting college sports scene in the early 1990s. Devaney retired in 1993.

BOWL LOSS TO MIAMI | LANCER MANIA | CWS DOWNPOUR | HOMETOWN HERO TOM SIECKMANN

1992

"Bill and I are good friends. I don't understand everything he does, but he has a lot of good qualities, and I appreciate the work he does with young people. If saying things and telling Nebraska jokes helps his team win, it doesn't bother me."

— TOM OSBORNE ON COLORADO COACH BILL MCCARTNEY

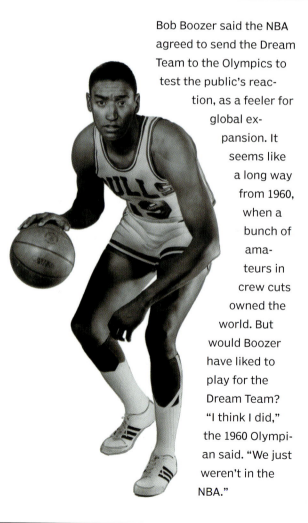

Bob Boozer said the NBA agreed to send the Dream Team to the Olympics to test the public's reaction, as a feeler for global expansion. It seems like a long way from 1960, when a bunch of amateurs in crew cuts owned the world. But would Boozer have liked to play for the Dream Team? "I think I did," the 1960 Olympian said. "We just weren't in the NBA."

▶ **MEMO:** To Tom Osborne, Bobby Bowden, Bill Walsh and Lou Holtz.

▶ **RE:** Directions to the next great college quarterback.

▶ **GENTLEMEN:** Take Interstate 80, get off on exit 300 and head south. Go over two Platte River bridges. Loop around a 90-degree curve to the left. Get to another curve, only head left instead down a gravel road for about a half-mile. The Frost house sits by itself, on the right. Finding Scott Frost figures to be easier than landing him.

Jack Pierce says this really happened. Pierce, Nebraska's off-campus recruiting coordinator, said he and assistant coach Tony Samuel were talking to recruiting analyst Max Emfinger a few years ago. The topic turned to a high school player on Nebraska's list. "We mentioned that he was someone we really liked," Pierce said. "All of a sudden, Max went to his chart and moved the kid all the way to the top of his position in the top 100." Presto. This is just something to keep in mind when Johnny B. Goode signs away his soul to universities all across the country: Give Johnny a break.

How bad was it? With 14 minutes left, Connecticut was ahead 71-46 and a first-round NCAA men's tournament game between eighth and ninth seeds had turned into a hopeless game of garbage time. Nebraska was throwing up most of the garbage. (NU eventually lost 86-65.)

12 • 20 YEARS WITH TOM SHATEL

THE OLYMPICS IN BARCELONA | CREIGHTON SOCCER SUCCESS | BOB DEVANEY'S RETIREMENT

The "N" on the Husker helmet stands for "nice." These are the most accommodating and classiest fans in the country, which are two words Buff Belchers don't comprehend.

Stephanie Thater is the Patrick Ewing of her sport, gliding up and down the net, blocking kills and unleashing her white heat. If there were a pro volleyball league with a draft, Thater might be the No. 1 pick. But there isn't, and that's OK. Thater's post-graduation goals include a shot at the U.S. national team and maybe a few gigs in pro beach volleyball, but none of the above is lucrative enough to pay the bills. Thater's degree in psychology will be her self-fulfilling validation of success at NU, not whether she turns pro.

Omaha obviously has made an impression on Martina Navratilova, who squeezed in an exhibition here between one in Columbus, Ohio, and a trip to Chicago for a tournament. "It's nice now because I feel like the home team," said Navratilova, who played exhibitions with Pam Shriver and Warren Buffett. "It's easier to play places like here because you know they don't get to see this. But it does add pressure." It was about education: Shriver gave a clinic for boys and girls from Boys Town and Boys Clubs in Omaha. It was about money: The players signed pictures and tennis rackets at a VIP party for the various sponsors of the $150,000 event. A check for $8,397 was given to the American Heart Association of Omaha.

20 YEARS WITH TOM SHATEL • 13

JANUARY 3, 1992 • NEBRASKA FOOTBALL

Give Osborne Time to Heal

MIAMI, FLA.

MAYBE IT WILL be next June. Maybe Tom Osborne will be sitting in his favorite boat on his favorite lake in Nebraska before he will be able to smile again. Maybe, by then, he will have forgotten the 22-0 loss in the Orange Bowl. You have to wonder.

The day after his Cornhuskers got folded, spindled and mutilated by No. 1-ranked Miami on a mission, Osborne looked like a man who hadn't slept many winks, if any. Then again, after what he had just been through, who could blame him?

There have been five bowl losses in a row now, and they only get harder to take for Osborne, who confesses his bowl hangover requires slow healing.

"I don't feel very good for a long time," Osborne said. "I guess I'm crazy, but I kind of hypnotized myself into thinking we could win this game."

Even for the most optimistic Husker fans, the aftershock from this one was not in the actual loss. It was how the blow was delivered. Like a hammer.

Nebraska played the game as if it were lost, like a mouse inside a maze. Everywhere Keithen McCant or Derek Brown turned, Hurricanes pounced like cats. It was a long, painful night in the dentist's chair. The Miami defense's total destruction of Nebraska's running machine was the reason Osborne was so down the morning after NU was shut out for the second time in his 19 years as a head coach.

Tom Osborne suffered through his fifth straight bowl loss in the 1992 Orange Bowl.

Oh, yes, and in a couple of hours he had to go talk to recruits in Fort Lauderdale. How do you suppose that conversation went?

"I don't know what impact it will have on recruiting," Osborne said. "It can't help. We have 15 or 16 commitments right now, and I don't know how many might change. Young people are impressionable. This thing didn't help any."

Washington coach Don James, one of the few coaching dinosaurs left, was awarded his first national championship this week. James changed. Osborne may have to, too. And amid the rubble, he hinted that he knew how.

"If people are upset with me," Osborne said, "they should be unhappy with the way I recruit."

Soon, he would have to go explain the unexplainable to Florida recruits.

Are we having fun yet?

"I don't have fun on the bowl trips that we win," Osborne said. "If you want to have fun, wait until recruiting is over."

Maybe that will be June in that boat on the lake. You have to wonder.

2011 INSIGHT *This was one of my all-time favorite moments at The World-Herald. We didn't know it at the time, but we were witnessing a crossroads of Nebraska football history. The morning after every bowl game, Tom Osborne met the Nebraska media at the team hotel before going home. It was just three of us back then. I'll never forget how low Osborne was. He was really despondent after losing to Miami yet again in the Orange Bowl and looking overmatched. When we were finished talking, Osborne said he was driving up to some town in Florida to see a recruit. I found out later the kid's name was Tommie Frazier.*

Lancer Aura Grips Omaha

YOU HAD TO be there. There is no other way to explain the phenomenon of Omaha Lancers hockey. Yes, phenomenon.

From the rowdy "Red Ice Rooters" to the mass of groupies waiting outside a locker room door for 16- to 19-year-old hockey players. And the older crowd, the legacy of a time when Knights lived in Omaha, who see more than mere teenage bodies gliding along the ice. They see hockey.

You had to be there. They come in cult fashion, a parade of orange and black. Girlfriends in oversized hockey jerseys, grandfathers in black Lancer jackets. They march to the tune of their own drum. Don't try to explain.

Bud Kerns, an Omahan in Lancer wear, stood outside Ak-Sar-Ben's west ticket gate before a game. He had one finger raised in the air, as in "need one ticket."

Why? "It's hockey," said Kerns, in a way that suggests you need not ask further. "I think this is a surprisingly big hockey town."

Why? "Omaha has always been a hockey town," said Jerry Huelshoist of La Vista. "Hockey is a good, exciting sport. This is the only exposure Omaha gets to hockey. And it is a very reasonable place to bring a family."

Why? "Hockey is a lot more exciting than other sports," said Jack Spencer of Omaha. "I only missed one game all of last year, because my mother got married. I gave her heck for it."

Why? "Hockey is unique here, whereas there are a lot of places to watch basketball," said Ron Grear of Omaha. "I watched the Omaha Knights since 1955. There's not much difference here. It's a different level, but hockey is hockey. It's a good game, though I never played it."

Some cities are magnetic to a sport. Denver is a football town. Kansas City, baseball. For whatever reason, the Lancers have struck a chord with Omaha. For whatever reason, there is a hockey mentality here. Don't try to explain.

Which brings us to the beer stand. No question, drinking is part of the appeal of the Lancers games. And Blues games in St. Louis, Blackhawks in Chicago and Rangers in New York. Etc. Hockey and beer go together.

I expected to see a drunken brawl at my first Lancers' game. There was nothing of the kind. The atmosphere was electric and orderly. The beer lines were virtually nil during the game; people didn't want to miss anything.

The people-go-to-drink theory is part of the Lancers' aura. But, let's face it, if you want to drink, there are several nice establishments in Omaha that don't charge Lancer prices.

And though fisticuffs have been known to occur once in a while at a Lancers game, the only fists thrown by the crowd of 5,908 came during the Arsenio Hall "Dog Pound" cheer after a goal.

You had to be there. Still, there is enough contact — the usual hard-checking and shoving — to lure what Lancers president Ted Baer calls the "football mentality."

And they do their share of promotional gimmicks, though they probably don't have to. Hockey is hockey.

"This is a great hockey town," Baer said.

The Lancers, who made national headlines by going 0-48 in their inaugural 1986-87 season, were regularly selling out the Ak-Sar-Ben Coliseum in the 1990s.

JUNE 6, 1992 • COLLEGE WORLD SERIES

TV Deal Rained on Ron Fraser's Parade

IT STARTED FRIDAY night as a farce, in the ridiculous rain, with University of Miami players shifting helplessly on their top step, with Ron Fraser's team getting outhit and outpitched, with Fraser getting booed at one point.

It ended with a loss. Not at all how we thought it would.

After all, this was his tournament. His farewell. His party. The other CWS coaches joked about it last week, saying they would let Fraser win, but didn't you expect it? Saturday, you would show up and Miami green and orange would still be around.

So, too, would the king of college baseball. The CBS Gods would give the sign, and Fraser might ride up to home plate in a limo. Pepperdine is hot, but this is his show. The Hurricanes would find a way to win — for him — and the only matter left to settle would be whether the Canes would douse him in champagne.

Instead, he walked away in a wet uniform, under a wet cap.

It would have made such great theater, something the folks from L.A. surely could appreciate. Fraser always enjoyed good theater. Whether it was "General Hospital" night at Mark Light Stadium in Miami or introducing such staples as bat girls and giveaway nights, Fraser was always about fun, entertainment and winning.

There was none of that for Fraser at Rosenblatt Stadium. For that, we have a bullish, undeniable Cal State Fullerton team to thank.

And the NCAA and CBS, two interchangeable money-grubbers who, as we speak, are all wet.

The man who has done so much to bring college baseball into the 20th century spent the last hours of a brilliant career watching the NCAA undo much of his work. The rain started lightly, but as it began to steadily fall harder and harder, it didn't take a hydrologist to see players were slipping, grips were impossible and this was no night for baseball — even for Hurricanes.

Yet the show went on. Neither rain, tornadoes nor one of our freak Nebraska snowstorms will keep the NCAA and CBS from making their attended rounds at 12:06 p.m. Saturday. Don't be late. The CBS Gods will start without you.

"I was upset," Fraser said. "I can't believe they continued the ballgame. You have a lot of student-athletes who worked very hard in September, started in February, played a lot of games and do a lot of good things. They go to the World Series and it should be the ultimate in baseball, a great showcase with great fans in Omaha who support it. To have to subject your players to that is not fair. The conditions should be ideal.

"I can't understand what they were trying to prove tonight. I'm not saying we would have won if it were dry. I'm not using that as an excuse. We got beat. But the games committee, I don't know if they were here or out to dinner."

Somebody was out to lunch. Afterward, the NCAA said that money was not a factor — right, and we're all going to Bellevue Beach on Sunday — because of rain insurance. So why was it that this game was crammed into Friday night like the last pair of socks in a suitcase? Why not wait until better weather Saturday and play the championship on Sunday? Ask your local senator or network programming exec.

"We didn't do a lot for college baseball tonight," Fraser said.

His words had an ironic ring to them. Here was Fraser, frustrated by the monster he helped create.

Yet even Fraser would tell you that college baseball has to be bigger than this. Those who worship this event talk of it in glowing, almost religious terms, a slice of Americana that is how sports should be. Impervious from corporate meddling. How hollow it all sounds now.

The rains came, and Ron Fraser left. It was a sad night for college baseball.

Miami legend Ron Fraser's last game was a rain-soaked 8-1 loss to Cal State Fullerton.

2011 INSIGHT *This was my first College World Series, so I didn't really have emotional ties to the event, and I didn't know Ron Fraser, though he seemed like a good guy. But I laid it on thick in this one because it seemed like an important moment for the event, and a travesty to have a legend like that play his last game in a driving rainstorm. It was late on a Friday night, and I remember there was a leak in that old Rosenblatt press box. Welcome to Omaha.*

JULY 5, 1992 • GOLF

Tom Sieckmann won the PGA Tour's 1988 Anheuser-Busch Classic and finished second in the 1991 Bay Hill Invitational and the 1993 Bell South Classic.

'Bringing the Show to Omaha'

IF ANYONE CAN understand Omaha, the sports town — and we're not saying it's entirely possible — it would be Tom Sieckmann.

The Big O's ambassador to the PGA Tour was born in York, Neb., but he lived in Omaha from the fourth grade on. It was while he attended Millard High School (now Millard South) that he came upon the reality that some things work in this town, and some things don't.

"When I was in high school, I was a big Kansas City-Omaha Kings fan," Sieckmann said. "But to my disappointment, they were never supported.

"Omaha is basically a conservative town. You have to prove to them that it's going to be good, that it's going to be well-organized and worth their time.

"You just have to keep after it. The people of Omaha are loyal. But they want you to prove to them first, and then they will support it."

Omaha is lucky to have a pro golfing son who keeps after it.

Sieckmann lives in Austin, Texas, now — he knows Omaha weather, too — but he remains one of those loyal Omahans.

Sieckmann's most visible — and significant — gift back to his hometown comes at the Mutual of Omaha Nebraska Pro-Am.

Tom Kite, two weeks after winning his first major golf championship, will play Highland Country Club. Ian Baker-Finch, one week away from defending his British Open title, will also be in town. Not to mention 20 more of the top golfers in the world.

For this, we have Mr. Sieckmann to thank.

It's no small deal, really. How many times do you leave your driveway, go a few miles and bump into professional athletes? Unless the K.C. Royals are at Rosenblatt for their annual go-through-the-motions appearance, you generally have to load up the car, spend a small mint on gas, food and Cubs, Twins or Royals tickets to get the big-league feel.

"All this evolved from Tom wanting to get the pros in here in return for all the good things he got from Omaha," said Bob Krohn, tournament director for the pro-am.

"Some people have asked me if this is a prelude to getting a tour event here," Sieckmann said. "We're bringing the show to Omaha. I think that makes it a better place to live. We can't do anything about the weather."

20 YEARS WITH TOM SHATEL • 17

Olympic Spirit Is Alive and Well

BARCELONA, SPAIN

HERE IT IS, the last day, and I am finally filled with the Olympic spirit. I have seen Jim Redmond carry his injured son, Derek, across the finish line. I have seen Charles Barkley embrace his gold medal like a kid on Christmas morning. I have heard badminton players complain about no air conditioning.

And I have this great idea. I'm bringing the Olympics to Omaha.

Mike Moran and I have it all figured out. Moran, an Omaha native (University of Omaha, class of 1966), is the chief spokesman for the U.S. Olympic Committee. He has connections. We have a plan. The Omaha-Lincoln Olympics. We're shooting for the year 2008.

The sports will be divided between Omaha and Lincoln. Track and field at Ed Weir field in Lincoln. Gymnastics in the Devaney Center. Weightlifting? At Boyd Epley's playground.

Baseball — where else? — at Rosenblatt Stadium, home of amateur baseball. Basketball will be at the new Ak-Sar-Ben Arena, which should be built by 2008 (we hope). Boxing and wrestling at the Civic Auditorium. Equestrian? The Ak. Fencing at the Orpheum Theater. Judo and team handball at the UNO fieldhouse. Shooting? We've got plenty of open space. Swimming and diving? OK, so we have to build a complex big enough to seat 20,000.

Moran said tennis should be in a clublike atmosphere. He suggests building a stadium at Happy Hollow. We're putting canoe/kayak on the Platte River, rowing at the Omaha Riverfront Marina. Yachting? Bet you didn't think we'd get the Missouri River involved.

"Just pray for wind," Moran says.

Soccer — futbol to the rest of the world — will take place in Memorial Stadium, where Moran predicts sellouts because "we'll call it football and unsuspecting Nebraskans will show up for it."

Our official mascot will be Herbie Husker. The opening ceremonies will be at Memorial Stadium. But instead of an archer shooting a burning arrow into the flame pit, I've got a better idea: Light up a football and have somebody punt it up there.

OK, so maybe I've been here too long. My batteries are low. My brain is out of film. But I have taken many pictures over two weeks of the XXV Olympics. Some I will keep forever. Others I won't.

Derek Redmond belongs in a gold frame. His is the image that won't go away, the British runner competing in the 400 meters. This is one lap. But Redmond is lying on the track writhing in pain, his hamstring snapped in two like a twig. But he has to finish. So he gets up and limps around the track.

His father, Jim, is running down out of the stands and onto the track. Security guards are chasing him. The old man, who owns a machinery shop, gets to his son, hoists him up over his shoulder and they finish the one lap together.

The Olympic Games never fail to produce these kinds of human dramas. They seemed to happen nightly at track and field. I'll remember that incredible night at the relays, with Carl Lewis showing he's still the fastest man alive. I'll remember poor Richard Chelimo of Kenya, who got boxed out of a gold medal in the 10,000 meters by two Moroccans — one of whom was in last place.

I'll try to remember Derek Redmond and forget how U.S. sprinter Gwen Torrance dragged her sport into the gutter with petty, irresponsible insinuations that athletes who beat her — no names given — were doped up.

I'll remember Francis Allen, the piece-of-work gymnastics coach at Nebraska, kicking back in a seat while his U.S. men's gymnastics team performed. Allen might as well have been in Lincoln. He was trading pins and stories and telling jokes to anyone who would listen — drinking in his Olympic experience the way he gulps down the rest of life.

I'll remember Henry Coimbra, the Angolan forward who took the unnecessary elbow from Charles Barkley and then put that NBA experience to good use. The next week a fight broke out in the Angola-Spain game after Coimbra threw a Barkleyesque elbow.

I'll remember the wonderful Lithuanian basketball team, which spent 54 years under the iron thumb of Russia, until 1990. When the Lithuanians lost to the Unified Team (the former Soviet republics except the Baltic states) in the pool round, they sat in the locker room for 10 minutes in silence. But after winning the rematch, they had the celebration of their lives.

For the award ceremony, they showed up in crazy green, red and purple tie-dye shirts — and matching pants — made for them by the Grateful Dead rock group. Even their president, Vytautas Landsbergis, showed up in a tie-dye shirt afterward. He was asked if George H.W. Bush would ever wear a tie-dye Grateful Dead shirt.

"I got wet," Landsbergis said about being doused with champagne in the locker room. "So I change clothes."

I'll remember Larry Donald, the "Cincinnati Lip" heavyweight who idolizes Muhammad Ali to the point of writing poetry. One of Donald's best lines: "It may sound like slander, but one day I'm going

U.S. Olympic Committee official Mike Moran.

AUGUST 10, 1992 • OLYMPICS

to knock out Evander (Holyfield)." Too bad Donald couldn't get out of the third round.

I'll remember the Iranian boxer who missed his bus at the Olympic Village and frantically arrived for his match in shorts and nothing else, standing there ready to fight. But he was disqualified. I'll remember the British woman in judo, dislocating her shoulder and pressing on. I'll remember the archer of the opening ceremonies and the shot of a lifetime.

I'll remember the awesome personality of the Cuban baseball team, which plays the game like a fast-break basketball team, but I'll forget the antics of Oscar Linares, the Cuban who stopped the Cuba-U.S. game five times to tie his shoe. I'll remember the fascinating female gymnasts — little girls who look like porcelain dolls — and their grace and beauty, but forget some of their sad faces — expressions from hardened athletes who never had a childhood.

Mostly, I'll remember the day-to-day adventures. The incredible people of Barcelona, who work hard and play harder. The maids who asked for pins. The women working in the press village gift shop, singing along with "YMCA" by the Village People at the top of their lungs.

When I think of Barcelona 10 years from now, I will think of an ashtray. Not for smoking, but it came in handy as a soap dish. Pizza. Thanks to a Pizza Hut near the press center, I ate enough pizza — with goat cheese — to last me another four years.

And, lest I forget, the laundry. The price you pay for wearing clean underwear in the press village is 3,000 pesestas. That's $30. Welcome to the Olym-

pics, where every day presents a dilemma: Do I eat today or wear clean underwear?

It is exhilarating and frustrating all at once. While you are at one venue, 12 other stories are occurring elsewhere. Michael Jordan had the right idea: He spent time with his family, played golf and showed up to beat the world every other night.

"The Olympic dream can be whatever you want it to be," Jordan said.

M.J. was referring to the criticism that he and his teammates didn't stay in the village and acted above the Olympic ideal. Poppycock. I'm worried about future Olympics for the Americans. Leroy Walker, the incoming USOC president, held a press conference

and reiterated his belief that all athletes should stay in the village. He wants to trash the Dream Team concept for 1996.

"Weren't Oscar Robertson and Jerry West good enough in 1960?" Walker asked.

Walker lives in the past. These Games are in transition. The world wants professionals in. The idea of an athletes' village may be outdated. We may, in fact, have all professionals in the Olympics in 10 years.

Certainly, the face of the Olympics is changing along with the world. This was probably the last Olympics where the ex-Soviet Union and Germany will be major factors. Their developmental structures of sport schools are falling with their economies, and athletes are defecting to places where they can train. The United States, with 106 medals (12 more than 1988), did itself proud, particularly in swimming, track and basketball.

There will be complaints all the way to Atlanta in 1996 that the Dream Team overshadowed other deserving athletes. Perhaps. But the Dreamers themselves learned what the Olympics were about — even the cantankerous Barkley, who coyly used the games to promote his image internationally and wound up hugging everyone in sight and staring mystically into his gold medal. He is sending it to his high school in Leeds, Ala., where it will be put on display.

"It shows that a fat little black kid from a small Southern town can make it somehow," Barkley said.

The Olympics still works. Which is why I'm shooting for 2008. I think we need to get on this right away.

2011 INSIGHT *When I look back on some of the things I covered early in my World-Herald career, it's like a dream. Did I really go to Barcelona, Spain, and cover the 1992 Olympics? Kudos to my editors for doing that. I think Nebraskans appreciated having a writer there, and I know I appreciated the chance to do it. When people ask what was the best thing you ever covered, those two weeks in Barcelona are my answer. It was like sports column fantasy camp. Every day was like Christmas; you woke up knowing you would be covering a great story that day but you had no idea what. My roommate those two weeks was Marc Hansen, the columnist from the Des Moines Register. I worked until 1 a.m. every night, stayed up until 4, slept until noon and had the time of my life. As a Magic Johnson and Larry Bird fan, the best part was covering the first Dream Team. U.S. Olympics official Mike Moran, a Westside and Omaha University guy, made sure I got into all the events. We had a blast doing the "Omaha Olympics" at the end.*

20 YEARS WITH TOM SHATEL • 19

OCTOBER 25, 1992 • NEBRASKA FOOTBALL

NU's Frazier Shows Cool in First Start

COLUMBIA, MO.

HIS YOUNG FACE was pasted with beads of sweat, yet Tommie Frazier looked cool. Confident. As he stood amid the hot, bright television lights while fielding a pepper-game of questions, you couldn't help but notice that The Kid has the look. The look of a gunslinger. The look of a winner. More important, the look of Nebraska's next great quarterback.

Even those Nebraskans present at Faurot Field who couldn't look inside Frazier's helmet, much less his head, had to sense it. The Kid is something special. On a day when Nebraska's secondary hardly looked ready for the Colorado challenge ahead, Frazier appeared more than up to the task as he led the eighth-ranked Huskers to a 34-24 victory over Missouri that was somehow bigger than expected. It was the day The Kid became The Man.

He trotted out as somewhat of a surprise starter for senior Mike Grant, whose stiff back had knocked him out of the lineup. But then The Kid immediately blended in. And whether he was diving in for a touchdown from 5 yards out like an Olympic high jumper to ice the victory or discussing his first start afterward with a face void of emotion, he looked like he belonged.

"I think I played well," Frazier said. "I made a couple of mistakes on audibles, but other than that, it was an A." So spoke Professor Frazier. Nobody dared argue.

"At this age," defensive coordinator Charlie McBride said, "Tommie Frazier is in the Turner Gill category. He showed a lot of poise. He showed the look of a winner."

In fact, it looked like Déjà MU. Eleven years ago, Gill survived a blitzkrieg on this very field in a 6-0 victory that served as the springboard to Gill's three-year legacy as one of the best quarterbacks in NU history.

"I think it does parallel that," said Gill, now Frazier's mentor as quarterbacks coach. "A young guy had to come in here and win a tough game. This will give him confidence in himself and confidence from the team.

"He has that something you can't describe. He has an air about him. He knows how to lead. Some people have it, and some don't."

Air Frazier was enough to persuade the conservative Tom Osborne to do the equivalent of putting on a wig and dancing the twist in the end zone: Hand the keys to his complex offense to a true freshman.

"I called in Turner Gill in the middle of his freshman year to ask him if he wanted to play varsity, and he said he wasn't ready," Osborne said. "But Tommie seemed to have enough confidence that it didn't faze him."

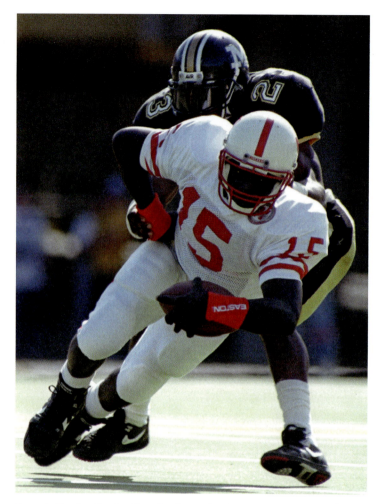

Tommie Frazier, the first true freshman to start a game at quarterback for Nebraska, produced 234 yards of total offense against Missouri.

2011 INSIGHT *The week before this Missouri game, there had been a lot of speculation that Tommie Frazier would make his Husker debut in Columbia. The night before the game, our beat writer, Lee Barfknecht, nailed it. And I'll take an assist. See, we were staying at the Kansas City Airport Marriott on Friday night, probably because the Big Eight basketball media day was there on Sunday. Anyway, Lee, myself and a writer from the Lincoln paper were in the hotel bar hanging out. Lee pulled me aside and said he had to go up to his room and call his source on Frazier starting the next day. He said, keep the Lincoln guy busy. So while Lee was upstairs breaking the Frazier story, I was down in the trenches making sure the Lincoln guy's glass was full. Tough job, but somebody had to do it.*

NOVEMBER 1, 1992 • NEBRASKA FOOTBALL

Nebraska's Trev Alberts (34) and John Parrella (92) bring the heat against Colorado freshman quarterback Koy Detmer.

Husker 'Blood Factor' Stuffs the Buffs

IN CASE YOU hadn't heard, technology stumbled into the prehistoric Big Eight Conference this year. Colorado and Oklahoma are driving new souped-up sports cars. The road to the Orange Bowl in the 1990s goes through the Nebraska secondary.

The Huskers threw up a roadblock.

Technology will be back another day. Technology wore a Band-Aid and an ice pack. Nebraska brutalized Colorado and its one-back offense at Memorial Stadium 52-7, proving that, even in an era of no huddles and four receivers, one thing remains timeless in college football.

The blood factor.

"You line up against a guy, and you beat him or he beats you," Nebraska senior defensive tackle John Parrella said. "There's no stalemate. Your heart is either pumping blood or Kool-Aid."

Nebraska's defense played like a destructive whirlwind on two missions:

To end Colorado's 25-game Big Eight undefeated streak.

To end Nebraska's eight-game losing string against top-10 teams.

Consider the roadblock successful.

Creighton's Dream Comes True

IT STARTED ON a soccer field, cold and empty, with nobody around but a dreamer and anybody else who would listen. This is how Bob Warming built his Creighton soccer power. He would take his first recruits to a lonely Tranquility Park and try to get them to see art where there was only a blank canvas.

"We'd stand out there in this open field and talk about what we wanted to do, the crowds we were going to have and what it would be like," said Warming, the Creighton coach. "You could see some of them daydreaming about it. Some of the kids would just look at the ground like, 'Yeah, right. Let's go. It's cold and I want something to eat.'

"The guys who dreamed along with me were the ones who came. They were idealists."

Warming and his idealists have arrived faster than even they might have envisioned on those afternoons in 1990. Creighton's soccer team is ranked second in the nation and, with a first-round bye in the coming NCAA tournament, sits four victories away from a national championship. All this in three years. With no junior college players, Prop 48s or Brazilian foreign-exchange students.

It may not rank on the local scale with Derek Brown galloping for six points, but it's a major accomplishment in its own right. Start-from-scratch Creighton was almost ranked No. 1 this week, but No. 5 Virginia, more established and visible in college soccer circles, leaped up over the Bluejays. And Warming understood.

"People don't know what to make of us," he said. "Look at the teams that got byes: Virginia, N.C. State, UCLA and Creighton. It's like the song on 'Sesame Street' that my daughter sings: 'One of these things is not like the others . . . can you guess which one?'"

When Warming arrived from North Carolina-Charlotte in 1989, with one year to recruit and plan before playing, he didn't have the Dead Poets Society in mind. When his first group of freshmen checked into Swanson dormitory in August 1990, Warming told them they were here to be role models to the soccer community. And win a national championship.

"I've done exactly what (Creighton) wanted to do," Warming said. "I've gotten student-athletes. I've gotten role models.

"I could have gotten jucos and done a lot better. But they weren't the kind of people that I want to start a program with. A good beginning takes you a long way. A bad beginning can take a long time to overcome."

Bob Warming produced a winning record in 1990, his first season as Creighton soccer coach, and led the Jays to the NCAA tournament in his third year.

NOVEMBER 13, 1992 • NEBRASKA BASKETBALL

Chubick's Job Is Enforcer

WHILE HIS NEBRASKA teammates had assembled on the floor for the cameras and happy-talk of preseason media day, Bruce Chubick was running late. He was back in the training room. He had to pop a blister. Typical.

In what was an unexpected metaphor of Husker basketball, Chubick was once again in the background, preparing his armor. As long as the 6-foot-7 junior forward is surrounded by blood and pain — hopefully dishing out the two — then all is well with Husker hoops.

"All great teams have that guy who works hard and does the little things," Nebraska senior center Derrick Chandler said. "Chubick is our guy. He's our worker. Nobody outworks him."

On a team of smooth, silky racehorses, he is the blacksmith. Amid jumpers and shooters and slashers, Chubick is relegated to the role of bouncer. He sets picks. He rebounds. He passes. He rebounds. He dives on the floor. He rebounds. But in his own quiet sort of way, Chubick has emerged as an early MVP of this collage of talent and personalities that is in need of some glue.

He will provide Jamar Johnson and Eric Piatkowski with screens and passes. And as for the new kids on the block, there is no better role model on the floor than Chubick showing up for work early and leaving late.

The junior from Atkinson, Neb., is the backbone of Nebraska basketball, whether it's providing his toughness on the court or as off-the-floor conscience — as he did last year when a midseason slump evoked thoughts of the postseason NIT. Nobody was more vocal about waking up the team than Chubick.

"People say, 'Who is this guy from Atkinson, Neb.? He can't play,'" coach Danny Nee said. "He's heard that. When you tell Bruce Chubick he can't do something, he gets determined. His goal is to prove to everybody that he can play and that he deserves to be here."

He has proved that over and over. But the best compliment one can pay Chubick is to tell him that he parallels the work ethic and impact on a game of his idol, another small-town gym rat named Larry Bird. To hear the comparison is to make all the bruises and blood blisters worth it.

Bruce Chubick, known for doing "the little things," takes a charge against Missouri's Jevon Crudup.

NOVEMBER 22, 1992 • NEBRASKA ATHLETICS

Bob Devaney Says Thanks

WHEN BOB DEVANEY calls, you answer.

So when Devaney phoned the office this week to request a meeting in his office, our curiosity not only was piqued, it drove to Lincoln to see what was up. Devaney announcing a new conference for Nebraska? A lifetime contract for Tom Osborne? Maybe firing some last salvos at the Nebraska administration?

Hardly. Seems he just wanted to say thanks.

"I can't thank everybody individually," Devaney said. "I just wanted to thank everybody for all the attention and all the parties and the banquets and everything. Let people know I appreciate it and not just take it for granted."

Well, thank you. Thank you for the football power that has given this state so much perpetual pride and pleasure; one that many do take for granted. Thank you for hiring Danny Nee and bringing Nebraska basketball into a new era. Nebraska may not have mountains, but the university funds every sport possible. Thanks to the guy named Bob.

He leaves as athletic director next month. It will be quietly, with the office being cleaned out over the holidays and then, when everyone returns from the bowl game, he will be down the hall, raising funds from the many friends and contacts made over the years and beers.

It is best that he go now, too. College football, and athletics in general, are not as he knew them. You have to be a CPA, not an old tackle, to know your way around. Soon, athletes will be wanting their piece of the pie, if not firing the very coaches who brought them to campus. Strange days, indeed.

"Shoot, that happened here," Devaney said. "In 1968, after we had lost big to Kansas State, the players came in here and wanted a meeting. There were gripes. If we hadn't won the next year, 1969, I was gone."

He stayed, of course. Until now. But before he moves down the hall — and since as he did call — let's take one last opportunity to ask the man who has transcended so many eras and changes to look into his crystal ball.

The future of Nebraska football: "As long as Tom stays as head football coach, then I think football is going to be tops. But the more restrictive the rules become, the more pressure there will be on the schools with the least population. We can't make as many visits.

"I have the feeling, too, that I don't think we should be too restrictive academically. If a kid wants to go to college, he should have a chance to go to college. Every day a kid is in college, he's better off than if he wasn't there. So I'm not concerned about having all valedictorians come over into your campus."

The future of NU athletics: "I did not vote for tiering the sports, which is a big push for a lot of schools in the Big Eight. That is, having some sports compete for championships nationally, having some in the Big Eight and having some like intramurals. I'm not for that. We're not for slamming the lid down and not giving the tennis team or golf team any money or not do any more for swimming or wrestling."

But can Nebraska keep funding all 21 sports?

"We're going to try as long as we can. But as far as I'm concerned, I think we should keep all of our sports programs. It will depend on how much these fundraisers, and myself, can raise."

The future of the Big Eight: "This talk about joining the Southwest Conference is not healthy. If you joined with, say, Texas, Texas A&M, Houston and Texas Tech — four public institutions — that would be fine. But to go down and play Rice and SMU and Texas Christian, where they don't draw flies, it's a losing proposition. If we want to pick teams out of other conferences and mix them up, I'm not against that.

"I called the Big Ten, talked to (Commissioner) Jim Delany two or three months ago and asked if they were interested in Nebraska joining the Big Ten and he said they were not interested."

But do you trust Colorado, Missouri or Oklahoma to stay put?

Bob Devaney came to Nebraska in 1962 to coach, but his impact extended to his role as athletic director.

2011 INSIGHT *One of the regrets of my career is that I never got to cover Bob Devaney. I would have enjoyed that. As it was, I loved my year or so talking with the legendary figure. After this particular interview, Devaney said, "I know it's your job to stir things up once in a while, but I appreciate that you tell it like it is." That really made my day, especially when a lot of Nebraskans weren't quite so agreeable with Bob on that topic. This is also one of those columns where you look back and go "wow," especially Devaney's comments on the Texas schools and Jim Delany and the Big Ten.*

NOVEMBER 22, 1992 • NEBRASKA ATHLETICS

Bob Devaney acknowledges the crowd's salute at the Colorado game during his final year as athletic director.

"We have to take them at their word. Colorado said it's all rumor, and that they are not making any plans to join the Pac-10, and Oklahoma has said the same thing. I think right now everybody has declared themselves as to wanting to keep the Big Eight intact. I think the Big Eight's a good conference, and will get along well without joining other conferences, as long as we keep playing well."

The future of gender equity and its effects on Nebraska: "I believe in it. (But) I don't want it to destroy any of the programs that we have here that have been successful. I want to try to help where help is needed without destroying what is good, what has been good. Football and basketball, the two revenue sports, will be the two last ones that are affected. But we'd like to keep all the sports strong."

The chance of a national college playoff: "I think it possibly will happen. But if they can work it out through the bowl games, it can happen pretty quick. If they could do that, I would be all for it. I don't feel that I want to destroy bowl games. I'd rather have everybody sitting around guessing who's the national champion than lose that."

Reselling Memorial Stadium based on donations made to NU: "I don't think we'll do that. As far as I'm concerned, I'm not in favor of it. I'm in favor of trying to rework the seating situation within the same general policy, except try to get money from everybody that can afford it that's sitting there. Try to get them to join some club."

And on the upcoming game at OU, possibly your last trip to Norman, site of your most famous conquest: "It could be. I would hope that in two years when we go down there again and (if) I'm with the university that I'd be able to bum a ride down."

Count on it. It's the least we can do for the ride you've given Nebraska.

20 YEARS WITH TOM SHATEL • 25

TOM'S TAKE
REFLECTIONS ON

Tom Osborne as Nebraska's Athletic Director? Not Just Yet

IT WAS ANOTHER reminder why Tom Osborne can't be the next director of athletics at the University of Nebraska.

The sun was out, footballs were flying through Memorial Stadium — please make note: these were passes — and Osborne was in Big Red heaven. At 55, Osborne is right where he should be: In gray cotton sweats, a red windbreaker and a red Nebraska football cap as he moves from instruction to instruction.

The athletic director's chair will have to wait. Osborne is not ready. You may disagree. You may have a handful of bowl tapes that suggest otherwise. Let's rephrase that: Osborne says he's not ready. And, frankly, he's not.

This is not to say that Osborne would not be a competent administrator. He could step in tomorrow and do it — provided he learn to better delegate authority — and Nebraska athletics would not miss a beat. But Osborne would miss his chalkboard, his players and his game too much. Osborne himself admitted he wants to get his program back to the upper echelon of college football. He can't do that as part-time athletic director or part-time football coach. So the athletic director's chair will wait.

But will it still be there when Osborne is ready? That's an intriguing question as the search for Bob Devaney's successor began with, curiously, Osborne on the outside looking in.

University of Nebraska Chancellor Graham Spanier announced at a press conference that the university will conduct a "national" search. But make no mistake: This is Spanier's hire, not Osborne's.

Yet you have to wonder what type of influence Osborne will have on whom his new boss will be. Why wasn't he included on a committee that will search during his off-season?

Maybe the new guy will leave Osborne and football alone. Maybe they won't be speaking in two years. Maybe Osborne will get mad and leave. Maybe their relationship is not important.

"It's damn important," Devaney said.

For his part, Osborne is staying out of this political football game. At least publicly. The sensitive Osborne is ultra-sensitive here, not wanting to give anyone the impression he's trying to craft a puppet.

"I don't have anything to say about the A.D. situation," Osborne said.

Nor, Osborne says, is he concerned about whether the chair will be open when he's ready to ascend. "I'm not sure how I'll feel in a few years," Osborne said. "I'm not going to coach forever. I'd like to do it sometime, I know.

"I'd like to get us back into the top two, three or four in the country, if possible, in the next two to three years. That's going to take some doing."

The job of athletic director today is more difficult than ever, and that includes Nebraska. Devaney did an admirable job, but Nebraska needs to get better — at fundraising in particular — just to keep pace.

If a professional A.D. — a "magic man" — can be found out there, it's worth the search. It also would be worth a call to Osborne — and Devaney, too — for advice. For all their blood, sweat and expertise, they are conspicuous by their absence in this process.

Osborne is not ready for the chair, but he deserves to be in the huddle. This is a big call.

— APRIL 1, 1992

> "I'm not going to coach forever. I'd like to do it sometime, I know."
>
> — TOM OSBORNE ON BEING ATHLETIC DIRECTOR

THE CHANGING SPORTS LANDSCAPE 1992

Omaha Goes to Bat to Keep the College World Series

HE WAS TALKING about his first recollection of the College World Series. Appropriately, the thing that stuck in Mayor P.J. Morgan's mind all these years had to do with leadership.

"It was in 1953," said Morgan, who was 13 at the time. "The thing I remember was seeing this man — I can't remember his name — who was responsible for the success of the College World Series, being introduced a lot and everybody cheering for him."

Through the years there were many more memories, June keepsakes to store away and take out each year to polish and admire. In this way, Morgan is like any other Omahan: So many memories have been stored that there is a foundation of pride that made him feel the CWS partially belonged to him. And when there was noise in his first year of office, 1989, that cities with big domes might make a run at Omaha's crown jewel, he also felt a sense of urgency.

Unlike other Omahans, though, he had the power to do something about it. "It's a tradition," Morgan said. "It's family entertainment. It's a nice June night, eating a hot dog. Omaha does not have as much going on as Minneapolis, but we have this and we appreciate what we have.

"Once you have something, you don't want to lose it."

Morgan didn't. So he did the only thing he could: He got involved.

Understand, he is not Jack Diesing Sr. or Jack Jr. — the father-son duo who have been so vital to the growth of the CWS — or any of the other countless faces and volunteers who have pumped life into this staple of Omaha. Instead, Morgan became a frontman for Omaha, doing what a mayor does best: showing his support and offering a front-view gesture to the NCAA that the Big O is paying attention.

He has driven to Kansas City several times for NCAA baseball meetings in the summer and fall. He has attended dinners, met with officials and talked baseball and the politics of keeping the CWS where it belongs. The message: Omaha will do whatever it takes to keep the CWS. The NCAA noticed.

"It's unbelievable how involved your mayor is," said Jim Wright, NCAA assistant director of communications who has worked with the CWS for several years. "It is very impressive."

Dennis Poppe, NCAA director of championships, was impressed enough to write Morgan a letter April 21 praising the mayor and the CWS board of directors and saying, "I don't think we've ever had a

NCAA officials were impressed by Mayor P.J. Morgan's efforts to keep the College World Series in Omaha.

better working relationship with the City of Omaha and CWS Inc."

You put a CWS inside a major league stadium and market, and 15,000 — if that — looks like an Indians-Mariners game. In the friendly confines of Rosenblatt, with tradition dripping on a sunny day, it looks like a big event. There's a perfect fit at work here. Just as the Super Bowl belongs in a garish setting with all the trimmings of excess and Corporate America, the College World Series belongs in Omaha's finely trimmed backyard.

"The tradition and support that this has in Omaha is unmatched, as far as I'm concerned, with any other championship we run," Poppe said.

"The thing I've always enjoyed is you go there and see the sons sitting with their fathers, who went there with their fathers, who went there with theirs. Little babies sleeping in the stands can say one day they were at a College World Series. You see some lady down on the third-base line, sewing and eating hot dogs, just as she does every year.

"It's unique. And I really think if there were eight teams there that nobody had ever heard of, as long as they knew it was the College World Series, I still believe Omaha would support the series."

— MAY 29, 1992

WAHOO HIGH SCHOOL BASKETBALL | RACERS' CBA CHAMPIONSHIP | THE VOICE OF OMAHA

1993

> "I still have people out there who are somewhat surprised to see me and they'll call me Bob. When I first took over, it happened maybe 15 times a year. Now it happens maybe four or five times a year. It's kind of a subconscious thing. It's always been symbolic to me."
>
> — NEBRASKA FOOTBALL COACH TOM OSBORNE

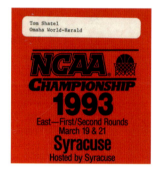

They could tell themselves, over and over, that this NCAA tournament trip would be different for Nebraska. But, of course, none of that mattered when the Huskers played New Mexico State in the Carrier Dome. The one thing they couldn't do was become human grasshoppers overnight. That mattered. Perhaps that explained the almost relieved look on Derrick Chandler's face afterward in the NU locker room. It was over. His career at Nebraska. And the barrage of Aggies who fell like paratroopers out of the sky onto the Nebraska defense. And Chandler's head. At some point in the NCAA tournament, they catch up with you. The leapers. You may be able to hide for a game or two in the bracket, playing halfcourt and living off breaks. But eventually, the men on pogo sticks find you. If you can't play with them, match them athlete for athlete, they exploit you. It just so happened that coach Danny Nee's third NCAA team caught the leapers in the first round. New Mexico State, a team of seasoned athletes playing with a crisp purpose, beat the Huskers 93-79 and in doing so often made it look easy.

Nebraska basketball coach Danny Nee is proposing a double-dip of Huskers and Bluejays each year. Two games. Two sites. "Philosophically, I was always against playing any team twice in one year," said Nee, whose team played CU twice in his first year (1986-87). "It would be good for both of us, with the limited time we have to get all your nonconference games in. Nobody wants to play those in the middle of conference season. If we could get dates during the week where we wouldn't miss classes and if we could draw and if it would be good for both Creighton and Nebraska, then I think we should do it."

With blond hair and a rugged face, Trev Alberts should have been cast as a quarterback. He looks like he should be a lifeguard on "Baywatch." No, Alberts doesn't sound or look like a carnivorous consumer of quarterback flesh. He just plays like one.

28 • 20 YEARS WITH TOM SHATEL

AK-SAR-BEN FADING AWAY | THE BIG MAN IN KEARNEY | WILD GAME WITH THE WILDCATS

On the Omaha Royals' 25th anniversary all-time team, Bill Gorman is the all-time GM, hands down. A Class AAA GM doesn't have to be Branch Rickey — or even Herk Robinson. He puts fannies in seats even when his players can't. He knows how to run the shop for owners who are either out of town or out of touch. Gorman has done so in three decades for three owners, all the while becoming an "Omaha institution," according to the Royals press guide.

Bill McCartney, eat your heart out. Nebraska's rival is coming to town this weekend. It goes by the initials CU. But it's not Colorado. The name is Creighton. The sport is baseball. What makes a rivalry? Big school vs. small school. Public vs. private. Different resources. Different recruiting philosophies. Jealousy.

"It's the ninth inning," said one pro scout behind the plate, "and he's still showing us the cheese." That's cheese, as in heat, as in Alan Benes, the Bluejays' Big Cheese. Why is the Creighton junior still humming as if his team were in the College World Series, instead of out of the Missouri Valley Conference race? Because it's a baseball game and he has a ball in his hand? Bingo.

One of the recommendations that came out of the American Football Coaches Convention in Atlanta has to make you wonder. There are so many other things these molders of young men could focus on. So what do they do? They push to outlaw the fumblerooksy. You know, the play made famous by Nebraska coach Tom Osborne. The center makes a semi-snap to the quarterback, takes the ball back and lays it on the ground for a guard to pick up before rumbling downfield. The crisis, as some coaches see it, is that the play is hard for officials to enforce. Did the quarterback really touch the ball? Did they sneak in an illegal play? Does anybody else care? This is much ado about a play used once every millennium, or at least whenever Nebraska needs some yards. It's not like it's killing the game. Take it away, and you take some of the color and imagination — yes, some of the fun — out of the game.

JANUARY 27, 1993 • HIGH SCHOOL BASKETBALL

Wahoo Loves Its 'Wahoops'

WAHOO, NEB.

TO FIND ONE of the hot spots of Nebraska high school basketball, enter Wahoo High School and go past the office and library until you find the room labeled "Mr. Anderson, Social Studies."

And when you do find coach Mick Anderson, don't bother telling him his Class B Warriors shouldn't be ranked fourth in the state, among the Class A giants. He already can hear the voices of doubt.

"I'm sure it's a subject at coffee shops around the state," Anderson said. "It's one of those deals where we feel honored by it, but we don't get caught up in it. We have enough to worry about in our own class."

Every coach should have such worries.

Anderson's Army had won four straight Class B state titles until losing in the state semifinals last March, which also ended a 114-game winning streak. Though his Warriors are 12-0 and leading all classes in scoring (95 points a game), Anderson constantly seeks ways to keep the monster happy.

Not everyone is. His critics say he runs up the score. They say he doesn't play enough Class B teams, let alone no Class A competition.

That's life in Wahoo, which probably deserves a spot in the Nebraska Top 10 just because it is such a phenomenon. For a town of 3,700 — with two high schools, no less — to produce the teams and results it has the last five years is uncanny.

But that's life in Wahoo, where basketball is such a mission that they should petition the state to add a "ps" to the end of the town name.

It wasn't always that way. Wahoo had won one state title (1926) and hadn't made the playoffs since 1948 when Anderson, an assistant at Ralston, took over in 1976. It took 10 seasons, with five winning seasons, before Wahoo's program arrived in defeat: a district final loss to Omaha Cathedral in 1986 that Anderson said "made us hungry."

The appetite was there all along. It took something special to bring it out.

It took "Wahoops."

That's the name of the youth program that was the foundation of the Wahoo dynasty. The catapult. It was back in 1981 when Anderson, Rett Inbody and Jerry Volin organized the boys and girls winter programs to supplement the junior high programs.

"We could see our kids were not playing as much basketball as teams we were competing against," Anderson said.

Now they may play more than anyone.

"Maybe if our program takes a downturn, we'll just be thankful to be where we are," Anderson said. "It doesn't last forever."

In Wahoops, Neb., they are too busy playing to worry about that.

Coach Mick Anderson and his Wahoo Warriors had a state-record 114-game winning streak that ended in the 1992 Class B semifinals.

FEBRUARY 8, 1993 • NEBRASKA BASKETBALL

Vitale Gets Assist in Win Over KU

IT TOOK DICK Vitale. It took a visit from the blue dragon, the Kansas Jayhawks. And it took every ounce of sweat and brains and guts that the Nebraska basketball team had, just when you thought the Huskers were lacking in all three categories.

With those forces at work, the fog over Lincoln lifted and a basketball season arrived. After two months of uncertainties, growing pains and ugly victories over uglier opponents, Nebraska was looking for a beacon.

Nebraska 68, No. 3 Kansas 64. The patient is alert.

And how. The Huskers had it all on the line at the Devaney Center. Their biggest crowd. Their loudest crowd. Their best chance at a "quality" win. And, finally, their best effort of the season — a second half of cat-burglar defense and even gutsier offense that allowed them to claw back into the game and end up on top.

"It was," Nebraska coach Danny Nee said, "a superhuman effort."

Of course. We had expected superhumans all year. The Huskers had, too. The hype surrounding this team — with a top-10 recruiting class — had come from all sides.

Appropriately enough, the team came together at the urging of the hype-master himself, Vitale, the broadcaster who gave the Huskers a pep talk.

"He got our attention," forward Terrance Badgett said. "One thing he said was that a lot of playground legends will be at home watching on TV. Not everybody gets a chance to play on national TV, so when you get the chance, you'd better play hard."

Added forward Bruce Chubick: "He used a few choice words which I'm sure he'll never say on TV. He basically told us to stop crying to the coach about playing time and start working hard for our shots. Nothing we didn't already know."

The Huskers followed his advice against KU. There's nothing like the presence of Goliath to make you put everything you have into your slingshot.

Eric Piatkowski and Derrick Chandler congratulate Terrance Badgett, whose dunk with three seconds to play clinched the victory over third-ranked Kansas.

20 YEARS WITH TOM SHATEL • 31

APRIL 28, 1993 • OMAHA RACERS

Bart Kofoed Plays the Enforcer

THERE WAS LESS than one minute left in the third quarter. The Omaha Racers were trailing Grand Rapids 82-75 — their biggest deficit in two nights. And Ak-Sar-Ben Coliseum was quickly making the transformation from discothéque to morgue.

But all was well. Bart Kofoed had not yet begun to fight.

Time for something drastic. Time for Kofoed, the smartest street fighter in the building, to reach into his repertoire of mind games and turn this thing around.

The target was Darren Henrie, who was hot to the touch from three-point range. Kofoed had something special in mind for Mr. Henrie. The old playground special: a blind pick designed to shake, rattle and roll Henrie. Mission accomplished. Henrie took a swing at Kofoed. They both got technical fouls.

Back to disco. The patient responded.

What's more, after a 119-111 victory, the patient is one win from a CBA championship.

What did we learn, class? Never count out the Racers. And never turn your back on Kofoed, the Racers' assassin and brilliant baiter.

"I wasn't trying to pick a fight," said Kofoed, not exactly convincing as the choirboy. "He (Henrie) was on a tremendous roll hitting threes. I had a chance for a good, legal screen, and I wanted to jar him up a little bit."

Kofoed would nail a three-pointer with 5:07 left that tied the score — a shot that the Racers said was his biggest play of the night. But it was the wake-up call — the backside hammer-job — that was more of Kofoed's calling card.

The Racers are a collage of roles and hard work and journeymen playing out of their minds. But it can be argued that Kofoed's acquisition in March was the ignition to this drive. The Racers have never had a player like him: a cocky, scrappy enforcer who won't take no for an answer. Danny Ainge? You read my mind.

He has become a local hero for the fans to rally around, and that is an ironic twist. Kofoed is not the point guard — in fact, he comes off the bench — but he is every bit the catalyst that another local hero, Cedric Hunter, was before he was traded to Sioux Falls. Kofoed might be the missing piece the Racers haven't had since Hunter.

"He's that tough guy who will do whatever it takes to win that night," Racers coach Mike Thibault said. "A guy like that from a small college (Kearney State, 1987) has to make it by being tough, be willing to take on the odds."

In a sense, Kofoed is what the CBA is all about: dreams. A 6-4 small-college guard bounces around the NBA and CBA for seven years, gets cut yet again and comes back to help take the hometown team to a championship?

The Omaha Racers wrapped up the CBA championship with a 106-98 victory over Grand Rapids. Bart Kofoed, center in sports coat, played at Omaha Westside and Kearney State and joined the team for the stretch run of the 1992-93 season. At right are coach Mike Thibault and owner Steve Idelman.

JUNE 4, 1993 • COLLEGE WORLD SERIES

Jack Payne: The Voice of Omaha

JACK PAYNE STORIES have their own flavor. They should be told out on the front porch, with the smell of fried chicken cooking and the family gathered around. Tell us another one about the voice of the College World Series.

"Only in Omaha could this happen, and only Jack Payne could get away with this," says Dennis Poppe, director of championships for the NCAA, prefacing a story.

"It was a couple of years ago and Creighton and Wichita State were playing and we were really packing them in. It was jammed full, and you could see we had a couple thousand still in the parking lot trying to get in.

"So Jack says, 'OK, everybody. We want everybody to come in and see the game. So scoot a little closer and get to know your neighbor.' I'm on the field. I turn around and I can't believe it. Everybody in the stands is scooting closer together. Because Jack says so.

"Can you imagine if they tried that in New York? What would the crowd do? If you want to describe what Omaha is, what the College World Series is, that's it."

The story is mostly true.

"I told them to 'oogie' up," Payne says.

Oogie? Is that a word?

"I don't know," Payne said. "But it worked."

Much has changed since Payne took over the public address system at Rosenblatt Stadium. The bats are permanently aluminum. National TV has added a glow.

But the basic fibers remain. Including Jack Payne's omnipresent voice, bellowing out into a warm night.

"You're doing swell. Now just bring somebody with you tomorrow. Come on, declare a truce. Bring your mother-in-law."

He has been called the narrator of the CWS. A down-home town crier with corny advice and even cornier jokes. With a touch right out of Will Rogers, the native Oklahoman provides much of the charm and flavor that make the CWS the family picnic of sporting events.

Jack Payne, the voice of the College World Series from 1964 to 2000, is a member of the 2011 class of the Omaha Sports Hall of Fame.

A writer from Minneapolis attending his first CWS last year compared Payne to the P.A. voice in the movie "M*A*S*H" that strings the film along in comedic tones. That's Payne. He is the cornball constant that holds the week of endless baseball innings together.

When a pair of headlights shine in the parking lot, Payne is there to warn the forgetful owner. But "Hurry back!" he adds. He used to have an "applause meter" in which he asked the crowd which team they liked the best. Payne would make sure nobody won, and even when there was a favorite, Payne would say, "Sorry, my machine's broken."

Before one game, Payne prepped the crowd by saying, "OK, these umpires have had a tough series, let's give 'em a hand." When the umps stepped up on the field, they were dumbfounded by the huge ovation.

"Now," Payne blared out to the umps, "don't blow it."

It works.

"Jack typifies what Omaha is to the College World Series," Poppe said. "His homespun humor and down-home approach gives the event the charm it has. We laugh at the same jokes every year. It's like going to see your old friend every year."

If there is still an innocence, or perspective, to the CWS, it's upheld mostly by Payne, who still insists on three rules: Never embarrass the players, never interfere with play and make the crowd feel involved.

"I don't think it's a narrative," Payne says. "I like the term 'folksy.' I try to make them feel welcome and stay out of the way.

"This is just a great thing. It's like . . . Ebbets Field or something. The old ballpark. I think people are happy having it here."

That's because a slice of Jack Payne goes a long way on a hot day. Go ahead. Bring your mother-in-law.

JULY 2, 1993 • **HORSE RACING**

Racing Dying as Fans Gray

A DAY AT the races . . . Old men in short sleeves sit behind tiny grade-school desks, seemingly hypnotized by racing forms spread before them. An occasional customer buys a hot dog or a beer from bored vendors. During the dead time between races, the echo of the announcer in the concourse rocks you to sleep.

This is Ak-Sar-Ben on a Wednesday afternoon in late June. Not exactly a happenin' place. More like a nappin' place.

Horse racing in Omaha is dying. Then again, you know that. You know because you've either been out to see the doldrums firsthand, or you've heard the doom-saying voice of Douglas County Board member Steve Rosenblatt, who says horse racing at Ak could hit the finish line in less than two years.

You've heard the opinions and the theories. There's too much competition from new rival tracks, and now the weekend buses from out of town don't come around anymore. There's keno and lotto and Powerball and most any other way for a gambler to get his fix. And, yes, the quality of horses is down.

These are all nice, neat reasons that have contributed in their own little ways. But they don't reach the core of the problem, which was evident again and which Ak-Sar-Ben may never be able to cure.

To quote The Who: Talkin' 'bout my generation.

I am a sports fan. I can hum the theme from "SportsCenter" on command. So why is it the only time I've been to Ak this year was on the way to a Racers game (next door)? (And I put $5 down on a horse because it had the name Dodger Fan.)

Could it be because I — and countless others — can't relate?

I appreciate the fact that, for years, thousands of racing fans came from throughout the Midwest, making Ak-Sar-Ben a bustling center of activity and giving Omaha a proud identity. I appreciate the tradition. Tradition is good.

What I don't appreciate is having to wait 20 to 30 minutes between races with nothing to do or see except old paint dry. A day at the races can be tedium. But that's my generation. Things today move fast, sometimes too fast. Meanwhile, a day at the races is a day in a time capsule. Going to Ak-Sar-Ben is like being in an old movie.

Omaha, too, has changed. In the glory years, Ak-Sar-Ben was the place to be. Now, we can sip wine in the Old Market. See movies. Play softball. Go to a sports bar. Stay home and watch cable.

I have a colleague in Kansas City, a columnist who knows a thing or two about the horse game. He says the future of horse racing in this country is a handful of major tracks simulcasting to the rest of the country. In other words, Ak-Sar-Ben of the future will have horses on the screen, not the dirt.

If I were a betting man, I'd say he's right.

The crowds at Ak-Sar-Ben dwindled as competition grew from other gambling outlets, and racing came to an end in 1995.

2011 INSIGHT *The truth is, I like horse racing, in doses. I don't follow it. My parents didn't take me to the track and show me the finer points of the horse game or the betting game. But I would always tune in to the Triple Crown races. When I lived in Kansas City, I would trek up to Ak-Sar-Ben once a summer on a bus with other friends to hit the track. The Star sent me up to cover a big race, maybe the Cornhusker Cup, in July 1983, and I remember meeting World-Herald racing writer Don Lee. I remember staying in a motel somewhere near 72nd and Dodge and going out to a place called the Bombay Bicycle Club, but that's neither here nor there. So I respected the horse game, the trainers and jockeys and the beautiful beasts that ran gallantly around the track. But this column touched a nerve with horse people in Omaha. I was labeled an anti-horse guy, maybe for pointing out the old guys sitting around at their desks. It was a tough time for Ak-Sar-Ben. Horse racing was starting to fade, and the push to start a casino in Omaha was going nowhere. There was frustration and some desperation. Maybe the wrong column at the wrong time. Or the right one.*

Small Town Suits Kropp

KEARNEY, NEB.

DON'T LET THE title fool you. Dr. Tom Kropp still plays a mean game of pickup basketball with the faculty three times a week. He may not weigh 250 pounds or run a 4.9 40-yard dash anymore. But the younger teacher assistants are the ones who have to guard him.

The University of Nebraska at Kearney's Dr. Tom still has the handshake of a legend, too. His vise grip is so firm that you find yourself looking at your hand, not him.

One thing is clear after a visit with Kropp: He still enjoys life in the small pond.

Kropp always did. The 1971 Aurora high school great bypassed a chance to play both football and basketball at the University of Nebraska to go to Kearney State. After a professional basketball career that took him to the NBA and Europe, he returned to easy-living Kearney. Here, on a Division II campus, is where he was comfortable.

In that way, he is Nebraska's version of Larry Bird, the small-town Indiana legend who went to Indiana State because he considered the University of Indiana too big. Like Bird, Kropp was good enough to do it his way, no questions asked. Like Bird, the game was the thing for Kropp. Like Bird, his small-town will and determination overcame the lack of speed or jumping ability.

The cheering has stopped for Kropp. But not the competitiveness. He spends his days channeling that spirit into coaching and the classroom. Kropp also teaches a course in sports psychology, where students are provided the rare treat of entering Kropp's keen, competitive mind.

"I've enjoyed it," Kropp said. "You see athletes that are not as physically gifted that must learn they can still make a difference. It's because of the attitude, the mental part that is as important as the physical. To me, athletics are taking the best you have and trying to win with that."

It's an intriguing thought: Tom Kropp teaching a course on being competitive. That's like Henry Kissinger teaching a course on world politics. "It's hard to teach competitiveness," Kropp said.

But if anybody can do it, it's Kropp. He has been honored as one of the top 25 football players and one of the top five basketball players in Nebraska high school history. He is in the Nebraska Football Hall of Fame and the National Association of Intercollegiate Athletics Hall.

His legend is such that you can go anywhere in Nebraska, say the name "Tom Kropp" and true sports fans nod. They know.

He thrived on competition. Anything and everything, though in high school at Aurora, Neb., he was limited to football, basketball, baseball and track.

Kropp would take anything on. He had the distinction of getting scholarship offers from both football coach Bob Devaney and basketball coach Joe Cipriano. Kropp, the 6-foot-3, 250-pound linebacker, and Kropp the basketball guard would play both for a year, then decide.

But after three days, he turned to his freshman roommate, Tom Humm (quarterback Dave's brother), and said, "I'm leaving."

"I got there and saw how big it was. I'm really close to my family and I missed them. I began to wonder if I had made a mistake. I was just more comfortable playing at this level."

And he has never looked back.

"I figured that out a long time ago. Don't second-guess yourself. I kind of have my own life here. Here in little Kearney, Nebraska, I'm very satisfied."

Maybe you can't teach competitiveness. But Kropp can still teach happiness.

Tom Kropp, drafted by the NFL's Pittsburgh Steelers and the NBA's Washington Bullets, returned to the University of Nebraska at Kearney to coach.

2011 INSIGHT *When I interviewed for this job in August 1991, I promised that I would do a tour of Nebraska every summer, digging out good stories and lost heroes. I did it for a few years and stopped. Anyway, the tour was great for me. I got to see a lot of Nebraska via the back roads. I met Chuck Jura at his Pizza Hut in Schuyler and Jerry List up in Valentine and went to Scott Frost's house in Wood River in July 1992. This was one of my favorite columns, meeting Tom Kropp, the "Larry Bird of Nebraska." I remember he had a handshake like nobody I had ever met. My hand still hurts.*

OCTOBER 17, 1993 • NEBRASKA FOOTBALL

Thanks, KSU, for a Thriller

THANK YOU, Kansas State.

Thank you for showing up with your Purple Pride on your sleeve. Thank you for pushing Nebraska to the limit — and almost beyond. Thank you for turning this annual snooze job into an honest-to-goodness football game.

With drama and all the trimmings.

This is not meant to be condescending. But too often Nebraska-Kansas State has been a one-way street, where Willie the Wildcat steps in front of a semi. Too often, this series has been an embarrassment to college football.

Not this time. Kansas State didn't go down until Ernie Beler intercepted a KSU pass with 1:35 left. This time, NU won 45-28, but K-State had to be dragged out of the stadium kicking and screaming.

Thank you, Kansas State.

I-back Calvin Jones posted his second consecutive 100-yard rushing day with 138 on 29 carries and two scores against Kansas State.

OCTOBER 31, 1993 • NEBRASKA FOOTBALL

Donta Jones had one of four sacks of Kordell Stewart. Stewart completed just 8 of 28 passing attempts for 115 yards, threw three interceptions and suffered through 13 QB hurries, in addition to the sacks.

NU Holds On to Its Dream

BOULDER, COLO.

THE THUNDER OF the mountains was crashing down on the Nebraska football team. Colorado was through playing possum, and the Buffs were in position to snatch away the envelope containing the invitation to the Jan. 1 Orange Bowl.

Colorado scored to cut the Cornhuskers' lead to 21-17 with 2:54 left in the game. Suddenly, the Folsom Field crowd was awake and on its feet, ready to pounce.

The Nebraska offense, battered and bruised and trying to limp away with this game, failed to make a first down.

The Colorado offense had the ball at its own 47-yard line with 1:41 left. Plenty of time to break Husker hearts. Here we go again.

Suddenly, Nebraska was backed into a corner like a wounded animal.

Who you gonna call? Charlie McBride?

The same Nebraska defensive coordinator who was put in front of the firing squad just two weeks ago after beating — surviving — Kansas State? The very same. Maybe McBride got lucky Saturday. Maybe he was just good. Maybe he was prepared to be both.

"That's part of the fun of it," McBride said. "I was ready to throw up."

Instead, McBride walked over to his defense and smiled. That's right. Smiled. "Here we go," McBride told his huddled defense on the sideline. "We've got to win this game. This is what we want. That's our job."

Nebraska fans had seen too many big games where the Husker defense slipped on the banana peel. The opportunity was there to slip again.

This is what the Huskers got: First and 10 at the Nebraska 40. Colorado's Kordell Stewart, otherwise known as the Big Eight's best passing arm, throws a weak sparrow across the middle. The sparrow dies in the arms of Nebraska cornerback John Reece, whom Stewart apparently did not see.

Now see this: Nebraska wins 21-17. Nebraska holds on to this season, the dream, the Orange Bowl.

"Today's game shows we can go anywhere and fight adversity," said quarterback Tommie Frazier. "And win."

20 YEARS WITH TOM SHATEL • 37

TOM'S TAKE — REFLECTIONS ON

Big Eight Needs to Have a Plan Before the Dominoes Start to Fall

WHAT WOULD WE do without Billy Tubbs?

Stop the presses, full-court or otherwise. We'd be left to hear the hypnotic monotone of other Big Eight coaches, clichés at no extra cost. Find a new occupation.

I don't want to write in a world without Billy Tubbs.

The very possibility was raised just the other day.

> "I don't sound like Jack Nicholson. He sounds like me."
>
> — BILLY TUBBS, WHO COACHED OKLAHOMA TO FOUR REGULAR-SEASON BIG EIGHT TITLES

The latest rumor came out of Houston: The Big Eight and Southwest Conferences are huddling again about a possible merger. This time, supposedly, it's serious. This time BYU's invited, too.

On the weekly news media conference call, each Big Eight basketball coach was asked his opinion. Most, as usual, had none. Except, as usual, for one familiar voice.

Tubbs said it was time for Oklahoma to bolt the Big Eight. Perfect.

Tubbs' complaint, unfortunately, was that the conference postseason basketball tournament is in Kansas City.

Too bad. The rest of the Big Eight hierarchy immediately shrugged and said, "That's just Billy."

This time, maybe they should listen.

We've heard this talk before. With each alarm, the bell has rung false, and each school hurriedly has claimed there was never any intention to mutiny. Funny thing about the Big Eight breaking up: You never actually hear anybody say they want to leave. Until our man Billy.

Maybe it was the usual Billy Babble. And maybe it was Tubbs playing spokesman for a lot of sentiment behind the scenes. Maybe it was the most outspoken man in the Big Eight saying what's on everybody's mind: We should look for a different alignment.

The problem is that only Tubbs knows his agenda.

But the Big Eight should know this: Rumors like these don't just appear out of thin air. You can be sure Colorado had — has — interest in the Pac-10, Missouri did more than just check road maps of Indiana, and Oklahoma is thinking about burning its membership card as we speak. Know that everyone — yes, even Nebraska — has a secret agenda in case the Big Eight dominoes start to fall.

The question is: Does the Big Eight have an agenda ready?

In Texas are a plethora of half-empty arenas and stadiums, popular professional teams and a religious zeal for high school football. The Big Eight as a half brother to an apathetic league would mean a watered-down product. The Big Eight can only improve the SWC's product, especially in basketball.

But can the SWC return the favor? It offers bountiful recruiting territory and the generic phrase "TV sets," which implies that Houston-Iowa State somehow would be more attractive to the networks than Notre Dame-Penn State. That's questionable.

For this reason, the Big Eight turns a cold shoulder to the south. The commissioner's office in Kansas City is quiet. Too quiet. It's time, perhaps, for the keepers of this league to come up with a tornado drill — in case one hits.

The forecast is for 1995. That's when the College Football Association TV package expires, when every conference is going to play musical chairs with a network and the last one standing is out.

Anything or nothing could happen. But the Big Eight, along with the Southwest and Big East, sits like a vulnerable plot on someone's master plan. It would behoove the Big Eight to have a plan, to talk to the SWC at this year's NCAA convention and see who wants in and who wants out.

The Big Eight should plan because Nebraska vs. Oklahoma for the North Division title of the Big Southwest Conference is better than Nebraska vs. Rice. Because a merged league is better than no league. Because this merger talk, like Billy Babble, is not going to go away.

— DECEMBER 8, 1993

THE CHANGING SPORTS LANDSCAPE — 1993

Ignore the Dire Warning About the Racers Leaving — for Now

THE SKY, AS it turns out, never did fall. The 3,500th Omaha Racer season-ticket holder is still at large, walking the streets, but at least he has hope. The Racers are staying.

And Steve Idelman still is co-owner of the reigning Continental Basketball Association champions. He held a press conference to tell us the news and, in case you haven't heard, here's what he had to say: "Wolf." The Racers are staying. Silly us for thinking otherwise, that Idelman might stick to his promise to leave town or fold the franchise if 3,500 season tickets weren't sold by June 15.

It was never a threat, Idelman said. Just a fact. But since March, much has happened. The Racers won a crown, 6,000 showed up for championship games at Ak-Sar-Ben Coliseum, deadlines were juggled and facts and figures magically were transformed into projections.

Fact: Idelman said 3,500 or gone.

Fact: "Save the Racers" aroused much interest in the Omaha area but, with 2,300 tickets sold, came up woefully short.

Projection: Because the Racers have sold 50 tickets a week this summer, the club should hit 3,000 (not 3,500) by the start of the season (not June 15).

Conclusion: Idelman has lost his credibility with the Omaha sports community.

Which, really, is bad timing for the Racers. After three years of raising their hands, they finally got Omaha's attention. They won the title. They won fans. People took notice.

What they saw was a coach named Mike Thibault, who not only figures to be working in the NBA someday but is also a wonderful role model for Omaha. They saw hard-working, likable players who embraced the community.

The Racers are staying, and that's good for Omaha. But how it was handled is not. The circus started when Idelman called a press conference to announce the 3,500 goal. Among other things, Idelman said, "What if we sold 2,000? We'd call another press conference and say goodbye to everybody."

Well, hello, everybody.

Idelman later extended the deadline one month because the Racers had lost selling time during the playoffs. He said if tickets were coming in at 50 a week July 15, he could be talked into staying.

Idelman later was quoted as saying that $1.1 million in revenue — through corporate sales and ads as well as tickets — was really the bottom line and that the 3,500-ticket goal was just an easy-to-understand goal for the public.

Good thing. The ignorant masses might have just bought, say, 2,300 tickets if Idelman hadn't hung 3,500 over their heads.

The number most certainly was too ambitious. Back in June, Idelman said cutting the halftime budget, housing for players, etc., would not make much of a dent and therefore was not feasible. In this market, he had to have 3,500. So what happens? He makes the cuts anyway.

If the Racers do, in fact, reach 3,000 by the start of the season, it would be a phenomenal thing in the CBA. So maybe the deadline charades will work out for the best for Idelman, who quite possibly feared a local lynching had he removed a championship team from its fans.

But the backlash from this probably will be worse. All people remember is that Idelman said 3,500, didn't come close and stayed anyway. The good news is, the Racers are staying. And that this is it. The next time Idelman calls a press conference — or thinks he sees a wolf — he'll be talking to himself.

— JULY 21, 1993

2011 INSIGHT *I had a lot of fun covering Steve Idelman and the Racers. I think we were good for each other. He provided me with colorful copy in the non-Nebraska football months and I helped put a spotlight on his team, which he craved. This column was the pinnacle of our relationship, for better or worse. Idelman put out a season-ticket number he had to have by a certain day or he was moving the team. When it didn't happen and he stayed, I called him on it. Then, he called me – disguised as "Mike from Omaha" – while I was doing the Gary Java sports talk show. After a 15-minute tirade, which he ended by saying, "I'll be in Omaha longer than you will," I heard from various folks, including Idelman's daughter. The thing lasted about a week. When I think that a column about the CBA team could spark such controversy, I have to laugh. I miss those days. I miss having Idelman as part of the sports scene. Whatever happened to "Mike from Omaha," anyway?*

ORANGE BOWL | BIG EIGHT BASKETBALL TOURNEY TITLE | ALTMAN HIRING | SOONERS WIN CWS

1994

> "When I walked off I was thinking about how well the kids played. And how it was when I was on the other sideline, next to Tom. I was a great coach, then. Maybe I should have stayed there."
>
> — JIM WALDEN, A FORMER NEBRASKA ASSISTANT, AFTER COACHING HIS FINAL GAME AT IOWA STATE

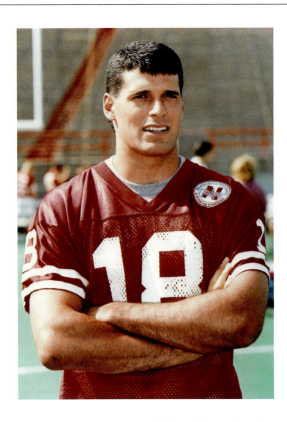

Brook Berringer was so efficient that Nebraska coach Tom Osborne didn't have to wait for rewind. "Brook was great today," said Osborne, who uses the word "great" about as often as he says "McCartney."

When it comes to the Big Dance, the Huskers still have two left feet. When the bright lights are turned on, they freeze like a deer. They can't shoot. They can't play defense. They suddenly forget to run the fast break. In four years, they've had four cups of coffee. Penn 90, Nebraska 80 — and it wasn't even that close — was the most bitter to swallow.

Not even Jim Bain, his former nemesis in zebra stripes, ever made Johnny Orr cry. So when "Coach" stepped up to a huge stage in Hilton Coliseum in Ames, Iowa, and couldn't say two words without the fault line in his emotions opening up, you knew something was up. There goes Johnny. For years — 14, to be exact — the theme was "Heeeere's Johnny." Orr was the only coach in America who had his own theme song. That was his magnitude. Before every home basketball game at Hilton, the Iowa State band would kick in "The Tonight Show" theme and out would pop Orr, walking the length of the floor and pumping his fists. But he turns 67 in June and so, before a crowd that gave him two standing ovations, he tried to tell the fans he was resigning. It wasn't easy. His face wrinkled up like a prune, his eyes grew red and his voice was like a sputtering car. "I think you come to a time — and I thought I wouldn't come to this time — when I didn't want to do this anymore," Orr said. "If I didn't want to give it everything, then I shouldn't be around doing it. That wouldn't be fair to anybody. I think I did this in a class way. A good way." In doing so, he preserved his legacy as the best thing to ever happen to Iowa State.

HOOP-IT-UP FEVER | VOLLEYBALL SELLOUTS | TOMMIE'S RECOVERY | BILL MCCARTNEY RETIRES

What exactly constitutes a pancake? Let's ask one of the chefs for a working definition. "It's taking your man off his feet and laying him on his back, where you can look right down over him," Nebraska right guard Brenden Stai said. "We take pride in that. We try to get as many as possible. We all strive to get the record." (Fifteen in a game by center Aaron Graham in 1995.)

Under Athletic Director Tom Moore, Creighton moved into new areas like marketing and compliance. CU moved into the 1990s, a time when college athletics is big business. The soccer program has taken off, new sports have been added and CU athletics are in a much better position than three years ago to foot that bill. That's assuming that basketball attendance will return, but with Dana Altman as the new coach, it's an assumption many at CU are making. Moore leaves optimism as his legacy, too. His greatest legacy is also his greatest accomplishment: training Bruce Rasmussen to do a job Moore himself was still learning. Now the job is done, the bridge built, and Moore can return to his perch in the stands. He should be proud of what he sees.

Dana Altman's not promising the moon. He talks of making Creighton "Omaha's team," and that's a good goal. If Altman can produce Tony Barone-type numbers, he might have the unequivocal popularity the demonstrative Barone never had.

Maybe the biggest mistake Kordell Stewart made was taunting the Werewolves of Lincoln, a fearsome enough bunch without the extra salivation. "Word got back to us this week that after the Kansas State game, Stewart went into their locker room and said, 'Let's go have fun with the Nebraska defense,' " Husker defensive tackle Christian Peter said. "That was not good."

20 YEARS WITH TOM SHATEL • 41

JANUARY 3, 1994 • NEBRASKA FOOTBALL

Respect Is Back for Huskers

MIAMI

HE LOOKED AT peace. That's the first thing you noticed the morning after.

At 8 a.m. Sunday, just hours after heartbreak, Tom Osborne sat on a lawn chair, beneath palm trees, taping his television show. But the look of satisfaction on Osborne's face was no act.

Across town, in a ballroom at a Miami airport hotel, the beatification of Saint Bobby Bowden had begun. A national championship trophy. A press conference with jokes and a thousand ways for Saint Bobby to tell us, by golly, how relieved he was to win the first big one. There was a different sort of satisfaction at work here. Now Saint Bobby could have a new image.

He was no longer the coach everyone felt sorry for.

That unfair label now belongs to the man named Osborne.

The man glowing with an eerie inner peace.

Some 12 hours earlier in the Orange Bowl, the two old legends had wrestled for their first national title like a game of tug-of-war. Back and forth. A classic game, maybe a candidate for "best ever" status.

But nobody knew until the final two minutes. Then, one of the longest bowl games in history (four hours exactly) suddenly became a rush hour of great moments. The lead was traded twice in the final 1:16, and almost a third time, but Nebraska kicker Byron Bennett's final-second 45-yard field goal attempt went wide left. Florida State, 18-16.

Again.

Ten years after losing the national title game to Miami, Osborne had lost another one. Somebody else had found a way to take it from his grasp.

"It was just our time," Bowden said.

Again.

The number of ways to lose would drive a lesser man crazy. The phantom illegal block that nullified a 71-yard punt return for a touchdown. A Florida State touchdown that looked like a fumble. And that maddening last-minute drive by FSU. Bennett's errant kick out of bounds, setting up FSU on its 35. The cheesy late-hit penalty call on Barron Miles. The pass interference on the next play. Always something.

But for all their miscalls and non-calls, the officials gave Nebraska what it earned by allowing the one second left in this drama of dramas. Osborne had a senior kicker with a makeable kick. He just missed.

And Osborne might have missed the boat for the national championship one last time. You never know. He's 57. It had been 10 years since his last shot. Still, the coach sat in peace Sunday morning, radiating a feeling of personal satisfaction and accomplishment that was somehow like his own secret.

"It may not happen again," Osborne said. "It's hard to say. But a lot of people get no satisfaction at all in that. They want the trophy. They want the ring. I feel a satisfaction in being able to play at the top level. That's very important to me."

There was, indeed, a much greater picture involved Saturday night than rings and history. It was all about respect.

Nebraska has it again.

For the past several years, Osborne has quietly hurt. The program he had helped build was no longer a major player on the national scene. It had dropped onto a lower shelf. Nebraska was to the national championship what the Washington Generals are to the Harlem Globetrotters: harmless fodder.

Until Saturday night.

With national television viewers waiting to see it play the joker one more time, Nebraska picked a wonderful time to bite back. The Huskers' relentless guts and execution under pressure were eye-opening. They got epic performances from sophomore quarterback Tommie Frazier, who outplayed Heisman Trophy winner Charlie Ward, and senior linebacker Trev Alberts, who left no doubt about who was Mr. Butkus Award.

They played most of the game without their top running back (Calvin Jones) and top receiver (Abdul Muhammad). Ward, who had been sacked 10 times all year, went down five times to the Husker wolves.

The Huskers should have won by two touchdowns.

They had a classic defensive game plan. Osborne's play-calling was at times brilliant and imaginative, using Frazier in different ways to offset the inability to run the option. Osborne, in fact, kept Bowden guessing most of the game. FSU was frustrated by Nebraska's ability to put pressure on Ward with only four men most of the game while the rest covered the receivers. Bowden looked flustered, and his team played like it. He started the game out of the I-formation and wasted a series. He tried a ridiculous trick play near the goal line that killed a potential touchdown.

He looked lost. He was. While the Huskers outplayed FSU, Osborne outcoached Bowden, proving himself the better big-game coach and showing Bowden for what he is: more of a news media star than coaching threat.

2011 INSIGHT *Like the post-Orange Bowl scene two years earlier, this was one of those moments in time that I'll always remember. Tom Osborne, at the team hotel, out by the pool, the morning after, replaying the game for his TV show and the Nebraska media. Only this was different. I had never seen Osborne quite like this. I had seen him crushed after losing the Big Eight title to Oklahoma in heartbreaking fashion. I had seen him befuddled after losing to Miami again and again. But I had never seen the man upbeat like this after a big-game loss. It was like he knew what was coming the next several years. I'll never forget feeling that.*

It was so obvious that, by halftime, many in the press box openly admitted to rooting for Osborne because, in the words of several, "He deserves it more than Bowden."

Honor in defeat. Respect out of losing. These are familiar themes for Osborne, who might go down as a greater man for losing big games than finally winning one. And while they might create a certain legend or aura, the close losses do little to console the 20-year-old hearts and minds whose chance comes but once or twice. "For the players, I feel pretty bad," Osborne said. "I told Barron Miles last night that a few years ago, Colorado lost to Notre Dame here and then the next year came back and beat them for the national championship. It doesn't mean you can't come back."

What happened here means Nebraska will be back.

This should go as no small consolation. Here was Saturday's signal: With a few adjustments in philosophy (offensive, defensive and in recruiting speed), Nebraska has caught up with the times and re-entered the national mix. The 4-3 defense is for real and still loaded. Frazier and Lawrence Phillips are ready for stardom.

They are back. And they are no fluke. By showing themselves — and the world — that they could have (should have) beaten mighty FSU, the Huskers have regained a certain swagger and confidence that they belong again. That is the legacy of this wonderful, unforgettable "We Refuse to Lose" bunch, which didn't win a national title but might pass along something as valuable: self-respect.

"I think the players have an appreciation for the fact they can play at a top level and play with everybody," Osborne said. "They will feel good about playing with anybody. But every season is a new adventure, and you have to build momentum and be fortunate. It takes a lot of things to get to this point."

They will be back. Tell it to the loudmouth national columnists who should know that, on Saturday night, Florida State was the true fraud. Tell it to the Las Vegas experts, who ought to consider a switch to keno. It's much safer.

You don't have to explain it to Saint Bobby, who dared underestimate a man and program on a mission.

"My hat's off to Tom," Bowden said Sunday. "I know how he felt. I've been there."

Osborne still is there. And you got the feeling he wouldn't mind staying there if he could have more Saturday nights. The smile said as much Sunday morning. At 9 a.m., the show was over and he walked away, into 1994, still empty-handed. But you knew he knew he would be back.

Tommie Frazier had 283 yards of total offense and put the Huskers in position to win at the end.

MARCH 14, 1994 • NEBRASKA BASKETBALL

Pike's Peak Has a Good View

KANSAS CITY, MO.

THIS WALK WAS real, but it could have been a dream. Any boy's dream.

Eric Piatkowski had finished the last interview and now he walked from Kemper Arena to a building across the street, where revelers from all corners of the Big Eight were congregating.

One by one, in black and gold, blue and red, orange and black, the fans recognized the man and his most recent accomplishment.

"Great game, Eric."

"There's Eric. Hey, way to go, Eric."

"God bless you, Eric."

Finally, Piatkowski reached the room where the Nebraska Rebounders Club was celebrating the Huskers' 105-88 victory over Oklahoma in the Big Eight postseason tournament.

As he walked in, the crowd erupted. Piatkowski smiled and held up a fist.

Welcome to Pike's peak.

At the moment, he can see forever. With a fourth straight NCAA tournament bid on the line, Pike didn't just deliver this season, he bought the rights.

With the clock ticking down on his brilliant Nebraska career, he had perhaps the best game ever by anyone in scarlet and cream.

He cut and slashed OU's tires. He bombed from outside (four of eight 3-pointers). Mostly, OU would miss, turn and see his blond blur going in for a fast-break layup.

When he was done, his 42 points were a career high, a school record and a Big Eight tournament record, beating the 38 by Oklahoma's Stacey King in 1989. But then, he knew that.

"Before the game, I was reading the Big Eight program, and I remember seeing Stacey King had the record for most points in a game," Piatkowski said. "Then, with about a minute and a half left, some of the guys called me over and said to go in there fast and get the ball and score.

"You know, most guys here are pretty tight. It's a media spectacle, and everyone's family's here. It's tough to go off and have a game like that."

The winning speaks loudest, of course: He now will be part of the first Nebraska senior class to go to four NCAA tournaments.

"He's the best basketball player that I've coached or been associated with," Nebraska coach Danny Nee said.

Eric Piatkowski's 42 points set a Big Eight tournament scoring record and led Nebraska to a first-round tournament win. The Huskers went on to win the championship.

2011 INSIGHT *I don't know why, but after Eric Piatkowski had the game of his life in the first round of the 1994 Big Eight tournament, I decided to follow him. After he dropped 42 points against Oklahoma from just about everywhere but the stockyards, I overheard someone saying Pike would be making an appearance at a Husker fan rally in the American Royal building next to Kemper Arena. So, I followed him. He walked, with his jersey hanging out, through a maze of fan tailgate parties. It was surreal to watch fans from Missouri, Kansas, Iowa State, etc., applaud Piatkowski and say "Nice job, Eric," as he walked to the Husker party. Big Eight tourney fans appreciate good hoops. But I couldn't help but think some of those fans considered Nebraska harmless. Two days later, they would find out otherwise. This Husker Hoops weekend to remember was just getting started.*

APRIL 1, 1994 • NEBRASKA BASKETBALL

Jamar Johnson Wears a New Label

KANSAS CITY, MO.

HE FIGURED HE had waited long enough. Through a Proposition 48 year. Through the junior year when he pouted and all but gave up on his NBA dream. Through the broken finger this season and the times when everyone had left him and his teammates for dead.

So when Jamar Johnson and his Nebraska Cornhuskers were still very much alive and, well, Big Eight tournament champions, there was nothing left for Johnson to do but take the first official snip of the net.

For the senior point guard, it was like cutting off a part of his past.

A horrid part. In 1990, his senior year at Concord High School in Elkhart, Ind., Johnson got to the state championship game. Before a national high school record crowd of 41,046 at the Hoosier Dome, Johnson lost to a team with future Indiana star Damon Bailey. But he didn't just lose.

He was labeled.

In the clutch, Bailey outplayed Johnson. Bailey was a winner, Johnson a loser. In Indiana basketball culture, it was like a tattoo on Johnson's chest.

Four years later — in Missouri and against a team from Oklahoma — Johnson washed away his pain.

"On the bus ride over today, I didn't say anything," Johnson said. "I knew it was the first time since that game that I had been in this situation. I knew that if it came down to it, I wasn't going to sit back and let someone else take over, like Damon did."

Johnson took over. He won. He made sure Nebraska won.

The maturing of Johnson arrived just in time. Nebraska's four seniors expected to win the conference title this season, but they were shortchanged by the failure to sign a big man. They could have quit.

But in red jerseys darkened by sweat, they outjumped Oklahoma State for rebounds, beat the Cowboys down the floor time and again, got the loose ball, made the defensive play. They showed that desire, poise and teamwork can make you play tall.

Standing on the press table, shaking his fist at the crowd, Johnson stood tallest.

Jamar Johnson carried Nebraska to the Big Eight basketball tournament title.

20 YEARS WITH TOM SHATEL • 45

APRIL 15, 1994 • CREIGHTON BASKETBALL

Good Move for Bluejays

CREIGHTON MADE A steal. With the world of college basketball congregated at the annual rite of passage known as the Final Four, Creighton made a move to return to the competitive mix.

In one of the most amazing searches for a Division I basketball coach in recent history, a school with suspect facilities in a mediocre conference and only a promise to upgrade its commitment interviewed just one man and got a Division I head coach to take the job.

The Bluejays and their fans should be celebrating at 24th and Burt Streets. Surely, Dana Altman is, too.

How? Creighton pulled off a mild stunner with its hiring of Altman, the former head coach at Kansas State. So much for the theory that Creighton was going to have to gamble on choosing the right top Division I assistant. Creighton not only got a head coach, it got a Big Eight head coach. From a land where basketball is sacred.

The question is, how?

You will hear that Altman was on the outs at Kansas State. A year from getting the ax. One step ahead of the posse.

It's a little more involved than that. True, despite improving his record in each of the past four seasons, Altman was not exactly a popular man in Manhattan, Kan. For three basic reasons:

He wasn't Kansas coach Roy Williams. He wasn't former K-State coach Lon Kruger, who has Florida in the Final Four. He wasn't Kansas State football coach Bill Snyder.

Now, these are not exactly crimes. But at Kansas State, they might as well have been felonies. And when you get compared to the football coach at Kansas State, you know things have slipped.

It's all relative. Creighton, of course, would take Altman's one NCAA appearance and two NIT berths. But at Kansas State, making the NCAA tournament every other year is unacceptable.

So it was a good time to leave.

Lucky for Altman, vanilla is the perpetual flavor of the month in Omaha. The city — and Creighton — seemingly ask only that a man be honest, hard-working and a family man, if possible. Flashy is not required. Charisma is a bonus. Winning solves most problems, if not Creighton attendance.

Altman ought to win at Creighton, where there will be slight pressure to do so. The Bluejays are making a commitment and will expect a return. But Altman should deliver in the Missouri Valley. He won at KU's Allen Field House this year, so Drake should be no sweat.

Dana Altman led Kansas State to three postseason tournament bids in four seasons, compiling a 68-54 record, before coming to Creighton.

2011 INSIGHT *I have known Dana Altman since about 1986. That was when he joined Lon Kruger's staff at Kansas State and I was covering the Wildcats for the Kansas City Star. Head coaches don't necessarily drink with writers, but assistants do. And Altman and I would meet up in Aggieville or at the Holidome bar after games. I kept in touch with Dana when he returned to K-State as head coach. So, suffice it to say, I was thrilled when Bruce Rasmussen shocked everyone, including me, by hiring Altman in 1994. I was at the Final Four in Charlotte when I heard. I immediately called our desk to say I knew the guy and would be writing live. I called a friend of mine in the K-State athletic department to get some background. I had no idea Dana would pull off the most successful run in Creighton hoops history. But I thought it was a good fit. And it wouldn't be bad for me, either.*

JUNE 12, 1994 • COLLEGE WORLD SERIES

Sooners Shed OSU's Shadow

GARY WARD'S YEAR is now complete. The Oklahoma State baseball czar spent much of the season bent over in the dugout with severe back pain. Then his Cowboys got a regional in Stillwater and blew the trip to Omaha when their pitcher hit a batter with the bases loaded.

And now this.

Oklahoma Sooners. National champions.

"I hope they're cheering in Long Beach," said OU second baseman Rick Gutierrez, speaking of his hometown in California. "I hope they're moaning, too, in Stillwater."

If the Sooners listened carefully, they could probably hear the pain in the wind.

In their immediate minds was the business of celebrating their first national baseball championship since 1951. The spoils of victory came in the form of some guy throwing T-shirts onto the growing dogpile of Sooners.

The national championship shirts came with this message: "No Respect."

What did you expect?

This was the year in sports when nobody got respect, from the Buffalo Bills, who didn't deserve it, to Arkansas basketball coach Nolan Richardson, who wouldn't accept it. But in the case of OU baseball, it is a theme embedded in red clay. From Tulsa to the Panhandle, the specter of Ward and his national program lurks over the Sooners.

Not today.

Ward's teams have been CWS regulars, but they have yet to have a T-shirt thrown at them.

"This will put OU on the map," said OU's Damon Minor. "At home, it's always Stillwater this, Stillwater that."

Minor, in particular, hoped Ward kept his TV set on long enough to see his three-run homer in the sixth, which landed somewhere in the zebra pen. A few years ago, when Damon and twin Ryan were going as a brother package, Ward wanted Ryan but waffled on Damon. That one's for you, Gary.

"That makes this a lot sweeter," Damon said. "When I got here last week, I hoped Oklahoma State was going to be here because I wanted to play them. I knew we'd beat them."

Oklahoma defeated Georgia Tech 13-5 to win the 1994 College World Series.

20 YEARS WITH TOM SHATEL • 47

JULY 2, 1994 • NEBRASKA BASEBALL

'Nebraska' Was a Bully

THE STORY THAT never should have been told is over. The verdict that never should have been called is in. "Nebraska" is guilty.

Guilty of apparent jealousy, desperation and, perhaps, even a misguided vindictiveness that has come back to haunt the biggest school on our block. But today, "Nebraska" just looks like a bully. Big Red in the face.

We say "Nebraska" because it's still unclear just who in Lincoln decided to turn Creighton's baseball program in to the NCAA on 33 allegations in 1993. Who is responsible for this cheap shot? Who is "Nebraska"?

Is it Nebraska Athletic Director Bill Byrne, who was the man in charge when the 33 allegations went to the NCAA?

Is it Nebraska baseball coach John Sanders, a veteran of 16 years at NU who saw Creighton's 1991 College World Series trip as a threat to his program?

Is it Nebraska assistant baseball coach Tim Seaton, a former Creighton player who admitted giving the NCAA information about rules violations at CU?

Will the real "Nebraska" please stand up?

Ever since this story broke in The World-Herald in 1993, the potential antagonists have hidden behind the label "Nebraska." Byrne was the initial spokesman, but he was in his first few months on the job. Why would he turn in Creighton? What would he gain? Why would he need the controversy? Answer: He wouldn't.

But now that the NCAA has doused this firecracker, it's time for somebody at "Nebraska" to take responsibility for this mess. You don't turn your neighbor in to the authorities and say "no harm, no foul" when it comes out that there was nothing substantial found in Creighton's closet. Somebody must pay.

Ah, Creighton. Those dirty birds. "Nebraska" blew the whistle on them for 33 allegations, though Creighton and its crack law firm could only find eight, including three that "Nebraska" didn't even see. But then, how could "Nebraska" know that

Creighton's Andy Vosik is forced out at second base, as Nebraska's Darin Petersen makes the relay throw to first in the Huskers' 7-6 victory over the Jays in 1994. NU's Darin Erstad hit a game-winning, three-run homer in the bottom of the seventh inning.

"Doc" (Lee) Bevilacqua, Creighton's volunteer team physician, was letting a sick player spend the night on his couch?

Goodness. A player is lent a car to drive back to Omaha after a medical appointment in Chicago. CU coach Jack Dahm picks up the lunch tab for a player who left his wallet at home and Dahm gets reimbursed. Bet you that Dahm probably jaywalked, too.

Fortunately for CU, it's over. The NCAA reviewed the findings of CU's investigation, made a few phone calls and decided this was much ado about nothing. All secondary violations. The NCAA took away a scholarship for one year, but ruled that Creighton did not gain an unfair recruiting or competitive advantage.

Queen and King on the Sidelines

IF NANCY LIEBERMAN-CLINE can't get to a hospital, she might as well have her baby right here.

This is, after all, her world. Her people. For as far as the eye could see at Bluffs Run, the world was hoops, basketballs, blacktop and high-tops. And the best female player in history, due to go into labor any day now, wishing she could play.

Indeed. The court was full at Omaha's Hoop-It-Up, but the Queen and King of Hoop-It-Up were not in their court. Their teams had won the Omaha and national 3-on-3 titles last year. But this summer the Queen, Lieberman-Cline, was walking around — slowly — helping run the tournament. The King, Dean Thompson, sat and judged a slam-dunk contest.

"Old age catches up with you," said Thompson, who blew out his knee last August in a game. "This tournament is tough. Two days, eight or nine games in the heat. And some of the games can really be wrestling matches. This (knee) is a good excuse not to play."

Hoop-It-Up is bigger and better than ever. Nearly 1,700 teams are entered. That's the third-largest Hoop-It-Up tournament in the country. And they said this was a football state. Now, if we can just get some of those sweaty bodies to shower and sit in a seat at a Creighton, UNO or Racers game, all of this will make perfect sense.

"I love this event," Thompson said. "Omaha is a participation town; when you give them a forum, they come out. But it's also a good basketball town, too. People here like hoops. They love to play."

And Hoop-It-Up is kind of a cult thing. But a huge cult. It's for anyone who ever had a basket standing on a pole in his driveway. It's for the people in the over-30 crowd who play on Sunday mornings or during their lunch hour. It's for anyone with a basketball, a pair of shoes and a dream. The population is booming.

Omaha boasted the third-largest number of teams in the Hoop-It-Up tournament of 1994.

Hoop-It-Up strikes a chord because it is the bare essence of sport. Teamwork. Hard work. Sportsmanship. A simple game. Play to 15, win by two. Call your own fouls. Play with your friends. Maybe make one or two while you're there.

Their slogan is printed on a T-shirt here. It reads, "Stop Hacking. Quit Crying. Play Ball." Enough said.

JULY 20, 1994 • DUNCAN FIELD

Duncan Field Stands Proud

HASTINGS, NEB.

SHE IS A wonderful old lady, full of charm and soul and a backbone made of brick.

Once upon a time, her brick wall probably was fire-engine red, but the games and years have taken some of the color. Still, Duncan Field stands proud as ever on a summer night, daring the hitters to scale the walls like some kind of prize to be won.

The prize would be to join the legend. The dimensions of the old ballpark are almost Ruthian. It's 408 to dead center, 405 to the power alleys, 370 down the left-field line and 367 to the right corner. The outfield is so big that the light standards are inside the wall. So big that St. Cecilia, a local high school, plays football games there.

But make no mistake, Duncan Field was made for baseball and making baseball nights special memories. Something to tell the kids. Yeah, I hit one out of Duncan. Well, OK, at least I saw one go out once.

The stories have come from all venues: semi-pro leagues, minor-league clubs (the Giants) and, mostly, American Legion teams. Dave McNally pitched here. Rusty Staub hit here. Yogi Berra even jacked one out. Or so they say.

The best part of Duncan Field is the myths that a place like this can perpetuate. It was made for nights like this one, when local faces like Bob Stickels, Butch Bienkowski and Pat Duggins sat around watching a Pony League game between Hastings and Hebron and tossed around Duncan Hall-of-Fame moments.

"I saw Gregg Olson pitch here for Omaha — I think it was 1985," Duggins said. "It was a Legion playoff game of some kind, and this place was full. I remember Bill Olson was the coach. They beat Hastings 2-1."

The myths and American Legion ball are alive and well at Duncan Field, the guardian of amateur baseball in Hastings and a monument to all that the sport has meant to this community.

It has been that way since the Great Depression, when Duncan Field was built as part of a Works Progress Administration project in the Roosevelt era, according to John Walsh, a reporter for Hastings TV station KHAS who researched a series on the field a year ago.

"People think this is football country," Walsh said. "But baseball has a lifeblood here."

Hastings residents are proud of the rich memories of Duncan Field.

2011 INSIGHT *I've always enjoyed getting in the car and driving west of Lincoln, not to mention north or south. Some of my best memories have been "outstate" Nebraska columns. My early tours. Ken Fischer, Tom Kropp, Bob Erickson, etc. There are a lot of hidden gems in the state, great stories and characters. This was one of my favorites. I like old stadiums. Duncan Field has a lot of baseball history. It also was fun to watch a high school football game there one night in 2006. These kinds of moments always make me feel like more of a Nebraskan.*

SEPTEMBER 2, 1994 • FOOTBALL

Football Fills Baseball Void

SPORTS MEMO
TO: Richard Ravitch and Donald Fehr.
RE: Baseball strike.

Who cares?
There may have been a time when those words would have been impossible to utter. When we still cared about Greg Maddux's ERA, Tony Gwynn's daily 2 for 4 and Cleveland at Seattle.

But that time is long gone.

Baseball's time is up. Expired. Over. This weekend, we find our oasis after weeks of channel-surfing through a wasteland of sports activity. I'll put it to you in six words, gentlemen.

Ahman Green. Notre Dame. John Madden.

Football has arrived. Baseball has gone from a season of dreams to its worst nightmare: a closed shop while football prepares to lap it in our everyday psyche. Good riddance. We can live without "Baseball Tonight," overpriced jerks and, most of all, your petty negotiating wars.

We live for the weekends.

We live for Friday Night Lights, sitting on a blanket next to a Thermos and watching neighborhood heroes — such as Omaha Central's Green — play for honest and emotional stakes.

We live for Indian summer Saturday afternoons, when we dress in our school colors, listen to a halftime show and go to the campus dive afterward to watch the nation's scores roll across the afternoon. We also live to stay at home, in an old shirt and an easy chair, cheering, cheering against old Notre Dame.

We live for Sunday afternoons and the sonic boom of Madden's voice telling us how that quarterback's decapitation actually felt. Sure, the NFL can be a tad clinical, but we have three fantasy teams each, so we live for each Sunday as if we were paying the schmucks.

Omaha Central's Ahman Green ran for 1,591 yards and 14 touchdowns as a senior, his third straight 1,000-yard season.

SEPTEMBER 27, 1994 • NEBRASKA VOLLEYBALL

Coliseum Is Just Like New

WILT CHAMBERLAIN PLAYED here. So did Cazzie Russell. Somewhere in the Nebraska Coliseum, the ghosts of Wilt and Cazzie are still hanging out along with the ghosts of Bob Boozer, Jerry Fort and Joe Cipriano. But the ghosts of the Nebraska Coliseum now have company.

The old relic is alive and well with the sounds of whistles, screams and a solid white ball that flies around the place like a pinball. Nebraska volleyball lives here now. And how.

That there is something special taking place here hits you the minute you walk in the door. Here you see a bronze statue called "The Players" — three women digging, setting and spiking a volleyball. At the time it was dedicated, in 1992, Nebraska volleyball coach Terry Pettit said, "This statue says, 'This is where women come to compete.'"

And people come to appreciate it.

A record Coliseum volleyball crowd of 4,577 crammed into the venerable building to watch Nebraska beat New Mexico and extend its home unbeaten streak to 31.

The fans hovered over the pitlike court, cheering and stomping, standing and hanging on every point. They stood in all the open areas at court level, their necks craning for a view. They sat along the back wall until the public address announcer asked them to move, lest they become the wrong end of a spike.

They were a sweaty, wonderful madhouse.

In the hallway is the trophy case showing off the countless Big Eight championships. From the rafters hang the banners. In the concourse is a concessions table selling only Nebraska volleyball merchandise. In the stands they cheer on cue, holding up giant cards with an "Ace" on one side and "K" (for a kill) on the other.

Move over, Wilt. Nebraska volleyball is setting traditions by the minute and spiking them in the building where college basketball once thrived.

"There are other places where they have enthusiastic crowds," Pettit said. "But in terms of atmosphere, this is without a doubt the best place in the country. These are the most knowledgeable fans in the country in a building that promotes crowd participation."

The Huskers have come a long way since 1977, Pettit's first year, when it was "40 people on folding chairs." They have become so huge that they brought renovations to the Coliseum: new lighting, scoreboard, floor and bleachers — and more bleachers have been ordered. The Coliseum is fresher and brighter than ever.

But what makes this work is the relationship between player and fan. The people sit so close they can see the color of the players' floor burns. Afterward, they can touch them. It's a tradition that Nebraska players hang around to mingle and sign autographs. This admiration society is most mutual.

"It's amazing," said senior Kelly Aspegren. "Tonight I got goose bumps from the crowd."

Together, they have built Nebraska volleyball into its own entity. There are only a handful of college nonrevenue programs in the country that can say this. What Pettit has built here in 18 years is a tribute to how far women's sports have come. And a glimpse of what they still can become.

The coach credits his administration for "taking a risk, making a leap and sticking with it." He credits the people and the volleyball leagues of Lincoln with nurturing the interest. He credits the high school programs around the state with fueling the pipeline.

But a large part of what is happening here belongs to the rejuvenated old Coliseum. So many of these antiquated structures of yesteryear sit on campuses nationwide, aging and lonely, with nothing but ghosts watching intramural games. At Nebraska, volleyball is pumping new life and traditions into a proud old lady. And she is returning the favor.

The University of Nebraska volleyball program enters the 2011 season with 149 straight sellouts at the Coliseum.

OCTOBER 16, 1994 • NEBRASKA FOOTBALL

Score One for Tradition

MANHATTAN, KAN.

THE WORDS ECHOED through the Flint Hills and beyond, a cold reminder to those who would rewrite history.

"Nebraska is still Nebraska," said Ed Stewart, the senior Nebraska linebacker. "And Kansas State is still Kansas State."

Was there ever any doubt?

Yes.

Fantasy met Tradition.

Fantasy was Kansas State, hypnotizing itself into thinking it would pick apart the Nebraska defense, stuff the run and send the Huskers home with a New Order.

Nebraska, meanwhile, had lost quarterback Tommie Frazier and had a nonconference schedule that suddenly had wilted in the September sun. What had Nebraska proved?

Was Tradition on the ropes?

No. Nebraska took this fork in the road and stuck it in Kansas State.

Every year is different; every team has its own personality. Every team must show it can carry on the tradition. With its 17-6 victory over K-State, the 1994 Huskers defined the kind of team — and season — they want to have.

"This showed a lot about our character," said walk-on quarterback Matt Turman, who should know.

"We sucked it up and showed a lot of courage," said quarterback Brook Berringer, who also should know.

Don't say Nebraska doesn't get the breaks. The steady mist and rain wasn't K-State weather. Then again, Nebraska didn't have its offense. It was almost as if Mother Nature wanted this one on equal terms. Let Fantasy beat Tradition straight-up.

One team came to redefine its tradition, but another one did. Nebraska is still Nebraska.

Jeff Makovicka's 15-yard touchdown run with 11:02 left in the game gave Nebraska a 13-6 lead.

20 YEARS WITH TOM SHATEL • 53

OCTOBER 30, 1994 • NEBRASKA FOOTBALL

Osborne Lets Actions Talk

NEBRASKA IS THE No. 1 team in the country. But don't quote Tom Osborne on that.

"I don't much care about the polls," said Nebraska's football coach minutes after his team showed that it did by thumping Colorado, 24-7. "I'll let you guys decide that."

On a day when the No. 2 (coaches poll) and No. 3 (Associated Press) Huskers decisively narrowed the national championship race to themselves and Penn State . . .

Moments after he put the finishing touch on perhaps his best coaching job in 22 years and staked a claim to his first national coach-of-the-year award . . .

And in a political process that often puts as much emphasis on press conference performances as on-the-field statements . . .

Maybe the best move Osborne made all day was excusing himself from his own press conference.

"Anything else I say," Osborne said, "might be counterproductive."

There's much to be said for the Oz approach. There's already too much lobbying for college football's top prize.

The Huskers could only try to make the process as objective as possible.

"I hope all the voters watched this game," senior offensive tackle Zach Wiegert said. "They say we don't play a tough schedule, but today we beat the team that supposedly played the toughest schedule, and it wasn't close. They say we can't win a big game, but was there a bigger game in college football this season than this one?"

"They" said this one was not only for poll position for the national title, but also a catapult to the Heisman Trophy.

This much we know: Colorado running back Rashaan Salaam (22 carries for 134 yards) was a nonfactor in what he'd called the "biggest game of my life."

Dittos for Colorado quarterback Kordell Stewart, who might win the Heisman every year if he could skip Nebraska. Stewart was his usual deer-in-the-headlights self again. He completed as many passes as the Nebraska quarterback — 12 — which wouldn't be bad except: 1, the Buffs supposedly had their best offense under coach Bill McCartney and 2, the NU quarterback, Brook Berringer, was making only his fourth start.

Osborne outcoached McCartney yet again with a series of "surprise" blitzes and offensive-line stunts that Nebraska hadn't shown and left McCartney again looking clueless on the sidelines. This isn't a rivalry, it's a rerun.

That Osborne won't campaign surely will fuel more talk that he doesn't want it bad enough. But did you ever know a fisherman who talked with the line in the water?

"He always taught us that words don't mean much," Wiegert said. "You've got to win by your actions."

Actions spoke louder than words. They said Nebraska is No. 1.

Quarterback Brook Berringer completed 12 of 17 passes for 142 yards in his fourth career start.

DECEMBER 14, 1994 • NEBRASKA FOOTBALL

Tommie Frazier sat out eight games before returning in the Orange Bowl. Running back Lawrence Phillips is behind him.

NU's Frazier Is a 'Miracle'

THE DREAM IS very much alive.

It was unthinkable that Nebraska quarterback Tommie Frazier could ever run another option this season. That was on Oct. 5. During an unforgettable press conference, Dr. Deepak Gangahar said that because of a second blood clot found in Frazier's leg, he was recommending that Frazier "be kept on blood thinners for three to six months as it stands now."

But something incredible has happened between then and now.

The blood clots that appeared so unexpectedly in Frazier's veins have left town just as quickly. Frazier now appears poised to play in the Orange Bowl.

And those experts — ahem — who wrote that this was "the death of a dream" may be wrong. Very much wrong.

Call it the miracle of modern medicine. Or the miracle that is Frazier.

You wonder if anything can stop this young man.

The story of the year is about to be rewritten before our eyes. If Frazier plays in the Orange Bowl, his legend will grow. If he makes a play to win a national championship, he should consider public office in 1996.

But is he OK? It will be human nature to cringe every time he gets hit. Is that blood on his leg? How can this be happening?

Back on Oct. 5, Dr. Gangahar called the blood clots "an enigma." Perhaps it just follows that their hasty disappearance is part of this enigma.

"It's definitely a faster recovery than the average person," Dr. Gangahar said. "But we're not talking about the average person, either."

Obviously.

TOM'S TAKE
REFLECTIONS ON

Battle of Survival Claims a Victim: The Nebraska-Oklahoma Game

KANSAS CITY, MO.

HERE IS HOW traditions are born today: A dozen men sit around a hotel conference room, kick around a few ideas, have them typed up on a piece of paper and then announce them to a room packed with reporters.

And this is how one tradition dies.

You probably thought the world would end before the Nebraska-Oklahoma football series. You may begin construction on that backyard bunker today.

> "We have other needs and commitments. Our fans might rather see Notre Dame."
>
> — DONNIE DUNCAN,
> OU ATHLETIC DIRECTOR

The Big 12 athletic directors didn't release the apocalypse, just their recommendation to divide the new conference into North and South Divisions when play begins in 1996. The proposal is expected to be approved by Big 12 football coaches and rubber-stamped by the league presidents in the near future, though Nebraska Chancellor Graham Spanier should leave his stamp at home.

As the fittest struggle to survive in this highly volatile and transient world of college sports, many old, time-honored traditions are expected to be squashed like so much roadkill along the way to the bank. As we speak, the Big 12 is bearing down on our Oklahoma rivalry.

That the Big 12 decided to split in two and draw the Mason-Dixon line at Bartlesville, Okla., is no surprise. The news came with the proposal that each school play eight conference games: five division games and three nondivision games.

Your favorite team will reside in the North with Kansas, Missouri, Kansas State, Iowa State and Colorado. The Huskers' three South Division games will be played on a rotation basis; each Big 12 school will be required to play each nondivision foe twice in four years. For NU, that means playing OU every other year or two years.

Where was this format when Tom Osborne needed it — in the 1970s?

Actually, NU Athletic Director Bill Byrne said he and Osborne both wanted an NU-OU guarantee written into the proposal but saw it shot down.

Such is the price of fame and fortune. And while the Big 12 is a natural, fertile new home for Nebraska, all the ABC money in the world can't replace the feeling of knowing that those dreaded, cocky Sooners are going to be waiting there at the end of each November. You can't replace Game-of-Every-Year atmosphere or the memories of Sims, Mildren and Switzer. This is tradition famous around the world.

"Nebraska is a great game for us, but to say it will be there every year, I can't say that," OU Athletic Director Donnie Duncan said. "We have other needs and commitments. Our fans might rather see Notre Dame."

Ditto for ABC, which likely would be content with OU vs. Notre Dame or Florida State instead of OU-Nebraska. The Huskers also have a full nonconference plate after 1996, including Iowa and Notre Dame. Oklahoma-Nebraska, the nonconference game, wouldn't feel right, anyway. Conference bragging rights are what founded this rivalry.

"I'm disappointed," Byrne said. "If we had our druthers, we would play them every year, but when we went to eight games, we got into problems because OU has other (nonconference) obligations, and so do we."

Which leads us to the really bad news.

"We could move Colorado to that last weekend," Byrne said. "Bill McCartney might get his wish."

Thanksgiving will never be the same.

— MAY 18, 1994

THE CHANGING SPORTS LANDSCAPE 1994

Believe It or Not, Nebraska Fans Will Miss Bill McCartney

ON THIS EVER-CHANGING Big Eight football landscape, that was only a tremor registered on the Big Red Seismograph.

Oklahoma coach Gary Gibbs' resigning is not a movement of earthquake proportions in Nebraska, unless the Sooners decide to win one for the Gibber.

But this state is still feeling the shock waves from Colorado coach Bill McCartney's resignation.

Gibbs will not be missed, primarily because nobody knew him. Gibbs was the unassuming, faceless coach who beat Nebraska once in five tries. In six generic seasons, he was never a threat.

McCartney was a serious threat to Big Red security.

Admit it: You either raised a toast or a high-five to McCartney's departure. Nebraska will miss McCartney like Dorothy misses the Wicked Witch of the West. Ding, dong, McCartney is gone.

I say Nebraska will miss Bill McCartney.

McCartney was the coach you loved to hate. He lighted the passions and fires inside Nebraskans like no other nemesis. Oklahoma-Nebraska was a rivalry built on mutual respect. Barry Switzer still gets invitations to speak at functions in Nebraska.

McCartney will never be invited to sit at Nebraska's dinner tables.

It wasn't so much that McCartney singled out Nebraska as his chief rival back in the mid-1980s. It was the way he did it. McCartney incited a riot.

"Nebraska" stood out in red ink on a mounted schedule. He evicted people from practice if they wore red during "Nebraska week."

The disdain for Nebraska turned into "McCartney-ism." The Colorado news media joined in with annual bashings of Nebraskans. Colorado fans took the Nebraska jokes a few ugly steps too far. Nebraska fans retaliated. It was everything college football should never be.

McCartney later tried to turn down the hysteria. It was never his intention, he said, to make it ugly. Right. And the Wicked Witch used that broom for cleaning.

But McCartney's scheme simply fit into his ability to be a magnet to controversy. That much was evident when, during one interview we had, McCartney said: "If I were in your profession, I would want to be a columnist." The implication being he loved to speak his mind.

And he didn't mind the consequences that came with walking wild-eyed down his own path.

— NOVEMBER 22, 1994

> **"If I were in your profession, I would want to be a columnist."**
>
> — COLORADO COACH BILL MCCARTNEY

Bill McCartney won 93 games and one national title in 13 seasons at Colorado.

NEBRASKA'S COMEBACK WIN IN MIAMI | SOME SERIOUS SOFTBALL | DARIN ERSTAD'S SWING

1995

"Sure, he gets mad once in a while. Actually, he doesn't like our dog very well. If he gets angry, he might kick the dog."

— NANCY OSBORNE, DESCRIBING STOIC HUSBAND TOM

Nebraska signee Tyronn Lue, the point guard from Raytown, Mo., canceled a trip to Memphis earlier this week and stuck with his first choice. One big reason, according to Lue: "They (Nebraska) said I could come in and start four years. I think I will be starting." No, Tyronn. We KNOW you will be starting.

Don't expect Nebraska coach Tom Osborne to flash his national football championship ring to recruits and boosters, as did Barry Switzer and Jimmy Johnson. Osborne isn't going to wear it. Osborne's No. 1 rock went into a collection of his numerous other Big Eight and national title (1970-71) rings that he keeps in a box in his house. The only ring on Osborne's hand is his wedding ring, and once that was almost too much to ask. "This is my second wedding ring," Osborne said. "The other one had to be replaced. I lost it in a baseball glove during a baseball game. Nancy wasn't very happy about that."

It's time for the Nebraska School Activities Association to do away with home fields as venues for state championship football games. The state association should consider moving all of the games to Lincoln and playing a doubleheader or tripleheader. Memorial Stadium comes to mind — what Nebraska-bred boy doesn't dream of one day playing a game in the shrine? Some have said Memorial Stadium is too big for the kind of crowd you would get. "My personal feeling is, I would like to see all the final games at one site," said Jim Riley, executive director of the NSAA. "It would be a great experience for the athletes." Exactly. Never mind how a small crowd would look in Memorial Stadium. Think how fair — and exciting — it would be for the players who worked all season to get there.

CWS STAR POWER | LAWRENCE PHILLIPS' ARREST | PETTIT'S TITLE TEAM | TOMMIE ONE OF THE BEST

Los Angeles Dodgers manager Tommy Lasorda on Creighton baseball coach Jack Dahm: "This young man is 27 years old. I've got shorts that old."

After he played in an exhibition game recently in Fort Dodge, Iowa, former Iowa State guard Fred Hoiberg saw his T-shirt auctioned for $475 — $225 more than the game ball went for.

To mark the Basketball Hall of Fame induction of Lew Alcindor (Kareem Abdul-Jabbar), we asked Nebraska coach Danny Nee — who was one year ahead of Alcindor at Power Memorial High School in New York — for his favorite Lew story. "I remember when he turned 7 feet, we threw a party for him, with cake and everything," Nee said. "People said he was one-dimensional, but he was a great athlete. He swam. I remember we played softball, and he was first base, and he caught everything you threw at him. I think if he had been 6-6, he still would have made the NBA. He was that good an athlete."

The Yoris — UNO's Mary (left) and Creighton's Connie — had a rooting interest in the Super Bowl. Chargers linebacker Dennis Gibson, also from Ankeny, Iowa, is their cousin. Gibson had 24 Super tickets, which, alas, ran out before Connie's and Mary's place in line.

The folks from Happy Valley should be downright giddy after hiring Graham Spanier as their president last week. True, this doesn't exactly make up for the national championship of college football. (12-0 Penn State finished second to 13-0 Nebraska in 1994.) But to those who know college athletics, stealing away Nebraska's chancellor represents a victory for the Nittany Lions.

Creighton has enlisted a new marketing strategy for the 1995-96 basketball season: selling beer at home games at the Civic Auditorium.

JANUARY 2, 1995 • NEBRASKA FOOTBALL

Nebraska fullback Cory Schlesinger barrels in for the go-ahead score in the Huskers' 24-17 victory over Miami in the Orange Bowl.

JANUARY 2, 1995 • NEBRASKA FOOTBALL

NU Exorcises Bowl Ghosts

MIAMI

JOE PATERNO WAS right. Coach Tom Osborne won his first national championship when he least expected it. And where he least expected it.

In the east end zone of the Orange Bowl.

The ghosts of the 1983 season, and the east end zone, were exorcised. There, in the place where so many Nebraska national championship dreams have died, Nebraska beat Miami 24-17 to hand Osborne his first national championship in a storied and often-frustrating career.

The east end zone can vouch for the latter.

There — where Turner Gill's pass to Jeff Smith Jan. 2, 1984, was tipped against Miami — quarterback Tommie Frazier hit tight end Eric Alford with a 2-point conversion pass that tied the Hurricanes at 17 with 7:38 to play.

There, where Byron Bennett's long field-goal try went wide left last year, Nebraska scored twice up the middle. There, where Florida State's William Floyd scored a controversial touchdown last year, Nebraska fullback Cory Schlesinger twice went in untouched.

Just like Nebraska at 13-0.

The Cornhuskers will have to wait one day for the final verdict to come from both the Associated Press and USA Today/CNN polls. But it will be easy, compared with the wait of 22 years for Osborne.

He overcame Miami in Miami. He overcame a 10-0 deficit in Miami.

Our ramblin', gamblin' coach reached for the dice and gave them a roll. Maybe that's what Paterno, the Penn State coach, meant by "when you least expect it." Who could expect so much Osborne caution being tossed to the Biscayne breezes?

He put Frazier back into the game for the first time since Nebraska's second series. And suddenly it all changed.

Nebraska's options worked. Nebraska moved the ball. Nebraska scored. In the east end zone.

Twice.

And suddenly, in a fourth quarter of an Orange Bowl, Miami was on the run. And on its back.

The east end zone was quivering. It had no chance. This was Osborne's night.

He moved All-America right guard Brenden Stai to the left side to combat Miami's Warren Sapp. While Sapp had his moments, it was clear on NU's two late scoring drives that Stai's pounding had taken its toll.

Bravo, Ozzie. He went back to the option and Schlesinger late when he felt his line would have the upper hand. Heavens. He even tossed out the quarterback slide rule and put Frazier in late "on a gut feeling."

Nebraska played solidly, its defense proud and courageous in holding the line.

And its coach pushed all the right buttons for admission into the national championship fraternity.

2011 INSIGHT *For years covering Tom Osborne and his journey to the top of the mountain, you couldn't help but wonder what the moment would be like and how you would write it. When it happened, I didn't have time to think or come up with a Pulitzer Prize nominee. Nebraska was down and it looked like another loss to Miami, then all of a sudden the fourth quarter came and Cory Schlesinger was scoring touchdowns. Then I had to have a column on the greatest moment of Osborne's career, the moment everyone had waited for, done in 40 minutes. I couldn't stop thinking about that east end zone, where the coach had gone for two 11 years earlier. I remember our World-Herald crew left the old Orange Bowl press box about 2 a.m. and got back to our hotel about 2:30 a.m. Got up a few hours later and went to Osborne's press conference, where he didn't act any differently than in any other press conference. I'm not sure what I expected. Osborne doing stand-up? Fireworks? It didn't happen. The moment got bigger once we returned home, and you saw the reaction here. And it's grown bigger with time. But back then, in the middle of it, it didn't seem different. That seems odd to say. But that's life on a tight deadline, I guess.*

FEBRUARY 21, 1995 • CREIGHTON BASKETBALL

Altman, Jays Aren't Quitting

DIARY OF TEAM Project: Today we laid another brick in the wall.

The sun blasts through the windows of the upstairs gym at Creighton's Vinardi Athletic Center, shining in on a dark season. Creighton coach Dana Altman talks to his basketball team. The Bluejays are 6-17. They have three games left.

Altman claps his hands together and says, "Let's go, fellas. We've got to get something done."

This was the year to get something done. That's how Altman's first season at Creighton was going to be judged. When the cupboard is bare, record can't be the issue. The foundation would be the thing. This was the year to set a tone, to establish all the corny things that show up in every championship game on every level.

This was the day to measure this season. The first practice after a ninth straight loss — the longest skid in school history. Have they quit? Are they getting anything done? Or is this year a total waste?

In a full-court, one-on-one drill, Joel Templeman tips the ball away from Adam Reid, and they both dive head-first after the ball, their bodies screeching against the wood floor like a car avoiding an accident. Senior guard Jason Bey gets beat by Marcus Lockett and throws the ball against the wall and curses.

"They are still working hard, but they've just lost their confidence," Altman said. "I'm glad they're continuing to play hard. It's our job to put a more athletic team together."

In the meantime, these late-season practices serve as a sort of tryout for next season. No coach will say he's going to run people off. But in their own subtle ways, every coach does just that. Sometimes, the player will decide it for him.

That's a big reason that this practice had the intensity of an NCAA tournament team. Bodies flying. Coaches shouting. Players bent over, gasping for oxygen.

"We're evaluating the people who are supposed to be back, to see how they fit in and if they fit in," Altman said. "I'm sure they're evaluating us, to see how we fit in. We're going to build this thing with a better work ethic. If they don't give it now, how can we believe they'll give it this summer, when we're not there?"

Randall Crutcher walks out to the line until Altman tells him to "hustle out." He misses, and they are running again. Bey wins the last sprint by diving over the baseline. Altman gathers the team and says, "Good job, Jason. That was a real quick lesson in not giving up."

Which is a daily victory for each Creighton player still out there every afternoon, laying the foundation for a future he may or may not see.

"It's all about pride," Bey said. "For me, being a senior, this is it. I want to play harder than ever and show the younger guys if you work as hard as you can, you can still walk away with your head up."

Looks like the foundation is beginning to take shape.

Coach Dana Altman finished with a 7-19 record in his first year at Creighton.

MARCH 24, 1995 • NEBRASKA BASKETBALL

Recruiting Is Key for Nee

THE BODY WAS not yet cold when The World-Herald's fax machine started warming up. Less than 12 hours after Nebraska's season ended with a 65-59 NIT loss to Penn State, there lay a stack of venom concerning one Danny Nee.

"Nee Must Go," read one fax, thus confirming what Nee has been saying all along: Nebraska basketball is fragile. The coach, then, must be made out of porcelain.

One year Nee's the hero, the next they want to string him up by one of his designer ties. One season he wins the Big Eight postseason basketball trophy, the next he's 18-14 in a most disappointing season that raises the question of the day.

Is that all there is? Has the Nee era peaked? Are three days of hot basketball in Kansas City going to be the crowning moments of Nee-braska? Nee raised the level of Nebraska basketball. But is this as high as he can go?

Nee is still the right coach for Nebraska, with one very big stipulation. That he hears the alarm blaring from a season that was mostly short of expectations, at times embarrassing and, in many ways, a huge wake-up call for the coach and his program.

A reality check.

The reality is that Nee offers certain limitations. He will never take Nebraska to the Final Four. He will never win a Big Eight title. But he can continue to meet the admirable standards he has set, such as going to the NCAA tournament and filling the Devaney Sports Center.

The reality is that Nee has carved a brilliant niche for himself at Nebraska, but even that popularity wanes with home losses to Colorado.

The reality is that Nee did not even produce his own bottom line this year. Nebraska started 11-1, but after Feb. 1, NU won three games. Sure, there were the bodies (Bruce Chubick and Eric Piatkowski) who weren't there anymore and the people out of position.

But those excuses didn't explain how the Huskers could look so flat and undisciplined so often. With Jaron Boone, Terrance Badgett and Erick Strickland, the Huskers had an opportunity to elevate their place in the Big Eight, with Oklahoma and Kansas State slipping in recent years. Make that a blown opportunity.

The reality is, Nee has to recruit better players.

He needs players as a form of discipline. Too often this year Nee couldn't bench a pouting Boone or cold Strickland because they had to play. In his best year, 1990-91, Nee had so much depth he was able to sit Tony Farmer and Rich King during the season as a motivational tool. It worked.

He needs players to offset his own game management. Nee is not a good bench coach. But when you have a point guard to run the show, a 6-6 gunner to blast open zones and a 6-10 behemoth to dunk on the break, who needs timeouts?

He needs players to effectively play this style, which is the perfect style for Nebraska. But you can't play a full-court pressure game with big men who can't run and guards who can't keep up. Nee gave too many quality minutes this year to too many players who aren't Big Eight caliber. But these were guys he recruited.

Some will say the potential here isn't that great. But if location means so much, then Colorado would never lose a basketball game and Oklahoma State and Iowa State would never win one.

The bottom line is that Nee is at a crossroads. He is the school's second-winningest basketball coach, with 164 wins in nine seasons, and if he sticks around, he could easily reach Joe Cipriano's mark of 253. Or, with a couple more seasons of 4-10 (in the Big Eight) and the NIT, he could be looking for new employment.

Danny Nee's streak of four straight NCAA tournament appearances ended in 1995.

20 YEARS WITH TOM SHATEL • 63

MAY 9, 1995 • SOFTBALL

This Softball Truly Serious

THE UNIVERSITY OF Nebraska at Omaha just won the North Central Conference tournament for the second straight year, wrapping up an NCAA Division II regional bid for the sixth straight year under coach Mary Yori. The big question this year for the Lady Mavs: Could they reload after making it to the Division II Final Six last year? Next question.

Meanwhile, Nebraska has won a school-record 42 games and expects to return to the NCAA tournament for the first time since 1988. But the Huskers have to sit and wait until bids come out Sunday night. The Big Eight doesn't have a softball tournament.

The Missouri Valley Conference does, and Creighton probably has to win it to get an NCAA bid. But the Lady Jays' proud tradition held up under second-year coach Brent Vigness, whose team beat both UNO and Nebraska this year.

Serious softball.

Not bad for a state whose high schools began playing the sport just four years ago. That's why many of the faces at NU, UNO and Creighton are from California, Iowa and Minnesota.

"Success breeds success," said Yori, a former All-America player and later an assistant coach at Creighton. "We are all in different situations, but I think there is a pride factor to be as good as or better than your neighbor. We haven't had high school softball that long, but we go out and find players and find ways to win. I have a little rivalry with myself, to put a better team on the field than Creighton or Nebraska."

UNO and Creighton have great commitment to softball. That commitment was one reason why NU coach Rhonda Revelle came back to her alma mater in 1993. Actually, it was a renewal of the commitment she found in coming to NU in 1981, when she followed coach Nancy Plantz from Oregon. A year later, Nebraska was in the Women's College World Series.

"When she (Plantz) came to ask me if I wanted to come with her to Nebraska, I literally had to get a map out to see where it was," Revelle said. "But when she said she was going to turn it into a nationally competitive program, I jumped at the chance."

She did again two years ago, when she was an assistant coach at San Jose State, and Nebraska called. The Huskers hadn't been to the NCAAs since Lori Sippel (now an NU assistant) was throwing strikes in 1988. They wanted to get back to the top. But Revelle got the commitment in dollars and cents, pumping up her budget to include at least four trips per year.

"I planted the seed early," Revelle said. "I wanted to be on the national scene, and there was no reason not to, with the luxuries we have with our schedule and ability to travel. I made a personal commitment that in three to five years if we didn't make a splash, I wasn't doing a very good job.

"There are the haves and the have-nots. We are one of the haves. We can't use the weather as an excuse."

Hmmmm. The "Haves" sounds like a good name for a summer team.

Nebraska coach Rhonda Revelle, who led the Huskers to an NCAA regional in 1995, shouts instructions as Tobin Echo-Hawk pulls up at third base. That season began a string of 13 consecutive NCAA tournament appearances.

MAY 12, 1995 • NEBRASKA BASEBALL

Measuring NU's Erstad

IT'S NOT AS if we should build a statue of The Swing, the bat extended, the hips square, the back heel lifting upward and the eyes of Darin Erstad looking outward toward a white rocket sent into orbit.

A ceremony for Darin Ballgame this weekend? Probably not. It's hard to imagine the image of Erstad standing near the mound, sobbing into a microphone, "I consider myselfffffff ... the luckiestttttt mannnnnn ...on the face of the earthhhhh."

Darin Erstad leaves Nebraska this weekend with a series against Oklahoma. If we're lucky, maybe he'll give us one more trip around the bags.

"I'm not real emotional," Erstad said. "You get a smile out of me, and you're doing pretty good."

Best Ever? He wants to leave the way he came, the way he's always been. Quiet. Humble. Efficient. Erstad has been all of those things for so long that now, after three years, 251 hits, 38 home runs, 175 RBIs — and a national championship ring in football — it's like we wake up and wonder what we have just seen.

The best baseball player in Nebraska history?

Maybe NU should build that statue or retire No. 17 at Buck Beltzer Stadium. It should definitely wait until after he leaves. There are still balls to be driven to the gap.

"Nah," Erstad said. "Just because you have your name on a bunch of records isn't nearly as important as being remembered for the kind of person you were."

He was the best. Maybe the best ever. He definitely is worth one last glimpse this weekend. Look close, you might even see a smile.

Darin Erstad, now Nebraska's baseball coach, hit .410 with 19 homers and 79 RBIs in his final season with the Huskers and was the first overall pick in the 1995 Major League draft.

20 YEARS WITH TOM SHATEL • 65

JUNE 4, 1995 • COLLEGE WORLD SERIES

Kevin Costner, a friend of Cal State Fullerton coach Augie Garrido's, got to take some swings with the team at Rosenblatt Stadium.

Costner Crashes CWS Party

HE CAME OUT of the dugout like a ghost. He had a bat, a navy Cal State Fullerton hat and a practice shirt. He was Shoeless Joe Jackson, emerging from the corn to take a few hacks.

Crash Davis was back. At the College World Series.

They had just opened the gates at Rosenblatt Stadium when Kevin Costner, movie star and Cal State Fullerton graduate, jumped into the batting cage. Those who arrived early were doing triple-takes. Isn't that Crash? No. This time, Costner was playing himself. Crash would have been proud.

Costner took a few rips, sending out hot grounders and line drives. Then he launched one. It went deep into the left corner, just going left of the foul pole by a few feet and entirely out of the stadium. The Titans roared. The batting practice pitcher then whizzed one high, over his head. They all laughed.

It was one of those unforgettable moments at the CWS. Dennis Poppe, the NCAA's director of championships, joked that he would probably never hear the end of this back at NCAA headquarters. Fine. That Costner could be one of the boys in the batting cage is what gives the CWS its unique, fresh flavor.

On the day Crash Davis came to the CWS, it made perfect sense.

Costner is here to cheer the Titans and take a break from "Waterworld," which is his new movie, not the weather forecast for Omaha. Cameras followed him around the dugout. In the stands, you heard the buzz. See the guy in the dugout, in the green shirt? Kevin Costner's here.

But he should be here. We have seen his passion for baseball and the innocence left in the game. In "Field of Dreams," he showed us how to play catch with our father. In "Bull Durham," he was Davis, chasing a dream that never would be caught. Yes, Costner should feel safe at home at the College World Series.

"He rode on the bus with us over to the game, just trying to relate to us," said outfielder Mark Kotsay. "It was neat to watch him at batting practice. It was like watching Crash Davis."

On the day Crash Davis came to the College World Series, he left his inspiration and maybe even took some away for himself. It was a special day. A day when life imitated art — over the foul pole, 332 feet.

"I was surprised at the way he was swinging it," Kotsay said. "I think he should stick to acting, though."

JUNE 11, 1995 • COLLEGE WORLD SERIES

Kotsay Excels at Rosenblatt

MAYBE THEY SHOULD rename it the Kotsay World Series.

Mark Kotsay comes to Omaha and is bigger than steak. He is hotter than a July afternoon on the Missouri River. So powerful he could bring professional hockey to Omaha.

It says he's a sophomore center fielder for Cal State Fullerton. He looks more like the mayor of Rosenblatt Stadium.

Something happens to Kotsay inside Rosenblatt, something he can't explain. He experiences one of the miracles of sports, in a place where every little thing he does is magic, where the baseball is as big as a beach ball dancing in the bleachers.

The Zone.

"It comes and goes as quickly as it comes," he said. "Things become . . . like being on the playground. The ball is slow. When it comes in, you can see the seams on the ball."

You can watch them leave the yard, too.

Kotsay did it again. He homered in his first two at-bats, made a head-first, body-extended, diving catch in right-center field and then came in to pitch. His Titans won the national championship, 11-5 over Southern Cal.

Kotsay won the outstanding player award. Mr. Omaha might be a more appropriate title.

Mark Kotsay, who hit .563 with 10 runs batted in during the 1995 series, finished with a .517 career average in the CWS.

OCTOBER 25, 1995 • NEBRASKA FOOTBALL

Osborne's Decision Was Bad

IN HIS ILLUSTRIOUS 23-year career as Nebraska's head coach, Tom Osborne has made more than his share of good calls. This is not one of them.

I have always respected Osborne as a man and, secondly, as a football coach. But some of that respect was lost when Osborne announced that Lawrence Phillips, who assaulted his ex-girlfriend, was reinstated to the team and would be allowed to play against Iowa State.

But I've lost even more respect for University of Nebraska-Lincoln officials, including Athletic Director Bill Byrne, who allowed Phillips to return this season. The University of Nebraska is a lesser-quality institution today than it was yesterday. And Byrne is less of an athletic administrator.

One of the school's students, a female, was beaten up by a male student. One of Byrne's female student-athletes was beaten up by one of his male student-athletes. And now we're supposed to all return to the field and pretend this never happened.

There was plenty of time to deliberate this decision, plenty of time to mull the consequences. This was no knee-jerk reaction. But as soon as Phillips was reinstated as a student by the university, interim Chancellor Joan Leitzel and Byrne stepped aside and let Osborne handle the tough decision, which was made in his mind long ago.

It's not surprising Leitzel wouldn't intervene; for an interim chancellor, this was one hot potato. But I thought Byrne would step in and hold up a stop sign. I thought wrong. As a UNL spokesperson said, "Coach Osborne has the ability to suspend somebody from the team or bring somebody back."

True. After all, Osborne is the football coach.

And maybe he's a lot more, too.

"What I saw was 35 years of good judgment," said Byrne, referring to Osborne, "and I had more access to information than the general public did. After I had access to that information, I was in complete agreement with Tom.

"This action doesn't say what happened was right. This action says that if this had happened to Joe Q.

Nebraska coach Tom Osborne defended his football program after a series of player arrests brought national attention to the Lincoln campus.

Student, he would not be banned from extracurricular activities as long as he was a student.

"Lawrence has had sanctions and is continuing to have sanctions. Now the question will be, are those sanctions severe enough? That is a debatable point. Everyone who looks at the case will look at it a different way."

What it looks like is carte blanche for future male students at Nebraska to harass or abuse females and get similar treatment. Byrne disagreed.

"This action does not condone what happened," Byrne said. "This action says if you commit acts of violence, there will be sanctions. I believe the previous and ongoing sanctions justify his return."

What we know is that Phillips must pay restitution for damage done at the apartment complex he broke into and medical or counseling fees for Kate McEwen. Those won't be inexpensive. He also must participate in regular meetings with his counselor and psychiatrist and perform two hours of community service a week. And any further violations of the Student Code of Conduct "will result in significantly more severe sanctions."

In other words, next time he may have to play on the scout team for two weeks.

If these are the university rules and sanctions, then they need to be updated. An action like this, whether premeditated or under "out-of-control" circumstances, should include a ban from all extracurricular activities — particularly for someone like Phillips, who was supposedly out of second chances. Expulsion may be a bit harsh. But maybe we should ask the victims of physical abuse about that.

So why would Osborne allow Phillips back? The image around the country will be that this is all about victories and championships, but that's not even close.

This is all about Osborne, as college football's Father Flanagan, looking at all the evidence and circumstances and trying to save a young life. This part of the job isn't in his contract — Osborne offers it strictly out of his heart.

As Spencer Tracy said in the movie "Boys Town": "There is no bad boy."

But Osborne said Phillips had been warned about staying away from McEwen and was out of chances when the incident occurred. Osborne's biggest mistake was initially dismissing Phillips, then reversing field and opening the door in order to give Phillips a carrot to shoot for.

Phillips' is a poignant story. He spent much of his childhood without parents, getting beaten down by life, without much female love to speak of. McEwen was apparently his first love, and he snapped. It's a sad story. But, again, none of that excuses what he did.

And when Osborne says football is a "major organizing strength" in Phillips' life, it should be remembered that Phillips had football in his life the night he scaled a wall and dragged McEwen down the stairs.

Osborne is gambling that that won't happen again, that weeks of counseling have changed a young man. He says, "I think we'll see a little different person."

We better see a lot different person.

One thing is for sure: The rest of the country will see Osborne in a different light. Just months ago, the entire nation seemingly embraced him for a stately career of service to young people and the game of football. When the cleanest coach finally won the "Big One," it gave America hope.

But today there is a spot on Osborne's image. He has taken a young man who committed physical violence against a woman and returned him to the field in two months. Osborne says, "I can take the heat." The heat will come, like never before.

Why bother? Because Osborne doesn't care about the public outcry and won't be swayed by the "popular thing." Osborne has always marched to his own drummer, always been stubborn about his ways and morals. He listens to his conscience, and it must be filled with emotion. His voice quivered and nearly cracked when he talked about Phillips.

"I really, really tried to do the right thing," Osborne said. "I'm prepared to live with it."

Perhaps the saddest part is that a young woman was violated here, then got lost in the debate.

Several people have wondered why Minnesota Vikings quarterback Warren Moon could beat his wife, apologize and play again without question, while Phillips is being held to another, higher standard. The best answer to that is that Phillips is still a college student and, we hope, colleges are in the business of preparing America's youths to become better people.

Today, the University of Nebraska has to ask itself if that is what happened here.

2011 INSIGHT

I have no idea how many columns I've written since Sept. 1, 1991. Whatever the number, no topic in all those years inspired more reader reaction than Lawrence Phillips. And none brought more than this column, the day after Tom Osborne announced he was bringing Phillips back. So, I guess you could say this column touched more nerves than anything I've ever written.

When you sit down to write a column like this, you ask yourself two questions. One, how strongly do you feel about it? And two, are you prepared to handle the heat that comes from taking on Tom Osborne, the icon of the state, who just won a national championship the year before?

The answers were that I felt very strongly that Phillips should not return to the playing field in 1995. And I was ready for the heat. Or so I thought.

Part of that was Osborne is a reasonable man, and he expected criticism on this topic, even from Nebraskans. Which he got. The other thing was, I'm not saying Nebraskans were split down the middle on LP, but there were many who were not happy with Osborne's decision. So it wasn't like I was all alone on the limb.

But it was a firestorm like no other. The phones started ringing early the morning the column ran. I felt sorry for our morning sports desk crew, who had to answer calls from irate readers every two minutes. I showed up about 11 a.m. and started taking the calls. How dare I question Osborne? Did I really know Phillips? Who was I to be judge and jury over a young man's career? On and on.

There were many more letters over the next few weeks. I can't imagine what it would have been like if email had been around then. It would have been at least 500. The most memorable letter I received came from an older woman who said she was a grandmother from Grand Island. She chastised me for taking on Tom, and she also said the young woman whom Phillips attacked deserved it, since she had been "cheating on" Phillips. I was taken aback by that one. Eventually things settled down. But not before the most unique form of reader response I've ever received or heard of.

One morning, not long after the Phillips column ran, I walked out to my driveway, about 8 a.m., to get my paper. I unwrapped the rubber band right there and read through the paper on the driveway, as I always did. My eyes popped out when I looked at my column that day. On my mug shot, someone had drawn a beard and mustache. And somehow delivered that exact paper to me.

I never did get to ask my paperboy about that. I assumed he was an Osborne fan.

SEPTEMBER 29, 1995 • NEBRASKA VOLLEYBALL

NU's Weston Breaks Ground

ALLISON WESTON IS "The Natural."

On the volleyball court, the Nebraska senior's talents flow almost effortlessly. Naturally. This season she could break the Big Eight Conference career record for kills and should become the first Nebraska volleyball player to be named first-team All-America three straight years. She makes it look simple.

Which is just how Weston likes it.

Off the court, Weston is a student of nature and a lover of the land. Give her a fishing pole, a secluded lake and about an hour with Lewis and Clark.

It says so in the 1995 NU volleyball press guide, in a survey designed to show what makes each player tick. After the question, "The person in history I would most like to meet would be:" Weston answered, "Lewis and Clark."

That's not Jerry Lewis and Roy Clark.

Why the famous explorers?

"I would just like to see what the Midwest, and especially Nebraska, looked like before settlers came in and moved in on the prairies and changed everything," Weston said. "I would just be curious to see that.

"Not so much because I like history. I love the outdoors. Fishing. I like simple things."

Simple. Natural. Dependable. Weston has never missed a college match. For Weston's final encore, she needs to move to one final level.

"In any team sport, you need that player who, in critical situations, takes over the match," coach Terry Pettit said. "They want the ball, everyone knows they're going to take it, and they still come through. She's always had that. But she has more willingness and eagerness to take on that role."

In 1995, three-time All-American Allison Weston led Nebraska to its first volleyball national championship.

Behrns' Class Is in Session

THE STUDENTS OF UNO Physical Education Class 377 — otherwise known as "Football Coaching Theory and Practice" — should consider themselves fortunate.

Their professor is not only a football coach, he's Pat Behrns. The University of Nebraska at Omaha football coach.

Twice a week, the would-be coaches learn everything from how to order equipment to how much Maalox to take after defeats. But if they are paying attention, they would raise their hands and ask the professor:

"What's it like to take over a program that some boosters want to kill, in a league that is the Southeastern Conference of Division II, where the facilities are worse than some high schools and your bosses change like the weather?"

After one year, "Professor" Behrns could give one heck of a lecture.

"It was a little scary when I got here," said Behrns, in his second year. "I figured if I stayed here five years and got fired, I would be 50 — and most colleges don't hire 50-year-old assistant coaches."

Ah, but what a difference about 10 scholarships, one legendary athletic director and some victories make. After getting up to the Division II limit of 36 scholarships and seeing some of Athletic Director Don Leahy's magic, the sun comes up most every day in Behrns' world.

"I underestimated how hard this job was going to be," Behrns said. "But I underestimated where we can go, too. We have always been told here what we can't do; we don't have facilities, don't have dorms. It was time to go out and sell our university and our community."

There were no tricks. Without sparkling facilities, dorms or recent tradition to sell, Behrns and his staff went out and made their pitch. Somebody listened.

"Recruiting is kind of like shaving," Behrns says. "You have to do it every day or you don't look very good."

Good line, professor. Students of football coaching and theory should all know that image and attitude work wonders until the blocking and tackling kick in.

Final lesson, class: Criticism can be a good thing.

"My daughter had two classmates tell her that her dad's team wasn't very good," Behrns said. "They had to write apologies, but you know what? I thought that was good. It's just like after the North Dakota State game, when people heard some fans complaining in the stands.

"I like that. It shows people care. That's better than the alternative."

Pay attention. That could be on the final.

"Recruiting is kind of like shaving," according to UNO football coach Pat Behrns. "You have to do it every day or you don't look very good."

DECEMBER 5, 1995 • NEBRASKA VOLLEYBALL

Pettit Puts Players First

HE IS NEBRASKA volleyball. He's only the sixth coach in the sport to win 600 matches. He has been to 14 straight NCAA tournaments and three final fours and played for two national championships.

He's been national coach of the year. His program regularly funnels in All-Americans and academic stars. He's produced Olympians. He could write a book on creating, and then feeding, a monster.

Christy Johnson

So after 19 years, there is only one thing left for Terry Pettit to accomplish.

"I want the president of Augusta National (golf club) to call and invite me and three guests to play a round of golf," Pettit said.

He probably has a better chance at a national championship. Nebraska volleyball is barreling toward a collision with history: the school's first volleyball championship. But Pettit chases his only obsession on a golf course.

"Maybe only coaches and players who compete understand this," Pettit said, "but if you're obsessed with the end result, you have no chance. The obsession is with the day-to-day things and doing them right."

But does the coach who's done everything else need a national title to validate an otherwise decorated career?

"I would hope not," Pettit said. "Would it alter my life? I don't think so. The reasons I would like to see it are mostly for my players. The players would enjoy it. It would be their national championship. And I think the players on our other teams would enjoy it, too."

Indeed, if there is a sense of urgency around Nebraska's team, it comes more from a group of seniors who want to leave a legacy like no other.

"I'm obsessed with it," senior setter Christy Johnson said. "But I think we're all a little obsessed with winning it all. But that's good. A lot of teams wouldn't even talk about it, figuring that they could get embarrassed if it doesn't happen. For us, we'll risk everything to get there. We'll die trying."

Pettit's motivation comes from deeper sources. The latest reminder was in a Sports Illustrated story about John Wooden's former players. In it, Pettit was riveted by a quote from the ex-UCLA basketball coach that said, "You won't know until 10 or 20 years later how good a coach you were."

"The things that make me feel good are seeing former players come back, and I can tell they feel good about what happened to them," Pettit said. "That is far and away the most important thing. Billie Winsett said something the other day: that nobody is going to remember whether she played hitter or blocker, but they'll remember that she played for Nebraska volleyball.

"It's a pretty special sorority. That's what it's all about."

Terry Pettit's 1995 Nebraska volleyball team finished with a 32-1 record and the national championship.

72 • 20 YEARS WITH TOM SHATEL

Frazier One of the Best

NEW YORK

WHETHER HE WON or lost the Heisman Trophy, that moment could never define Tommie Frazier. There is a higher standard, even above the mighty Heisman, to which the Nebraska senior quarterback holds himself and his four-year career.

The national championship.

The Heisman recognizes individual achievement. The criteria are not spelled out by the Downtown Athletic Club, but, traditionally, the Heisman goes home with the lad who has produced the biggest numbers and projects into a long and fruitful career in the National Football League.

Frazier fits neither of these categories and, therefore, it could be called a minor upset if he won.

Jan. 2 is another story. There, on the Tostitos Fiesta Bowl turf, Frazier will take a shot at a second straight national championship. He will be favored to win because that's what he does best. Win.

That will be Frazier's epitaph when he leaves Nebraska, and he knows that being the leader — reason — for college football's first repeat national championship since 1978-79 would have more staying power than carting home the Heisman.

By the way, can you name the Heisman winner of 1989? If he can wrestle down the Florida Gators, Frazier's name will be embedded in the granite of college football history instead of washed away like the name of Andre Ware. You remember Ware, the 1989 Heis-man.

Frazier may have no more success in the NFL than did Ware, who had none at all. But two rings would make him the richest man in the world.

"I look at everything as a team thing," Frazier said. "All the honors I've won are because of the team."

Frazier has made his teams far better. He has turned it into such an art that most of the time you don't even notice his subtle magic.

Frazier's highlights don't make SportsCenter. Instead of the 80-yard gallop or the picture-postcard pass, he offers the glare in the huddle, the impossible throw off his back foot that somehow moves the chains. He commands victory, and victory has disobeyed only three times in four years.

Frazier is the consummate money player. He is the Michael Jordan and Reggie Jackson of college football. He was made for the defining moment, when the team and hopes rest on him. He always delivers. For that, he is surely one of the greatest "college" quarterbacks of all time.

We've been blessed observers, watching him start as a freshman, win the 1994 Orange Bowl MVP award in a loss (though he just ran out of time) and come off the bench in last year's Orange Bowl, a sign that gave Nebraskans confidence that the championship could be, would be, had.

And nobody will ever forget him taking a shot and still completing a pass against Colorado. That's the kind of leadership and impact that should win Heismans. But Frazier will gladly settle for a national championship.

His impact is such that NU can reach for those brass rings again. It's not a stretch to say Frazier is the single biggest reason Nebraska went from spectator to player again in the national big-game hunt.

"My whole career has been like a storybook career," Frazier said. "I'm a Husker, and I'll always be a Husker. Wherever I am, I'll always have room for Nebraska."

Then again, his legacy is not his concern.

"I don't want to leave a legacy," Frazier said. "I want to be known as a quarterback who came here and performed well. I don't care about a legacy. That's the kind of person I am. If anything, I'd want to be known as a team player."

There must be some way to honor his time here. But how? Nebraska doesn't retire numbers. And it's not going to be Frazier Stadium. Not unless he comes up with a few million, anyway.

How about an award? The "Tommie Frazier" award for leadership and impact on a team. That is the legacy Frazier leaves, a legacy stronger than any Heisman or All-America plaque could offer. Think about this: What if he'd never come to Nebraska?

"I've never even thought about it," Frazier said. "Everything that happened, happened for a reason. I've been in the right place at the right time."

That place is Tempe, Ariz. That time is Jan. 2. Frazier can pick up his trophy there.

Tommie Frazier quarterbacked Nebraska to two national titles and was named to the Sports Illustrated All-Century Team. He finished second to Ohio State's Eddie George in Heisman voting.

TOM'S TAKE | REFLECTIONS ON

The riverfront, 1995: The cleared area at the upper right, the site of the Union Pacific shops, became the home of Omaha's arena. In the foreground is the Asarco lead refinery, now Lewis & Clark Landing.

'New Arena's Time Is Now'

OMAHA NEEDS A new place to play.

Once upon a time, the Civic Auditorium and Ak-Sar-Ben Coliseum were more than adequate in housing sporting events and activities. But now they are just antiquated. It's time to move on. Time for a new state-of-the-art something.

Dome or arena? Downtown or Ak-Sar-Ben or farther west?

Just do something, Omaha.

I admire Mayor Hal Daub's vision for the riverfront. It's big. It's ambitious.

My major concern, however, is whether this thing will ever get off the ground.

This is Daub's baby. What happens, however, if Daub doesn't get another term in 1997? Does the project go on permanent hold in a file cabinet, lost forever? What if the entire riverfront development price tag is too big for Omaha's appetite? Then a sports facility gets lost in the shuffle.

The thing is, we've all heard this before. What we need is a new twist: action. A sports commission. A game plan. A new arena. And then tenants and activities to improve our quality of life. Yes, sports does that.

A new arena and a bright sports future would not only entertain generations of future Omahans, it would teach us a great lesson: that we can put down our individual agendas and work together toward a common goal.

End of sermon. But this is not the end of the issue. In so many ways, it's only the beginning.

— **JULY 9, 1995**

2011 INSIGHT *I like to call my first 10 years or so here, when Ak-Sar-Ben was still around, Creighton played at the Civic, etc., the Old Omaha Years. Back then, I occasionally liked to rant and rave about Omaha needing this or that. I never really thought it would happen. I thought most Omahans were pretty old-school in their approach and didn't like change. I'm certainly not claiming to be any kind of visionary. But I could see how people in this town were active sports fans and liked to get out if they were going to see something good. I certainly never envisioned that we would actually be where we are today. I'd like to take credit for being a genius, but I'm surprised, I really am. Building the Qwest Center changed everything. It showed everyone what could be done. I also remember railing about how Omaha needed a CHL hockey team. Nobody ever suspected UNO would play hockey. Well, maybe Don Leahy. He's the real genius.*

THE CHANGING SPORTS LANDSCAPE 1995

Texas Is Acting Like a Bully

THE CRYSTAL BALL is clearing now, and life in the Big 12 Conference in the 21st century is beginning to come into focus.

The Big 12 presidents meet at the NCAA convention Jan. 7 in Dallas for a little game of high-stakes conference poker.

Texas President Robert Berdahl threw down the gauntlet, telling the Dallas Morning News that UT will not accept a policy that allows recruitment of nonqualifiers under NCAA freshman eligibility requirements. Berdahl, tossing around some heavy-handed hints, said if the Big 12 allowed nonqualifiers "we would have to review our options at that point."

Can you say, "12-Pack?"

Big 12 observers say Texas has support from Colorado, Missouri, Texas A&M, Texas Tech and Baylor — the latter three who also did not accept Proposition 48 athletes while in the Southwest Conference. Kansas State is thought to be leaning with Nebraska, which is carrying the flag to allow nonqualifiers in the new league. The rest is up for grabs.

You would think a compromise would be in order. You would be wrong. Texas is in favor of allowing some "partial qualifiers," students who have either the required entrance score or grade-point average on a sliding scale. Nebraska has argued that, under that sliding scale, a "partial" is virtually impossible. Nebraska has researched the high school transcripts of 300 recruits and found none who qualified as a "partial."

That would suit Texas and Co. just fine. There is a school of thought that their aim is to knock the Nebraska football machine down to everyone else's level. There may be some truth to that. But closer to reality is that this is not about academics and whether the Big 12's reputation wears ivy or mud.

This is all about power.

Academia is the mere vehicle being used by Texas, which wants to see how far it can push the envelope. Texas doesn't want to run the league. Bully is the more appropriate word.

There is probably panic in some corners of the Big Eight, which is traditionally a passive group and had to be talked into the Big 12 arrangement just to save its own carcass from being picked apart by other leagues. It isn't used to pushy members like Texas. Now, they have to decide how much they want Texas.

The power of UT is not to be underestimated. UT brings the Dallas and Houston markets, and it will take them to the West Coast, along with Colorado, which would no doubt see the Big 12 as a lesser entity without Texas. How and where the dominoes fall from there is anybody's guess.

It's a risk the Big 12 will have to take. The Big 12 should call Texas' bluff. If Texas walks, fine. You can't have Texas holding the league hostage every week. Better to have a lesser league than Texas and the 11 "Yes Men."

— DECEMBER 17, 1995

2011 INSIGHT *When it first happened, I wrote that the Big 12 would be a good deal for Nebraska. But then Oklahoma pulled out of the Nebraska series and then Texas started being Texas. This column depicted the mood at the time. Reading this, it's no surprise at all that Nebraska is in the Big Ten now.*

FIESTA BOWL ROUT OF FLORIDA | NEBRASKA'S NIT TITLE | DEATH OF BROOK BERRINGER

1996

"I understand our fans being so excited. For the last four years they've seen a lot of not very good basketball. I'm more of a realist. If you even want to dream about those things (NCAA or NIT) happening, we better get better at rebounding, defense and shooting free throws."

— CREIGHTON COACH DANA ALTMAN

Not all of the blue chips were cashed in when college football national letters of intent were signed and sealed. Ben Walker, a running back at Oak Creek High School in Milwaukee, told seven Big Ten Conference schools "no." That's because Walker is going to Creighton. Credit a big assist to Creighton freshman Rodney Buford, a fellow Milwaukee prep star who played with Walker on an AAU team. "People down there are going to like Ben Walker," said Tom Diener, Buford's coach at Milwaukee Vincent High. "He's a kid who plays to win."

As the Blackshirts have grown into something almost inhuman, defensive coordinator Charlie McBride has gone from late-night phone calls from anonymous cowards who wanted him gone to fans who now say, "Nebraska's defense is so good the Huskers should punt when they get the ball."

Just a few hours after many of the Olympic athletes got home from the long-winded Opening Ceremonies, Bret Erickson strolled up to his shooting station in a secluded pine forest known as Wolf Creek. He bent over in a slight crouch, called for the first "bird" and let his MX 8 shotgun blast the thing out of the sky. And the Atlanta Games began. Erickson, the Nebraska native son from Bennington, is one of those competitors often referred to as the "real Olympians." In other words, he doesn't have a shoe contract or a Jacuzzi in his Atlanta hotel room.

WARREN MORRIS' HOME RUN | SCOTT FROST'S STRUGGLES | THE BIRTH OF UNO HOCKEY

Usually, I rank soccer somewhere below Brussels sprouts and equestrian. But this year is different. Creighton's classy monster of a program looks like a national championship contender. Time to give the Bluejays their due.

Back before the invasion of the riverboats, before it was fashionable for Nebraskans to sneak to Iowa, Andre Woolridge took considerable heat for heading east. But now it's time to cut the cord, cut Woolridge some slack and admit the truth: Woolridge knew what he was doing by transferring to Iowa. After a 24-hour span in which I watched his former basketball team lose its fifth straight game and then saw his current team pound Indiana by 26 — after watching Woolridge equal the total number of Nebraska assists (nine) against Iowa State by himself — I was ready to concede. Andre, you were right. Asked if good buddies Jaron Boone, Erick Strickland and Terrance Badgett have told him they are unhappy at NU, Woolridge said, "They don't have to say it. I know. It's a joke there, man. Everybody who talked bad about me — who said I couldn't play Division I, that I was a baby, I was just a street player — when I go back those people now say, 'That was the best move you ever made,' " Woolridge said. "You know. You trashed me, too." Guilty. You were right, Andre. But then, you already knew that.

You are waiting to do an interview with Nebraska heavyweight Tolly Thompson. And you are amazed. Thompson is the last one off the mat. Three days before the start of the NCAA wrestling championships in Minneapolis, Thompson is the Niagara Falls of sweat. "Every day, he doesn't leave until he thinks he's worked harder than every heavyweight in the country," Nebraska head coach Tim Neumann says.

Best Season of All Time?

WE IN THE sporting press have an obsession with superlatives. Perhaps we too often throw around the term "best ever," as in "they're the best team ever that plays its games on grass and has a left-footed kicker." But it keeps us off the streets.

Where it concerns the 1995 Nebraska football team, a superlative or two is only appropriate.

For what they did, how they did it and who they did it against, the 1995 Huskers have to be the best team in college football history.

Any arguments out there?

All you can do is look at paper. And offer opinion.

Opinion: I can't imagine any team ever having a more dominating season than Nebraska in 1995.

For starters, the Huskers trailed only once during the regular season. Nobody got closer than 11 points to Nebraska at the half, or closer than 10 in any second half.

The Huskers beat their opponents by 426 points, or an average of 38.7 per game. That, fittingly, was the spread in the Fiesta Bowl.

And they outnumbered the 1983 Nebraska team, which previously led the nation in "best evers." While the 1995 offense averaged two yards less per game rushing than 1983, it averaged 11.5 more yards passing per game than 1983. The 1995 team also outscored 1983's, 52.4-52.0. And the 1995 version was far and away the better defensive team. It was, all around, a more balanced team.

But enough numbers. They don't tell the story of 1995, anyway.

When we say the 1995 team had the best season because it was the most balanced, we aren't talking about offense, defense and special teams. We're talking about courage, heart and character. The pillars of a champion.

Time and again, the Huskers were single-minded piranhas in a season that had all the drama of C-SPAN.

This wasn't Northwestern, captivating a nation with a fairy tale. It was a group of men doing drywall every Saturday afternoon.

It was last winter and spring's commitment to a goal — repeat as champions — that hadn't been accomplished in two decades. It was commitment in an age when responsibility usually takes a back seat to short-term gratification with today's youth.

It was having to replace the guts of last year's team — the offensive line — and making it better.

It was choosing one quarterback over another deserving quarterback and not losing a thing in team chemistry. Brook Berringer, high-five for you.

It was waking up Monday morning, Sept. 11, to the shocking news that Lawrence Phillips had been suspended from the team.

It was the media circus that ensued and the roller coaster of Phillips being off the team, then back on. It was every member of the Nebraska team keeping his focus and eye on the prize, no matter how he felt about what Phillips did.

It was no penalties, no turnovers and no problem in Boulder, where the Huskers raised their level when it counted.

It was Tommie Frazier being hit by a Colorado linebacker, keeping his feet and composure and deflating the Buffs by completing a pass in the second-most defining play of the season.

It was Nebraska not playing its best at Kansas and winning by 38.

It was surviving Bernard Goldberg and "48 Hours."

It was a brilliant defensive game plan in the Fiesta Bowl, the greatest moment ever for Charlie McBride and his Blackshirts.

It was the combination of poise, depth and talent that overwhelmed Florida and were the staples of this incredible 36-1 three-year era.

It was Frazier, galloping, sneaking and then sprinting 75 yards through a maze of Florida defenders in

Tommie Frazier capped off his brilliant career with a 75-yard touchdown run in the Fiesta Bowl.

the play that most defined Frazier — and his era. It's time now to call Frazier the greatest quarterback in Nebraska history.

It was the steady hand of Tom Osborne, who rode out the controversy he helped create, with his typical consistency and resiliency.

Mostly, it was a season made up of the unassuming hard work and unbending excellence that characterizes what this program has been about for more than 30 years.

The best season.

JANUARY 5, 1996 • NEBRASKA FOOTBALL

Nebraska's Jamel Williams sacks Florida quarterback Danny Wuerffel for a safety in the Huskers' 62-24 victory in the Fiesta Bowl.

FEBRUARY 11, 1996 • NEBRASKA BASKETBALL

2011 INSIGHT *This column was a historical mile marker for Nebraska basketball. This was a turning-point day for Danny Nee. It was the day it all started going south for the program's winningest coach, when he started to lose his grip on not only the team but also the fans. After this loss to Iowa State – an up-and-coming Cyclone team – Nee and the players could be heard yelling at each other in the locker room. We weren't allowed in the locker room, but we were allowed to stand outside and wait for Nee to come out. The visitors' locker room at Hilton Coliseum is like a large closet in the corner of the arena. The area outside it is packed in tight. So we were right next to the door and could hear everything. In the next few days, Nee's image took several hits, including negative comments from Andre Woolridge, then at Iowa, and the famous "walkout" by the Huskers to Athletic Director Bill Byrne's office. To his credit, Byrne told the players to go back and work it out with their coach. Nebraska would win the NIT in an incredible run. And Nee would return to the NCAA tourney in 1998. But it was never the same after this one. I spent the next few weeks being really hard on Nee and this dysfunctional cast of characters. But in the process I missed out on a great story, them banding together to win the NIT. I'm not a big NIT guy. That came out in my column the day after they won it. But I wish now I had written more about the players rising above their issues and winning it. That's one I can't get back.*

Nee Lost His Team in Ames

AMES, IOWA

YES, THERE WAS good news from Hilton Coliseum. Nebraska basketball has a much-needed week off.

The Huskers have a Nee injury. Whether this is a temporary condition that can be salvaged or one that could damage a coach's career remains to be seen.

But this much we know after seeing – and hearing – Nebraska's 74-59 defeat to No. 21 Iowa State: Coach Danny Nee not only lost a fifth straight game, he has lost his team, too.

Should he lose his job as well? Incredibly, those words will be spoken this week around Nebraska, from the coffee shops to the radio talk-show airwaves. It's still early to be writing obits for this Nebraska season. But then again, it's also getting late for players who began the season with good intentions and have unraveled to the point where they do not respect their coach and, worse, themselves.

Nebraska basketball has become a joke. The worst part is, the Huskers themselves are laughing. That was the story on a Saturday when a well-coached, overachieving Iowa State team separated itself as the clear-cut No. 2 team in the Big Eight, and Nebraska went looking for the Cyclones' chair at the bottom.

It wasn't the Huskers' 39.3 percent shooting, their 19 turnovers, their being outrebounded by ISU, 41-34. It wasn't their season-low first-half total of 23 points. Numbers don't tell the story of Nebraska basketball. Faces, voices and images do.

It was forward Bernard Garner leaving the Nebraska huddle during a timeout with 7:45 left in the game and refusing to rejoin the huddle. Nee later said something to Garner, who scowled back at Nee. Garner never went back into the game or listened to another timeout huddle.

"No comment," Garner said.

"He's upset about losing," Nee said. "There are 11 other guys who feel the same way."

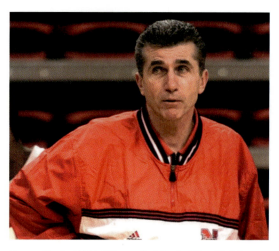

Danny Nee's 1995-96 team finished with a 21-14 record and an NIT championship.

It was also Nee and at least two players in the locker room afterward, who could be heard shouting expletives. One player yelled, "We're playing like individuals! We're not playing like a team!" Nee was heard to yell, "What are you going to do about it?!" over and over.

And it was a five-minute team meeting — moreover, what that meeting produced. The Nebraska locker room sounded like a frat party. Players sang. There was loud laughing and chattering. You would have thought the Huskers won the NCAA championship. Ridiculous. This is a team that can't be controlled by its coach. Players who have no respect for the man, the game of basketball or themselves.

There were few comments afterward, except for senior Tom Wald, who said the Huskers had several capable leaders, but "we're all waiting for someone to step forward." Including the coach.

True, Nee did not start Erick Strickland because the senior got himself thrown out of the last game. He didn't play freshman Venson Hamilton because Hamilton missed practice. But these disciplinary acts roll off the players like sweat. It's too little, too late for a coach who over the years has given his team too much leash.

It all starts with coaching. For Nee, the writing was on the wall — or chalkboard — in the Huskers' locker room, where the words "Teamwork, Hustle, Listen to Coaches" were displayed. You think Bobby Knight and Roy Williams have "Listen to Coaches" scrawled on their chalkboards? Not hardly. Some messages are ingrained by day one. Some coaches don't put up with locker room cabarets.

Like Tim Floyd. Funny thing about the second-year Iowa State coach, who is the odds-on favorite to win Big Eight Coach of the Year honors: We all thought his band of junior-college players and transfers would lend itself to the kind of circus currently playing in Lincoln. But Floyd doesn't even let his players argue with a ref, much less him. The results are obvious.

Ask Cyclone star Dedric Willoughby, a Floyd disciple who marvels at how talented Nebraska is, but knows why ISU is in second place.

"There is a difference between athleticism and hearing and listening to what the coach wants," Willoughby said. "He's a teacher. He gets people to believe in him. We know he won't steer us wrong. He's a master of the game."

The Huskers? They are being steered into the swamp of underachievement.

"It's absolutely unraveled," Nee said. "Now we have to put it back together."

Nebraska fans will be hard on the team and Nee. Blame the football program. Not the winning. Nebraska basketball can't meet that standard. Moreover, it's the way the football team presents itself: hard-working, intelligent, humble and classy. Those are the standards Nebraska fans expect, the ones this NU basketball team doesn't meet.

Mikki Moore is second in career block shots at Nebraska.

Huskers Hold Garden Party

NEW YORK

WE'RE NO. 65! We're No. 65!

The Nebraska Cornhuskers completed one of the most improbable postseason runs on any level, beating St. Joseph's 60-56 for the National Invitation Tournament title at Madison Square Garden.

Congratulations, Nebraska, the consolation champions of the world. This is no small consolation. Three weeks ago, this team had lost to Iowa State in the Big Eight tournament and should have been looking for a hole to crawl into. Instead, the Huskers staged a Garden party.

After the final buzzer, Tyronn Lue heaved the basketball up into the thick arena air. The players who couldn't get along and didn't want to play for their coach were suddenly hugging each other, high-fiving fans, congratulating the coach's wife. One big happy family.

We're No. 65!

It was a great scene. A positive image for a team that had searched the haystack feverishly for one. And yet it was a bittersweet moment for one very obvious reason.

Where were these guys in February? Where was the defense? Where was the sweet passing, the monster inside play by Mikki Moore and Bernard Garner, the unselfish play by Jaron Boone, the inside-out half-court game, the zone pressure that smothered each opponent? Where? Where? Where?

Why ask why? This team finally resembled a team again, and that's all that mattered.

APRIL 19, 1996 • NEBRASKA FOOTBALL

Nebraska Lost a Champion

THIS IS NOT supposed to happen. Not two days before the National Football League draft. Not ever.

Brook Berringer is dead. I can barely write those words. We have lost a champion and a friend. This is the shock of shocks, the nightmare of nightmares. It will take a long time for this hurt to heal. Brook Berringer is dead.

He would have been 23 in July. He was on his way toward what everyone knew would be a successful future in the NFL, starting with the draft, the first day of the rest of his life. But today Brook is reunited with his father, Warren. They are probably fishing. What stories the son has for the father, who he always called "my hero, my friend, my idol."

Brook, you were our hero, our friend, our idol. You taught us how to handle adversity with class. You showed us how to be patient with a quiet dignity. You gave us true grit when it was your turn at the front of the line. You embodied the spirit of Nebraska football. Brook, you were Nebraska football.

Of course, we weren't always good about telling you that. We were usually marveling at the latest accomplishment by Tommie Frazier. But we knew you were there, Brook. We knew you were pushing Frazier to be his best. If only we could tell you again.

But a small Piper Cub airplane went down in an alfalfa field, taking with it a young man's hopes and dreams. Life may be unfair, but death is downright dirty. Of course, Brook would never say he got cheated out of life. He lived it to its fullest, to the end.

It made no sense, his climbing into a two-seat plane for another joy ride 48 hours before the NFL draft. But this was right in line with Brook's character. He was a true sportsman and an able adventurer. Gusto oozed out of his pores. There wasn't a challenge he didn't welcome, whether it was hunting antelope or taking over for Frazier. Flying was his latest craze.

In many ways, he left the earth the way he arrived. Brook got a fishing license on the day he was born. It was given to him by his father, who knew he was dying of cancer. For the next seven years, Warren tried to cram a lifetime's worth of father's lessons and love into his son's memory.

His mother, Jan, an elementary school teacher in Goodland, Kan., laughed when she told the story about the fishing license.

"He (Warren) went to the place to get the license and the guy asked him for the date of birth and (Warren) said 'July 9.' The guy said, 'No, not today's date. The date of birth.' They went round and round until finally the guy said, 'OK, but you have to pay for it.' Warren did. And he hung it up on the wall in Brook's room."

Two years later, 2-year-old Brook caught his first fish. His father took a picture of it and they took it home, cleaned it and fried it. Brook made sure everyone had a bite.

When he was 20 months old, Jan would pack a lunch bag and a diaper bag, and father and son would go hunting. When he was 7, Brook aced the hunting safety course and, later that year, bagged his first pheasant.

"He's probably the only kindergarten student to

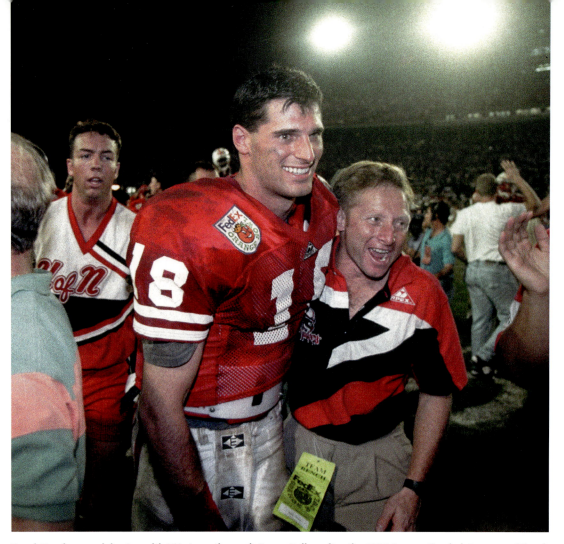

Brook Berringer celebrates with NU strength coach Bryan Bailey after the 1995 Orange Bowl victory over Miami.

get out of school for three days to go antelope hunting in Montana with his father," said Jan, in 1994.

When he was 3, Brook unhooked the training wheels on his new bike and flew off down the street, born to be wild. There was nothing in life that he was afraid to face, and that made him the perfect person to take on the impossible task of replacing Frazier in 1994. But for so long nobody knew this unassuming kid in the back of the class. His confidence grew as we grew to know him. It was exciting to watch. He was like Michael Corleone in the "Godfather," the way he transformed before our eyes. He gave us so many special moments.

Who could forget that debut, when Wyoming was threatening the upset in Lincoln and nobody knew if Brook could save the day? He played with a collapsed lung. And nobody found out until afterward, when he had already left. Typical Brook.

Who could forget his coming off the bench to help beat Kansas State and throwing a touchdown pass with that bad lung? Above all else, we will cherish his victory over Colorado, his rite of quarterbackhood. Before that game, former CU coach Bill McCartney had dared to wonder aloud what was on everyone's mind: Could this kid run the option?

I will always remember the kid scoring on an option early. From that point on, nobody worried about Frazier being out. It was his finest moment, the day Nebraska knew it could win with Brook.

The 1994 season was a team effort. But that national championship was all about Brook becoming a man. He showed us when Frazier came back to start the Orange Bowl, exited, and then returned to lead the Huskers in the climactic fourth quarter. When Brook said, "I don't think there's any question I would have gotten the job done," we believed him.

That he was a team player may have been the single most important ingredient in that national championship. I always wondered if Brook felt like Frazier was getting a break over him in the pre-Orange Bowl scrimmage and even last spring, when the two competed. Frazier proved to be the best quarterback. But if Brook was upset, he never let on. And he never backed down.

"I paid my dues," Brook said last spring. "I've worked my tail off since I stepped on campus. I don't think I'll let it stop here. I'm going to go out and try to be the best I can be."

Our hero, our friend, our idol. He arrived at Nebraska as a guy with a strong arm in a running man's offense — a long shot surrounded by "13 quarterbacks," he once joked. But as the others dropped off, one by one, Brook remained. Never transferred. Never complained. Just waited.

The budding Huskers who think they are stuck on the assembly line of Nebraska football should all hear about Brook. He was a winner. He had the heart of a lion, the courage of a champion. He was a Nebraska success story. Like all of the young men who wear the Big Red, he is family.

Today we mourn the loss of family. It began as the sobering news hit the airwaves. Brook was to speak at a Fellowship of Christian Athletes banquet in Lincoln, which went on as planned. NU coach Tom Osborne, his eyes red with grief and disbelief, spoke quietly and softly of one of his boys. Osborne no doubt said a prayer for Brook. And no doubt he was joined by an entire state.

I was in west Omaha when I heard the news. I drove to Oak View Mall, to the "Red Zone" Husker memorabilia store. For some reason, I wanted to see a photo of Brook. I felt I needed to be there. But when I arrived, the store clerk, Dan Wagner, had already removed everything with Brook's name, face or number from the shelves.

"I don't think it's right to make money off him now," Wagner said.

There were two patrons in the store. But it felt empty. No one spoke.

"I feel like closing it up, to tell you the truth," Wagner said.

Everyone can relate. They called off the "Night of Champions" at Memorial Stadium, and that was the best and only decision. Nebraska does not feel like celebrating. We may have two national championships, but today we have lost a champion and a friend.

2011 INSIGHT *I heard the news about Brook Berringer about 5 p.m. I was sitting at the old Scoreboard sports bar, which is now D.J.'s Dugout, doing a radio show with Gary Java and Randy Eccker. It was a Thursday afternoon. Nebraska had won back-to-back national championships. The spring game and NFL draft were two days away. Life was good. And then it wasn't. Gary got a message from the producer to go to commercial. That's when we got the news about Berringer and the plane crash. I thought about driving out to the crash scene, and now I wish I had. It was off limits. But I still wish I would have tried. In any case, we didn't have a lot of details. This is one of those columns you tend to overwrite, because you know it's going to be read by everyone. So you try for the big hyperbole, the over-the-top drama. As I sat in the office that night, in front of a blank screen, something inside me said to just go with your emotions. Write the emotions of the moment. So I did. It took about 30 minutes to write this. I just cruised right through it. I didn't change a lot. I was emotionally spent. I remember watching the news that night, waiting for more answers about the crash. There were none. I left The World-Herald about 10:30 p.m. and headed to Pauli's. I needed a beer. Nobody at the bar that night said much. I remember sitting at the bar and crying.*

JUNE 9, 1996 • COLLEGE WORLD SERIES

A Swing, a Title, a Legend

THIS IS WHY God created the College World Series.

So a kid like LSU's Warren Morris, who missed 40 games this year with a wrist injury, who tumbled in the draft like a falling star, whose status on the 1996 Olympic team suddenly was in doubt, who had hit 12 home runs in his life, and who couldn't take a full swing two weeks ago, can change the world with one swing.

They have played the College World Series 50 times. But none ended with any more drama or poetry than this one, the day Warren Morris took the fullest swing of his young life.

Two outs. Bottom of the ninth. Man on third. Miami up, 8-7. National championship blowing in the wind. Here's the first pitch. . . .

"I wasn't trying to think 'One out and the season's over,'" Morris said. "I was thinking it was an intrasquad game."

It looks like a curve ball. . . .

"I wasn't trying to be a hero," said Morris. "I was just trying to get Tim (Lanier) . . . or Justin Bowles . . . no, it was Chad Wilson, in."

Morris swings. There's a line drive toward the right field fence. . . .

"I thought it was going foul," he said. "Thank God it stayed fair. Unbelievable."

Bill Mazeroski. Kirk Gibson. Joe Carter. Maybe they know what was going on inside Morris after his two-run homer won the 1996 CWS for LSU. There are some emotions you can't communicate. Sometimes the rewind button jams in the euphoria.

"It feels like it happened to somebody else," Morris said. "I don't remember what happened from the time I got to first base until I touched home. The only reason I remember home plate is because I had to fight off 25 guys.

"And then excitement took me over."

Morris met the fan who caught his memory and traded a ball for the keepsake. A small price to pay for a treasure his grandkids will one day get to touch while grandpa relives the story.

"The guy in the stands who made the play, he's the MVP of the game," Morris said.

Morris was the MUH: most unlikely hero. For too many reasons.

For one, there's that build. At 5-11, 190 pounds, Morris looks like a guy who, well, has hit 13 home runs in his life. The Alexandria, La., native showed up at LSU four years ago with 160 pounds to his frame and no home runs to his name. One problem: he was replacing icon Todd Walker, the power-hitting second baseman who was most outstanding player of the Tigers' 1993 CWS championship and the school's all-time leading home-run hitter with 52.

"I knew I was in trouble my first meeting at LSU," Morris said. "I looked around and the only guy I was bigger than was the equipment manager."

But Morris had the leather, as they say, and used it to turn himself into a second-team All-American.

Then it happened: His right wrist started to bother him last fall. After 12 games this season, the soreness was back. He could only put the bat on the ball. A full swing was too painful. CAT scans and MRI tests were inconclusive. But six games later, during a mid-April series with Arkansas, Morris could hardly swing a bat. One more CAT scan showed a break in a bone in the wrist. He had surgery April 24. The prognosis: a return in four to six weeks.

"I decided to go ahead and have it done," Morris said. "And get back in time for Omaha."

That's how LSU Tigers are recruited and trained to think: Omaha will be there. That's what got them through a season of injuries and late-season underachievement in the Southeastern Conference.

That Tiger toughness won this CWS. It got Warren Morris through the pain and to the plate with two out in the bottom of the ninth. Morris said he finally felt comfortable swinging the last two games. Uh-huh.

"In baseball, many kids are defeated by the game itself," LSU coach Skip Bertman said. "It's such an unforgiving game. You have to be very tough to handle all the things that happen. Warren is one of those tough kids."

On the day he etched his name in CWS history, baseball forgave Warren Morris.

Facing page: LSU's Warren Morris touches home plate with the winning run of the 1996 College World Series.

JUNE 9, 1996 • COLLEGE WORLD SERIES

2011 INSIGHT *This is my favorite College World Series memory. At the end of the championship game each year, they let the media come onto the field. In the bottom of the ninth, we would go downstairs and sit on the steps behind home plate, right behind the gate to go onto the field. I was sitting on those steps when LSU came up to bat in the bottom of the ninth. I remember thinking about the column I was going to write, about Miami head coach Jim Morris winning his first national title, and carrying the torch from Ron Fraser. Anyway, here come the Tigers. And here comes Warren Morris. Two outs, LSU down, 8-7. Anyway, you know what happened. When Morris swung the bat and it lifted toward right field, the crowd stood and roared. I stood up and yelled, "Oh, my God, you gotta be kidding." After those moments you kind of train yourself to watch the reactions around the scene, look for little things you can recall for your column. But this moment was all about the shock, the unthinkable surprise that just happened. A light-hitting second baseman hits the biggest homer ever. The Miami players lying face down on the turf. Morris was mobbed by the media afterward. The quotes weren't that good, but this column didn't need quotes. I sat there for about 20 minutes trying to think of a lead. I came up with an over-the-top line, but I didn't care. The moment called for over-the-top. Hell, the moment was over-the-top. That was another one I wrote in 40 minutes. I love those moments, and those kinds of columns. It's why I love what I do.*

Golf Season or Football?

SO, WHO'S NO. 1? Well, before the third round of the Nike Omaha Classic, it was Mike Sposa. But he hadn't even played Colorado yet, much less the bowl game.

This is confusing. We are at Champions Club, surrounded by great golfers, a real professional tournament in our midst. But out of the corner of our eyes we look for it. Yes, Saturday is the big day.

The Associated Press top 25 comes out. Poll position for Jan. 2. Nebraska is No. 1 in both the AP and the USA Today/CNN Coaches' poll.

Joe Durant is No. 2 on the money list.

So, so confusing.

This is a great sports week here. Nebraska golf on the map. The U.S. Women's Amateur putting on a show at Firethorn in Lincoln, and Omaha and Champions knocking the ankle socks off the Nike boys. But the timing is all wrong. These are the PGA Tour stars of the future. But in the distance, you can hear somebody yell, "You the Ahman!"

When you play the Nike Tour for a year, is it like a redshirt?

Of course, Nebraska should be No. 1. Everyone who left skid marks on Steve Spurrier's visor is back. The Blackshirts are nastier than the 16th at Champions. Sure, that No. 15 guy is gone. But this new kid, Scott Frost, looks healthy. Just don't fumble, Scott. Just play within your game, like Sposa says.

But how is Jared Tomich's short game?

We are walking around in a daze. Matt Delaney isn't helping matters. Delaney, a Nike Tour official, has been having fun with Champions volunteers all week since they found out he was a Florida State fan. Delaney wears a Nebraska hat he was given, but he wrote, "OLES" after the huge red "N." He put "Go Noles" stickers on everyone's walkie-talkie and can be heard frequently moaning the "Tomahawk Chop" chant into his walkie-talkie.

Who's No. 1? "It breaks up the nervousness you get with the volunteers and the tour officials who come in," Delaney says. "We've been going at it all week. They still think they won that game (1994 Orange Bowl). I tell them the scoreboard says something else."

You go to the locker room. You are looking for the great golf story. You see Jeff Brehaut, the blond Nike veteran from Vacaville, Calif. You want to impress him with the ultimate golf question.

"So, who's No. 1?"

"Probably Nebraska," Brehaut said, "But we just played at Knoxville a while back, and everyone there said Tennessee."

What does he know? Brehaut went to Pacific, where he says "football was just a party." The party's over: Pacific dropped football. Then again, Brehaut's heard of Nebraska.

Sposa wants to say something about golf. This is good. My notepad is filled with scribblings about college football. I let him speak.

"The tournament has been run amazingly well," Sposa said. "Considering they had such short notice. From the transportation to everything, it's very well-organized. We see other tournaments that have been around for a long time not as organized as this. The people have been great."

A crowd wanted to watch Jeff Brehaut after he grabbed the third-round lead — or was it to hear his football predictions?

UNO Football a Pure Delight

SIXTY-EIGHT BEAUTIFUL, crisp autumnesque degrees. Trees. The Arts and Sciences Building (the old Administration Building, the first built on campus) with the white cupola against the blue sky.

No skyboxes or reserved seats. A university president who sits in the stands. An athletic director who paces the sidelines. A head coach who does interviews on the field immediately after the game. No TV timeouts.

Those are just a few of the reasons why an afternoon of UNO football is absolute perfection. It's a hidden gem on Saturday's America. Nebraska football is a happening. UNO is college football at its purest and finest core. But those reasons aren't always enough to fill the metal bleachers — or keep the program from having to defend itself to regents looking for a financial scapegoat.

Fortunately for UNO, on a picture-postcard Saturday at Al F. Caniglia Field, the Mavericks offered still more reasons to come into their world.

Bryon Holston, a 5-foot-11, 310-pound world of hurt who had three sacks, nine tackles and recovered one University of Nebraska at Kearney fumble.

The punishing, straight-up, try-and-tackle-me running style of sophomore Melvin McPhaull, a diamond in the rough from Flanagan High School.

The playmaking of sophomore quarterback Ed Thompson, whether he's running 43 yards off the option for a touchdown or hitting an open MarTay Jenkins streaking across the middle for an 89-yard touchdown.

The excitement any time senior Jake Young gets the ball.

Those heroes and more made the Mavs' 39-14 victory over UNK special.

There were 6,400 people in the stands, not only to enjoy the fine day but to become convinced of why they should come back soon. Among those 6,400 were a handful of Nebraska regents, who voted last June to keep the program going (despite the insistence of a couple that the plug be pulled) and were looking for reassurance that they made the right call.

"We had a lot of the regents here today," UNO Athletic Director Don Leahy said. "They saw a great showcase for Division II football in the state of Nebraska. Not everyone can play in Lincoln."

On a picture-postcard Saturday when even the old facilities couldn't get in the way of euphoria, coach Pat Behrns did his postgame press conference next to the men's room and joked, "This is Division II football at its best."

Star UNO receiver MarTay Jenkins was a sixth-round selection in the 1999 NFL draft.

SEPTEMBER 23, 1996 • NEBRASKA FOOTBALL

What's Next for Huskers?

TEMPE, ARIZ.

THE MOMENT THEY had dreaded, if they had even imagined it at all, had arrived. Unannounced and definitely uninvited. The Arizona State madhouse had swept over the field and the goal posts and left them to pick up the debris of their dreams.

Slowly, they trickled out of the locker room and into the late Saturday night. Down a ramp, toward the bus and they were waiting for them. Parents. Relatives. Friends. Just folks in red, 30 strong, pressed up against a chain-link fence by the bus. Their hearts had been ripped out, too. But they stood there, trying to soothe an open wound that they understood all too well.

"You're the best! Hang in there! We love you! Hey, it's a long season!"

You got that right. The Nebraska Cornhuskers, formerly the No. 1 team in the country, signed a few autographs, exchanged a few thank-yous and hugs and loaded up their first defeat in 27 games onto three large buses. Finally, everyone was aboard. And the buses left into the darkest of nights.

To where? Interesting question for the Nebraska football team. Somehow, they plod forward. But to what? The chance of a three-peat is all but gone. A Bowl Alliance game is an iffy proposition. The Big 12 Conference championship (and boy, there's something to be proud of)? That doesn't have quite the appeal, thank you.

If it's any consolation, they're hurting across the states of Tennessee and Iowa, too. But Tennesseans and Iowans haven't sipped from the Holy Grail of college football. Iowa loses to Tulsa and says, "We wanted to win the Big Ten, anyway."

Nebraska loses to Arizona State, 19-0, and wonders if there is reason to go on. Somehow, they will. And it will be one of the hardest things they've had to do in their young lives. Can they keep their interest for nine more games when the 10th isn't going to be what they had in mind?

"Our theme is perseverance," said Jack Stark, who is in his ninth year as the Huskers' sports psychologist. "Tom (Osborne) is a master at that. I think you'll see us work harder. We'll have a team meeting and see what the Unity Council wants to do."

Long talks. Long faces. Long season. It all happened because of a long night, perhaps the most shocking defeat in Nebraska history. Sure, there were the Oklahoma losses. And the Missouri game in 1978. And those gut-wrenching bowl losses of the early 1990s.

But those teams carried a shadow of doubt. This was arguably the greatest team in Nebraska history, coming off back-to-back national championships and having played in a third, the 1994 Orange Bowl loss that was their last loss. This was a team that had a patent on swagger and confidence and had the secret recipe to total domination.

But what they found out on the same field on which they celebrated their championship last Jan. 2 were two things:

1. This isn't the same team as last year's. Not even close.

2. The distance from the penthouse to humiliation is about nine months.

"Empty," is the one-word description senior I-back Damon Benning used for the moment the Huskers discovered they were mere mortal.

"Tears were shed in that locker room," Benning said. "Especially for the seniors experiencing a regular-season loss for the first time. We just didn't think this day would come."

But when it rained, it poured. Indeed, when the loss came, it wasn't a fluke. It wasn't a Hail Mary by Colorado's Koy Detmer. It wasn't Kansas State recovering an onside kick and booting a 57-yard field goal at the gun. It was total embarrassment. It was Nebraska and Arizona State, trading places. The Blackshirt defense played hard, perhaps well enough to win. But the offense? To paraphrase Butch Cassidy, "Who were those guys?"

The men in red and white were impostors. The black and white numbers said it all: 13 first downs, 226 total yards, 130 rushing yards on 44 attempts, 96 passing yards, three of six fumbles lost, and 23 minutes, 32 seconds of possession time. And eight punts. When Nebraska punts eight times in one game, the world is off its axis.

This was a mad, mad, mad, mad, mad world.

2011 INSIGHT *Some columns I've done taught me lessons. This one falls into that category. I came down pretty hard on Scott Frost after the Arizona State game. A lot of people did. But the folks on the team, the coaches, knew better. There were issues on the offensive line. There were a lot of rebuilding things going on. Nebraska had built a pretty high standard by the time of this crash in the desert in September 1996. The last loss was the 1994 Orange Bowl. We weren't used to seeing Nebraska look like this, and so the easy scapegoat was the new quarterback. Frost held a pretty good grudge against me for a while, and so did his parents. That's fine. That's part of the deal. We had a good talk later on about it, and I think we ironed some things out. I've changed since this column. Call it soft, but I don't think college players should necessarily be ripped or held to an NFL standard. These days, whenever I think about taking apart a college player, I think about this column. I later learned from listening to a couple of old coaching gurus, Milt Tenopir and Charlie McBride, that there are a lot of reasons for why things happen in a game, good and bad, and they aren't necessarily what you think you see from the press box or the stands. That was the lesson from this experience.*

SEPTEMBER 23, 1996 • NEBRASKA FOOTBALL

Scott Frost sits in the end zone after being sacked for a safety in a 19-0 loss to Arizona State.

This was the Husker offense, starring in its own version of "Clueless." Three times, they had only 10 men on the field and twice it cost them timeouts. They gave up three safeties. Three! We heard quarterback Scott Frost could play some safety, but this was ridiculous. Frost's best play of the night came after the third safety when, lying in the end zone, he fired the ball at the goalpost.

Bull's eye! It was the worst offensive performance since, well, before Tommie Frazier showed up on campus. Oops. There, we said it.

It may be taboo. But the fact is, if Frazier had been out there, you wouldn't have seen the mistakes and ineptness. Blocks would have been made. The offense would have moved. Nebraska would have won. No. 15's magic was appreciated once again.

Nobody expects Frost to do a Tommie imitation. But what you do expect Frost to do is something. Curiously, the guy coveted by offensive genius Bill Walsh doesn't have an accurate cannon. And while ASU's Jake Plummer was picking apart Nebraska with crossing passes, it became apparent that the Huskers don't have a passing game. Throw in the shocking development that the option game is almost nonexistent with Frost and it's no wonder Osborne was grasping for trick plays and straws early in the game — even giving up a chance for a field goal late in the first half by throwing deep (incomplete) when a 20-yard pass might have set up an encouraging three-pointer.

But it wasn't just about Frost melting in the desert heat. It goes deeper than Frost's growing pains. Nebraska couldn't even run over or wear down an ASU defense that gave up 42 points to Washington two weeks ago. The bottom line: Nebraska's offensive line has a problem. Do real men still wear red?

"It will be interesting to see their reaction," Osborne said. "I'm looking for a positive reaction. We need to think through exactly where we are and where we're going."

The answers were on a bus on a late Saturday night. And as they pulled away, leaving behind history, they drove off into a darker, more uncertain night.

20 YEARS WITH TOM SHATEL • 89

DECEMBER 8, 1996 • NEBRASKA FOOTBALL

Texas Coach Rolls the Dice

ST. LOUIS

NOW NEBRASKA KNOWS all about the new neighbors to the south. Texas talks a big game. Texas plays a big game. Its quarterback isn't afraid to make predictions. Its quarterback isn't afraid to back it up.

Fourth and one. No, fourth and inches. Mere inches.

Texas ball on the Texas 28-yard line. Texas 30, Nebraska 27. There was 2:38 left in the game. And not a craps-roller nor a blackjack player a few blocks away on the Admiral riverboat casino could dare to watch Texas coach John Mackovic. You don't roll the dice when the odds say punt and take your chances with a sporadic Nebraska offense. You don't ask for a card when you're sitting on 16.

Not unless you feel lucky. Not unless you feel good.

James Brown felt good. Mackovic knew it. Mackovic went for it, and all Nebraska could do was watch and survey the stakes.

Make it, and Nebraska fails to win a conference championship for the first time in six years.

Make it, and Nebraska loses a chance at a third national title and falls to the fate of possibly playing Virginia Tech in the Orange Bowl. Ugh.

Make it, and Brown, who dared to predict Texas might just win this game, is in-your-face right.

Make it, and the Big 12 championship game was a terrible idea. Miss it, great idea.

Make it, this is the gutsiest, most terrific call in a long time. Miss it, Mackovic's an idiot.

Make that genius.

Brown takes the dice, er, the snap. Doesn't sneak. Doesn't even hand off. He rolls out. It is a run-pass option. Brown looks to run. No, Derek Lewis has sneaked open down the sidelines. Brown stops and lobs him the ball and suddenly, the 30,000-plus Nebraska fans in the Trans World Dome are holding their breath and have their hands over their mouths and the horror that unfolds before them — Lewis running 61 yards to the Nebraska 11 — seems to go in slow motion. Next play, Longhorns score. Longhorns win, 37-27.

Rush end Grant Wistrom said: "If it hadn't worked, it would have been a real dumb call. I guess coach Mackovic's a genius."

Texas coach John Mackovic gambled and won in the Big 12 championship game.

UNO Blooms in Volleyball

NATIONAL CHAMPIONSHIPS COME in all shapes and sizes. The common denominators are the glazed eyes, the I-haven't-slept-in-two-days-and-I-don't-care giddy aura about a person and, of course, the gifts. Win a national title and get gifts. Lots of gifts.

In the case of UNO volleyball, that would be a nice floral arrangement. Welcome to Rose Shires' Flower Shop. You walk into Shires' cubbyhole office, and the place is dominated by flowers. Welcome to our funeral home, Shires jokes. But there was no funeral here. It was more like a birth. A bouncing baby national title came into her life this week. Where are the cigars?

"Come on in," Shires says. "You want some cookies?"

Tom Osborne has won two national championships. Tom Osborne has never invited me into his office and offered cookies.

The Lady Mavs won the lottery. They haven't stopped cheering, or started sleeping, yet. Maybe not as many people have heard them, or noticed. But there in the UNO athletic hallway, it still counts.

"The people of Nebraska don't really know all these other sports that aren't Husker football," Shires said. "These girls work just as hard as the football players, train as hard and play as hard. And we usually have to sleep three or four to a room. They're eating Froot Loops for breakfast in their rooms before games."

But the reward – the feeling – is something they all share.

"After years of watching these celebrations on TV, I'd sit there and bawl because, as a coach, I wanted one so bad," Shires said. "Now that it's here, I can tell you the feeling is even better than I imagined.

"I have a lot more respect for Tom Osborne and his staff now, too, for challenging for a national championship every year. It's so hard. At one point this year, we sat there and said, 'If this doesn't work, we can't imagine what else we could do.'

"People of Nebraska should understand, this is

Rose Shires led her 1996 UNO volleyball team to a 35-2 record and an NCAA Division II national championship.

not something you should expect every year. It's something you should appreciate when it happens."

Shires tells a story: It was media day and the Lady Mavs had a good team coming back, a team worth telling the world about. It should have been called "Writer's Day." One World-Herald writer showed up.

"I felt bad for our girls," Shires said. "It was kind of an in-your-face thing. Then I found out it was on the same day as Nebraska football media day."

That's a battle Shires will never win. She knows it. Next year, maybe two or three more bodies will show up for media day. But it will be back to the same song, next verse. Enjoy this, Shires is told. This is your 15 minutes of fame. Then you go back to the cubbyhole and wait, along with the rest of the world, to see if Nebraska can beat Texas next year.

Those 15 minutes, though, are always worth the trouble.

"It's definitely worth it," Shires said. "The people who were involved in this national championship will always have the title of being national champions. That is what's worth it. Not the press we're getting now. Not the flowers. Not even the trophy. The prize is the road. It's not getting what you want, it's getting there."

TOM'S TAKE   REFLECTIONS ON

Time Is Right for Hockey

THIS IS THE biggest natural since Robert Redford.

University of Nebraska at Omaha Athletic Director Don Leahy and a host of local corporate investors unveiled a sparkling new gift for the city: UNO hockey.

College. Hockey. What a concept. This is a great hockey town. This city loves college sports. Why haven't we thought of this before?

"It's come up a few times," Leahy said. "I tried to get it started here in 1974. I presented a plan to the chancellor, and he was in favor of it, but he said the timing wasn't right. The Knights had just left Omaha and we were going to need new ice-making equipment. There were other things. Now, the timing is perfect."

> "It's come up a few times. . . .
> Now, the timing is perfect."
>
> — DON LEAHY, UNO ATHLETIC DIRECTOR

Perfect doesn't begin to describe UNO hockey. You could see it and feel it at the UNO Alumni House press conference, which attracted curious visitors from the Omaha Royals and Racers and all corners of the city. There was an unusual electricity in the room. As Chancellor Del Weber and Leahy explained the incredible future before them, the looks on the faces in the room all screamed the same thing.

WOW. Is this really happening? In Omaha? Where can I get tickets?

It was a great day for Omaha, a day for positive thinkers who look for a reason to achieve, not search for an excuse to tear down potential. It was the dawn of our sports future.

It's a way for Omaha to give UNO a place on the local sports map. UNO hockey would be the school's flagship sport, one that would be UNO's answer to Nebraska football and Creighton basketball in local stature and pride. It would boost interest in all UNO sports, not just hockey.

— MAY 2, 1996

UNO Athletic Director Don Leahy said he first tried to get a UNO hockey program started in 1974.

THE CHANGING SPORTS LANDSCAPE 1996

NU, OU See Rivalry Die

NORMAN, OKLA.

SOMETIME EARLY SATURDAY morning, when this proud, old rivalry still had its last breath, Jerry Tagge walked onto the sun-splashed field at Memorial Stadium and took a step back in time.

Here was the place where Tagge, the former Nebraska quarterback, and so many others had been immortalized on a cold, gray day so long ago. How long? Twenty-five years ago. And 25 years since Tagge had been in this stadium. Like an old soldier returning to a field of battle, he could feel the memories, maybe see a few of the old ghosts still running around out there.

Johnny Rodgers turning a punt return into a magic carpet ride. Jack Mildren to Jon Harrison. Rich Glover grappling with Tom Brahaney. And the frantic, breathless last drive of "The Game of the Century," with Jeff Kinney dragging himself into the end zone for Nebraska's 35-31 victory.

"I had goose bumps," said Tagge, the man who led that final drive to destiny. "I got to the 50-yard line, and I remembered being there 25 years ago on that spot. It gave me goose bumps."

And then Nebraska-Oklahoma, circa 1996, started. And Tagge's trip into the Time Tunnel became a jaunt through the Twilight Zone. As a sideline reporter for the Husker radio network, he had news to report.

"When I was down there, I could tell they didn't have the same emotion we had," Tagge said.

This just in: The Nebraska-Oklahoma rivalry is officially dead.

It died a very slow, and mostly sad, death. It had lived a full life. It was a rivalry built on championships and coincidence, not geography. It was as American as apple pie. Dessert on Thanksgiving.

But a quarter of a century later, and countless great moments and thrills later, the poor thing was beyond recognition. Early November date. The worst Oklahoma team ever. And the carnage. Oh, the brutal carnage.

Never mind the particulars, the missed tackles, the incompetence of Oklahoma's offense, the general ineptitude of Sooner

Nebraska's Jason Peter puts a bear hug on OU quarterback Justin Fuente in the Huskers' 73-21 rout.

football. The score, for once, said it all. Nebraska 73, Oklahoma 21. Yes, the biggest victory by Nebraska over Oklahoma ever. Yes, the worst defeat for Oklahoma ever.

Worse than a 45-point loss to Oklahoma A&M in 1945. The most points ever scored on Oklahoma. The most points scored by Nebraska since the 73 put up against Iowa State last year.

So now Oklahoma stands with Iowa State in the annals of Nebraska football. How appropriate. Because this game has become just another game. Exactly 25 years after "The Game of the Century." How ironic. How sad.

Once upon a time, in a storybook game that transcended the ages, a rivalry came to life. Twenty-five years later, on the same field of battle, it closed its weary eyes. You had to be there to believe it.

— NOVEMBER 3, 1996

BOB DEVANEY'S DEATH | BIG GOLF CROWDS | SCOTT FROST ARRIVES | FIRST UNO HOCKEY GAME

1997

> "He has the Midas touch. He gets things done. He has the respect of so many people who helped get things done. He treats everyone with respect."
>
> — CONNIE CLAUSSEN, UNO ASSOCIATE ATHLETIC DIRECTOR, DESCRIBING ATHLETIC DIRECTOR DON LEAHY

Osborne Era Ending Soon?

A tale of two Tom Osborne questions: Will Nebraska's football coach wear a denim shirt with his new "An Era of Excellence" logo? And is that era about to end?

The latter speculative question is worth asking because of a comment Osborne threw out while discussing his 25th anniversary as coach with a group of local and national writers. When asked about the future of the program, Osborne volunteered that he would prefer "a Nebraska guy" to follow him someday. Huh? Those who have followed the 25 years with a magnifying glass — including World-Herald Sports Editor Steve Sinclair and longtime NU beat writer Lee Barfknecht — were stunned to hear such a revelation from a coach who never hinted (at least publicly) about his preference on a successor.

"People talk about corporate culture, well, football programs have a culture," Osborne said. "It's unsettling for a team to have that culture, that atmosphere, change. . . . Having someone who understands the peculiarities of the program would be helpful. We rely on walk-ons. I think you need someone who understands the recruiting difficulties here." The alternative, Osborne said, is "having somebody learn the hard way two or three years down the road that certain things don't work in Nebraska."

The comments make you wonder if Osborne is heading down the road soon. Is he laying groundwork, planting a seed in Athletic Director Bill Byrne's head that a current or former staff member is the preferred and only acceptable choice? Or is it all totally innocent?

— AUGUST 12, 1997

Always, the basketball barometer for Dana Altman has been Mitch Richmond. Mitch the All-American. Mitch the NBA All-Star. Mitch the Dream Teamer. Mitch the self-made player. Mitch the best player Altman ever coached. But then came something Altman, the Creighton head basketball coach, had never seen. At least by someone wearing one of his uniforms. The alley-oop pass was high. Too high to catch for most players. But Rodney Buford is not just your ordinary jumping jack. He is a budding creative genius. So he reached back and caught the errant pass behind his head with his right hand and, in one fluid motion, slammed it home while still in orbit. The Creighton crowd roared. And Altman saw a new standard taking shape. "Mitch could do some dunking," Altman said. "But Mitch never did that."

MIRACLE IN MISSOURI | OSBORNE'S RETIREMENT | BIG 12 FOOTBALL TITLE | OUTLAND TO OMAHA

Jesse Cuevas' official title is Rosenblatt Stadium superintendent. But he is more of a gardener to a field that sprouts dreams. Cuevas calls Rosenblatt Stadium "Omaha's front yard." It's his job to make sure the front yard looks like an oil painting. During the College World Series, a few million people looking in on TV will be driving by the yard. It's a grass thing. It's a pride thing.

Cubs Director of Scouting Jim Hendry, the man who transformed Creighton baseball into a College World Series program, said it's time to stop comparing Creighton coaches to the standard Hendry set. "It's going to be hard to do it at the highest level, maybe again," Hendry said. "But that's the reality of it. I don't want the coaching staff there to be compared to me. I don't want people there to say, 'Why can't they be like (Hendry)?' People like to put me on this pedestal, but it's unfair for the people after me. It's a lot harder now than it was then."

Grant Wistrom stays. Shocking news? Slightly. Good news? Most definitely. Maybe this shouldn't be such a big surprise. But the list of underclassmen jumping to the National Football League has become so unwieldy and the moves are so commonplace that you naturally assume any junior with half a résumé is gone. Wistrom, the All-American, stays. But why? For the love of college? For the joy of college football? Who is this guy, anyway? Our newest hero. Thank you, Grant. Thanks for returning some faith and life to the college game that has treated you well. Thanks for standing up for what you wanted and ignoring the word of all the "experts" — from Mel Kiper right down to this column — who said you were crazy if you didn't take advantage of your current stock. The Blackshirts thank you, too. Even though Wistrom may or may not break through double-teams to match his junior-year numbers, his experience and leadership alone will help develop a young defense. Talk about good omens. Suddenly, some of the fog over the 1997 season is clearing.

Hockey boys are regular guys. You can talk to them. Buy them a beer. Just don't ask them if they're hurt. Most of these guys don't play football because it's not physical enough.

Here was a loving grandson whose grandmother, Ella Kemp, had died the day before. What to do? For Tyronn Lue, there was no question. He would play for his team. He would think of his grandmother. Such a heavy heart, but then, the big tickers usually are. The kid went out and played 29 minutes and scored 11 points with five assists in a 71-52 win over Creighton in Lincoln.

20 YEARS WITH TOM SHATEL • 95

JANUARY 1, 1997 • NEBRASKA FOOTBALL

NU Answers All Questions

MIAMI

SOME NEW YEAR'S Resolutions:

I won't say Scott Frost can't win a big game.

I will remember Damon Benning as someone who was an impact player.

I will never again question the Nebraska football program's desire to show up for a game that only a few thousand Virginians and a couple of daiquiri vendors outside Pro Player Stadium seemed to care about.

Never mind that it wasn't the national championship. Never mind that it wasn't even a real Orange Bowl. This was New Year's Eve, in a strange stadium, a pro stadium. Frost will take it. Benning will cherish it. The Huskers needed it.

Nebraska 41, Virginia Tech 21 was the largest margin of victory in an Orange Bowl for Nebraska since the Huskers thumped Notre Dame 40-6 in Bob Devaney's last hurrah on Jan. 1, 1973. It was also one of the largest bowl victories for coach Tom Osborne, a man who hasn't had many, period. He had to feel good about this one, as satisfied and proud as he did three years ago, in that gutsy 18-16 loss to Florida State or after either of the last two national championship wins. Because Osborne is all about performance.

The Huskers, with two explosive I-backs injured and a defense fast running out of gas, won the war of resiliency. Which made the heroes even more appropriate.

Nobody could question Benning's heart or soul. But in a long career marred by injuries and younger, more talented I-backs stepping over him, the question was whether the Omaha Northwest star would ever make an impact. A real impact.

Finally, it was the other guys who were hurt.

Finally, fate found Benning. It opened the door and begged him to come in. And he stormed through, knocking down the door on a 33-yard run — make that sprint — up the middle for a third-quarter touchdown that was Nebraska's most important play of the night. It made a statement that

Damon Benning ran for 95 yards and two touchdowns and was named Orange Bowl MVP.

Nebraska's offense wasn't going to curl up in a ball, as it had against Arizona State and Colorado. Benning's two second-half scores were enough to make him Nebraska's MVP. This is how we will remember Benning: a head of steam going 33 yards toward the goal line that nothing, finally, could stop. Better late than never.

You, too, Mr. Frost. The beleaguered quarterback from Wood River could easily have been Nebraska's MVP. But it had nothing to do with numbers; Frost was 11-for-22 passing for 136 yards and rushed for 62 yards.

Those are Tommie Frazier-type numbers. And,

bottom line, Mr. Frost had a Frazier-type game. If he doesn't mind, we'll use the comparison again. It worked back in September, in the stop-the-presses loss to Arizona State. It works again now.

Somewhere at a water cooler or corner tavern in Nebraska today, somebody will complain because Frost threw a ball too high or didn't break 10 tackles on the way to a 75-yard touchdown run. Here's what Frost did: He won a big game.

"He did some things reminiscent of the guy we had last year that everyone is so quick to compare him to," said Benning, referring to No. 15. "He passed the test tonight."

Heyns True to Her Word

SHE HAS A ways to go to reach the celebrity quotient of, say, Scott Frost in this college town. But Penny Heyns is getting there.

"A couple of times I've gone somewhere and been recognized," Heyns said. "Like at the Barnes and Noble (bookstore), getting coffee and the guy said, 'You're the swimmer, aren't you?'"

Yeah, and Michael Jordan is the guy who shoots hoops. Heyns is more than just a swimmer. She was a two-time gold medal winner in the 1996 Olympic Games and, moreover, a hero and role model in her native South Africa who had the honor of meeting South African President Nelson Mandela three times in the past year. She has had parades in her benefit and pools renamed in her honor. South African children, black and white, flock to her side — and there is no barometer to gauge the significance of that. She's the MJ of South Africa.

So why, then, was she decked out in a "Nebraska Swimming" T-shirt, on the deck of the Devaney Center pool and cheering on her former teammates in a dual with Kansas?

Better question: Now that her eligibility at Nebraska is up, shouldn't Heyns be training at home? Or at an Olympic-training site, with an Olympic-sized (50-meter) pool?

Because Heyns was true to her word. After Heyns won the two golds last July in Atlanta, she spoke glowingly of her experience at Nebraska. She said she wanted to spend the next four years setting up the Heyns 2000 Summer Games Gold Medal Push right there in Lincoln.

"It's my second home," Heyns said. "The staff there, the other South African swimmers, they are like family to me. This is my comfort zone. I don't think I could swim in South Africa. I associate home with taking a break.

"I plan on coming back here frequently," Heyns said. "It's really hard to leave Nebraska. I'm comfortable with the weight room. I've met some football players there. They know who I am. They've said it's a pity (the Olympics) are only every four years."

Football players recognizing the South African queen? She's practically a Nebraska native.

University of Nebraska swimmer Penny Heyns, who captured 14 Big Eight conference titles, won two gold medals at the 1996 Olympics.

How One Life Touches Many

BEERRRINNGGGG!!!! The alarm clock pierced the dream of Big Red like a needle going through a balloon. Big Red looked at the clock. It was 7 a.m. Game day. Big day.

In an hour, Red was on the road, dressed in red, from his old 1972 cap with the white "N" on the front and the Jerry Tagge autograph still showing through the dirt stains to his obnoxious (yes, even Red knew it but didn't care) red cowboy boots. He was in his red Chevy Blazer, the third one he'd owned, tooling down Interstate 80 toward Lincoln. On this beautiful autumn Saturday, Big Red was going to worship. It was Saturday, but he was going to church. He was going to watch his beloved Nebraska Cornhuskers play, pray for a win and sing "Hallelujah" with the choir of 75,000 all the way home.

They called him Big Red because his name, like his thinning hair, was "Red." And he was, to be polite, "stocky." But the name fit. Big Red loved Husker football. He had an "office" at home that was more like a shrine. He had it all, everything from posters and pennants to the decanter in the shape of Bob Devaney with the head of Bob that screwed off and poured out, appropriately enough, a toddy that Bob himself would approve. Standing out, above his desk and looking down over him and all of Nebraska, was his favorite memento: a lovely, stunning painting of Devaney, dressed in his red coaching jacket and ball cap, hovering above a packed Memorial Stadium. At the bottom of the painting were the words, "He built it ... and they came."

And Big Red was on his way.

Except, on this Saturday, something was different. Strange. Eerie. Interstate 80 was empty.

It didn't strike Red until he hit Ashland (he was always going over the game plan or was paying attention to the pre-game babble on the radio). There wasn't a soul on the road. Did he have it right? Was this Saturday? He turned on the radio to the pre-game show. No show. An announcer talked about how cattle prices had dipped this week. He tried the

Bob Devaney left a giant footprint upon the University of Nebraska with two national football titles and a top-level athletic program.

other station. An auto mechanic was on the air, talking about antifreeze and winterizing your baby for the hard months ahead. An occasional truck whizzed by, going back toward Omaha. Where was everybody?

Finally. Lincoln. Strange. There were only two exits, one for downtown and the other for the airport. Red got downtown and his jaw dropped like an anvil. It was a ghost town. Nobody on the streets. No red. He parked and walked around. Finally, he saw an old geezer, sitting outside a barbershop. Red asked: "Where is everyone? Don't they know there's a game today?"

"Game?" asked the old man. "Who?"

Senile old guy, Red thought. So he walked his usual route, down 14th Street, past the Zoo Bar to O Street and then down to 10th where the red parade to the game usually started. Where were the thousands of his red lodge brothers? Where were the two fat guys who wore the tattered red jerseys underneath blue coveralls whose claim to fame was that they once bought Dean Steinkuhler a beer and Dean told them, "Thanks"? Where was the old woman who wore a sweatshirt that said, "God Loves the Huskers" and kissed everybody in red for good luck? Where was that crazy crimson Cadillac with the bumper sticker that said, "On the eighth day, God created the Huskers"?

The Zoo was closed up. So, in fact, were stores, restaurants and bars in every direction. The only things Red saw open were a couple of greasy-spoon cafes, the barbershop and a hardware store. Aha. Inside the window of the hardware store, there was a schedule placard. Red bent over to take a look and make sure he wasn't imagining that there was a game today.

There was. It said, "Nebraska vs. South Dakota. Saturday. 1 p.m."

Red shrieked. And ran inside Kinney's Hardware for a look. The owner, a burly man with a gut and a friendly smile, said, "Can I help you?"

"Yes," Red said. "Can you tell me what year this is."

"Why, it's 1997," said the owner. "What's the matter?"

Red began to ramble: "I don't know. I thought I was going to a Husker game today. But there's nobody here. Nobody. And now I see, on the schedule up front, that they're playing South Dakota today. What happened to Kansas State?"

"Aw," said the owner. "They haven't played Kansas State in 10 years or so, not since they dropped down to Division II. Sad day, that. But it was only inevitable. The state just couldn't support Division I sports."

Red scratched his balding head. Where was he, anyway? The "Twilight Zone"? When was Rod Serling going to come out from behind the back room and yell, "Surprise! Huskers 34, K-State 7"?

Red looked around the store, searching for proof: a 1970 or 1994 national championship poster, a photo of Jarvis Redwine, anything. Instead, he saw something that caught his eye but didn't register at first. Until it hit him like a ton of bricks. Red bricks, of course.

"BILL BARNES NAMED HUSKER COACH" screamed the headline, in big, bold print. Underneath was a smaller headline that read, "Dye says UCLA coach will be Nebraska Savior." Red almost choked when he saw the newspaper date: "Feb. 3, 1962." It sent chills down Red's spine.

"That's the day they hired Devaney," said Red, who knew the date by heart.

"What's the matter, fella?" the store owner said. "Looks like you've seen a ghost."

"I have," Red said. "Say, have you ever heard of a coach named Devaney? Bob Devaney?"

"Sure, everyone has," said Jeff Kinney, the hardware man. "He's the coach at Kansas State. Led them to two national championships before he turned it over to the next guy. I hear he was a wonderful old guy, full of spit and vinegar and magic. He turned K-State into a football power. Then he became A.D. and made them into a sports power. Now, they run the Big 12."

"But didn't he coach at Nebraska?" Red asked, almost pleading.

"Nah," said Kinney. "He turned us down. Said the commitment wasn't enough. He stayed at Wyoming for a few more years. We got Barnes. Poor guy. Came from the West Coast thinking he could turn it around here. He got spooked by the lack of players, had a bad personality, made some enemies and then bolted after two 5-6 seasons. It's been downhill ever since. Coaches were afraid to touch Nebraska. Thought it was the impossible job, what with Oklahoma and Kansas State and Missouri dominating the Big Eight."

"You mean, no Nebraska national championships?" Red asked.

"Fella," Kinney said, laughing, "I don't know what you been drinking, but let me know if you got any more."

And then Kinney began to fill Red's head with an incredible story, an unthinkable, horrible tale. Of how Nebraska went to one bowl game, that 1982 Independence Bowl, and left Division I two years later because it couldn't support enough sports. Of how there was no Devaney Center; the athletic folks were lucky just to scrape enough together to touch up the old Coliseum. They got about 7,000 for basketball games, Kinney said. But the basketball team did go to the Division II playoffs last year.

Volleyball national champions? Heck, Kinney said, there was no volleyball team, unless you counted the one at the YWCA. Nebraska had women's basketball, track and softball. Red couldn't believe it. He thanked Kinney for his time and took off for Memorial Stadium, where he was in for another shock: no South or North Stadium additions. A crowd of 25,000 showed up on this brilliant Saturday.

Suddenly, a South Dakota player broke through the line and was streaking down the sidelines, ahead of the red pack of players, who were so small and slow it was disgusting. Then Red looked up at the scoreboard that read, "Visitors 63, Nebraska 0" and before he could let out a huge scream ...

BRRRINNGGGG!!!! He woke up.

Red bounced out of bed. He was in a cold sweat. He raced into the living room and picked up the front page, where a headline said, "Legend Devaney Dies." He was relieved at first, then felt suddenly filled with regret. Of how he took Devaney for granted all this time. Of how he saw the old man over the years and never once stopped and told him, "Thanks." Not even a stupid card or a letter.

Red bent over and cried his eyes out. Then he went into his office and stared up at the old coach, looking down from the painting. He somehow felt connected with the man. He began to pray, right there to the Bobfather. Thanks, Bob, he said. Thanks for the championships and the winning and the joy and the fun and the Saturdays filled with red and the courage you made me feel and the sheer life and pride you single-handedly pumped into this state. Take care, Bob. Don't let St. Peter give you any grief, and if he does, then put Jerry List or Wayne Meylan or Ben Gregory or Brook Berringer on him. You had a great life, Bob. Most men never get to be giants. You wore it as naturally as a red blazer.

And then Red smiled and said one last prayer, to the guy even Devaney calls "Coach."

"You can have him, Lord," Red said. "But thanks for sharing him with us first."

2011 INSIGHT *When Bob Devaney died, I had a few options as a columnist. One, write about what the man meant to the state. Which was obvious. Two, reach into a deep reservoir of Devaney tales and spin one after another for old times' sake. Three, find Devaney friends, players and colleagues and let them tell the story of the great coach. Well, I hadn't been around the man long enough to know a lot of great stories. And I wasn't familiar enough with Devaney cronies to get the really good, vintage stuff. So, I chose option one. And I knew if I tried to write it with authority, it wouldn't come off believable. Because I hadn't been in Nebraska that long. So, rather than do the obvious here's-what-he-meant column, I came up with this idea, which borrows from the "It's a Wonderful Life" concept. I thought it would be effective. What if Devaney hadn't come to Nebraska? What if they had hired some other guy, a coach who would have gone 8-3 or 7-4 every year? I thought it put the Devaney legacy into perspective. The problem was finding a name for my character. I probably could have gone with something other than "Red."*

JUNE 8, 1997 • COLLEGE WORLD SERIES

Loving the Long Ball

THE FUTURE OF college baseball showed up at Rosenblatt Stadium for the championship of the College World Series. The future speaks with a bit of an accent. The future swings a big aluminum stick and has been known to hit home runs that scare the lions at the Henry Doorly Zoo. Mostly, the future of college baseball wears purple and gold these days.

LSU, the past and still champion of college baseball, sure looks like the future. The Tigers, aka the Bayou Bombers, won their second straight CWS title with a 13-6 victory over Alabama. It was the fourth title of the decade for LSU, the self-proclaimed "Team of the '90s" that backs it up. Don't look now, but they look like they're just getting warmed up.

LSU's win wasn't that close. But it was that boring. And long. Is that bad for college baseball? Or do we expect too much?

If you pitch, period, you have the least desirable job in college sports, right behind Western Athletic Conference Commissioner and Gender Equity Compliance Director. The future of baseball is batters going deep in games that last too long because the pitchers are trying to figure out a way to sneak off the mound without getting noticed.

The game took 3 hours and 15 minutes, and that wasn't all that unusual, considering the average CWS game this week took 3:01. Shoot, the last time a national title game didn't take at least 2:50 to play was 1986 (2:44).

Hey, but it plays in Omaha. The numbers that mattered most this week were 204,309 and 24,401 — the largest total and single-game crowds in CWS history. People apparently love catching those home runs.

"Sure, it's good for the game," LSU hitting coach Jim Schwanke said. "Run-scoring is a lot of fun for the fans."

LSU outfielder Wes Davis can't get high enough to snag a home run by Alabama's Joe Caruso.

Nike Classic Hits an Ace

MIKE WEST, NIKE Omaha Classic tournament director and director of attendance, stopped his golf cart on the median outside Champions Club and admired the view.

Out on the ninth hole, following leader Chris Smith, was a sight for a tourney director's eyes: people, people and more people.

Young, old, 5 handicaps and 22s, kids on their dads' shoulders and golfing buds laughing in amazement at how Smith drove the par-4 ninth green without hesitation. West was in the middle of his daily rounds, driving around the course to guesstimate the attendance. But he had to take a deep breath at the monster being created before his eyes.

"This is a PGA gallery," West said. "A couple of the (Nike Tour) players said they don't even see these galleries on some of the PGA (Tour) stops and nowhere on the Nike except maybe Boise.

"This is cool. This is what we've been waiting for."

Indeed. This was Arrival Day at the Champions Club. Smith won the second annual Nike Omaha Classic with a tour-record 26-under-par week. Now he can give somebody else a chance.

But if Omaha witnessed the launching of a great golf career, then Smith, too, can say he was there when the Omaha Classic became an official big-time event.

With Sunday's estimated crowd of 14,000, the Omaha Classic drew a terrific 39,700 in its second year (eclipsing last year by 12,700). And if some November weather hadn't decided to drop in a few months early, you could have had 3,000 more dropping by to catch some rays and birdies.

"It's fantastic," Smith said. "For a second-year tournament, it's unbelievable. It's fun.

"To hear that kind of roar when you make a putt, and hear roars from around the course, that's how it is on the big tour."

Could you have guessed it? Yes. The people here get up for big events. The Omaha Classic is on the fast track toward becoming our golfing College World Series (which is why we build a sports arena and fill up the calendar with big events).

People came for the fireworks, for the nightly social tent that is the city's biggest cocktail party and, yes, for the golf. They came because West and Co. have turned this into the place to be.

A crowd of 14,000 watched Chris Smith capture the Nike Omaha Classic.

Torres a Star Off Field, Too

JOHNNY TORRES REMEMBERS standing there, at the Houston airport, his heart ripped apart, saying goodbye to his parents, maybe forever.

Who knew then? Torres was a confused 9-year-old, torn between the love for his parents and two brothers and the gut feeling that he could not — no way — get on that plane and go back to South America with them.

To this day, his mother's parting words stay with him: "You are here for a reason. Make the best of this opportunity."

Today Torres is making the best of his opportunity. He is a senior on Creighton's soccer team, an All-American and, at 5-8, is quite possibly the tallest man in Omaha.

The way Torres performs on a soccer field pales in comparison to the magic he works off it. In the day care centers and shelters of Omaha and as a Big Brother, Torres offers kids his time, his hope and his proof.

Johnny Torres was born in Medellin, Colombia. He lived with his family in an apartment with one small bedroom and one living room. The family — father, mother, three boys — slept in the same bed.

Outside, Johnny kicked a soccer ball in the streets and tried to dodge the daily rush of crime and drugs.

When Torres was 5, his parents sought to take their children out of that environment. They moved to Dickinson, Texas, just outside Houston.

There, Torres found his first organized soccer team, and it was like his eyes were opened and his world became full of color.

"I still have a photo of me in my first soccer uniform," said Torres, his face beaming.

"I have a maroon top with yellow stripes and maroon socks. I had my first pair of soccer shoes — white Converses with a blue star."

But soon, when Torres was 9, his parents grew homesick for Colombia. They prepared to take their sons back. One problem: Young Johnny had been taught to dream by his first soccer coach, Carlos Clark.

"He told me that I had an opportunity here in the States to become successful, to get an education by playing soccer, and to make something good of myself," Torres said.

"It was really hard. But I knew I didn't want to live there (Colombia). I knew I was on a mission. I wasn't just getting adopted. I was getting something done. I was getting another chance."

That chance came from Clark and his wife, Marcella, who adopted Torres and put him on the path to Creighton and U.S. citizenship.

It was when he went to visit his adopted mother's day care classes that something inside clicked: He loved kids. The ultimate Big Brother was born.

As a social work major, Torres spends four to six hours a day at Guadalupe Hall in South Omaha and at two other shelters in Council Bluffs and Omaha ("between soccer and classes"), talking to young teens who want someone to listen and to others sitting on the brink of delinquency.

"A lot of kids I work with are prisoners of their environment," Torres said. "There was this one art session I went to. I remember when I painted things it was of birds or soccer balls. These kids, 7- and 8-year-olds, were painting gang signs and handguns.

"I try to teach them there are other things outside their community, a whole other world out there. I tell them they can never expect to get out of there if they don't work hard, go to school and take care of themselves."

Creighton's Johnny Torres was twice named national player of the year in college soccer.

SEPTEMBER 21, 1997 • NEBRASKA FOOTBALL

...he Has Arrived

WHO? There is no question of the identi... Nebraska quarterback, or who it should ... name is Frost. Scott Frost. Finally.

... he has been out there, for a year now. But not ... a breathtaking September Saturday at Husky ...dium did Frost fully arrive, wings spread, in full ...om. In the biggest Husker game of the season, with ...hampionship stakes and in front of a national and ...hostile stage, Frost was The Star. The Show. The Man.

Nebraska 27, Washington 14. That will make for a nice mantelpiece in the Frost home. But now we must get busy. The Scott Frost Fan Club is now forming. For the past few years, Nebraska's prodigal son has been bashed, doubted, scorned, blamed and finally booed. He will return home the Favorite Son in many corners. Frost for senator. Frost for governor. Frost for Heisman. Frost forgiven.

You know, I knew all along this kid was going to be something special. He will hear that a lot this week. He will be greeted by legions of new friends. The way he has been treated, like the plague, the problem, the anti-Frazier — by news media and fans alike — it would be his right to brush everyone off this week. To walk around campus wearing a T-shirt that said, "I told you so."

But Frost is taking the high road. Looks like it might go to the Orange Bowl.

"I don't care," Frost said about his forthcoming new popularity in the state. "The friends I have and the friends I want have been the friends with me through everything."

Nebraska coach Tom Osborne said, "It's been disturbing to me as a coach to see him treated the way he's been treated when all he's done is the best he can. He has a scholarship worth $7,000 a year. He's not a pro quarterback. He's 22 years old.

"I think he was a little apprehensive about this game, that if we lost, people would say it was his fault. I'm glad, for his sake, it went well for him. Tommie Frazier had a great supporting cast. Last year, we had only three returning starters on offense. And Scott was still learning the offense. It wasn't like he had started for four years. It's taken a lot personally for him to handle it the way he has. He's kept his head up. I was very appreciative of the way he's handled it."

Osborne's faith in Frost was such that he put in two new plays for him. In a big game. Plays that would work if executed well. The first was a fake trap play, with a fake hand-off to Joel Makovicka designed to suck in the defense while the quarterback found room to run. Frost did, in an unforgettable 34-yard streak to the end zone on NU's first possession. The second was a quarterback draw out of the shotgun formation. Frost eluded a tackler and went 30 yards for the second score. Huskers, 14-0. Husky crowd, out of the game. Scott Frost, front and center.

"Great play-calling. Great line play," Frost said.

Great quarterbacking, too.

"My focus is the football team and the football game," Frost said when asked about vindication. "What other people say doesn't matter."

Many of those people never would have believed this day would happen. I was one. But this day was for those people who did believe in Frost through thin and, finally, thick.

Scott Frost left Husky Stadium with a victory and a legion of new supporters.

OCTOBER 18, 1997 • UNO HOCKEY

Mav Fans Make It Memorable

U-N-O! U-N-O! U-N-O! The chant is still bouncing off the roof, skipping down the catwalks, echoing through the halls and cascading down toward the bright ice as I sit here, an hour after the fact, trying to put this incredible story into perspective. U-N-O! U-N-O! U-N-O!

If there is one image, one memory for the UNO hockey and Omaha sports scrapbooks from this unforgettable night — the night UNO hockey was born — it was 8,000 people standing and chanting, in unison, at the end of the first UNO hockey game at the Civic Auditorium.

The chant started after the first UNO goal in history, by James Chalmers, with 10:09 left in the second period. They chanted after the next goal. They chanted because they were wired, stoked, juiced for this night. They chanted because all the anticipation of 18 months came spilling out at once in one glorious burst. They chanted because it was a game like no other for UNO, the first-ever UNO game as a Division I member. They chanted because this whole college and hockey marriage makes so much sense in Omaha and, finally, the bride and groom were together before them, a sight for sore eyes.

And, finally, they chanted because, after all the pomp and circumstance and banquets and golf outings and stories and countdowns, they got a game out of the deal. Suddenly. UNO had cut the lead to 3-2. There were four, three, two minutes left. UNO kept scrambling, shooting, skating, missing. If the Mavs could score, if only they could score, they could forget about this remodeled Civic Auditorium. All that money would be down the drain. Because if UNO scores, the place comes down.

Instead, the place stays up. But so, too, did the crowd. The buzzer went off. The University of Manitoba went off a happy and nervous winner. And as the boys in white and red skated around, dejected, the largest crowd in Omaha hockey history stood and chanted, spontaneously.

U-N-O! U-N-O! U-N-O!

"It was overwhelming," said right wing Jeff Edwards. "Fantastic. This town is a hockey hotbed, I've said it all along. I'm proud to be part of this organization and this community."

"Unbelievable," said goaltender Jason Mitchell. "That's the reason we played, well, pretty well."

"I was wondering what the crowd would chant after we scored a goal," said UNO coach Mike Kemp. "That's a terrific chant. That's great. I can't say enough about the crowd. We can't wait to play here again in two weeks."

At the inaugural Blue Line Club lunch on Friday at the Holiday Inn, Manitoba coach Mike Sirant told the crowd, "We're going to try to spoil the fairy-tale ending." And the Bison were, indeed, less-than-perfect guests, winning 3-2. But then again, it was almost beside the point, or goal.

The Mavericks can't join a league or participate in NCAA postseason play for two seasons. For now, the experience is the thing. And what an experience! UNO hockey public address announcer Fred Brooks told the crowd, "Welcome to the most anticipated sporting event in city history."

And who could argue? This night had more hype than a Nebraska football spring game. Eighteen months' worth. After all the talk and recruiting and talk and banquets and talk and wondering what the new jerseys would look like and more and more talk, you began to think there would be this big letdown. Nothing could live up to this.

"Certainly, the people got their money's worth," Sirant said.

Certainly. It was worth the wait. It was the greatest sporting event in UNO history, with apologies to the Omaha University football team that played in the Tangerine Bowl on Jan. 1, 1955. Call it the greatest sporting event for UNO, ATB. After Tangerine Bowl. U-N-O! U-N-O! U-N-O!

It was 534 days ago that UNO's then-athletic director, Don Leahy, held a press conference to announce the Division II commuter school on Dodge Street was going big-time. Some scoffed that the day would never come. When the 535th day had come and gone, Leahy was by himself, walking the empty Civic Auditorium, yelling up at the press row, "Not bad. Losing, and 8,000 fans are standing and cheering at the end."

Not bad at all.

2011 INSIGHT *I don't think anyone, maybe even Don Leahy, knew what UNO hockey would be when it was created. We found out on that Friday night. The atmosphere was amazing. We were toward the end of the Racers era, and the Lancers were the Lancers, and Dana Altman hadn't cranked up his machine yet, so Omaha was ready for something new, something big. This was it. As I sat up on press row at the Civic Auditorium that night, listening to the chants of "U-N-O! U-N-O!" it was clear this had touched a nerve with the city, in a positive way. With apologies to Sandy Buda and Pat Behrns, the Mavs really didn't have much of a profile in our sports town. This changed everything. UNO would supplant the Lancers as the big dog in hockey, and the Mavs would find a bell-cow sport for their athletic department, their Nebraska football and Creighton basketball, and it was a niche the other guys didn't have. I'll always hear that crowd and that chant.*

OCTOBER 18, 1997 • UNO HOCKEY

James Chalmers, center, celebrates the first goal in UNO hockey history, joined by teammates Mike Skogland and Ryan Bencurik.

Cornhusker Magic Saves Season

COLUMBIA, MO.

IT WAS JUDGMENT Down. On Judgment Day. Third down. Last down. Scott Frost dropped back to pass and as the clock — shoot, the season — wound down . . . 4 . . . 3 . . . 2 . . . 1 . . . he threw the ball toward the end zone. A stadium full of black-and-gold dreamers held their breath. About 10,000 dressed in red had their hearts in their throats.

It was like a movie, in slow motion. One receiver, Shevin Wiggins, dropped the ball. It bounced off his outstretched foot and landed miraculously in the cradling arms of freshman Matt Davison. This was the Immaculate Reception, Nebraska style. This was Husker Magic. A minute ago, it was all gone: the national championship, the Orange Bowl, their reason for being. Now, just like that, it was somehow back. How? Why? Who knew?

"All I saw," Frost said, "was the brown thing bouncing around and the ref raised his hands."

Husker Magic.

Dozens of Missouri students who had prematurely run out to tear down the goal post had to go back. The goal posts would stay up.

The return of the Missouri Upset would have to wait. Nebraska would get the brown thing in overtime and win, 45-38. Of course, overtime. Husker coach Tom Osborne had the momentum and unbelievable faith in a defense that got kicked around all day. If Osborne had had this option available at the 1984 Orange Bowl, he would have kicked and taken Miami into OT. He might have won his first national championship that night, too.

This year's title is another story.

As they walked to the locker room afterward, their faces drained of emotion, the Huskers looked up to a row of adoring fans and yelled, "We're still No. 1! We're still No. 1!" Uh, maybe not. On ESPN's self-proclaimed and self-serving "Judgment Day," the voters would have to make the call. Michigan's domination of No. 2 Penn State in Happy Valley — coupled with Washington losing at home to Oregon

Nebraska wingback Shevin Wiggins (5) put his foot to the ball, and freshman wide receiver Matt Davison (3) was in the right spot to complete one of the most miraculous plays in Husker football history.

— is now the best victory of the season. The Wolverines probably deserve to be No. 1. But what of Florida State, which won at North Carolina? Would Michigan and FSU split a lot of votes?

Would Nebraska get credit for showing national championship heart, if not defense?

Chances are, the Huskers will drop. That would be appropriate.

Nebraska played like only half of a national title team.

In the MU interview area, Nebraska Athletic Director Bill Byrne hugged Cheryl Smith, the wife of Missouri coach Larry Smith, and whispered to her, "You deserved to win." Osborne told Smith, "We were lucky to win." Smith later said, "They were lucky to win. I wish we were lucky, too."

Better to be lucky than good? Sure. The football gods have a few more offerings to go, but maybe this was their way of paying Osborne back for all the bad bounces, the Sooner Magic and the poor luck the old coach has swallowed over the years. What the gods provided was the most breathless and exciting, if not the best, comeback in Nebraska football history. A classic victory. Husker Magic.

"That game was so emotionally draining," said Frost, the game's hero. "They played great. We played great. It's something we'll always remember."

Husker defensive coordinator Charlie McBride said: "Nobody gave up. It's a game that we'll always remember."

NOVEMBER 9, 1997 • NEBRASKA FOOTBALL

Quarterback Scott Frost (7) directed a 10-play, fourth-quarter scoring drive with no timeouts.

There would be a fumble by Ahman Green in the third quarter to kill one drive. Five careless penalties that gave MU life. A Nebraska defense playing scared. But the Huskers kept coming. Green, with 189 yards and a touchdown. Frost, relentless as an October snowstorm, with 141 yards rushing and 175 passing and five touchdowns. Five. Above all, a 10-play, 67-yard, no-timeout touchdown drive conducted by Frost that will live forever in Big Red history. Think of Frost years from now and remember his poise and guts. Frost has the heart, if not arm, of John Elway.

All anyone at Missouri knows is that that north end zone is haunted. The same one where Davison grabbed a dream was the same end zone where Colorado scored on a fifth down en route to the 1990 national championship. Fate? For now, you can call it Husker Magic.

2011 INSIGHT The thing you forget about Matt Davison's catch is that it was the second surprise of the day. Nebraska was coming off a complete demolition of Oklahoma the week before at home. The Huskers of 1997 had mauled everyone in their path. And the last several Nebraska-Mizzou games were Husker romps. So when this game started, there was no reason to think it would be a game that would become a regular on ESPN Classic. But the game started, and the Blackshirts couldn't stop Corby Jones. And back and forth it went.

Finally, it grew dark, and I was standing in the south end zone at Faurot Field, just down the ramp from the Nebraska locker room. I had come to record the sad story of the day: the No. 1-ranked Huskers getting upset by Missouri in Columbia and the undefeated season being ruined, just like that.

The Missouri football historian in me noted that this would be the greatest home win in Mizzou history, if not the greatest win, period. The Omaha columnist in me said, wow, this will be one of Tom Osborne's toughest losses. There weren't rumors of Osborne leaving yet, but with Scott Frost, Grant Wistrom and Jason Peter leaving, 1997 felt like an important opportunity.

So Missouri's leading, and the Nebraska last-ditch drive is stalling, and I'm standing next to Mike Babcock, a Nebraska football historian in his own right. Frost and the Huskers have one play left. It looked bleak. The ball is snapped, and here comes the Missouri student section, out of the stands and onto the end zone near us. They're ready to tear down the south goal post. We're watching that happen, and watching the last play on the far, north end. You could see Frost throw the ball toward the end zone over a pile of arms. The ball disappeared. The crowd roared. I saw the ball pop up in the air and then land. The roar stopped. The Nebraska players in white and red started hopping up and down and hugging.

"Oh my God," I said to Babcock. "What the hell just happened?"

"I don't know," he said. "Nebraska must have scored."

What happened was one of the greatest plays, and signature moments, in Nebraska football history. And we didn't see it. Not exactly. I got the low-down on what happened at the press conference outside the Mizzou locker room. I was also introduced to this wide-eyed freshman named Matt Davison. I finally saw the play on a replay up in the press box.

And then I had to write about the play I didn't see but heard — heard from the silence of the crowd. It was a very strange way to witness something big.

After I filed my column, I joined my wife-to-be and my sportswriter friend Dennis Dodd for a late drink at Harpo's, the famous Mizzou watering hole. What a scene at midnight. Mizzou fans were in shock, not saying much. Husker fans wore sheepish looks and didn't say much. Some Nebraska fans consoled their Tiger friends, saying, "We were lucky today." I heard a Mizzou guy saying, "That's going to cost you in the polls." I saw something you don't see much anymore: the game's would-be hero, Mizzou quarterback Corby Jones, was standing at the front door of the bar, holding the door open with his back. He looked absolutely drained. A Nebraska fan shook his hand on the way out the door and said, "You deserved better." Jones just smiled and shook his head.

To this day, Jones, Davison and Frost are good friends who stay in touch. Tiger and Husker fans may or may not share that sentiment. But nobody who was there that day will ever forget it.

DECEMBER 10, 1997 • NEBRASKA FOOTBALL

What Will Osborne Do?

HE SPOKE LIKE a man who is ready to retire, saying only, "It could happen any time." He sounded like a man talking with a heavy mind and heart, taking deep breaths between sentences. Some would even say Tom Osborne, the face of exhaustion, looks like a man who needs a permanent vacation from his job.

So, is Tom Osborne going to retire any time soon?

He wouldn't say yes. He wouldn't say no.

That in itself was a startling revelation from what was going to be an ordinary pre-Orange Bowl press conference in the South Stadium "N" Club lounge. Three weeks before the bowl game, and in the midst of recruiting season in which impressionable recruits might be looking for a sign, Osborne wouldn't commit past Tuesday.

He's here today, he said. That's the main thing. Tomorrow never knows.

It was a rather shocking non-denial denial.

The day started with Osborne upset. People were calling his house, calling the assistant coaches' houses, calling the football secretaries at home. All about the rumors that Osborne had decided to retire. The final call. He was leaving after this season. It was like a brush fire that was heading for a forest.

There was no shortage of people throughout Omaha and Lincoln who had heard from their neighbors who heard from their co-workers who read it on the Internet that an inside source in Lincoln who heard it from someone who was in with the regents had said that Osborne was leaving. Suddenly, out of nowhere, Nebraska was abuzz. Heard the news? T.O.'s leaving.

And so the man himself was called upon to put out the fire. Except what he was carrying looked like a gasoline can.

Frank Solich, Nancy Osborne and Tom Osborne at the press conference announcing that Solich would replace Osborne.

He began with a personal plea. Sort of an ode to the little people. Osborne said he was standing on turf at the Alamodome, before the Big 12 Conference championship game, thinking about how out of control the whole 250th victory, 25-season thing had gotten.

Don't forget the assistant coaches, Osborne said. And their assistants. And wives. And secretaries. And the people in the academic centers and ticket offices and everyone in red. It's their program, too, Osborne said. This incredible run has been a team effort.

As he spoke, his voice cracked. These are the kinds of things a man says before dropping the big one. More than one media type in the room thought Osborne was about to say good-bye.

Except Osborne never did it. If he had planned to, he decided to back off. If that wasn't the plan, then the ode to the little people was a strange coincidence, considering what was said the next 10 minutes. Here is how Osborne addressed the rumors of his departure:

"The thing you need to know," Osborne said, "is the first thing I'll do is talk to the assistant coaches, then I'll talk to the players. Then I'll talk to you. Once that happens . . . it's kind of like the stars and moon lining up."

When will that happen?

"I don't know," Osborne said. "It could happen anytime."

2011 INSIGHT *I've never been good at playing hunches. That's the best way to start this little story about how I missed the day Tom Osborne retired. I mean, there was no excuse. The rumors had been out there since August of 1997. I even wrote a column about the signals the coach was sending before the season. Then, came this Tuesday press conference, a few days after NU had won the Big 12 title over Texas A&M. Osborne was in a cranky mood. He complained about his hours, the workload, this and that. He sounded like someone who had hit the wall. The red flags were up everywhere. So I wrote this column saying that, you know, he didn't exactly deny anything. So this could happen anytime. Good advice. Too bad I didn't take it. The next day, Wednesday, I got on a plane for Orlando, Fla., to attend the ESPN Awards Show at Disney World. It was Omaha's first year as the host of the Outland Trophy dinner. Huskers Aaron Taylor and Jason Peter were finalists (Taylor would win). They were on my flight. So was Ahman Green. I spent most of the flight from St. Louis to Orlando talking to them. And what a terrific acting job, with all of them knowing that Osborne was retiring that day and me playing the clueless sportswriter. When our flight landed, I went to my hotel. Turned on ESPN. They had a "Special Report: Tom Osborne retires as Nebraska football coach." Brilliant. Absolutely brilliant. So I called the office, got some quotes and went to work in my hotel room. I had missed the big press conference in Lincoln, missed the big day. After that, I swore to play my own hunches. My next hunch was that Steve Pederson would be a terrific athletic director. I give up.*

It could happen anytime. Not exactly squashing rumors. Not exactly an adamant declaration. It could happen anytime.

It would have been easier to be skeptical, to write this off as a rumor that is going to come up every December from now until he hangs it up. He'll be 61 in February. Annual speculation is natural.

But the way Osborne continued raised red flags. He talked — and he almost seemed to be complaining — of how he still gets to work at 7 a.m. and doesn't quit until 10 or 10:30 p.m., "with 45 minutes for lunch and 45 minutes for dinner." He said he does this seven days a week. Worse, he admitted that he averages only "five hours of sleep" per night. Except for Saturday nights, when he's so wound up after a game that he watches film until 2 a.m. and gets only three hours of shut-eye.

But, he said: "If you want to call plays, make adjustments on Saturday, be actively involved in everything, that's what you have to do. Another way to do it, turn it over to coordinators and be a supervisor . . . that would be self-defeating. That's not what I enjoy.

"It's a pretty good pace we keep," Osborne continued. "You need a guy that does that (hands-on head coach) around here. You're not in a geographic region where you have 25 recruitable players in that region. We think we need to put out great effort."

As for how much longer he could go, Osborne said, "I don't think I can do that until I'm 70. I know I can't."

That's nine years away. But here's why it might come nine days from now: Osborne's heart. He underwent double bypass surgery, to clear blockage, in 1985. His routine makes him healthier than a raw carrot. But the week of the Iowa State game, three weeks ago, Osborne felt his heart racing during his daily workouts. He checked himself into a Lincoln hospital after the game for tests, and doctors found an irregular heartbeat. Medication was prescribed. Then it was on to Colorado.

But Osborne was obviously shaken by that "episode" and by the condition of his heart.

"What happened to me is something people can live with," Osborne said. "It can also cause strokes. It's not a good condition to have."

Asked if his health would affect his decision, Osborne said, "I've had some warning signals, no question. I'm here today. That's the main thing."

When you think about it, there are other reasons why it would make sense for him to walk away on Jan. 3. The death of Bob Devaney last spring had to make Osborne feel a tinge of not only emptiness but mortality.

There is the loss of his support system at NU with folks like Don Bryant, Steve Pederson and soon-to-retire Al Papik leaving the department. And there is Osborne sounding like a corporate CEO late in life, feeling guilty about the time spent away from his family and ready to give something back.

"You don't want your family to go through the dregs," Osborne said, "where you can't talk or walk or anything."

What also makes perfect sense in these scenarios is a perfect sense of timing. If Nebraska beats Tennessee, Osborne could walk away a tall and proud 13-0, having done the best he could. No. 1 or no, he would leave with his program setting the standard for college football. He would leave on top.

If nothing else, it makes for a good rumor. But it looks and sounds like so much more.

"I just know that when the time comes," Osborne said, "you'll be told."

Just then, a TV reporter said, "Well, coach, now that you've told us you're not leaving, let's go on to football."

The thing was, he never said he was or wasn't leaving. It was what Osborne didn't say that has everyone hanging. He certainly sounds and looks like a man who may be coaching his last game.

Solich Takes T.O.'s Pitch

TOM OSBORNE, THE master of the triple-option play, called his own option play. He pitched off.

Next September, when the Huskers open against Alabama-Birmingham, Osborne will be in a boat with a line looking to sack some unsuspecting bass. Or playing with his grandkids, William, Catey and Haley. Frank Solich will be playing with Huskies, Longhorns and Wildcats.

On the first day of the rest of Tom Osborne's life, we wonder: Is there life after Osborne?

Of course. Remember 1973. Who was Osborne then? He was a squeaky-clean, quiet, polite, redheaded assistant coach who got the job over more popular Devaney assistants. But Bob Devaney picked him. Today the monster is happy and healthy, the model program in college football. Bob erected it. Tom perfected it. So here we are, in 1997, déjà vu all over again. Who is Solich?

This squeaky-clean, quiet, polite assistant who looks like he's 30 even though he's over 50. Solich has been on Osborne's staff for 19 years. Nebraska football is a program of routines. Solich knows the routines. But can he coach? Can he work the living rooms? Well, sure he can. What were Mike Rozier and Irving Fryar, chopped liver? But now Solich has to close deals. He has to be a presence against the Joe Paternos and Bobby Bowdens and John Coopers and Rick Neuheisels. At first, that won't be easy. Kids don't know Frank Solich. For now, Solich will have to sell Nebraska football, Nebraska tradition, Nebraska's weight room, not his name.

Osborne will leave on top, like Devaney. Solich will have to continue, like Osborne. It won't be easy. What this does automatically is give the rest of the league hope, particularly at Kansas State, Texas and Colorado. Osborne was so far above everyone. Will K-State coach Bill Snyder be intimidated by Solich the way he was by Osborne? Not likely. As a San Antonio sports columnist wrote, coincidentally, last week, "If Tom Osborne retires, now that's a coaching change."

The past is unforgettable. The future is now uncertain. The day you never thought would happen has arrived.

Solich takes the pitch . . .

TOM'S TAKE — REFLECTIONS ON

NU Settles Big 12 Score

SAN ANTONIO

FINALLY, IT'S THE Big Red Conference. After two years of being outscored 11-1 in important conference votes, the numbers that counted for the Huskers were 54-15.

Nebraska folded, spindled and mutilated the Big 12 Conference. Oh, sure, Texas A&M drew the unfortunate short straw in the South Division and had to show up for the actual flogging. But this whipping was for the entire Big 12. The Huskers can't beat 11 men in a boardroom. But 11 Aggies on artificial turf were no problem whatsoever.

What did we learn? The Huskers are the best program in the Big 12, and it's not as close as the score indicated.

This was for all the votes that didn't go their way. This was for the league's founding fathers having the audacity to create a championship playoff game and one more dadgum hurdle on the way to the national championship. This was for 1996, when Nebraska fell over that hurdle in a stunning 37-27 loss to Texas in St. Louis that kept it out of a fourth straight national title game.

Nebraska assistant coach Nelson Barnes and senior Grant Wistrom leave the field as Big 12 champions.

Now the Huskers are headed for the Orange Bowl and another national title shot. Because they finally learned, and accepted, that the road to Miami goes through San Antonio.

"Last year against Texas, we didn't get that excited and looked ahead to the next game," said Nebraska coach Tom Osborne, "and we goofed up."

There is a nasty element in the air throughout Nebraska. It's this national championship phobia. It's a feeling by fans that there is No. 1 or nothing else. It's the main reason Nebraskans can't and won't accept their Big 12 fate. The league is viewed not as a competitive commodity but a conspiracy to knock down the Big Red and keep it from precious national championships.

But the Huskers left wearing red Big 12 champions ball caps and carrying a conference championship trophy that is either a crystal bedpan or taco-salad shell. They also left wearing smiles. Good thing. They need to embrace this conference title, especially this season.

Nebraska can win the Orange Bowl, and it might not matter. If No. 1 Michigan wins the Rose Bowl, then the Huskers could be left with a hollow feeling of what could-have-been but could-not-be-played. But it shouldn't be hollow. Finishing 13-0 and No. 2 shouldn't ruin the season. Conference titles should mean something.

"I've always heard that the journey is better than the end," said senior Grant Wistrom, who probably heard it from Osborne. "At the end of the season, we'll remember all the hard work and the fun we had. If it doesn't happen, it's not going to take away the enjoyment we had this season."

It shouldn't. The Huskers should not take lightly being the best in a conference, even if it's a weak conference. The Huskers might not win the national championship trophy. The bedpan might be all they get. But that's better than no bedpan.

"The losses hurt more than the wins feel good at Nebraska," said quarterback Scott Frost, talking about last year's loss to Texas. "You expect to win the national championship and conference championship at Nebraska. But this definitely feels good today."

Good. No matter what happens from here, the Huskers should always remember the Alamodome.

— **DECEMBER 7, 1997**

THE CHANGING SPORTS LANDSCAPE 1997

Outland, Omaha Are Great Fit

WELCOME HOME, MR. OUTLAND. This is where you belong. This is where you will be given proper care and attention. This is where your legend will live for a long, long time.

Omaha meets the Outland Trophy. This is the perfect marriage of city and event. It was announced that the Outland Trophy, which is awarded to the top interior lineman in college football, will be presented annually in Omaha.

Why Omaha? Because of the local legends, carved in Outland granite. Larry Jacobson. Rich Glover. Dave Rimington. Dean Steinkuhler. Will Shields. Zach Wiegert. Nebraska has more Outland winners than any school. Nebraska was already home to the Outland. What happened was like signing for the deed.

Because nobody appreciates linemen and what they stand for better than Nebraskans. Linemen toil in the trenches. Work hard without any fanfare. Don't say much about it. Don't care because you get that warm, inner satisfaction of knowing a job was well done. That's a lineman. That's Nebraskans. Now they can gather each January to throw one whale of a dinner for their man of the year — whether he be a Cornhusker, Buckeye, Hawkeye, Seminole or Trojan — and let him know there is someone out there who appreciates his quiet efforts. Someone who understands.

Why Omaha? Because funny things can happen when sportswriters get together to eat nachos and drink their favorite beverages. This was back in the spring, last May. This was in Dallas. Steve Richardson, a good friend and longtime colleague, and I are in some joint spilling salsa on our shirts. Steve, now the executive director of the Football Writers Association of America, is overhauling the FWAA and its various awards. Trying to make each award the best award it can be. Somehow, the Outland came up. It has been in Oklahoma City for years, on the same dinner table with the Jim Thorpe (best defensive back) Award.

Overshadowed? You bet. The Outland was definitely not its own man with its own spotlight.

Which is what it deserves. The Outland is the best college football award. The Heisman is so much hype and blather; quarterbacks and running backs get it every year. They already get all the girls. The Outland says linemen are special, too.

Could Omaha have it? Make a bid, said Steve. The next thing I knew, I was home, calling Don Bryant, the former NU sports information director and Mr. College Football, telling him how the Outland belonged here. Asking for ideas.

"Give me some time. I'm going to make some phone calls," Bryant said. "We can't be outbid on this!"

Soon, the phone rings. It's Bob Mancuso, a longtime Bryant chum and chairman of the Greater Omaha Sports Committee. He is excited. Mancuso gets Jay Baum, executive director of the Greater Omaha Convention and Visitors Bureau, involved. Soon, they have a game plan. They make their bid. They win. Omaha wins.

It was not that easy, of course. Months of work, dreaming and scheming went into this. Mancuso and Baum are the heroes here. They made it happen. They stepped to the plate and hit a huge home run. They delivered a gem that will become an Omaha sports classic. When people in sports think of Omaha, they will also think "the home of the Outland Trophy." The College World Series of the winter.

What a menu. Besides the Outland presentation, there will be former Outland winners, from Nebraska and other schools, at various tables, telling old war stories. There will be the Omaha Sportscasters Association's main awards. Moreover, The World-Herald's All-Nebraska, all-class high school football team will be introduced. They will get photos with the Outland winner. Maybe some drive-blocking tips.

A group including Mancuso and Baum will make its way to Orlando, Fla., for the ESPN College Football Awards show. There, the FWAA will name the Outland winner on national TV. Mancuso and Co. will shake the winner's hand and tell him, "We'll see you in Omaha." They will bring the trophy back to Omaha. Back home.

— **NOVEMBER 25, 1997**

Husker senior guard Aaron Taylor became the seventh player in University of Nebraska football history to win the Outland, which is given to the top interior lineman in college football by the Football Writers Association of America. It was the first trophy presented in Omaha.

TOM OSBORNE'S FINAL GAME | LUE PUTS ON A SHOW | CWS SLUGFEST | BOB GIBSON GOLF EVENT

1998

"I said, 'Doc, this is the College World Series.' It's more important than taking that shot. I mean, the shot may work, but we don't know. The College World Series always works."

— LSU FAN AND CANCER PATIENT RUSSELL MENDOZA OF BATON ROUGE, WHO CANCELED HIS WEEKLY CHEMO SHOT SO HE COULD TRAVEL TO OMAHA

Eddie Sutton was talking about his favorite memories of Creighton, and one of the first things he mentioned was . . . baseball? "One of the best things about Creighton was that, at that time, the basketball coach was also the athletic director, so I was the tournament director of the College World Series," Sutton said. "I got to watch every inning of every game for five years. I like baseball."

In the end, nobody cares that Dave Van Horn compiled a 106-65 record and won two conference championships in three seasons at Northwestern (La.) State or that Van Horn is "one of the rising superstars in college baseball," as Nebraska Athletic Director Bill Byrne introduced him. Nor did anybody come to hear the new baseball coach's play-defense-play-hard-and-pitch-a-little philosophy or that he would "rather have a high school kid" than a junior-college kid any time. No, what Nebraska was waiting to know from Van Horn was: Would he sign the very best Nebraska high school kids? "There are kids in this area, and we need to keep them here," Van Horn said at his press conference. "We don't want them going south or going to junior colleges or wherever. We want to see that end. We've got to get them interested in the University of Nebraska's baseball program." And, above all, the Nebraska baseball coach's imagination must be able to stretch at least 50 miles to the east. "It (College World Series) has got to be feasible," Van Horn said. "That's why I'm here. We have to have those goals. You know how it would be if we were up in Omaha." It's an image Van Horn can start selling today. First, he must convince Nebraska kids that they will be safe at home.

The thing about Nebraska football, and maybe the thing that fuels the whole machine, is that nobody in the state ever looks back. People are always asking about the next recruiting class — in July. People are always looking for the next national championship. That sense of uncommon urgency filters down — or up — to the players and coaches. "Every year is a test for this program," senior fullback Joel Makovicka said. "You can never be satisfied with how you played the year before. We have to go out every week, every game, and perform."

112 • 20 YEARS WITH TOM SHATEL

THOMPSON LEADS MAVS | K-STATE ENDS STREAK | HAYDEN FRY'S EXIT | ODE TO A PRESS BOX

Go Lil' Red! This is not an easy thing to admit. The first time I saw this eight-foot boy, this Stay Puft marshmallow wrapper, this bouncing bundle of plastic joy, I groaned. Another corporate promotional toy from Nebraska Athletic Director Bill Byrne. Herbie Husker on steroids. But Lil' Red grows on you. It's the bouncing. The gyrations. The slick dance moves. The routines. OK, it's the standing-on-his-head schtick. How does he do that, anyway?

There are no secrets in recruiting. That's what was worrying Creighton basketball coach Dana Altman two summers ago. Here was this 6-foot, 150-pound kid from Ankeny, Iowa, in an AAU summer tournament. The kid looked great. He had amazing quickness. He could shoot the 3. He played defense. Dived on the floor. Looked like a real bulldog. The kind of point guard Altman wanted and needed for his construction job at Creighton. There was only one problem with Ryan Sears. Nobody else wanted him. Was Sears that bad? No. To the contrary, Altman thought he was that good. And Altman was that lucky. "In recruiting there is such a herd mentality," Altman said. "You're thinking, 'Am I wrong here?' Obviously, in this case, we weren't. There were no doubts in my mind about him. He had all the intangibles. And he wanted to be a player."

Creighton had a death in the family, the first day of practice, the last day of Lee "Doc" Bevilacqua's life. Bluejay coach Dana Altman had the distinct displeasure of gathering the troops and relaying the bad news. "Everybody was pretty shook up," Altman said. All this for a 71-year-old volunteer team doctor? In his 32 years of service for Creighton's sports teams, Doc was that and a lot more. "We needed Doc. He was the balance," said CU Athletic Director Bruce Rasmussen. "As coaches, you're always saying, 'You gotta get better.' You harp on the negative so much. Doc would always hug every player he saw and say, 'I love you, man.'" One of Doc's more famous diagnoses came before the 1978 Indiana State game, for the MVC title, when he spent the night working on Larry Bird's bad back. Bird had a brilliant game. Creighton won. And nobody was mad at Doc. "That's just Doc," CU assistant Kevin McKenna said. "He was competitive, but he wanted to do things right."

Life begins in August. That's the first rule for being a sports fan here in the land of the Husker helmet lamp and stadium-turf coasters, a place where college football never dies, it just takes long naps.

20 YEARS WITH TOM SHATEL • 113

JANUARY 4, 1998 • NEBRASKA FOOTBALL

Journey Ends for Osborne

MIAMI

ALWAYS, TOM OSBORNE has maintained that it was the journey, and not the destination, that carried the most weight. It was the relationships with people and the impact upon them along the way that mattered most, not the pot of gold, silver or bronze that could gather dust in a coliseum trophy case. Osborne's first book was titled "More Than Winning." Here was the rarest of men, who coached against the game, not for the glory.

So late on a Jan. 2 night in south Florida, Osborne probably thought his standards were about to be put to the ultimate test.

Here his Husker football team had just polished off a 13-0 record with a rather convincing 42-17 demolition of Tennessee's third-ranked Volunteers.

And there, the day before, No. 1 Michigan had beaten Washington State 21-16, and Brian and Bob Griese were crying and hugging and the Wolverines were wearing "National Championship" hats. It looked like such a done deal, like what Osborne's team did in the Orange Bowl might not matter. Like Osborne would finish 13-0 and have to settle for a No. 2 ranking.

Like the journey might have to be the only thing Osborne got out of this 1997 season. His last season. The final journey.

But Osborne should have known better. He has seen and heard just about everything on his fantastic journey. Howard Schnellenberger dropping out of the sky in a helicopter. The 4 a.m. call that Lawrence Phillips had gone Spider-Man up an apartment building and attacked former girlfriend Kate McEwen.

So what he saw about 2:30 a.m. Saturday in his hotel room shouldn't have surprised him one bit.

He and wife Nancy and their children and NU Sports Information Director Chris Anderson were in the Osborne room, watching ESPN.

And suddenly there was anchor Chris Fowler's face, saying, "This just in . . . Nebraska is No. 1 in the coaches' poll." And for a minute, it was like time froze in the room. And then there were hugs and tears and cries of joy.

There was the "Miracle in Missouri." But this surely was a smaller "Miracle in Miami." Or, perhaps, "Pandemonium in PJs."

"By that time, I was seriously thinking about going to bed," Osborne said. "But then some players called. I even had a few come by the room and say hello, even though I was packing my suitcase and in my pajamas."

While most of Nebraska was asleep or running around naked at 72nd and Dodge, Osborne won his third national championship in his pajamas. It will be known in some corners as a farewell present from the coaches, but let's get real.

Anyone who saw Nebraska in the Orange Bowl can't deny the Huskers deserve at least a share of the title. They can't say some great injustice was done to Michigan.

Why would the Wolverines deserve it more than Nebraska? They wouldn't. If anyone should feel jilted, it's Penn State coach Joe Paterno, who wasn't on the coaches' bouquet list in 1994.

For Osborne, it's a fitting and perfect ending to a 25-year career. But these national titles are only bookmarks to the body of work, reference points that come up first but don't define the man or the career. They are mere signposts on the journey, a journey that always has been about coaching and teaching and preparation and doing your best on each and every play assignment.

That was Osborne's message. Again. The players had just watched the Rose Bowl and were a little down in the dumps, Osborne noticed. So he called them into a meeting.

He showed them a short video of their season, with inspirational messages from the seniors. He reminded them that they, too, were on a journey, a journey of effort and camaraderie and memories of each other that would last a lifetime, national title or not. He reminded them to play their best. He

Tom Osborne leaves the field after coaching his last game, an Orange Bowl victory that propelled him to his third national title.

reminded them that their true prize would be in looking one another in the eye and knowing they had left every bead of sweat on that patch of south Florida sand-turf. And he reminded them that if they did all that, by 30 points or so, maybe someone would throw them a bone.

"I told them you know Michigan didn't win by two or three touchdowns, so the door is open just a crack," Osborne said. "We've got to take advantage of that. We've got to make sure it's wide open."

His players didn't disappoint. Osborne's last game was a collage of his career: hard-running backs, bulldozing linemen, smothering defense. And a terrific leader in quarterback Scott Frost.

The Wood River Wonder became the poster boy for Osborne's farewell.

More than Tommie Frazier before him, Frost became a mirror-image of his coach and his own career: maligned early, resilient and strong-willed throughout and successful walking out of the arena.

And while Osborne said little afterward about the poll situation, it was Frosty who stepped up to the plate and delivered a speech that probably was scribbled out on his hotel-room stationery.

Frost's near-perfect Orange Bowl and his now-famous "Why you should vote for us" monologue afterward were a fine tribute to Osborne's unbending faith in him.

It was Frosty's finest moment. And now he has his name on a national championship to boot. He may also surge in local popularity polls, particularly after the man whose shoes he could never fill — Frazier — bluntly said this week he thought Michigan should be No. 1 if it won.

And Frost used to be the guy they called disloyal. How ironic.

Another sight of irony was in the back of the Westin Resort Hotel ballroom as Osborne gave his final press conference. Nancy Osborne, sitting in the back of the room for more than three decades now, smiled as she watched her husband fumble like a man searching for his keys in the dark when the question came up about his immediate future. Osborne said he has no specific plans.

His wife probably has at least 25 years' worth.

"It's hard for me to really believe this is happening," Nancy said. "It's difficult to imagine not seeing Tom doing X's and O's on some piece of paper, in church or wherever. I'm happy for him. It's going to be different for him."

Scott Frost stated his case for No. 1 with his play and his postgame remarks.

2011 INSIGHT *This was a national championship column unlike the previous two. Actually, it was an Orange Bowl trip like no other. For starters, I got engaged on this trip. Popped the question on Dec. 31, 1997, at the News Cafe in South Beach. My wife, Jennifer, can provide the details. I'm told I was there.*

Then, the next day, at the pre-Orange Bowl press conference, my friend Blair Kerkhoff of the Kansas City Star told Osborne that I had gotten engaged the night before. I asked Osborne the last question of the press conference, about whether he expected the coaches to vote him No. 1 – if he beat Tennessee – as a going-away gift for his retirement. Tom gave a really good, thoughtful answer. Then he said, "By the way, I understand Tom got engaged last night. Now, there's an upset!" And everyone roared.

There was certainly some hate mail involved that week, after I wrote that Nebraska had no chance of winning the national title after Michigan beat Washington State in the Rose Bowl. My thought was, Michigan was No. 1 and even though the Rose Bowl had been a close game, I didn't see any way the Huskers could leap up. One wise guy noted, "He gets engaged and already he talks about no hope."

Finally, there was the Orange Bowl game, and it took a back seat to the two big stories of the night: Osborne's last game and NU trying to finish undefeated and stake a claim to a third title in the '90s. I remember writing on deadline in the back of the press box, and listening to Scott Frost's impromptu speech about how the voters should give Osborne a national championship. There were some catcalls and sneers in the press box after that. That little speech may have been big in Gothenburg and Nebraska City, but it didn't go over well with the national media. Personally, I thought it was over the top, but honest and full of real emotions on Frost's part. I had no problem with it.

The World-Herald gang packed up for the media hotel about 1 a.m. on Jan. 3. There was still no word about the polls. We assumed the AP would go with Michigan. The writers weren't prone to mood swings with their poll. So we decided to stay up until the coaches' poll was announced, which was about 2:30 a.m. Eastern. It was too late for me to write something then, though The W-H got a story in the morning paper. Everybody came to my room, and we watched ESPN until Chris Fowler broke the news that Nebraska was indeed the coaches' choice. We stayed up another hour or so talking about that, and then hit the sack for a few hours of sleep before the early morning press conference, Tom's last one as coach.

JANUARY 12, 1998 • NEBRASKA BASKETBALL

Lue, Huskers Worth a Look

SURE, SUNDAY WAS a big day. There was church. And John Elway breaking steel hearts on the tube and Cheeseheads to wear. And the replay of the Orange Bowl to watch; you know, you can never get enough of that third quarter. And the Mercedes Championships. If you have Phil Mickelson in the golf pool, you definitely had to see how the Mercedes Championships turned out.

What only 8,807 people decided to do was go watch a Nebraska basketball game. That was a striking ring of empty seats around the Devaney Center.

Coach Danny Nee said it was nice to come home to the "sea of red." This looked more like a pond.

Wasn't it just four years ago that Nebraska basketball attracted 100,973 fans, an average of 14,475, the most in the history of Husker Hoops? Yes. They were loud. They were proud. They had embraced Nebraska's alternative sport. But much has happened in four years.

Nebrasketball fans got spoiled. But then they got spurned, too. After four straight NCAA tournament appearances, they got more NIT apples for the orchard. They saw teams that didn't play like teams.

They saw players who pouted. They saw student-athletes who talked back to their coach, who wouldn't go into games upon command.

Suddenly, it seems all the support and goodwill Nee has built is eroding before everyone's eyes.

The irony is, it shouldn't be that way. Not this year. This is a Nebraska basketball team fans can fall for and embrace all the way to March Madness.

This team has chemistry. The Huskers have some heart. They play hard. They don't pout. They are too thin and will suffer the trials and tribulations of the marathon that is college basketball. They may fall short. But they will dive trying.

This is a team that manufactures floor burns. The Huskers have Andy Markowski diving into the press table for a pass he can't possibly hope to get. They appear devoid of clubhouse lawyers and the bad apples who soured this program the last few years. When their coach says something, they do it.

Nebraska point guard Tyronn Lue later played on two NBA championship teams with the Los Angeles Lakers.

They have five, six guys passing to one another and nobody caring who gets the minutes or the shots or the numbers. That's because there are so few of them that everyone will get his share. Maybe that was the problem.

But now, here it is, a team that, if it stays healthy, is talented enough to rip through a mediocre Big 12 Conference and return to the NCAA tournament. Win or lose, it will make watching basketball at the Devaney Center fun again.

"We don't have the most talented team," Markowski said. "But we play hard and we're all unselfish. Our attitude is so much better. This is the closest group of guys I've been around. We really enjoy being around each other. This is a fun team to be around."

Perhaps the biggest irony is that this huge falloff in interest comes when maybe the best player in Nebraska history — that would be junior point guard Tyronn Lue — could be taking his farewell tour before he gets paid for doing amazing things night in and night out.

"If nothing else, just come out and watch Tyronn play," Markowski said. "That's a treat in itself. I tell you what, I'd be out here if I was a fan. This is a fun team to watch."

Where have the Huskers been all this time? Don't ask. Just enjoy.

JUNE 7, 1998 • COLLEGE WORLD SERIES

It's Trojans by a Touchdown

USC 21, ARIZONA STATE 14. Thank goodness Arizona State football coach Bruce Snyder was up in the press box watching. Snyder was overheard to say, "I thought we did some nice hitting, but our passing game needs some work."

OK, OK, this was baseball(?). And that was the final score. USC is the College World Series champion for the first time in 20 years, and the Trojans made up for lost time. They had 23 hits and five home runs and stole home. Twenty-one runs? There are some Big 12 Conference football teams who would take that many points tomorrow.

But please, yes, this was baseball. College baseball. Sure, there's a difference. We'd seen it all week at the College World Series. This was the year we learned the difference between creatine and Ovaltine. The year of "Gorilla Ball." And just because the LSU Geaux-rillas had gone home didn't mean the fireworks show was over.

It was only beginning. There were nine home runs, by eight players, including ASU's 5-foot-10, 170-pound shortstop, Michael Collins. There were 39 hits. There were 10 pitchers who were dragged out to the mound. USC's Jack Krawczyk got his NCAA-record 23rd save, but he should have been given an extra save — for saving the crowd.

There were too many records to count. Ask Jim Wright of the NCAA.

I asked him about records at 4 p.m. and he said, "It'll be at least an hour, and I may not have all of them then." He came up with 68.

For starters: There were records for runs in a game, home runs in a game, home runs by one team, RBIs by one player, funnel cakes sold in one inning and trips to the bathroom by both fathers and sons.

Don't forget the most important records of all: attendance. The championship game crowd of 24,456 was a record, as was the total CWS gate of 204,361.

And they stayed through the 3-hour, 59-minute marathon. That's the amazing thing. Sure, there were mini-bars set up in the backs of pickup trucks. But the people stayed. The purists can cry about how messed up college baseball is and how wrong the aluminum is, but the bottom line was: The people stayed.

USC leadoff hitter Wes Rachels set a championship game record with seven RBIs and tied another with five hits, including a three-run homer. Rachels' RBI total also tied the one-game CWS record. "I don't think I ever had seven RBIs, even in Little League," he said.

20 YEARS WITH TOM SHATEL • 117

JUNE 14, 1998 • GOLF

Gibson Fires Charity Pitch

FIRST OF ALL, Bob Gibson would not knock down Mark McGwire. Because, as Gibson says, it's not necessary. McGwire doesn't crowd the plate, he likes balls over the plate, and Gibson would see if Mr. McGwire could touch some of his moving heat.

Now, secondly, Gibson resents the question. But you ask because in baseball today too many batters have short fuses and there's too much stupid fighting and, meanwhile, McGwire is just making a mockery of pitching. So you ask. But you understand, too, Gibson's ire. Everybody asks Gibson about knockdowns and purpose pitches.

Thirty years later, he's still the official spokesman for Headhunters Anonymous.

"If that's all I did, how ... did I ever do everything I did?" Gibson asked. "The thing nobody understands is, I was never trying to hit a batter. Why hit a guy? I was trying to make him think here (inside) so he wouldn't be thinking there (outside) the next pitch."

Gibson, of course, is right. It's unfair. He set World Series records and in 1968 had the greatest season ever for a pitcher, and he's still known as the Bach of chin music.

But if Gibson has an image problem, it's because he's the man who made intensity an art form. And who really knows Gibson? Even now, living in Bellevue, he cherishes his privacy. The real crime is that there's nothing in town with Gibson's name on it. No park. No stadium. No buildings. Nothing to let us know the legend who grew up here and still lives here.

Which is why the Bob Gibson All-Star Classic Golf tournament is so special.

For one day a year, Omaha gets to see its native legend up close and personal. Of course, you won't see him pitch, except sometimes short of the green, but that's another story.

Golf isn't the story of this event, anyway. It's about baseball. It's about camaraderie. It's about fun. It's about stars. Big, big baseball stars. If there is a bigger selection of Hall of Fame talent on the same golf course in the country, Classic Sports just went off the air. But what makes the event is the atmosphere. It's laid back, not Gibson-like intense. Autographs and conversation are the order, not the obligation, and — get this — they're free.

The moral of the story is that while baseball may not know how to act in the 1990s, it can take a few lessons from the 1960s and 1970s. The beauty of it is that Gibson brought us these former stars who serve as goodwill ambassadors.

Hall of Fame pitcher Bob Gibson hosted his golf event for eight years, raising $2.5 million for local charities and the Baseball Assistance Team.

With This Column . . .

ONCE UPON A TIME, at a college newspaper where the best stories were graffiti scribbled on the walls, a message inscribed above the sports department read, "And now, for a halftime score . . . Life 63, Shatel 0."

Today, I rally. Today, in a church that has agreed to allow several other ink-stained sports wretches in the stained-glass door, I am going deep on Maddux, acing Sampras, closing out Tiger 5 and 4 and dunking on Michael. At approximately 3:05 p.m. (hey, blame the networks), I will close up the laptop, put down the remote, lay down the sand wedge and marry the woman of my dreams, Jennifer Phillip. I will get a wife and a life. That's a full day.

Till "SportsCenter" do we part.

Sports and marriage generally make strange locker mates. Most husbands go home after the game. They talk sports at the health club. But sports is not their life. Life is their life.

Sportswriters are different. Sportswriters live in a press box. They're afraid to eat unless they get a press pass punched. They can't talk unless it's in sportsuguese. Some people worry about taxes or world peace. Sportswriters are either plotting how they can get the "Sports VIP" rate at the Marriott or who's going to be in the Fiesta Bowl.

By all rights, sportswriters shouldn't be married. It's dangerous. For one thing, there are the papers. Ever seen a sportswriter's house? Newspapers everywhere. Or Sports Illustrateds. Or media guides. Don't light a match. And please, don't open the fridge. Mike Ditka might jump out.

No sane woman would ever actually live full time with a sportswriter. Talk about the Odd Couple. Think about it. Did you ever see Oscar Madison with a wife? Of course not. He was always at a Mets or Rangers game. Oscar Madison was divorced. Why? Because even TV Land knows: Sportswriters and marriage are a fumble waiting to happen.

And sometimes you get lucky. I hit a home run, as they say in sportsuguese. As the 10 o'clock news producer for KETV, Jen understands bad hours. Sports?

I married the perfect woman, Jennifer Phillip, who loves to watch football and plays golf. She also agreed to a honeymoon at Pebble Beach. Here, we're on the tee box at the famous No. 7, minutes before I sliced my 8-iron into the ocean.

At Valley High School, she lettered in volleyball and tennis and got a letter in basketball for keeping stats all season (so she knows her way around the press table). While growing up in Lincoln, she was a grade-school playmate of Annie and Susie Osborne and a sorority sister of Cindy Solich's at NU. She and her father, Jary, love football so much they sit 96 rows up in the south end zone at Memorial Stadium each Saturday through rain, sleet and Akron. Her apartment has more red than "Husker Heaven."

Part of which explains why I got away with the following at today's wedding: a 3:05 starting time, entering the reception to the "Husker Tunnel" music and naming the food stations after sporting events. (Cake table is the "Sugar Bowl.") I was going to ask to have an "Ashworth" logo sewn on my tuxedo sleeve, but, hey, why push it?

They say love is patient, love is kind. But love never had to sit in a press room until 11:30 p.m., sifting through bad quotes. But from now on, this sportswriter will have to edit his life. Write faster. Maybe there's a movie at home she wants to watch. Like "Bull Durham."

Here is what "I do" vow:

To listen to my wife more than I listen to Dan Patrick.

To not take off my ring and twirl it on the table when I write, like the columnist sitting next to me at the U.S. Open.

To not watch the Oklahoma Pom Poms (for more than 10 seconds).

To not go to the "It's Nebraska tennis media day" excuse on "yardwork day."

To take my wife to Boulder, Colo., and Austin, Texas, and Tempe, Ariz., and leave her behind when I go to Lubbock, Texas, and Manhattan, Kan.

To love my wife forever, even when it's tough in the trenches, the count's 3-and-2 with two on and two out and the fans behind the basket are waving their arms like a thousand windshield wipers.

After all, there will be no free agency in this marriage. Today, I'm signing her to a lifetime contract.

SEPTEMBER 19, 1998 • KANSAS STATE FOOTBALL

Kansas State a Football Power?

"BARTENDER, BEER PLEASE. Make it Olympia."

"Excuse me? Olympia? They don't make that anymore. Where have you been for the past 10 years, on the moon?"

"Close. I graduated from the University of Nebraska in 1988. I was going to be an environmentalist. I went on a whale-saving expedition off the Pacific Coast and we got lost in a storm. Ended up on this desert island. It was supposed to be a three-hour tour.

Anyway, we finally got rescued. Say, what time do the Huskers play today?"

"Sorry, Gilligan, they're off. The big game of the day is Texas and Kansas State."

"You gotta be kidding me. What, did the rest of the Big Eight go on probation? Who wants to watch that?"

"Tell you what. I'll give you Texas and you give me 25 points."

"Wait a minute. Give me the sports section. Let's see the spread.

WHAT? Kansas State is favored by 25 points?"

"That's not a misprint. Kansas State should more than cover today. K-State is ranked fifth in the nation. K-State might win the national championship."

"Kansas State? National championship?"

"It all started back in 1989. This guy named Bill Snyder came from Iowa, recruited like crazy, threw the ball around and played the Little Sisters of the Poor and some of their cousins. They've won nine games the last few years. Texas has mismanaged their program. They brought in John Mackovic and he alienated everyone except his favorite restaurant in Austin. Now they have Mack Brown.

He's supposed to lead them back. Not today."

"What about Nebraska?"

"Coach Solich will do a great job."

"Frank Solich, the old running backs coach?"

"Right. He took over when Tom Osborne resigned last year."

"Resigned? Did he ever win a bowl game?"

"Boy, Gilligan, you have been out to lunch with Mary Ann. Osborne won his last four bowl games,

A Gatorade bath for a K-State football coach: Who would have thought?

three of them for national championships. He retired a hero."

"Well, when's the Oklahoma game?"

"Nebraska won't play Oklahoma again until the year 2000. That's Big 12 rules."

"Big 12?"

"That happened in 1996, when the Big Eight merged with four schools from the Southwest Conference — Texas, A&M, Baylor and Texas Tech. The SWC was drowning in red ink. The Big Eight was threatened with losing Colorado, Oklahoma and Missouri to other leagues. So the strong merged into this alliance. It made everybody richer, but some of the old rivalries took a hit. It's just as well. Now that Oklahoma is in the outhouse."

"You're telling me Oklahoma football is bad? How could Barry Switzer let that happen?"

"Barry got run out of town in 1989. Now that the Cowboys ran him out of Dallas, he's in Hollywood, making films. Boy, the Cowboys sure do miss Jimmy Johnson."

"I thought Jimmy was in Miami."

"Nope. And when he left, the Hurricane dynasty went down the tubes with NCAA problems. Hard to believe. But hey, it happened at Notre Dame, too."

"Notre Dame went on NCAA probation?"

"No, no. But the Irish went into the gutter with Miami. Not only that, but Lou Holtz got pushed out and the new guy, Bob Davie, testified in a nasty public case this summer that Lou was a little lu-lu."

"Next thing you're going to tell me is that Northwestern went to a Rose Bowl."

"Yep. In 1995."

"Let me get this straight. Miami and Notre Dame are struggling to go bowling. Switzer coached the Dallas Cowboys. Northwestern went to the Rose Bowl. The Big Eight merged with Texas. Oklahoma stinks."

"And Kansas State might win the national championship."

"You got it. Hey, you need another drink?"

"Yeah. Scotch on the rocks. Make it a double."

120 • 20 YEARS WITH TOM SHATEL

OCTOBER 2, 1998 • UNO FOOTBALL

Dreams Come True for Thompson With Mavs

ED THOMPSON IS nobody's reject. Oh sure, he could be in Lincoln, somewhere on the depth chart. He could be wearing the shiny white helmet with the red N, just like he always dreamed, just like every Nebraska boy in every Nebraska town dreams underneath a cottonwood on a lazy summer's day. He could be a Cornhusker.

But then Thompson wouldn't be one of the key players in this UNO football revival. He wouldn't have his name in the NCAA record books for being the first player in Division II to rush and pass for 1,000 yards in the same season.

He wouldn't be 914 yards from breaking the University of Nebraska at Omaha record for total yards in a career, held by Marlin Briscoe, perhaps the school's most illustrious football alum. And he wouldn't be a hero at UNO, helping the Mavs chase the impossible dream of a national championship. He wouldn't be ready to go down in history as one of the school's all-time greats.

Mostly, Thompson, who dances and jukes through the autumn like a boy in his backyard, wouldn't be having this much fun.

"I always dreamed of going to play for the Cornhuskers," Thompson said. "Everybody else in Cambridge (Neb.) wanted me to go there, too. There are some who still wish I would have done it.

"But I never wanted to go sit there and wait. It would have been nice to be part of a national championship team for two, three years. But being able to play, that's something I'll remember more than just sitting and watching."

That is the dilemma of the Nebraska schoolboy, from towns large and small. There are so many good football players, drilled by good coaches. The byproduct of the Bob Devaney era was that it created a state filled with good high school football, better than most and certainly the best in the country for its population base. But they can't all play in Lincoln. Not all fit the cookie-cutter dimensions to make the Big Red Machine. Where do they go?

They are called the "rejects," mainly by themselves. The cream of the leftover crop get offers to walk on at NU and fill the legions of practice players trying to grab someone's attention, maybe step onto the field for one kickoff return in four years. But that's a lot of work — and waiting — for a championship ring and the right to tell your grandkids you once wore the Cornhusker helmet.

Guys such as Thompson are different. There are many of them, too.

Thompson came from Cambridge, a town just east of McCook, as a second-team all-class quarterback. A guy with speed, a nice arm and letters in basketball and track. But he was no Scott Frost or Frankie London. And NU coaches were after big-name recruits like Eric Crouch and Bobby Newcombe. Thompson was faced with the age-old question: Walk on at Lincoln and watch, or go somewhere to play before smaller crowds and for smaller stakes.

Fortunately for UNO, the University of Nebraska at Kearney wanted him to redshirt as a freshman. Shoot, Thompson could go to Lincoln and do that. But the alternative was a rebuilding program in a "big" city that looked downright intimidating for a kid out of western Nebraska. Still, coach Pat Behrns was selling dreams. And playing time.

"Initially, I didn't want to go to UNO," Thompson said. "They were 1-10 (in 1994) and there was a lot of uncertainty about where they were going. Plus, I had heard so much about Omaha. You hear about the negative things, the bad influences, the crimes that go on there."

After one year, in 1995, spent at receiver, the Thompson Era started. That's when the magic began. His arm and legs are equally dangerous. He is a killer on the option. He is UNO's Tommie Frazier, if that is a fair comparison. OK, it's fair.

"Tommie put them (Nebraska) in and out of a lot of things," Behrns said. "That's what Ed does. He sees the defense and knows what play to call. He gets the job done. Whatever you need, he'll get it."

The obvious question in watching Thompson the past three seasons is: Could he play at Nebraska? Could he have beaten out Scott Frost or Bobby Newcombe? No. But Thompson says, "I think I could have played there." Chances are, he could have played at Iowa State or Kansas or any Division I programs that ran the option.

"There are some places he could have played if they ran the same offense we're running," Behrns said. "I'm glad we didn't have to find out."

Quarterback Ed Thompson, who dreamed of being a Cornhusker, broke records at UNO.

20 YEARS WITH TOM SHATEL • 121

NOVEMBER 15, 1998 • KANSAS STATE FOOTBALL

Time to Give Cats Credit

MANHATTAN, KAN.

SOMETIMES YOU DON'T lose so much as the other guy wins. Sometimes it's just somebody else's turn. Sometimes the best thing to do is just tip your hat and get out of the way before you get clocked with a piece of flying goal post.

Every dog has his day, and now Kansas State can join the club.

And what a day. What a game. The Wildcats, awash in a sea of purple passion, beat Nebraska, 40-30, to end 30 years of futility against Big Red. On a classic autumn day for football, it was classic football. Back and forth. Up, down. Emotional waves with whitecaps.

Forget that ridiculous talk of a blowout. Nebraska pride came out smoking. K-State answered. Nebraska could have put K-State away early, but the Wildcats wouldn't have it. Then KSU tried to bury the Huskers in the third quarter, but the Big Red was going nowhere. NU played well, K-State played better. The Huskers didn't lose, Kansas State won.

Uncle.

And now — drumroll, please — it's time to give Kansas State credit.

Yes, now the check is due. Forget all the jokes about the nonconference cupcakes. Forget all the rips of coach Bill Snyder and his quaint little Stalag on the plains. Kansas State finally won a big game.

Darnell McDonald's touchdown catch with 5:25 left put Kansas State ahead for good.

Kansas State beat a good team and a great program. Kansas State answered every question, every doubt, every bell.

The Wildcats declared this the biggest game in their history, and then they had the guts to go out and win it, in front of God, America and Keith Jackson. The Wildcats fell behind 7-0, but even as the air seeped out of Wagner Field, they came back and came back. They gave up five turnovers and kept coming back and coming back.

Their emotional fire, quarterback Michael Bishop, fumbled three times and threw an interception and looked like he was about to melt down in the second quarter. But Bishop gathered his wits and finished with 446 total yards and four touchdowns. If Bishop loses it in the first half, Kansas State is done. But he didn't.

The Wildcats bagged their biggest game in style. They circled this game last winter, listened all season to their fans tell them that they had to win it and then, as their worst nightmare appeared — a Nebraska team that threatened to win — stared down all the demons of the last 30 years.

"It hurts to know that you are the team to give up that streak (29 wins over K-State)," said NU rush end Chad Kelsay. "It's something that hurts more than you can know. I'm a senior, a captain, a small-town boy from Nebraska. Nebraska football is more than just Saturday. It's a way of life. What hurts the most is that (the streaks) are something we didn't start."

Perhaps it eased the pain knowing that the better team simply won. Perhaps not.

"I thought we rattled Bishop early, but good players bounce back," Kelsay said. "That's the sign of a good team. We've been part of those teams. I knew Kansas State was a good team. I wish them the best of luck."

That's all that was left to do as one of the goal posts finally came down after 40 minutes. Kansas State fans figured it was worth the wait. This was their year. Their turn.

2011 INSIGHT *If you had put me in a time machine and sent me back to 1979 or 1988 or even 1994 and told me I would be writing this column one day, I'd have said you were fit for Jack Nicholson's posse in "One Flew Over the Cuckoo's Nest." But it happened. And the way Bill Snyder was building his program, inching closer each year, you figured it was bound to happen. Still, it was a surreal scene at KSU Stadium on that early evening in November. Part of me was happy for Kansas State. I had covered many, many awful days of K-State football in the 1980s. Just hapless, helpless games. Nebraska would always be Nebraska. This was Kansas State's turn. This was also history. I love college football history, and we were witnessing it up close and personal. Maybe too close. I remember getting bumped and knocked down going to the locker room. There was a security guard standing right by the Nebraska locker room who was supposed to keep people away, but he was too busy celebrating. Anyway, I felt it was necessary to take this angle on the column. I knew Husker fans would be very upset with finally losing to Kansas State. I knew some would be like Jay Foreman, after the game, saying, "We're still the better team." I felt it was important to say it was time to give K-State credit. The Wildcats were the better team, for once. Sometimes, you have to tip your cap to the other guy. And get the hell out of the way of the students storming the field.*

A Sad Day for Iowa Fans

WELL, COLLEGE FOOTBALL lost another one.

Hayden Fry, the patriarch of Iowa football, stepped down after 20 years as the Head Hawk. Fry could barely get through his farewell press conference, breaking down at times, his eyes red, voice quivering, head bowed. Fry kept crying, and you knew it was a melancholy moment for Iowa. The game of college football could use a Kleenex, too.

The game keeps losing its wonderful old warhorses. The legends keep leaving. Last year it was Tom Osborne and Eddie Robinson. Don James and Bo Schembechler left long ago. Only a few remain who remember freshman ineligibility and no scholarship limits. LaVell Edwards. Bobby Bowden. Joe Paterno. One day, it will hit them.

They'll know they can't coach forever. They'll want more out of life than the lousy hours and the roller-coaster rides. Just like Fry.

They don't make them like Fry anymore. The coaches with swagger. Coaches who are so powerful that you joke they have more pull than the governor. But the thing is, it's true.

They are a dying breed, these football coaches who are icons.

Heroes. You may not agree with his play-calling, but you would defend him to the death. His picture is on the bedroom wall of every boy and girl in Iowa. All he does is win football games, but he's a role model in every classroom and Rotary Club and fire station in the state. When he comes to town, time stops. Nebraska had Bob Devaney and Osborne. Iowa had Fry.

We miss them in college football. Nobody ever stays around long enough to warrant hero status anymore. If a guy wins, he leaves right away for a better job or salary. Coaches are more mercenary than missionary. College presidents created this shallow atmosphere by tightening the rules on coaches and then hypocritically firing them for not winning enough. There's less and less loyalty in college football. Less and less color. Less fun, too.

Fry gave Iowa all of that and more. Nile Kinnick,

Hayden Fry turned a struggling Iowa football program into a Big Ten champion.

the 1939 Heisman Trophy winner, was an Iowa legend. But Fry put the Hawkeyes on the map for good. When he arrived in 1979, with his Texas drawl and cowboy boots, he took over a program that had had 17 straight non-winning seasons and had been to only two bowls (1957 and 1959 Rose Bowls). He won 143 games and took Iowa to 14 bowls, including three Rose Bowls.

But it wasn't the winning that made Fry so unique, so special. It was his relationship with Iowa fans. He loved them, and they idolized him. They filled each other with such enormous pride. They were the perfect match, this Texan with the homespun humor who when he arrived promised only "to be competitive, tough and colorful," and the hard-working folk of Iowa, who wanted a team they could be proud of.

Fry gave them reasons immediately. His target was Iowa's fragile mental state. He changed the uniforms to look like the Pittsburgh Steelers, who, in 1979, were the model of excellence and intimidation.

He created the "Tiger Hawk" logo that fed the frenzy. He threw the ball like a West Coast coach. There was the "swarm," the slow-jog intro onto the field. The visitors' locker room painted in pink. He gave Iowans a cause, an identity, a road map to Pasadena.

Last spring, at a Hawk Club golf outing in Council Bluffs, Fry took six hours to play his round of golf. It's not that he's a hack. He spent most of the day wandering through fairways, shaking every hand he could find and saying, "Hi, I'm Hayden Fry. Thanks for your support."

That love was genuine and that's a love you don't find much of these days in college football.

It was a love that Fry kept giving, to the teary end.

NOVEMBER 26, 1998 • NEBRASKA FOOTBALL

Some Memories Won't Fade

ODE TO A press box: The following story is true. The names have been changed to protect the innocently wacko. The year was 1985. It was July. It was hot. Lincoln was dead. Any questions?

Yes. What to do on a Monday night in Collegetown, U.S.A.? I was in the Capital City to do some preseason football interviews for the Kansas City Star. I was also thirsty. So I called up a couple of friends: a sportswriter for the Omaha World-Herald (we'll call him "Scoop") and the other a guy who worked for the University of Nebraska (we'll call him "Red").

We decided to meet later that night at Barry's Bar and Grill, which was before they had a warehouse dance hall and pinball games and their own traveling trailer. Back then, the only people who went to Barry's were out-of-town sportswriters. That night, we owned the place.

We stayed until closing, and this is where the story gets weird.

For some reason, I said, "Let's go to the stadium."

Now, at 1 a.m. on a Monday night in July, there are lots of places you should be, and home is probably tops on the list.

Memorial Stadium ranks down there just below White Castle. But there we went, the three amigos, traipsing down to Memorial Stadium. Well, the gate was locked. Red didn't have the key. But we did get into the main concourse, and Red could get us into the elevator.

"Great," I said. "Let's go to the press box."

That's just what we did. Like three little kids walking through some abandoned old building. We went up to the broadcast level. The windows were open and you could see the full moon and a shower of stars above the Nebraska night. We started doing Keith Jackson.

"FUMBBBLEEE! NEBRASKA'S GOT IT!" "HERE COME THE HOGS OUT OF THE CHUTE." "WHOAAA NELLIEEE."

Finally, enough. We turned to leave. Oops. Somebody, perhaps a late-night security guy, had shut the elevator off.

We were trapped in the press box. In July. On Monday night.

("Now, on to other news. Two sportswriters and a university official were found this morning locked in the Memorial Stadium press box. One writer claimed to be looking for the great line he misplaced there last November. Bail has been set at ...")

What do you do when you're locked in a press box at 1 a.m.?

First, you panic. Then you call your nearest relative or sportswriter friend. In this case, it was Ken and Ryly Jane Hambleton, the sportswriting couple at the Lincoln Journal Star (who, ironically, now own Barry's). We pleaded with Ken to come down and find the security guard to get us down.

"Where are you going?" Ryly Jane asked Ken.

"I'm going down to the stadium. Shatel and two guys are locked in the press box."

Workers tear out the old press box at Memorial Stadium to make way for the new West Stadium addition.

"Oh, OK. Have a safe trip," Ryly Jane said, or something to that effect.

Five minutes later, she was running out the door to stop her husband in the driveway. The three amigos just called. The elevator magically came back on. I think we ran home.

That's how I'll remember the Memorial Stadium press box.

Next year, the news media will have new digs. The old digs will be missed.

Not because it's a luxury box. I have friends who are dying to go up and see the press box, and I keep telling them it's nothing special.

As press boxes go, Nebraska's is functional. There are three rows, with 131 seats, a few TV sets, lots of phones and a small lunch bar in the back. We sit on small metal folding chairs. But the Nebraska press box is special because of the games, the people, the memories.

'98 Huskers Never Quit

THEY PLAY FOR pride about as often as Dennis Rodman marries for love.

They weren't on the same planet as the national championship this year. They won't call the jewelers for a conference championship ring for the first time since 1990. They lost at home. They lost to Kansas State. They had the gall to lose three games. They will play their bowl game in the month of December. They played Colorado in a bizarre setting known as the Thanksgiving Leftover Bowl.

And it was a good season. The Huskers ensured that, surviving Colorado 16-14 in a game in which the car rolled home into the driveway on empty. But for all the broken streaks and legacies left in the rubble this year, Nebraska kept a most important streak alive and kicking. The Huskers won their ninth game, and if first-year coach Frank Solich could have torn down a goal post by himself, well, he would have done it.

You may have tossed this one in the nearest container on the way home, but for a rookie coach replacing a legend, this victory was golden. Lose, and the Huskers have no guaranteed ninth victory in the Holiday Bowl. Lose, and Solich's first team might break the mother of all Nebraska streaks: 21 years of nine-win seasons. That was Tom Osborne's signature collection. Lose, and NU has four losses for the first time since Bob Devaney was on the sidelines and maybe a fifth loss in the bowl game. Lose, and there's no confidence going into 1999 and people are saying, "Well, Frankie's a good guy and all, but he didn't win nine games like Tom always did."

This one was so big that Solich admitted it.

"That was really big," Solich said of winning nine games. "I tried to downplay it myself, because you need to focus on the game at hand and trying to prepare the kids for the game.

"Every time these players turned around this year, there was something (a streak) like that being thrown at them. I'm relieved they were able to get nine victories. They wanted that badly. If I look at everything that's happened to them this year, I feel good about

Senior fullback Joel Makovicka leaves the field at Memorial Stadium for the last time.

9-3. That sounds pretty good to me."

It should to all of them. Considering the circumstances — and how can you not? — this was an effort, if not a season, to remember.

"It's been a rough season," said rush end Mike Rucker. "We've been kind of hard on ourselves. But we've never lost three games. At least we left them with a win."

Yes, indeed. This senior class has taken way too much heat this season, most of it self-inflicted. After each loss, they've walked out, shoulders slumped, accepting full responsibility. After each streak was broken, senior rush end Chad Kelsay acted like he was about to be deported. He talked of being from small-town Nebraska, of letting down generations of Huskers, of being the bane of Husker society.

Bullfeathers.

This senior class has nothing to be ashamed of. They have national championship rings, some with three, and contributed to each and every diamond. They had nothing to do with the inexperience and lack of push in the offensive line, the slump in the secondary, the injuries at quarterback and I-back and the inexperience of the head coach. They weren't the best leaders Nebraska's ever had, but neither were they the worst.

In fact, what they accomplished, in the face of tempting apathy, showed great leadership. Nebraska kept fighting. Pride may be a cliché. It's also not a bad streak to keep alive.

"I think it showed a lot of character," Kelsay said. "We're not going to make any excuses. We've had to overcome some things, but every team goes through those things.

"The season hasn't gone the way we planned. And this senior class has gone through a lot. We have a couple national championship rings. We had three losses this year. None of us are satisfied with three losses. But each week we came out to play."

The Husker seniors never gave up. They finished the job. That's the most important legacy they can pass on. 1998? It was a very good year.

TOM'S TAKE   REFLECTIONS ON

Politicos Stall New Arena

I THINK MOST Omahans agree we need something. The arena and convention center aren't about sports, they're about this area's growth. Where, and how much we should pay, are other issues. But we need to figure out a plan, and get behind that plan, and soon.

— APRIL 17, 1998

Even with a wind chill reading of 39 at game time, 19,000 College World Series fans cheered on Arizona State and Long Beach State.

No Fair-Weather CWS Fans

IT WILL BE a cold day in Phoenix before the College World Series ever leaves Omaha.

That was the stone-cold message on a lovely night for ice-fishing at the CWS. I'm not saying it was cold at Rosenblatt Stadium, but they had a seventh-inning thaw instead of a stretch. The balls leaving the infield were literally frozen ropes.

While the concession stands were running out of coffee, hot chocolate and parkas, Long Beach State was running out of season.

The Dirtbags were swept up by the Arizona State Dirt Devils, 14-4.

And anyone who was there to see the end deserved a medal, a blanket and a frostbite checkup — not necessarily in that order.

I don't care what dome you come up with or what city the NCAA moving van shows up at next. Everyone knows this event isn't going anywhere.

Not after 19,002 fans braved the wintry June elements for a baseball game between teams from Long Beach, Calif., and Tempe, Ariz. At game time, the official CWS Doppler radar reading was 50 degrees with a wind chill of 39. That must have felt like Antarctica weather to the visitors. To Nebraskans, it was simply Makovicka weather.

That surely was part of it. Nebraskans are a hardy lot, used to sitting through a lot worse to watch walk-ons walk over the Husker entrée of the week. Nebraskans show up in Lincoln every other week, no matter the opponent or conditions, because that's what they are supposed to do. It's tradition.

So, too, is the CWS. This is Omaha's Super Bowl. Omaha shows up, no matter if it's 91 degrees and humidity off the faint meter or if nature decides to turn on the air conditioner.

— JUNE 4, 1998

THE CHANGING SPORTS LANDSCAPE 1998

Simon, Jays Need Facility

BEFORE HE LEFT four years ago, former Creighton soccer coach Bob Warming offered his successor some words of wisdom. "Ride the wave as much as you can."

Bret Simon's Bluejays are doing just that. Again. For the seventh straight year, Creighton soccer is in the NCAA tournament. The Jays are Road Warriors. Their midfielder should be named Mel Gibson. They have won eight straight NCAA games on the road, dating to 1996.

Bret Simon

Some wave. But what Warming was warning Simon about was the wave of success. He knew that CU would have to find most of its players out of state. He knew that the Tranquility Park "facility" was a nice place to start a program but not necessarily maintain one. He knew that something, someday, would have to be done or this breaker would crash with a thud.

Not yet. The Jays' program is too good, too solid. But make no mistake: The lack of a quality college soccer facility is starting to bite the Jays. Simon is certain it's why the NCAA three times this postseason has turned down CU's bid to host a game. A deteriorated Tranquility field sent CU on the road in the NCAAs in 1996. There's no reason for CU fans to think that will change in the future.

"It has something to do with the facility," Simon said. "The shape of the field this time of year, no locker rooms, no press box, the lack of parking. Our field is nice and cozy. But there are certain requirements you need to keep getting the top players here. Just because you're near the top now doesn't mean it will always be this way."

Father Michael Morrison, Creighton's president, needs to decide how important Division I sports are at CU. The Jays need to have updated, if not completely new, fully equipped facilities to compete in Division I athletics here in Omaha, Neb., USA.

"It's easy to sell (recruits) on the great soccer community here," Simon said. "But it's important to show them (a stadium) when they ask, 'Does soccer matter here?'"

— **DECEMBER 2, 1998**

Creighton's nationally ranked soccer program was unable to host NCAA tournament games because of the inadequacy of its Tranquility Park field. The school's new soccer facility, Morrison Stadium, opened in 2003.

WIN AT ALLEN FIELD HOUSE | JAYS WIN NCAA TOURNEY GAME | NU'S BIG 12 BASEBALL TITLE

1999

> "When we were coming onto the field, it was a very emotional time for me. I looked around, and I asked myself, 'Do I belong here?' There was Carl Yastrzemski, Willie Mays, Henry Aaron. I said, 'I struck all of those guys out. I guess I do belong here.'"
>
> — BOB GIBSON, ON BEING PART OF THE ALL-STAR PRE-GAME INTRODUCTIONS

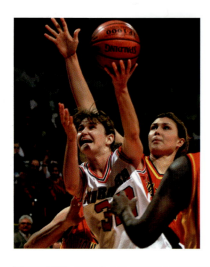

Nebraska clawed back against Texas behind Nicole Kubik, who was hitting jump shots, making defensive plays and driving, always driving, to the basket. Late in the game, she faked left, crossed to the right and dribbled through the defense for an open layup to give NU a 53-46 lead. She scored nine of the team's last 10 points. Kubik was third in the league in scoring (18.9) and became the first player in Big 12 history to record 1,000 points, 300 assists and 300 steals in a career. Nobody was better on both ends. But she was left off the All-Big 12 first team, and it seemed that she was trying to prove a point against Texas and first-teamer Edwina Brown. "I don't have to prove anything to anybody," said Kubik, a junior from Cambridge, Neb. "I'm a total team player. I'm playing to win. I'm playing for my team, my coaches and myself."

"You can feed a chicken a kernel of corn, but you can't teach it to play the piano." Missouri's Norm Stewart once said that. The writers there just shook our heads. It didn't have to make sense. It was Norm. Well, he did it again. Stormin' Norman Stewart up and retired, leaving us bemused and puzzled. You always figured Norm would coach until one day he'd just keel over, in the heat of battle, right there on the sideline at Allen Field House. But now the old sheriff of the Big Eight rides into the sunset without warning.

You don't tell Charlie McBride that his defense isn't exactly calculus. Texas quarterback Major Applewhite made that ill-advised statement after the Longhorns had beaten Nebraska in Austin. Well, McBride came back swinging in the Huskers' 22-6 Big 12 championship game victory. The Blackshirts blitzed everyone but Lil' Red. "I told them to come after (Applewhite) hard," McBride said. "I wanted to see the skin peeling off their eyeballs." That is, Nebraska players' eyeballs. It was certainly an eye-opening experience for Texas and Applewhite, who finally saw the real Nebraska.

128 • 20 YEARS WITH TOM SHATEL

OSBORNE IN HALL OF FAME | TERRY PETTIT'S DEPARTURE | A SPECIAL DECADE FOR HUSKERS

Somehow, some way, a column questioning Creighton's toughness ends up in the Jays' game plan for Southwest Missouri State. "To be honest, a certain columnist got them going when he questioned their toughness," Creighton coach Dana Altman said. My first assist. I'm so proud. When does the letter jacket come? Truth be told, no sports columnist ever won or lost a game. The Jays scratched out a 79-76 win over Southwest Missouri State on their own.

Rodney Buford's modest 13 points against Maryland in the second round of the NCAA tournament were enough to break Bob Harstad's Creighton career scoring mark (2,110) by six (2,116). Buford played it down, but you know he takes great satisfaction in one-upping Harstad. Buford heard so much about Harstad's work ethic and leadership during his career. Well, even Harstad would have been proud of the way Buford matured. And finished. "Nobody wanted me out of high school," Buford said. "People have said I'm an underachiever. To score 2,000 points is a great experience. I wish I had another game left." Anyone not satisfied with the end of this story should remember where it all began. "When Rodney got here, we were awful," coach Dana Altman said. "Non-athletic. We didn't have a good basketball team. We had to start somewhere. Rodney came here and gave us something to start with. He helped us recruit other players. Because of him, we were able to build some things. He started it."

So you want to build a college baseball program? You want people to sit up and take notice? Here's what you do: Score 50 runs. Yes, in one game. You do that and everyone but Letterman will call. Do that, and folks will pencil you in for second place in the National League Central. You say "Nebraska Baseball" and everyone knows who you're talking about. Yeah, that team that dropped 50 runs on somebody. Fifty! With one game, Nebraska baseball coach Dave Van Horn got more juice than a Big 12 title or NCAA appearance could ever provide. The only thing better than the crazy and totally unintentional 50-3 victory over Chicago State (or was it the White Sox?) would be a College World Series berth. Impossible? Tell it to the Chicago State pitchers.

Great Crowd Thrills Coach

THEY WERE YOUNG and old, tall and short, male and female, animal and mineral. They came from Kearney and Gering and Omaha and every two-lane road in between. They came from Ames, Iowa, by the busloads, dressed in red and gold.

They were here, at the Bob Devaney Sports Center, to watch Nebraska and Iowa State play a little game of women's college hoops. But never mind the grand game itself, a manicure special, right down to the nail-gnawing end with the Huskers finally exhaling with a 68-67 win over the 15th-ranked Cyclones — a candidate for Big 12 game of the year.

Paul Sanderford

This was the biggest crowd of any year in the Big 12. The crowd of 13,135 at the Sports Center was not only a Nebraska feat, but supposedly the all-time women's basketball crowd for any Big 12 Conference school, including, and especially, Texas. A peek in the Big 12 women's basketball record book did not show any such records listed, but a Nebraska official claimed it was true, and on this phenomenal day, nobody was about to argue.

Then again, if the claim to a Big 12 record was just another marketing ploy by Husker coach Paul Sanderford to sell his program, nobody would be surprised, either. Sanderford is a master promoter who can coach a lick or two in his spare time. But even this surreal atmosphere — with fans in the aisle near the top of the arena — impressed the man whose basketball standards are a few light years ahead of his program.

"It was by far the best atmosphere at Nebraska," Sanderford said. "I don't usually come out before the game. When the players came into the locker room after warm-ups, I could see it in their faces. I knew the crowd was special."

It made the players feel special, like a giant party

Nebraska's Cori McDill drives between Iowa State's Monica Huelman and Megan Taylor.

thrown for them. Nebraska is like most Division I women's programs: They get a few thousand folks, the diehards, to watch their games. Their stories get played below the men's. They usually play in the shadows, and that's fine, because that's not why they play the game. But then they walked out Sunday and saw every seat filled and people jumping up and down screaming for them ...

"When I came out of the tunnel I tried to be cool and not smile," said Nebraska junior guard Brooke Schwartz, from Gering. "But my face just lights up."

You want to know the secret? Come closer, and we'll whisper: They Gave Out Free Tickets! That's right. Like a good neighbor, the local State Farm insurance company bought up a reported 20,000 tickets and gave them out in the surrounding communities. And so what? It's one thing to get a free ticket. It's quite another to actually show up — and then stand up and yell. The crowd was a rock concert compared with the library at Nebraska men's games.

"You can talk about giving out free tickets," Sanderford said. "But aren't free tickets better than empty seats?"

FEBRUARY 11, 1999 • NEBRASKA BASKETBALL

Huskers Cut Into 'Phog'

LAWRENCE, KAN.

THE PHOG FINALLY lifted and, man, the view was incredible.

After 15 seasons of walking out of Allen Field House in a fog, the Nebraska basketball team danced and whooped its way into school history with a 64-59 victory over Kansas. They did it by coming back from 11 points and 15 years down. They did it, and it wasn't a fluke. They did it with the ghosts of Beau Reid and Henry T. Buchanan and Eric Piatkowski on their backs. They did it in the face of the ghosts of Danny Manning and Rex Walters and Jacque Vaughn.

They did it in "Phog" Allen Field House, for crying out loud, which, by the way, is what Kansas fans were heard doing afterward.

And by the time there was a minute left, those KU fans were seen leaving early.

The Phog was indeed lifting, finally, and what the Huskers saw had to stun even the most myopic sort: They beat Kansas twice in one season. And they produced a war story for the Markowski grandkids some 30 years from now.

"To have the (guts) to dig out a win here. ... I'd go to the mouth of hell with the devil with these guys," Andy Markowski said.

John Wayne never said it better. Walk into storied Allen, where the tradition is so thick you need a fork, and you see a banner that warns, "Beware the Phog." That's F.C. "Phog" Allen, the legendary former KU coach. And it's a lot more.

The Phog is when you walk out for warm-ups — some 90 minutes before tipoff — and the place is half full of students who taunt and tease you. The Phog is the noise level; folks here walk through the turnstiles screaming. The Phog is the retired numbers, the museum of basketball history in the corridors, the drive down Naismith Drive to the arena.

To emerge from the Phog victorious is huge. How big? The Huskers' win was so big that Nebraska is now a basketball school. OK, maybe not. But at least today people will stop talking about Bobby Newcombe for 10 minutes.

For a Nebraska team looking for reasons to believe, that was a start.

"It was a David and Goliath story," Markowski said. "In the past, when you're down 11 here, it's like there goes the coffin. But they are beatable here.

"When you've got good chemistry, you can do anything."

Andy Markowski helped Nebraska to its first victory at Allen Field House since 1983.

MARCH 12, 1999 • CREIGHTON BASKETBALL

This Dive Was Perfect

ORLANDO, FLA.

RODNEY BUFORD DID it again. He had them talking in the locker room. He had their eyes popping way out of their sockets there on the Creighton bench. Once again, he showed them something they had never seen before.

But no, dear no, it wasn't that late 3-point dagger he stuck in Louisville's heart that made Buford the talk of the Jays' 62-58 NCAA victory. This was better.

This was Buford diving. On the floor. After a ball. After a victory.

"FIRST LEGITIMATE DIVE!" yelled Creighton coach Dana Altman, as he and Buford walked off the floor at the Orlando Arena after talking to CBS. Altman had his arms around Buford's neck and wore a smile as big as Disney World. He was a father hugging his son after his first hit, his first time on a bike without falling or his first A on the report card.

Buford took a dive. Creighton didn't.

No one could remember just when it happened — they say it was the first half — or if Buford even got his hands on the ball. No matter. What was stop-the-presses news was that Buford had gotten his Bluejay feathers dirty.

And though the coaching staff claims they don't keep such stats, everyone knew it was a Buford first. Oh, there was that lame attempt against Evansville in the Missouri Valley tournament.

"That was a pseudo-dive," said Creighton senior forward Doug Swenson. "In that one, he kind of laid on top of somebody. That didn't count. This time he actually dove. There was a possibility of a floor burn. The judges gave him a point."

And his harshest judge, Altman, had to be giddy. Those little hustle plays score the most points with Altman. For four years, he has been trying to get Buford to hustle, to play hard. To dive. Just once. He would trade all those points and dunks and highlights by Buford for one dive. Finally, so did Buford.

"I didn't want to lose," Buford said. "It's do or die right now. I didn't want to die."

Buford said he couldn't remember, but he "might have dived once a couple of years ago." We'll take Altman's word for it: This was probably his first. Regardless, nobody will forget this one. It came with the Jays flustered, tight, nervous, going down in the NCAA tourney in the worst possible way. It's OK to lose in the NCAAs. Just be competitive. Just show up. The Jays weren't even showing up. Then Buford took flight with a twist — he flew downward.

"It was a big dive," said sophomore guard Ben Walker. "Rodney's not the kind of guy who will throw his body on the floor if he can help it. When we saw that, that fired us up."

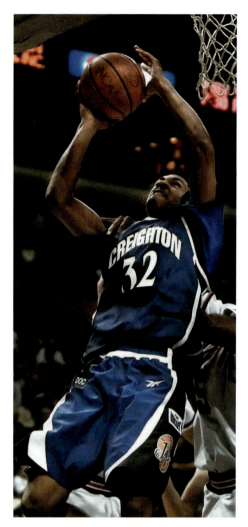

Creighton's Rodney Buford got the Bluejays into the 1999 NCAA tournament by delivering 21 points and 13 rebounds in the Missouri Valley Conference tournament title game.

2011 INSIGHT *This was the day that Dana Altman's Creighton arrived, the day you knew it was going to be special, and it totally fell out of the sky. Nobody predicted this. Nobody saw it coming. Beat writer Rich Kaipust and I were on this trip, and we packed for a short stay. That was by habit, from my covering too many Nebraska basketball one-and-dones in the NCAAs. My angle here came from a little trick I've used over the years: stand by the court or the path to the locker room after the game and see what you might pick up. Most of the time, nothing. But here, I heard Altman yell "First legitimate dive!" to Rodney Buford, and I knew I had my angle. Now I needed a pair of clean underwear. We were staying two more nights.*

Right Move for Van Horn

OKLAHOMA CITY

THEY LAUGHED AT him when he said he was going to play ball in the great white north. They told him he was a fool, taking a job at Nebraska, where football scrimmaging is the No. 1 spring sport. They said it would be a career-killer — trying to win in the Big 12, where all the good weather and facilities and players live south of Wichita.

Good thing Dave Van Horn believed in himself, and not the naysayers.

And now all of Nebraska believes, too.

The proof was everywhere on a late Oklahoma Sunday, when the last out landed safely in left fielder John Cole's extended glove and 25 bulldogs in red and white made a dogpile in center field. Would you believe Big 12 baseball champs, the first NU baseball league title since the Big Seven title in 1950? Would you believe a sweep of Oklahoma State, Oklahoma, Texas A&M and Baylor, the latter two ranked in the top 10?

Would you believe 41 wins? A No. 2 seed in the school's first NCAA regional since 1985?

Maybe the only guy who wouldn't believe it isn't here anymore.

"The biggest difference between coach (John) Sanders and coach Van Horn is that coach Van Horn is a motivator," NU first baseman Ken Harvey said. "From day one, he's been telling us we could win. You start to believe it."

Van Horn took a team picked to finish eighth and led it through rain, sleet and snow to 41 wins and a fifth-place finish. His team started seven new regulars, including true freshmen Cole, Will Bolt and Shane Komine. He mixed junior-college players with some of the best Nebraska American Legion ball has to offer.

He brought in speed and won with stolen bases, bunts and kitchen sinks. He kept Mike Anderson from the Sanders staff and brought with him pitching coach Rob Childress, who did wonders with a staff of Nebraskans that the Sanders regime didn't want.

He taught them all to believe baseball could work in Nebraska.

Van Horn has put Nebraska baseball on the map, most importantly at home. Let the bandwagon begin.

"People are talking about us," Van Horn said. "They've got talk-radio shows, and I'll be flipping the dial on the way home from practice or somewhere and people are talking about our program. It puts a smile on your face.

"Sometimes you're going, 'Wow. This happened pretty quick,' " Van Horn said. "We're surprised we've gone this far. We knew we had a chance to win 35 games, but to get up to 40 in these last few weeks and then win the tournament with all these top-ranked teams, that's an awesome feeling for myself, the other coaches and the players."

Nobody knew Van Horn when he showed up at that first press conference in January 1998. He wasn't the hot coach in the country. He wasn't coming from a College World Series program. He'd won a couple of Southland Conference titles. But you looked at his record, and he'd won everywhere he'd been, at every level.

Now Nebraska knows. Now everyone, south, east and west, knows. The man is a winner.

"For me, personally, I made the right move," Van Horn said. "I had people telling me, 'You might be crazy going up there.' I said, 'Hey, they want to win, and we can do it.' "

Dave Van Horn and wife Karen watch the selections for the NCAA baseball tournament.

JUNE 20, 1999 • COLLEGE WORLD SERIES

Varnes Joins CWS Lore

AFTER A HALF century, we think we have this College World Series thing figured out.

We all know about the effort, the boyish exuberance, the pride, the charm of these players. We've seen them play their hearts out, spill their guts, jump over fences, dive headfirst, reach into their soul and hit game-winning homers. We've seen them laugh, cry, yell and dogpile. We've seen them go four hours-plus just to stay one more night in our hometown.

And just when we thought we'd seen it all in 50 years in Omaha, along comes Blair Varnes.

The Florida State redshirt freshman pitcher taught us something new about the human spirit and how it fits into our little world known as the College World Series.

Varnes was the special surprise guest at the FSU-Miami national championship game. When he limped out to the mound, Florida State fans stood and cheered. Some couldn't believe it. Hey, that's No. 21. Isn't that Blair Varnes? Is he really going to pitch?

Florida State's Blair Varnes injured his knee in a dogpile after the Seminoles won their NCAA super regional.

Oh, yes. Varnes pitched. He went six innings, giving up eight hits, six runs and more guts than you can ever imagine. By the time he left, after a leadoff walk in the sixth to Miami's Bobby Hill, he knew he was done. FSU coach Mike Martin came to get him. Varnes left. The FSU fans stood and cheered his valor. A few thousand Omahans joined in, and you wonder if they knew what was going on or if it was just polite applause.

What was going on was Varnes giving us all a new definition of what the CWS is all about.

"Was he gutty?" Martin asked. "Boy, he was gutty."

Do you ever wonder whether anybody ever gets hurt in those college baseball celebration dogpiles? Two weeks ago, Varnes was on top of the world. One year after having "Tommy John surgery" on his right elbow, Varnes had bounced back. Strong. He was 11-1 with an ERA of 3.84 and 75 strikeouts. He was named freshman All-American. And then the Seminoles won their super regional and Varnes was suddenly on top of the dogpile.

He landed on his knee wrong. Very wrong.

"It hurt a little," Varnes said. "But I didn't think it was anything. A couple days later it was still hurting, and I decided to go to the doctor. I was bored. Just watching TV. He looked at it and said, 'I don't think you want to hear what I think it is.'"

A torn anterior cruciate ligament in his left knee.

Ouch.

Double ouch.

Varnes was hurt almost more emotionally than physically. Here it was, the week of going to Omaha, and he was out.

Then it happened. FSU stayed alive this year in Omaha. The 'Noles kept hitting, and pitching, and winning. They beat Stanford in a 13-inning marathon. But Martin had used seven pitchers.

He'd used up every available arm. How about that: FSU finally gets to the CWS final and there's nobody left to pitch. It would either be Martin or the bus driver.

Martin and pitching coach Jamey Shouppe had an idea. A crazy idea. Maybe it would work. Varnes had thrown some during practice that week. He couldn't run. But he could throw. Maybe he could get them five or six innings. Maybe he would last one inning and hurt himself worse.

The only thing they knew was that Varnes wouldn't say no.

"Coach Shouppe looked at me, and I could tell what he was going to ask," Varnes said. "I said, 'Yes, I can pitch.'"

Oh, yes, he could. Varnes limped out there. He wore a sleeve and two special braces over the knee. Instead of rotating off his leg after the pitch, he "just fell forward." The knee could have buckled on the mound. It could have given out at any time. Career over? All for a CWS game?

Varnes couldn't think about that. Nor could he think about the pain. He took strong painkillers before the game. He was doing fine until he got out of the third inning on a double play and did a little celebration jump. From now on, Varnes should just stick to handshakes.

He went six innings, 100 pitches. He gave up five runs in the fifth, including a backbreaking double by Kevin Brown. But he gave back so much more.

"I didn't really look at it like that," Varnes said. "I was mad that I hadn't pitched yet. I'm not saying I wasn't hurting, but more than anything it just changed my delivery. No excuses.

"Sure, I could have torn my cartilage or something. I could have blown it all out. But I'm having surgery on Thursday anyway. It was the national championship game. I didn't want to look back and say I didn't try."

Nobody could ever accuse Varnes of that. He tried. Miami was the better team. The Hurricanes deserved to win the national championship. They beat FSU for the sixth time, five in one-run games. But the Seminoles left here with a lot of pride, if not the trophy. They showed a lot of heart. We've seen heart. We know heart. But what we saw from Varnes was something else.

Face to Face With Koufax

I CAN ONLY speak for the male species here. But there is a place in every man's heart, a never-never land he crosses into, where the man becomes a boy; the hardened journalist turns into a slobbering, goo-goo-eyed fanatic with a black Sharpie pen.

I went to that place and never looked back.

They say we Oscar Madison types aren't supposed to be fans. But then the public relations guy at the Bob Gibson All-Star Classic says, "I'd like you to meet Sandy Koufax," and you can kiss all those journalism school ethics goodbye. You try to be professional, but Sandy is the pro and you, well, you are a 7-year-old boy with a baseball card.

There are two special moments in every man's life: the day he gets married and the day he becomes a father. For me, there's a third: the day I got to meet Sandy Koufax.

I'd love to report that I got the full scoop on Koufax, why he all but disappeared from society. I'd love to be able to call up Sports Illustrated and brag, "I not only found Sandy, I got an interview, and he gave me all this great stuff about the demise of the curveball. ..."

Except, well, I really can't remember much that he said. I wish I could have told him about my father, who grew up a Brooklyn fan in New York and saw Koufax break in with the Dodgers.

Or how, as a 7-year-old living in Southern California, I took a blue marker to a T-shirt and inked in Sandy's name and number on the back. Or that magical night in September 1965 when my first trip to Dodger Stadium came on the very night Koufax tossed his fourth, and last, no-hitter.

But when you meet your childhood heroes, you generally say things like, "Ah, oh, well, uh, nice to meet you, too. How's the weather?"

He had a few minutes. He talked about how he does only a few of these events, how he and Gibson are closer, how nobody throws curveballs anymore.

The whole thing was surreal, like a dream. But that's the beauty of the Gibson event. All the legends out there are followed around by men acting like little boys, dressed in baseball jerseys and hats, getting autographs. Some will sell them. But most are there because they've been summoned by a higher power. Some of the big kids turn to their little kids and say, "That guy was my hero when I was your age."

Koufax drew a larger crowd of "kids" than most. What is it about Koufax, after all these years? Not just that he was the greatest pitcher of his era, maybe all eras, and his fastballs and wicked curveballs have become mythical over time. Was it how he disappeared from the game so abruptly? How he left on top? Or is it how he carries himself, almost regally, still tan and fit and looking like he could strike out Mark McGwire today on three pitches?

Or maybe it's because nobody could believe how approachable he was. Koufax would sign all day for the fans, talk to them like long-lost friends. One guy said, "I saw you pitch in the '65 Series on Classic Sports." Koufax said, "How'd we do?"

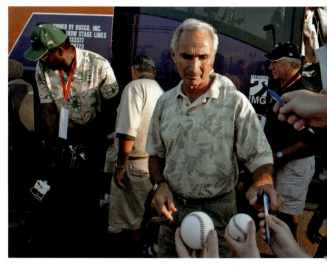

Sandy Koufax was popular with autograph seekers at Bob Gibson's golf events.

Koufax has been called a recluse, a legend who is more ghost than real. But where he lives and what he does with himself are not nearly as important as the idea that guys like him live in our memories. If you find out your hero is a good guy, too, well, that's a full day.

"Don't believe all the crap," Koufax says. "I haven't disappeared. I'm not lost. I'm not very mysterious."

You don't really know what to say to that, except, "Mr. Koufax, could you please sign this?"

2011 INSIGHT *I broke a couple of personal rules in this column. One, don't write about your childhood. It's only interesting to you. Two, you're a journalist and supposed to be professional – don't ask for autographs. And if you do, you sure as heck don't write about it. OK, that's three rules I broke. I put myself in detention later. My thought here was, why not? There's still a young kid living in most sports fans, and we still want to be around athletes and talk to them and get their autograph. Maybe you had a favorite player growing up you never got to meet, or you did but you wished you had asked for a signature. This column was for those people, more than me bragging about anything. Again, I looked foolish in the eyes of other journalists. The only thing I regret is that I didn't have a magazine cover or baseball card to sign. I had brought my favorite old, rumpled blue Dodger hat – which I had bought outside Riverfront Stadium in Cincinnati in 1979. I had Koufax sign the inside bill of the hat. So now I can't wear my favorite hat without someone seeing Sandy Koufax's signature and saying, "You idiot, why are you wearing that, you'll wear it off." So that's four rules I broke. Tough day. Great day.*

AUGUST 13, 1999 • NEBRASKA FOOTBALL

No Asterisk for Osborne

SOUTH BEND, IND.

THE FIRST TIME I met Tom Osborne, it was in a hot tub. OK, let's clarify the situation right now. Osborne was not in the hot tub, too. He was standing on a staircase in the Manhattan, Kan., Holidome on a Saturday morning in October 1988, looking down on a pair of sportswriters who were using warm bubbles to exorcise the demons of a night in Aggieville gone wrong.

This was the Nebraska team hotel, on the day of a Husker-Kansas State game, back in the days when a Wildcat was still Husker roadkill. Osborne probably had just left a pre-game meeting, where he no doubt went over for the umpteenth time how Ken Clark was going to go 80 yards off-tackle on the first play, when he spied the writer from Kansas City.

"Hi, Tom . . . I'm Tom Osborne," said Tom Osborne. "You got a minute?"

I always said getting chewed out by Osborne was like getting scolded by Ward Cleaver. He'd send you to bed without supper without so much as a high octave. He would talk, in that brown-jacket tone of his, and he almost seemed more nervous about the spanking than you were. Osborne would try to reason with you. He would tell his side of the story and then thank you as he walked away. He was so dadgummed nice about it that he made you feel guilty, even if you weren't. Man, he was good.

That was the case again that Saturday morning, when Osborne approached this reporter about a story I had done on a former NU academic adviser who had threatened to blow the lid off an alleged Husker football academic scandal. The day I had gone to Lincoln to meet the adviser, Osborne had been busy. I called up Assistant Athletic Director Al Papik instead and called it good.

"I wish you would have called me before you did the story," Osborne said.

I told Osborne that next time I would. He thanked me and went on his way. Our paths wouldn't cross again until August 1991, when I showed up with a World-Herald press badge and introduced myself as the new sports columnist. This time Coach Cleaver shook my hand and said, "I know sometimes you'll be controversial, but as long as you get my side of the story first, that's fine with me."

Even when the story was about a hard-nosed kid from L.A. who had done wrong, and the story wasn't very complimentary to Osborne, he was right. I never heard a peep. Not one protest. Why? Later, Osborne said, "Because I felt like you got my side of the story."

Consistent. That's the word to best describe Osborne, with "courageous," "brilliant" and "sensitive" close behind. Osborne was all those things and more in an amazing 25-year career that was as understated as the man. And as he prepares to receive a final validation, by being inducted into the College Football Hall of Fame, what stands out the most about this unique, unwavering man was that he was consistent with his values and beliefs, whether it was dealing with people or pounding the Big Eight.

I hope that's how he's remembered, and not for a kid named Lawrence Phillips.

Yet I can't help but think the two will be tied together by some strange, invisible cord.

It's not fair. But ever since Phillips ran amok in Lincoln on that early September morning in 1995, and Osborne later granted him a pardon by bringing him back on the team, the two were destined to be linked through history. So loud was the national outcry, so stinging the criticism over Osborne's decision, that you knew Phillips would be attached to his hip as long as Phillips was playing. Or, worse, if Phillips were found in a gutter someday and never got around to repaying his former coach by joining the Good Citizen Club.

"I really don't know what my legacy will be," Osborne said. "You can't see the forest for the trees when you're close to something. I hope people will see me as an honest person with a good level of integrity."

The problem with today's world, with people, with news media knuckleheads like myself, is that we are drawn to the negative like a 15-year-old to Ricky Martin. We make Phillips the asterisk when for every L.P. or Christian Peter there were a few hundred good men who became men under Osborne's watch. The countless, faceless good guys who ate all their vegetables and graduated on time and never harassed society once. The guys who went on to become ministers and doctors and teachers and good fathers. They are the ones who should erase the asterisk and put the man's name in all caps: TOM OSBORNE, HALL OF FAME COACH AND MAN!

"When you win a national championship in 1994 and have another great team in 1995, and win another one in 1997, some people who hadn't paid

---

2011 INSIGHT *For years, or since that day in 1988, I had been waiting to use that hot-tub story. Sure, it happened. It's the absolute truth. It's too strange to make up. Anyway, Osborne going into the Hall of Fame seemed like the perfect time. The Lawrence Phillips hook was also timely and very useful here. It had been only four years since the L.P. days, but enough time to have Tom add some perspective to it. I liked how he compared it to calling a play. You take the information you have and make the best decision you can and live with it. That comparison was perfect and summarized his career and how he coached and has lived his life. You tell somebody to write the Tom Osborne story, and there's not going to be a lot of new material in there. But I had a couple of different angles here. That made this one memorable for me.*

attention to us in a while were starting to pay attention," Osborne said. "And Lawrence Phillips was the focus of that.

"For people at a distance, that's all they were seeing, and they were saying I was a win-at-all-costs coach. They didn't know that we went through the unity council on the thing, just like we had with everyone else. Nobody talked about how we stood by other guys, too, like Scott Baldwin, when he got in trouble. And he couldn't play anymore. Hopefully, the people closer to the program, the people who know me, they will know that that wasn't the deal."

A silent majority of the news media who didn't know Osborne believed that he was doing what he thought was right — even if they didn't agree with his method.

If it's any comfort to Osborne, the people who write college football history — and not necessarily make it — see Phillips as one chapter in an intriguing, if not colorful, career.

"It's a blip on the radar screen," said Mark Blaudschun, a Boston Globe writer who has covered college football for two decades and was one of Osborne's sternest critics in 1995.

"You can't diminish the consistency over that time span. He had some problems with players, but the overall mark of greatness is he did it year after year. And you argue that Nebraska could have won five national championships in the '90s."

Indeed. Combine Osborne's NCAA record of 25 consecutive nine-win seasons and bowl appearances with his three national titles, sterling academic record, his community service and his hand in developing strength and conditioning in college sports, and you have a guy who can sit with Amos Alonzo Stagg, Pop Warner, Bear Bryant, Bud Wilkinson and Joe Paterno any time. In the front row.

"It's nice to hear people say that," Osborne said. "But I really never thought about where I am in history. I still don't. Bob Devaney turned this program around. I didn't have to do that."

Osborne, who joins Devaney in the Hall of Fame, brings up a good point. He took the baton from Devaney in 1973, after the Huskers had ended their strongest era to date. You could say he had it easier, because Devaney had to start a winning tradition from scratch, but you wouldn't have had the gall to tell Osborne that in 1978, when Barry Switzer was running roughshod over T.O.'s legacy.

What's tougher? Lighting the torch or keeping it lit?

"Both are difficult," Osborne said. "When Bob came here (in 1962), he was one of the first to admit there were some really good players already here. What Bob did was instill pride and a belief they hadn't had before.

"In a sense, I was jump-started. I didn't have it like Bill Snyder at Kansas State, where things were at a terrible level. But it is true that expectations were great and the margin for error was slim. Those first years, I was trying to survive. Expectations were high and the history books show that in following a legend, the odds of being highly successful were long.

"It was difficult to measure up. Those first few years, when we didn't beat Oklahoma (1973 through 1977), it was like we didn't have a good year. I realized then we better beat Oklahoma or I was going to get run out of town."

You know what? He beat Oklahoma. But in 25 years, it's always something. Osborne couldn't beat Miami, he couldn't win a bowl game, he couldn't recruit speed or Florida, he couldn't throw the ball, he couldn't stay with the times. Of course, he did all that, and maybe he compromised his program's image by bringing some hard characters to Lincoln. But he never compromised on his belief that he could make a difference in their lives, just like the farm boys and the other city boys before them.

"I can remember a lot of plays that were bonehead calls but for some reason they worked. And there were plays I thought were good calls but turned out bad. You can look back on them with 20-20 hindsight, but hopefully there was a thread of consistency there that we always tried to do the right thing."

That's how Coach Cleaver should be, and will be, remembered.

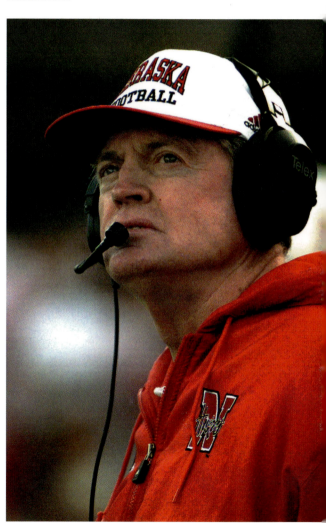

Tom Osborne, who entered the College Football Hall of Fame in 1999, won 255 games in 25 seasons.

SEPTEMBER 1, 1999 • NEBRASKA FOOTBALL

Tough Time for Solich

TOM SAID THERE'D be days like these.

But no matter how much prepping he got from former Nebraska football coach Tom Osborne, current NU coach Frank Solich probably never thought he'd be driving to Omaha to go to a high school to try to talk his No. 2 quarterback into staying in school.

If, in fact, that's what happened.

There's more speculation and rumors around whether Eric Crouch tried to quit the Huskers than an episode of "Entertainment Tonight." Here's what we know: Solich was at Millard North, and he didn't blow off a Big 12 teleconference and Extra Point Luncheon just to pop in and see how Fred Petito was doing.

Solich admitted he was off campus to talk to one of his players.

If Solich didn't know that damage control would be one of his job requirements, he found out quickly. The Husker Spin Doctors were at the Tuesday press conference. Crouch was a no-show. Solich took a question on Crouch and said, "Next question." How about them Hawkeyes?

But just because you name Bobby Newcombe your starting quarterback doesn't mean the controversy is over.

Solich is a good football man. He's a veteran. He knows the game. But there are head coaches, and there are assistants. More than anything else — the TV shows, the booster breakfasts, the press conferences, the recruiting trips — a head coach has to be able to make decisions.

Without hesitation. Without fail. Without hem or haw. Without looking back.

This is the most fascinating player competition at Nebraska in years, maybe since Van Brownson and Jerry Tagge. People are lined up behind their man. Heaven forbid what might happen should Nebraska actually lose a game.

So you wanted to be a head coach, Frank? Now you'll really find out what it's like.

Nebraska football coach Frank Solich was feeling the heat even before the first game of the 1999 season.

In Era of Skyboxes, Memorial Stadium Keeps Its Ambience

"NOT THE VICTORY, but the skybox; Not the game, but the mini-bar; In the drink the glory." — Unknown Skybox Owner

So I'd been up the spiffy new elevators. I tiptoed through the new press box, from which the Nebraska Cornhuskers are going to look like extras in the movie "Antz."

I gawked my way through the spacious, plush "Stadium View Club," which is big enough to hold most wedding receptions, not to give any prospective brides any ideas.

Saw the escalators. Yes, escalators. Perused one of the 42 skybox bachelor pads. Very groovy, baby.

But what I really wanted to see on the tour of the new, improved Memorial Stadium was a little history.

It was like Indiana Jones looking for the "Holy Grail," which, in this case, would be the inscription on the old southwest cornerstone that reads: "Not the victory but the action. Not the goal but the game. In the deed the glory."

Ah, there it is. Now they can play the game.

A new era is beginning. Call it the "Skybox Era." Directed by Steven Spielberg.

Nebraska's grand old lady has undergone a major face-lift. Talk about makeup. Memorial Stadium just got a $36.1 million concrete and steel job.

It looks like a professional stadium. It looks like something out of "Close Encounters of the Third Kind." The Mother Ship has landed. And the Lincoln skyline has changed forever.

But it works. The new addition is anything but subtle. Then again, neither is Big Red football. It screams, "HUSKER FOOTBALL IS REALLY BIG." Or "SOMETHING IMPORTANT IS HAPPENING HERE." Or "ICEBERG, STRAIGHT AHEAD."

This is Bill Byrne's ship of dreams and, sure, it had to be built. Nebraska was way behind the curve of college football's rich and famous and their fancy toys.

You want to raise money, you want to compete, you have to have one of these in your backyard. No argument there.

The trick was going to be whether Byrne could pull this off without trashing perhaps the most valuable entity of Nebraska football: tradition. You know, stuff like red on Saturdays, families and friends, Huskerburgers and blowouts of Kansas.

One of those most precious commodities is Memorial Stadium. Everyone from Knute Rockne to Joe Paterno has passed through. Not to mention every legend who ever donned the scarlet and cream.

Memorial Stadium is all about class and dignity, history and character. Memories. The challenge, then, was to build these donor condominiums and not chase out the ghosts.

Well, congratulations are in order to all. They did it. Beneath the fresh paint, Memorial Stadium still has that old-time ambience.

They've preserved the site of many classic battles.

Don't look now, but there might be a new one on the horizon. The downside to progress is that not everyone can afford it.

Nebraska's new era is one of two classes: have and have-not, royalty and serf, warm toes and frostbite. Will there be resentment?

You bet. But the "serfs" should be pleased to know that the condo owners have provided them with a stadium that is finally fan-friendly.

All the while, though, preserving the structure that holds so many memories. And all the old chills. Go to the southwest corner of the stadium, go up the new stairs leading into Gate Four, look up and you'll see it. "Not the victory but the action ... "

Some things are still free at Memorial Stadium. They're called goose bumps.

NOVEMBER 11, 1999 • NEBRASKA FOOTBALL

Quiet Husker Gets a Vote

WITH ALL DUE respect to the fine, upstanding and normally diligent folks at The World-Herald — the good people who sign the checks — I would like to take issue with our Nebraska football Millennium Team contest.

You forgot somebody.

The last name's Brown. No, not Kris Brown. Or Josh Brown. Or Lance Brown. Or Derek Brown. Or Todd Brown. Not big Bob Brown. And no, not Ralph Brown.

The name is Mike Brown.

You may have heard of him. He's the other Brown, the second Brown listed in the Husker secondary phone book. The Brown who lets his play do the talking for him.

The Brown you won't even find on The World-Herald's checklist of greatest all-time Huskers.

It's understandable, really. For one thing, M. Brown has the bad timing of having his career at Nebraska parallel that of Ralph, the preseason All-American, the four-year starter and school-record holder in pass breakups. You think Nebraska defensive back, and Brown, and you think Ralph. You wonder if Mike should have changed his name to "Green" or "Blue."

And then there's the anonymity that goes with his job description. Cornerbacks get all the glory (and grief) playing out there on the high wire, in front, for everyone to see.

Interceptions are sexier stats than tackles. Tackles are expected.

Tackles are part of the game. Except that Mike Brown has made 259 of them. That's good.

How good? Put it this way: Mike Brown not only deserves to be on any Husker millennium team, he probably should be in the top 10, next to Johnny Rodgers, Tommie Frazier, Turner Gill, Rich Glover, Tom Novak, Bobby Reynolds, Dave Rimington, Ed Weir, etc., etc.

In fact, it says here that Mike Brown ranks No. 2 behind Frazier on a list of the greatest Huskers of the 1990s, which is quite a list. But you don't have to take my word for it.

"He might be the best football player I've been around in college coaching," said NU defensive coordinator Charlie McBride, who has been at Nebraska since 1977.

"He might be the best football player I've ever played with," said Husker junior receiver Matt Davison, who played with Grant Wistrom, Scott Frost and Jason Peter.

Why?

"Instincts," Davison said. "You can't teach that. Nobody tackles like him. He's a motivator. He makes everyone around him better. He's just a ferocious football player."

He's also the most underrated Husker, maybe ever. But don't tell him that.

"Nah," Mike Brown says. "I don't feel that way. I don't even think about stuff like that. It's just the way I was brought up. I was taught by my parents to work hard and do your job every day, quietly, and do it well. Those values have carried on."

Brown learned well from his father, who has worked in a foundry for over 20 years, and his mother, a nurse. But other things couldn't be taught.

In four years, I've seen Brown run 50 yards across a football field to block a punt. I've looked on, in awe, as he drove a receiver five yards to get him out of bounds and stop the clock.

I've watched Brown breaking for a runner, smelling out screens like a crime dog.

"A lot of it is instinct," says Brown, smiling sheepishly. "It's natural. I can't explain it."

There have been only a handful of players in NU history who could single-handedly force their will upon a game.

M. Brown is one.

Safety Mike Brown "might be the best football player I've been around in college coaching," said NU defensive coordinator Charlie McBride.

140 • 20 YEARS WITH TOM SHATEL

'Good Coaching Is ... Invisible'

I HAVE A confession to make: I'm going to miss Terry Pettit.

Coaches come and go. Some of them tell you things you already know. Some tell you things you don't want to know. But Pettit is different.

After a conversation with the Nebraska volleyball coach, you feel like you've actually learned something. He's brilliant. He's fascinating. After you interview Pettit, you feel like you should keep the notes. Maybe write a book, something like "Tuesdays with Terry." Who else is going to talk to me about Norman Mailer?

Well, he did it again the other day in an interview, my last interview with Pettit as coach. After 23 seasons, Pettit is moving on.

And you want to know if Pettit will feel any different when he walks out of the Nebraska Coliseum, and the empire he's built, for the last time. You want to talk about his legacy. Oh, what a legacy.

Pettit has taken volleyball — the sport you play in gym class, the game you play on the beach or in the backyard — and developed it into a sport that fans follow and buy tickets to watch. He's raised the level of high school volleyball in Nebraska so high that his small-population state can feed his national-title program. Girls grow up wanting to play volleyball at NU. In fact, you can safely argue that Pettit's volleyball machine (along with Gary Pepin's track machine) has set the standard for women's athletics at Nebraska.

But, of course, none of that will be crossing Pettit's mind now.

"That's not my coaching mentality," Pettit said. "It's like a short story that Norman Mailer once wrote, about breaking up with a woman. As his girlfriend comes up and says it's the end of the relationship, he's writing down notes for the novel.

"I don't know how to do anything except stay focused on the task at hand. I do other things, husband, father. But I do them with the discipline of doing what we have to do for the next match. That may be my personality, but successful people I know tend to do it that way."

How would Pettit like to be remembered?

"Nebraska volleyball was modeled around a vision, a philosophy, that will continue," Pettit said. "It was built around opportunities and exceptional athletes growing in an environment where they learn to make better decisions.

"That's what separates us from being a great and good program. Training them to make decisions, not just in volleyball, but things that will work for them in life. It's not me. If a coach is the center of things like a three-ring circus, that doesn't happen. If everyone leaves the arena thinking they won because of the coach, you don't get very far. Good coaching is . . . invisible. It's teaching skills and then letting go, not doing it for them. Don't become the center of the enterprise. Certainly, (Tom) Osborne would fall into line with that."

Was this season, when a young team developed into a Big 12 champion, his best work?

"People listen to you every year," Pettit said. "It's like knocking on a door. Sometimes someone answers the door and says, 'I'm ready.' This group finally answered the door and said, 'We're ready.' As a coach, you have to have the discipline to keep knocking."

So when you walk off the floor, will you be thinking this could be the last time you do this? Will all the old players and faces flash back in your mind?

"I won't think about it," Pettit said. "If I was walking down the street and someone threw a baseball at me, I'd catch it. It's reflex. When that happens, the instincts will take over."

I'm really going to miss this man.

"If everyone leaves the arena thinking they won because of the coach, you don't get very far," Terry Pettit said.

TOM'S TAKE | REFLECTIONS ON

Ak Memories Worth Saving

THE SIGNS SAY "Pine Street." Maybe they should call it the Boulevard of Broken Dreams.

To get there, you can take Pacific Street east, past 72nd Street. Go two blocks, past the old Ak-Sar-Ben marquee sign that's gutted out, along the fence where the old barns and backside world lived in obscurity. Go to 67th Street, turn right and wind your way through progress. And then you see it.

The huge grandstand sits like a relic in an attic. Empty. Historic. It's the day before the Kentucky Derby, and the old Ak-Sar-Ben grandstand, surrounded by new office buildings, looks lonely. Searching for the past. Waiting for old friends who never come.

You turn right on Pine. You notice the green, grassy infield to your left and, suddenly, amazingly, it hits you.

Pine Street is on approximately the same spot as the racetrack, the same spot where those beautiful, powerful horses used to come thundering by, carrying jockeys, dreams and Omaha's place in the Midwest.

A different sort of horsepower zooms down this spot these days, complete with "Speed Limit 35" signs. You think Bersid or Gate Dancer ever held it back to 35 mph?

You close your eyes, just for a second (you're driving), and imagine you're a jockey and the stands are full and the Cornhusker Handicap is waiting on the other side. Somebody's coming. Fast. Who's that making a move on your right shoulder? Who Doctor Who?

No. It's a white Honda Civic, doing about 60.

You park your car outside the old grandstand. You walk up the ramp — admission's free now — and take a peek. The spot where they used to sell Racing Forms is now a puddle of water. Bird droppings own the place. A dozen or so birds fly out of a corner, scaring the daylights out of you. You walk into the apron area, where the railbirds, the real people, the hard-core gamblers, used to hang. In their place sit weeds and aging concrete.

You go back out and into the Coliseum, up the escalator and into the old grandstand. You see the signs "To Lawn Level," "To Grandstand" and "Approximate Odds, Minutes to Post, Race."

Workers put up fencing around the UNO soccer field north of the deserted Ak-Sar-Ben grandstand.

It's like being in a sunken ship, Omaha's Titanic. This is the Overlook Hotel in "The Shining." Empty but so many stories, so many ghosts, still living here. Close your eyes, and it's Derby Day, 1969, 1979 or 1985. There's a line at every window, a seat in every chair. The Cornhusker and Nebraska Rooms are jammed. Women are dressed to the hilt and men clutch Racing Forms and cigars. Ah, Ak-Sar-Ben. The folks who lived there still miss it.

"Just looking at it, sitting there by itself without a racetrack, it's a sickening feeling," said Butch Lindley, a longtime Ak supporter and worker. "So many memories come back. All those barns that were there. To be on the backside when the sun came up ... "

— **MAY 1, 1999**

THE CHANGING SPORTS LANDSCAPE 1999

1990s Were Special for Huskers

IT WAS THE best of times. It was the worst of times. It was the greatest decade in the history of Nebraska football.

The 1990s didn't start that way. Back in December 1990, a Husker fan had every right to be concerned. Colorado had won two straight from the Big Red. And Nebraska limped out of the season with losses to Oklahoma and Georgia Tech in which the Huskers all but admitted that they didn't care. What was next?

Well, for starters: four national championship games, three national titles and seven conference championships. All the while, Husker fans rode a roller coaster of emotions. They cheered for championships, they cried over the loss of a favorite son, they said goodbye to a favorite coach and wished another one a happy retirement.

They saw their national image go from national champions to a program of violence and back to proud champions. They watched with anxiety as a new coach found his way and exhaled when he proved he could win a couple of big ones.

They beamed as their program was the most dominant in college football for the decade. They felt fortunate to have seen some of the greatest players in NU history in one 10-year span; indeed, the Huskers' all-1990s team could almost hold up as an all-century team. Some fans kicked back on game days in a carpet-lined phenomenon called the "skybox."

Nebraska has never had a decade with so much sweet success. It may never have another one like it. Who knows? With increased recruiting limitations and a Big 12 Conference that looks to be as competitive as the New York Stock Exchange pits, it will be harder and harder for NU to repeat the kind of dominance it enjoyed in the 1990s. But after a reassuring 1999, Husker fans can always hope, as they remember a scrapbook full of memories, good and bad, sweet and bitter, and all unforgettable.

— DECEMBER 26, 1999

▶ **BEST VICTORY:** Nebraska's 24-17 victory over Miami in the 1995 Orange Bowl, which broke the Miami-in-Miami hex and gave Tom Osborne his first national title.

▶ **BEST MOVE:** Switching to the 4-3 defense, and recruiting faster linebackers, in 1992.

▶ **BEST CATCH:** Getting Tommie Frazier to sign a letter of intent in 1992.

▶ **BIGGEST SHOCKER:** Iowa State 19, Nebraska 10.

▶ **GREATEST ESCAPE:** Nebraska's overtime win at Missouri in 1997.

▶ **BEST-KEPT SECRET:** Osborne's retirement announcement.

▶ **WORST-KEPT SECRET:** Frank Solich hired to replace Osborne.

▶ **GREATEST INJUSTICE:** Frazier finishes second to Ohio State's Eddie George in the 1995 Heisman Trophy race.

▶ **BEST MEMORY:** Nebraska beats Tennessee 42-17 in the 1998 Orange Bowl to win a split of a national title in Osborne's last game.

▶ **WORST MEMORY:** Lawrence Phillips in 1995.

▶ **HAPPIEST MOMENT:** Osborne being carried off the field by his players after beating Miami in the Orange Bowl.

▶ **SADDEST MOMENT:** The day Brook Berringer died in a plane crash.

▶ **BIGGEST LUMP-IN-THE-THROAT, RED-EYE MOMENT:** Watching HuskerVision's excellent video tribute to Berringer at halftime of the 1996 spring game, two days after Berringer lost his life — especially the "Green Eggs and Ham" scene at the end.

▶ **MOST MELANCHOLY MOMENT:** Bob Devaney's funeral, where folks laughed as much as they cried.

▶ **GREATEST OFFENSIVE LINEMEN:** Three different Huskers — Will Shields, Zach Wiegert and Aaron Taylor — win Outland Trophies.

▶ **MOST SATISFYING MOMENT:** Defusing Florida's "Fun and Gun" offense in the 1996 Fiesta Bowl.

▶ **BEST SPEECH:** Scott Frost, begging for the coaches to vote Nebraska No. 1 after the 1998 Orange Bowl.

▶ **FUNNIEST NEW MASCOT WHO GROWS ON YOU:** Lil' Red.

▶ **TOUGHEST LOSS:** The ones to Texas, in 1996 and 1999.

▶ **TOUGHEST PERFORMANCE:** Phillips, playing with an injured thumb and carrying Nebraska, literally, between the tackles in a gutsy win at Kansas State in 1994.

▶ **MOST YOU-KNEW-IT-COULDN'T-LAST-FOREVER LOSS:** K-State 40, NU 30, in 1998.

▶ **BIGGEST OVERREACTION:** The criticism from fans, and from this columnist, of Frost after that Arizona State game in 1996.

▶ **BIGGEST STATEMENT:** Frost's performance to lead Nebraska to victory at Washington in 1997.

▶ **BEST CIRCUS ACT:** CBS's Bernard Goldberg, for his grandstanding performance at an Osborne press conference in 1995.

▶ **SIGNATURE PLAY:** Frazier's 75-yard touchdown run in the third quarter of the 1996 Fiesta Bowl, which broke eight tackles and symbolized Nebraska's drive through the '90s in one play.

▶ **BEST SIGN FOR THE FUTURE:** The Platte River-wide smile on Solich's face after beating Texas for the Big 12 title in December, the last month of the greatest decade.

MCBRIDE'S LAST GAME | SEARS LEADS JAYS TO TITLE | DANNY NEE'S EXIT | UNO HOCKEY MAGIC

2000

> "Who ever thought Nebraska would win the Big 12 tournament again and go to a super regional? Our seniors helped take this program to a new level. I told the young guys to learn from this. And go make the series next year for us."
>
> — NEBRASKA SHORTSTOP BRANDT VLIEGER

The Huskers are still seeing red over a column by Al Carter, the college baseball writer for the Dallas Morning News. Carter chastised Nebraska for saying in its media guide that last year's Big 12 tournament championship was the school's first conference baseball title in a half-century. Carter wrote, "Tournament trophies make nice doorstops. In a pinch, you can use them to pack the mound dirt. But what counts are those straight-up, regular-season conference titles, something no Big 12 school outside Texas has so far managed to win." Ouch. "That was a little arrogant and cocky," Nebraska coach Dave Van Horn said. "I don't think Texas or Texas A&M use them as doorstops. You get a ring and a trophy (with a tournament championship)."

The Jays lost to Auburn 72-69, and their magical ride was over, just like that, before half of the "Creighton NCAA" T-shirts were even out of the box. It was a great ride, but solace was hard to find in a Creighton locker room so quiet you could hear a tear drop. "It was a good season, but it will take a while for this one to go away," said senior forward Donnie Johnson (above left). "You always remember your last game."

He won't say it. He won't admit it. But at some point, as Nebraska tries to win a national volleyball championship, Terry Pettit will look down from the radio booth with an expression that says, "Man, I wish I was still out there." He is. The spirit, the legacy of the Husker volleyball coaching legend is alive and well in a season that is stunning, even by Nebraska standards. Congratulations, Terry. Sometimes the best legacy a coach can have doesn't lie behind him. It's not what he did. It's not the 697 wins for Pettit at Nebraska, the 21 conference titles, the six Final Fours, three national title games, one national championship. Not the sellout crowds. Not the building of a program that ranks with the best women's college programs in any sport. No, sometimes the measure of a coach is what happens after he leaves.

RED SEA IN SOUTH BEND | VOLLEYBALL CHAMPIONSHIP | ALAMO BOWL ROUT | CREIGHTON SOCCER

Anybody seen the prenup agreement? Just wondering, because the honeymoon is definitely over between Nebraska football coach Frank Solich and Husker fans. Now the marriage begins. Now they have to figure out if they can live with each other. Whatever happened to the patience and understanding that Husker fans like to boast about? Here's your irony: A sports columnist is asking fans to be patient and understanding with a coach. But please don't tell anybody. He could lose his second-guessing license.

Man, woman and child! He's all the way home! Perhaps that's what the late, great Lyell Bremser would have said on a day even Johnny Rodgers thought would never come. Rodgers, the greatest Nebraska football player in history, in fan polls and on turf, has made the College Football Hall of Fame. It's well-deserved. And so long overdue. It's been 28 years since Rodgers last played college football, too long for a man of Rodgers' stature and legend to wait. But wait and wait and wait he did, for various reasons, until the men who make such grandiose decisions each year finally relented and let one of the top 10 to 15 — arguably — players in college football history through the sacred glass doors. Where he belongs. How could they keep him out? How could they have a College Football Hall of Fame without Rodgers? You might as well not have Knute Rockne or Doak Walker or Tom Harmon or Earl Campbell or Bo Jackson, for that matter, in the building.

UNO 4, Michigan State 3. Even if you know nothing about hockey, that score caught your eye and snapped you to attention. UNO could beat Michigan State in tiddlywinks and it would be the biggest story of the day. "Mavs Upset Spartans!" "World To End ... Page Two." Call it the greatest win in UNO history. Until the next one.

Sure, Mike Schuchart believes in golf gods. Sooner or later, every golf junkie who's ever changed clothes out of his car and blown his beer money on a three-putt believes there's a guardian angel standing at the top of his swing. How else do you explain Schuchart's name on the first-round leader board of the Buy.com Omaha Classic? "I couldn't tell you," Schuchart said. How does a 39-year-old golf lifer finally get the guts to admit that it's time to get a real job so he can support his wife and son with a full-time salary — and then start hitting every green like he's Tiger Woods? "It's crazy," Schuchart said. No, it's just golf. Of all the sports, golf is the beautiful siren, teasing you, taunting you and then breaking your heart as you crash into the rocks. But it always brings you back. It always leaves you that sliver of hope.

20 YEARS WITH TOM SHATEL • 145

JANUARY 4, 2000 • NEBRASKA FOOTBALL

Mac's Saga: Style, Class

IF YOU ARE a Nebraska football fan, or just a fan of old-school values and bloodstains on football pants, then go to the kitchen and find a glass. Fill it with anything: orange juice, pop, preferably Old Style. Add a shot for good measure.

And raise a glass to Charlie McBride, a one-of-a-kind coach.

A retired football coach. McBride walked away from a long and colorful career as the leader of the Nebraska Blackshirt defense. He did it in typical McBride style, with no fanfare, all but sneaking out the back door on a late Fiesta Bowl night, when the crowds had long since gone home. He was replaced 12 hours later. Heck, Charlie's taken longer to kill a hangover.

We hardly even got to say goodbye. But that was only appropriate.

McBride was the Husker coach we never seemed to truly appreciate.

He was the coach fans loved to rag, the target of all fingers after a rare Husker loss because Tom Osborne's brilliant offenses couldn't be the reason. It was all unjustified, but that was OK, because nobody was harder on Charlie than Charlie. That was unjustified, too.

But that was Charlie. He was salt of the earth, regular guy, Joe Lunchbucket with a whistle. He didn't fit the button-down, cerebral image portrayed by Osborne and most of his staff. Charlie was gray sweatshirts and tough love. He taught his players how to tackle, cuss, fight back, love each other and respect the game. And how to win.

McBride was almost like a fictional character. He learned football in an era when crusty classics such as Woody Hayes, Frank Kush and Bob Devaney were the rule. McBride spewed venom at his share of players. But he would turn around and hug them. McBride's brutal honesty was not discriminatory.

Recruits always knew where Charlie stood. He once walked into a recruit's house and, before sitting down, said, "Here's the deal. Here's how far away Lincoln, Nebraska, is. If you're going to be home-

Charlie McBride hugs defensive tackle Jon Clanton after McBride's last game, a Fiesta Bowl victory over Tennessee.

sick, tell me now and I'll leave." And yet so many came to play for him. Five All-Americans, 17 pros.

He was a man of a thousand stories, most of which were suited for the end of the corner bar. One of Charlie's favorites was when he was facing Ohio State as a young assistant at Wisconsin in the early 1970s. The legendary Hayes, a buddy of McBride's father, was leaning on the goal post before a game. He saw Charlie and said, "Hey, McBride, are you as dumb as your old man?"

Charlie was no dummy. He was crazy like a fox. He coached emotion, heart and instincts. But he knew how to break down an offense. Just ask Steve Spurrier, Phil Fulmer, Bobby Bowden and others who got drummed by NU in the 1990s.

Speed and talent made McBride a genius in the '90s, but he was the same blood and guts he always had been, when NU was putting its best athletes on offense. He blamed himself for NU losing the national title in 1983. He never got over that one.

He took too much blame and never enough credit. And he wouldn't have had it any other way.

He was Nebraska's backbone, even while his was going out on him. Charlie was the attitude in this program, the raw nastiness in the game that fans don't like to acknowledge but appreciate just the same. But cry not for Charlie. He went out his way, surrounded by his favorite defense, guys cut from his gray cloth. Charlie silenced Major Applewhite, took Tee Martin down and decided it won't ever get better than this. Know what? It won't.

In the end, McBride was surrounded by the people and the game he loved. Who needs a parade? A toast is more fitting.

Here's to you, Charlie. Nebraska football won't ever be the same.

CU's Sears Stands Tall

ST. LOUIS

HE WOULD NEVER admit it. But Dana Altman knew. Deep down, the Creighton coach knew it could end like this, with Bluejay students storming the court and the Jays taking turns climbing up the ladder to cut down the nets to celebrate another Missouri Valley Conference tournament title and a return trip to the NCAA tournament.

All last week, Altman had that silly, cat-that-swallowed-the-canary grin on his face. To be sure, Altman wears a perpetual poker face. If he won the Nebraska lottery, he'd act like he just lost to Drake. But last week Altman acted like he knew something. It was the same sort of look Tom Osborne used to have before his Huskers beat Colorado or Florida.

Maybe Altman felt good about having senior forward Donnie Johnson healthy for the first time all year. Maybe he knew his team was as good as, or better than, any team in the Valley.

Or maybe he could see Ryan Sears growing up.

That's what we saw as Creighton, which lost two key seniors and finished fourth in the Valley regular-season race, returned to the NCAAs in stunning yet workmanlike fashion.

Sears, the Jays' junior point guard, had the game of his career. Creighton beat Southwest Missouri State 57-45, and Sears was the difference. It was his energy. His three-point shooting. His relentless defense. And, yes, his leadership.

We can make too big a deal about leadership, like it's passed on in a will by the previous senior class. We almost force it upon young athletes, who often aren't ready to handle it. But leadership often is something that just happens, at some point, inside someone. It can be a reaction you can't predict. But when it happens, it's a beautiful thing to watch.

Sears is listed at 6 feet, 185 pounds, but those figures might be a projection for 2002. He looks like the kid who sneaked into the pickup game because his big brother lost a bet.

But this weekend, Sears blossomed. He was named the tourney's most valuable player, and nobody else was even close.

In the title game, Sears had 15 points — including four three-pointers — four assists, five rebounds and three steals. But numbers don't tell the story. Sears led his team in heart, soul and big plays. Huge plays. That's how the Jays won this weekend. They bucked up on every single possession. They outfought, outrebounded, outdefended and outshot Bradley, Indiana State and SMS. After a season of ups and downs, they just refused to lose.

"Coach didn't say anything, but I think he knew there was a toughness about this team," said senior guard Matt West. "And we had the maturity to do this."

Much of that attitude came from Sears. Guards aren't supposed to dominate basketball games, but Sears broke the rule.

Point guard Ryan Sears contributed 15 points, four assists, five rebounds and three steals in Creighton's victory over Southwest Missouri State in the Valley basketball tournament final.

Sad Ending for Nee, NU

KANSAS CITY, MO.

IT WAS HARD to watch. It was hard to stomach. It was a classic example of why there will be a coaching change next week. Frankly, it was one of the darkest days in Nebraska basketball history, this 63-55 loss to Baylor and the end of Danny Nee's career.

No coach wants to walk off the court like this. But Nee's last game was a microcosm of his 14-year career: The Huskers built a lead in the first half, peaked midway through the second with a 14-point lead, couldn't sustain it and had it all crash down at the end.

Nee went down to his postgame press conference, alone, no players. Why bother? What could anyone say? The press conference lasted three questions. The last was about Nee's job status. He gave his standard "I'll talk to Bill Byrne" answer. Then, he left and, lo and behold, there was Byrne waiting to meet him. They met behind a blue curtain, in secrecy.

The flies on the wall inside that curtain had no comment.

Nee stopped to talk to a couple of writers, then was whisked through the pressroom up to an elevator, where he went to do his postgame radio show. Later, word circulated that Nee told radio analyst and director of basketball operations Nick Joos that it was over. But by the time that word had spread, nobody could ask Nee about it.

He was gone.

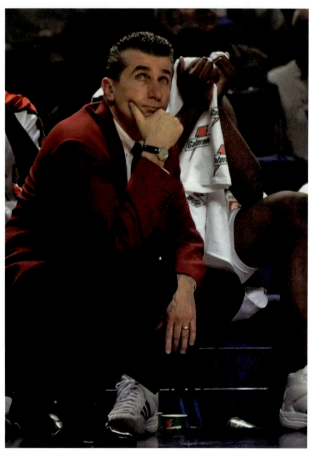

In 14 seasons, Danny Nee recorded 254 victories and took the Huskers to five NCAA tournaments.

What Could Have Been

THE YEAR WAS 1940. And Forrest "Phog" Allen, the Kansas basketball coach and one of the greatest coaches in college basketball history, was mad.

Allen had been removed as athletic director. So he wrote a letter to Nebraska Athletic Director Major L. McC. Jones. Phog wanted to come coach the Huskers.

Well, as history shows, Phog didn't get the job. It went to A.J. Lewandowski, who went 24-63 in five years. Phog at Nebraska? Who knows? Maybe Nebraska would have joined Kentucky, North Carolina and UCLA as basketball blue bloods.

Phog thought it could happen. In Blair Kerkhoff's book, "Phog Allen, the Father of Basketball Coaching," Phog lauded Nebraska's potential as a basketball giant. He said NU had everything you needed. Yes, including football.

In his letter, he wrote, "The prestige of one sport, especially football, aids the other sport considerably in national ranking."

— **MARCH 12, 2000**

Mavs, Crowd Make Magic

WELL, IT LOOKS like everyone better vote for the new arena and convention center. Because the old Civic Auditorium came down last night.

This was March Mavness. This was insane. This wasn't Omaha. This was Detroit. Philadelphia. Montreal. This was Chicago Stadium, the old Chicago Stadium, on steroids.

This was magic, pure and simple. The UNO hockey team, which is growing faster than a 6-foot 13-year-old, provided the magic. And the crowd threw it right back at them. They were partners on a singular mission. They were in perfect synch. They kept batting the magic back and forth to each other like a beach ball.

And both outdid themselves. The Mavs took care of Bowling Green 3-1 in a Central Collegiate Hockey Association playoff game. The Mavs, in their third year as a program and first year in the league, are going to the CCHA Final Four at Joe Louis Arena in Detroit.

Omaha has had its Knights and its Lancers. But this had to be one of the greatest, loudest, most special nights in Omaha hockey history. There were more people yelling, screaming, chanting and standing than you could shake a high-stick at.

"It was unreal," said sophomore Jeff Hoggan. "I can't even describe it."

The whole evening was wild. It was like something out of a dream. Veteran observers were saying it was the loudest noise in this building since Creighton's famous Larry Bird game against Indiana State in 1978.

They were just nuts. Totally nuts. The fans got here early. They stood and cheered during warm-ups. They got louder and louder. They kept standing and standing. There were 8,314 of them but they sounded like 18,000. So much for people not wanting to drive downtown. So much for good-life Nebraskans sitting on their hands. These people came to party and win a hockey game and they weren't going to leave until both were on ice.

This is what you call a home-ice advantage. This atmosphere is why UNO is going to rise like a hot Internet stock in the CCHA. The word is going to get around about this night, how 8,314 people lifted a team riddled with injuries and fatigue, playing its fourth intense game in five nights, to glory. Even the milk bottles will be hoarse today.

"The crowd was stirring," UNO coach Mike Kemp said. "It was the best crowd I can think of since opening night here (in 1997) against Manitoba. It was better than any place I've been, better than any place I can think of."

Their reward was victory. They saw a whale of an effort all around, terrific game between two evenly matched sides. Bowling Green goaltender Tyler Masters was a wall, stopping 39 shots. UNO's Kendall Sidoruk stopped 25. Back and forth the teams went, skating out of desperation, trying to get to "The Joe." Is there anything better than playoff hockey?

No, nothing better, especially when it's wrapped in a fairy tale. The winning goal was scored by Hoggan, who has scored the last three game-winning goals, who was told last December he would have to miss the season with a torn anterior cruciate ligament in his left knee. It would have sidelined Eric

Jeff Hoggan's goal sends the Civic Auditorium crowd into a frenzy.

Crouch or Ben Walker. But in hockey, the movements on skates allow an athlete to skate on the injury. That doesn't mean it doesn't hurt.

"It comes and goes," Hoggan said. "But on a night like this, it's easier to take."

It was the kind of night they'll be talking about for years. The accomplishment. Hoggan's game-winner trickling past Masters. And the crowd. They just wouldn't stop. It was 11 p.m., the place was empty, and you could still hear "U-N-O, U-N-O" somewhere in the arena.

"I always said I thought something special was going to happen to this team," said captain Jeff Edwards.

2011 INSIGHT *I didn't bring my computer to UNO's CCHA play-in game against Bowling Green. I was heading out to Minneapolis the next day for Creighton's NCAA tourney game against Auburn. I hadn't done a whole lot on hockey, but I wanted to see the playoff game live. There's nothing like playoff hockey. Well, then the game started. And the crowd started. It was unlike any crowd I'd heard at a winter sporting event in Omaha or Lincoln. Just crazy loud. When UNO won, and they turned the Civic into Chicago Stadium, I knew what I had to do. I called the office at 9:30 p.m. and said "I'm writing," which the editors always appreciate at 9:30 p.m. Then I went out to my car and got my laptop out of the trunk and came back in and knocked this column out in about 40 minutes. The moral to the story: Always bring a computer to playoff hockey. Or at least keep one in the trunk.*

MAY 12, 2000 • NEBRASKA BASEBALL

Komine and NU Dream Big

THE ONLY THING harder than hitting Shane Komine is pronouncing his last name.

He's been called "Co-Mine." "Co-Meaney." "Co-manay." There are more mispronunciations of his name than the Nebraska sophomore right-hander has "out" pitches.

Just call him "co-ME-nay." That's "nay," as in May.

As in the month of the season when a college team can feed off the energy and confidence from a dominant No. 1 pitcher.

Komine is the hottest arm in college baseball. He leads the nation with 131 strikeouts. His ERA is 1.66, and he's given up just two homers in a sport that should be renamed "Home Run Derby."

But the magic in Komine is how he's transformed this Nebraska baseball team.

It's a team with everything: hitting, fielding, speed, depth, chemistry. The best teams generally have that. But what separates pretenders from contenders, May from June, is pitching. You don't need to be the Atlanta Braves. Sometimes all it takes is one ace to bluff your way to Omaha.

The Huskers have that ace. They know he'll throw strikes. They know he won't give up many runs. Komine's arm is like having "Excalibur." The Huskers might just use it to cut a swath 40 miles east.

"It gives any team a chance to go deep in the playoffs," Nebraska pitching coach Rob Childress said. "It gives you so much confidence."

This year everyone's dreaming big. The reason is the little big man from Hawaii. His back is back, thanks to a summer of surfing. Now he hangs 10 strikeouts most every game.

"The difference is, he's healthy," Childress said. "But we didn't know he would be so dominant. As the conference season has gone along, a lot of it has been his reputation. Most teams won't pitch their No. 1 guy against him."

You'd never guess why. Komine, 5-9 and 165 pounds, looks like the batboy. He couldn't stare down a fly. He doesn't throw heat down a batter's neck. He's never laid a hand on a water cooler. You

Shane Komine, a two-time All-American, led Nebraska to two College World Series appearances.

don't know what he's thinking. Which is exactly the point.

"I'm not one to show emotions," Komine said. "I won't pump my fist or stare down some hitter so he can come back the next time and hit one out on me. Why would you do that? I like to keep them guessing."

Komine will make a great poker player some day. He's got the full house. Komine has five pitches, uncanny for a college pitcher: fastball, curve, change-up, slider and a split-fingered fastball he learned from a former California Angels pitching coach at a camp in Hawaii.

Komine can't remember the man's name, but it doesn't matter now. Komine's new mentor is Childress, who is teaching him the art of pitching, although at times it seems like chess. Childress calls the pitches from the dugout, but occasionally he'll let Komine do the honors. He's either creating a young Bobby Fischer or Greg Maddux. Or both.

"Shane is like a surgeon," Childress said. "He doesn't have one super pitch; he's got five good ones. And he can throw them all for strikes. He's very cerebral. He's like a sponge. We give him an idea on what pitch to throw, and he knows what to do with it."

The key to Komine's season, though, may be that he's able to do it.

"It's all due to the fact that I don't have a bad back," Komine said.

Which will come in handy if he's going to carry Nebraska through the crucial part of the season. As in May.

AUGUST 7, 2000 • GOLF

Chris Zambri putts out on the 18th hole on the final day of the Buy.com Omaha Classic.

18th Green Is the Place to Be

THE COLLEGE WORLD SERIES. A Saturday at Ak-Sar-Ben. UNO and Lancer hockey nights. Creighton hoops. Fireworks night at the Omaha Golden Spikes. The Rump Roasters.

Now let us add another staple to our sporting traditions: the 18th green at the Omaha Classic.

These guys are good. This tournament isn't so bad itself. The Omaha Classic is growing faster than the Champions Club rough. Just like the Buy.com pros, the Omaha Classic is getting closer to the big tour.

The reason would be the 18th hole.

They say that you can walk up the 18th hole on Sunday at the Omaha Classic, close your eyes and not know what tour you're on. OK, you know you're not at Pebble Beach or Hilton Head. But for all you know you could be at the Buick Classic or the Byron Nelson. And, by the way, you might want to keep your eyes open. Makes it easier to hit the green.

The point is, what Tournament Director Mike West and his staff have done in five short years is nothing short of amazing. They've created a monster on stilts.

The 18th green at Champions Club on the first Sunday in August is fast becoming tradition. It's a big-time scene, from the ring of skyboxes to the mini-bars in each skybox to the marshals holding up those "Quiet" signs around the green. Wonder if those marshals get to take those signs home. They'd be great at the dinner table when the kids get out of control.

There were an estimated 8,000 fans around the green on Sunday afternoon — about the size of a UNO hockey crowd — and it was a beautiful sight to see. Just ask the PGA Tour. The 18th green is so impressive that the tour wanted a photo taken on Sunday. It wants to paste the shot up on its roaming Buy.com truck, the one that says, "These guys are good."

This crowd is good. The 18th green is now the signature thing about the Omaha Classic. Sure, the players love the range, the card room and the Champions people and, of course, the 19th Hole. But when they think of Omaha, when they say it's the place to be on the Buy.com tour, they're seeing the 18th green. Too often the Buy.com players feel like forgotten men. The 18th green gives them PGA Tour-type love. It's the reason Omaha will always attract the cream of this tour.

Sure, Omaha loves a party. But the folks gathered in the natural amphitheater at Champions are golf-friendly, too. They have the golf clap down. They know when to be quiet and when to pop the tops to their beers. Omaha's junior golfers are particularly savvy. They swarm each golfer for golf balls and autographs as he leaves the scorer's tent.

Omaha's sports summer is all but over, and the Omaha Classic is entrenched as a nice bookend to the CWS. Unless, of course, the Beef are in the playoffs.

SEPTEMBER 10, 2000 • NEBRASKA FOOTBALL

South Bend Is Awash in Red

SOUTH BEND, IND.

OVERRATED? NOT A CHANCE. Those Nebraska fans are the real deal. They stormed Notre Dame Stadium like Omaha Beach. They set up tents. They overran the bars, coffee shops and hotel lobbies. They painted the town, and the stadium, red. Yes, those wacky, out-of-control, insatiable Husker fans are No. 1 in college football.

Their team is another story.

A story-in-progress, mind you. Nebraska beat/survived Notre Dame 27-24 in overtime on a glorious Saturday that produced a glorious game for storied programs that have waited so long to be reintroduced.

The No. 1 Huskers found themselves waking the echoes, shaking down the thunder and raising the eyebrows of poll voters from here to the Orange Bowl.

Are they a national championship squad as we speak? Probably not. Were they overrated? Who knows?

Who cares?

What mattered most, besides a very classic scene, is that the Huskers are 2-0 and know so much more about their identity. That's why you schedule Notre Dame.

Forget the predictions. Forget the expectations. Championships aren't won on paper — or in the paper. They're won when every Irish spirit, alive or otherwise, is roaring down and you've got to make nine yards. That's when you find out who you are.

Nebraska center Dominic Raiola celebrates quarterback Eric Crouch's game-winning touchdown against Notre Dame in overtime. Notre Dame officials said the game was witnessed by about 25,000 Husker fans — a record number for visiting fans in the stadium.

2011 INSIGHT *Of all the things that have happened in and around Nebraska football in the last 20 years, I think this game is underrated as a special event or memory. It's like pages of a scrapbook that get torn out or stuck together. I can still see and hear Nebraska's trip to Notre Dame. I can see that red – everywhere. Not just like a blanket over half of Notre Dame Stadium, but everywhere outside. I can still see the giant tailgate tent with the "Fahey For Mayor" sign out front. Yes, that Mike Fahey. There were two stories in this game, the crowd and the game. And I could have written a column about each. I tried to do both here, and it was probably a mistake. The overtime win was not against a great Irish squad, but it was thrilling nonetheless in this venue. NU would go on to lose at Oklahoma and Kansas State that year, miss the Big 12 title game for the next several years, lose big at Colorado and to Miami in the Rose Bowl the following year. That's why this one gets lost. But this day deserves to be remembered.*

DECEMBER 10, 2000 • COLLEGE AWARDS SHOW

Time to Slay the Dragon

"ARE YOU OK?" Chris Fowler asked.

Well, let's see. I'm standing on stage at the ESPN College Football Awards Show. I'm about to go on national television for the first time in my life. And I actually have to look into the cameras and speak. I feel like I'm naked up here. Everybody's laughing. I can't remember my lines, and even if I could, there's no way I'm going to be able to spit them out.

And so here comes Fowler, the smooth and likable personality for ESPN College Football, seconds before he "throws it to me." And he wants to know if I'm "OK?"

"Sure, I'm fine," I lied.

Everybody is afraid of something. Failure. Commitment. Heights. Beano Cook. We all have a dragon that torments and taunts. The thought of having to face that dragon can make you crazy. But one day you have to face it. It may not work. But you have to try. You can't run forever. That's no way to live.

I stutter. There, I admitted it. That's not exactly something you can hide. Unless, of course, you never talk, which, believe me, is something I've considered. Again, that's no way to live. You have to live with yourself.

For the past year, I've served as president of the Football Writers Association of America. It's an incredible honor. But there's a catch. Each December, you present the FWAA's Outland Trophy award. That means going on stage. On ESPN. For the last two years, I've dreaded this moment. But I had to do it. Because it was my duty as president. Because the dragon couldn't win again.

My dragon is going on stage. Talking in front of groups. I would rather pull a coach or player aside than ask a question in front of a press conference. How would I survive this?

Two months earlier, John Vassallo, the coordinating producer of the ESPN show, sent me a copy of the Outland speech. It was a nice 60-second bit on the history of the award. I phoned him back and explained I would be more comfortable with just saying "And the winner is ..." I explained that I stuttered. Had stage fright. Vassallo graciously agreed.

All week, I practiced my line out loud. You should have seen the looks from folks concerned about the man who was talking to himself. I thought about breaking the ice with a couple of jokes. I would start out, "And the Oscar goes to ..." or "Hey, folks, did you hear the one about the Tennessee lineman?"

None of that happened. An amazing thing did. As I was sitting in the audience, waiting to be called up and wondering how I would live this down, I wondered: Why did I have to stutter? Why couldn't I be like everyone else? The answer was, because nobody's like everybody else. My mother stuttered. Her father did, too. That's who they were. It's who I am. If you trip and fall in front of millions, so what? It's what I do. I'll probably do it tomorrow, too.

The next thing I knew, I was on stage. Talking. I don't remember a thing, except somehow saying, "On behalf of the Football Writers, it's my pleasure to announce the winner of the 2000 Outland Trophy is John Henderson....Tennnnnn...essee!"

As I walked off the stage, someone said, "That wasn't so bad, was it?" Well, yes, it was. But here's the thing: It was worth it. I discovered two things can happen when you stare into the eyes of your dragon: 1, You find out who you are and that it's not a bad thing. 2, You find that the dragon isn't so big and bad himself.

Take it from me. It's easier done than said.

"On behalf of the Football Writers, it's my pleasure to announce the winner of the 2000 Outland Trophy is John Henderson....Tennnnnn...essee!"

2011 INSIGHT *I've heard people say I should write about my life more, my family, my kids, my stuttering. I just don't think it's that interesting to people. That's not my job. I wasn't hired to write about myself. But a friend of mine convinced me that once in a while is good, that you open up a window into yourself for people. So this was one time I decided to open the window. Stuttering is not a painful topic for me to discuss. I don't care about it. At least, that's what I always told myself. Looking back on this column, I think I may have been living a myth. At the time of this column, I didn't admit it. And maybe I didn't even know it. But I regret glossing over the entire introduction I had to say on ESPN. I wish I'd read the whole thing and stumbled over myself on national TV and made the entire country wait for me to spit it out. This brilliant deduction didn't come to me until several years later, after I had interviewed another stutterer, Nebraska guard Matt Slauson. I wrote about that experience, too. But I remember watching Slauson do the postgame interview thing after a Nebraska game, and he was up there stuttering and falling over words. I got really uncomfortable. But as I looked around at the other Nebraska media, nobody else seemed to care or pay attention to Slauson's stutter. That was a real revelation to me: I've held back at press conferences myself because I was afraid of the reaction. The Slauson press conference made me realize it really was no big deal. I'd like to have that ESPN experience over. This column, too.*

DECEMBER 19, 2000 • NEBRASKA VOLLEYBALL

Huskers Enjoy Incredible Ride

WELL, NOW THE pressure's really on in the Alamo Bowl. This Northwestern game is huge. The Big Red really, really needs a victory. For recruiting. For pride. For the seniors.

Mostly, because Nebraska needs a football team its volleyball team can be proud of.

How 'bout them Huskers? And please notice we didn't say "Lady Huskers" or "Nebraska Women" or "Spikers." But feel free to say "world-class athletes." Or "champions." Or "national champions," for that matter.

You can call them "Huskers," too. They are, indeed.

Members of this NU volleyball squad showed they are all those things, and more, after a superlative season ended over the weekend in a riveting, breathless and glorious crescendo at the NCAA volleyball championship. The Huskers finished 34-0. It was their coach's first season. Most players on the team are underclassmen. What an incredible ride.

But perhaps the most amazing thing they did was remind us how far they — and we — have come. How far gender equity has come.

I saw it everywhere I looked all weekend, from the opening "kill" to the celebration at the Bob Devaney Sports Center. We watched. We cheered. We didn't see women. We weren't looking for ponytails. All we saw was a color. Red.

And, most of the time, I couldn't believe what I was seeing.

Not on the court. In the living room. I watched that championship match on ESPN2 with my 68-year-old father. He's not a Husker fan. He just moved to Omaha. He's a sports fan. He's a "the-way-it-used-to-be-and-ought-to-be" sports fan. Hates domes and turf. Loves grass fields, throwing the ball to the ref after you score and ESPN Classic.

In that generation, not everyone approved of girls playing sports. It just wasn't done. But as we sat watching the Huskers rally, he made a big admission: He enjoyed watching the women play now. They played the game with such heart.

Husker athletes celebrate another national title, this one in volleyball.

Skill. Fundamentals. And no showboating. He saw them as athletes.

How can you not?

Meanwhile, my wife the Husker fan was cheering and yelling for each point, as loud and proud as she does for Eric Crouch and Carlos Polk. Why not? They're all Huskers.

There are some guys I know. They like to talk sports and golf and politics. They watch "Hardball" every day. They turn it over to the Fox News channel to see which news babe is on next. Well, these guys were flipping channels and calling The World-Herald to see what channel the volleyball match was on. When they found it, they were yelling "Go Huskers" like it was the Orange Bowl. Or, Alamo Bowl.

Let's be honest. A lot of folks got caught up in NU volleyball because they were winning. Sure, there is something about these ladies, with their big smiles and home-grown work ethic. But Husker fans love a winner, no matter what the gender.

Which is exactly the point.

There is no place like Nebraska. Especially when it comes to gender equity. It doesn't make sense. This is a football school.

The women are supposed to be the enemy. They're cutting into funding and scholarships. At a lot of schools, the two sides are like Republicans and Democrats right now. They talk a good game. But they hate each other's guts.

Gender equity works. We see it all the time in Nebraska. We saw it again last weekend. We saw it on the beaming faces, in the hugs and the tears. And the trophy.

"I've been in locker rooms after football won a national championship, and the sheer joy is just the same," Athletic Director Bill Byrne said. "You dedicate your whole career to a goal, and when you achieve it, it's absolutely the best. It's a joyous celebration, no matter what the gender."

Thanks, Huskers, for the reminder.

DECEMBER 31, 2000 • NEBRASKA FOOTBALL

Huskers Vent Frustrations

SAN ANTONIO

THERE YOU ARE. A Nebraska offensive line that was going to four-wheel this offense all the way to January.

A defensive line that gave a great push and shove.

Dan Alexander breaking into the great wide open.

Bobby Newcombe making a catch, a juke, a spin and a dash to the end zone.

A Blackshirt defense with all its bases, and receivers, covered.

"Special" teams.

And, finally, that long-awaited pass by Newcombe. For a touchdown, in fact, to Matt Davison.

And wasn't that Newcombe sprinting downfield to jump into Davison's arms? And Eric Crouch joining them in a group hug? Hope somebody had a camera.

It was that kind of warm and fuzzy scene in the Alamodome. Nebraska put the wood to Northwestern — ouch! — in a big way, 66-17, to win the Alamo Bowl.

The Huskers beat the Wildcats like a piñata, over and over and over, until the game finally broke apart and spilled all over the rug.

What did it mean? Nada. Nobody's at the Orange Bowl saying, "Boy, I'm glad we don't have to play those guys." Nobody's going to vote Nebraska No. 1 next year based on this game. It looked like a second straight year in which the Huskers went to a bowl that wasn't in the plans and took out their frustrations against an overmatched opponent.

That they put it all together for one game so decisively can only add to their fans' frustrations. Where was this kind of game when they needed it? In Norman? Manhattan?

Well, obviously, the Huskers' problem this year was that they didn't play in the Big Ten.

Northwestern was a co-champion of the Big Ten. In fact, if the Wildcats had won at Iowa, they would have gone to the Rose Bowl.

They actually complained about having to fall to the Alamo Bowl, as if it were beneath them.

The only thing that was beneath the Wildcats was the hard green turf as they got their faces rubbed in it.

Nebraska's Bobby Newcombe cuts upfield to score a touchdown on a pass from Eric Crouch in the second quarter.

20 YEARS WITH TOM SHATEL • 155

TOM'S TAKE | REFLECTIONS ON

What's Ahead for Arena?

HMMMM. WAS IT fate? Or mere coincidence?

Maybe just a little of both on the first day of the rest of Omaha's life. The day after the city voted to build a new arena and convention center in downtown Big O.

And who should be in our fair city? None other than Dennis Poppe, the NCAA's director of championships. Yes, the man who can wield heavy influence on where NCAA championships end up. Yes, Dennis Poppe, Omaha's No. 1 fan at the NCAA.

Poppe was at Rosenblatt Stadium to announce a new "Opening Ceremony" night for this year's College World Series. But the fact that Poppe was here the day after the arena was approved, well, the irony was thicker than the grease on a funnel cake.

Anyway, Poppe couldn't make any promises on this day; each sport has a committee that chooses its championship venues. But you take the twinkle in his eye, the optimism in his tone and the fact that the NCAA loves how Omaha runs the CWS, and you do the math.

"There are 81 different championships," Poppe said. "Can you host water polo here? Skiiing? We might be able to do fencing here."

Well, the streets of the Old Market would make a great fencing venue. Maybe we'll just stick to basketball, hockey, wrestling and volleyball for now.

"I think it's very positive," Poppe said. "I live in a city (Indianapolis) that came alive because of sports facilities. You only have to go to Indy to see the results of a proactive city. Omaha has the commitment and the wherewithal to support events. They know how to run an event. All they needed was the facilities."

In other words, let's get those NCAA applications in the mail.

This will be great fun. I'll make you a prediction. This new facility will transform Omaha. There's an energy in this city right now looking for an outlet. Omaha will go from passive to aggressive, overnight.

Welcome to the 21st century. Welcome to the first day of the rest of your life.

— MAY 11, 2000

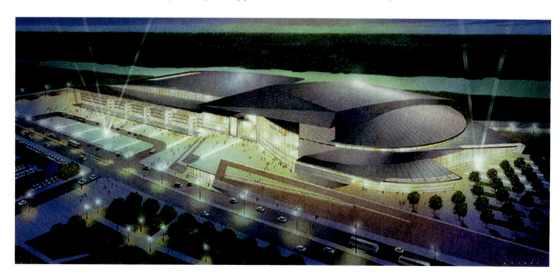

An artist's early rendering of the proposed arena and convention center for downtown Omaha.

156 • 20 YEARS WITH TOM SHATEL

THE CHANGING SPORTS LANDSCAPE 2000

Bluejay Run Is Amazing

AS I WATCHED the home team play for a national championship on ESPN, two things came immediately to mind:

1. The world would be a better place if every sport had soccer's running clock.

2. Creighton athletics is one of the truly great stories in college sports.

It's an amazing thing, this Creighton athletic department. These are amazing people, these Bluejays. They are the Green Bay Packers or Kansas City Royals of college sports. They are a low-budget outfit competing on a big-budget playing field. They should be the bottom-feeders of Division I. Everybody's Homecoming opponent.

Their athletic budget is $6 million (one-sixth the size of Nebraska's massive $37 million budget), with $2 million going to scholarships for 14 sports. They don't take in Prop 48s. Their academic standards are higher than NCAA requirements. You can't hide in an "Anatomy of the Jock" class or "Sports Illustrated Swimsuit 101."

They're a small Jesuit college in modest downtown Omaha stuck in a Division I recruiting no-man's land. They play in a league, the Missouri Valley, where the devil's bought another soul every time a Valley team plays on national TV.

Their women's basketball and volleyball teams play real-live games in high school gyms. Good thing the prom's in the spring, or Connie Yori's girls might never get a home game in. And yet those girls already have beaten Nebraska.

Then there's Jack Dahm's baseball team, whose field still lacks lights and doesn't have enough money to finish a renovation, yet has been to the past two NCAA tourneys.

And there's Dana Altman's basketball team, which is 13th in the Sagarin power ratings. But Altman has to beg a decent Division I team to come play in Omaha.

And Bret Simon's soccer team, which plays on a home field so bad it can't play host to an NCAA tournament match. All it did was get to the national championship game.

Nobody in college sports gets more out of less than Creighton.

"I do think it's amazing," Athletic Director Bruce Rasmussen said. "But when you look at our quality of academics, we have a good community to sell. And quality coaches who care about kids and do things the right way. So, in another way, it's not a surprise."

Maybe not, because what they lack in concrete resources, they make up for in human resources. Creighton is good people. These are winners, not whiners. No excuses. There is a philosophy that you may be outmanned, so outwork, out-teach and outfox everyone.

They hire good teachers. Altman and Simon, for what they have to recruit to, are among the best.

"It's a servant attitude," Rasmussen said. "What can I do for you now? And I think we've developed a good atmosphere. My grandpa said, 'A good job is a job where you work with good people and you like coming to work.' I think our coaches like coming to work here."

But camaraderie doesn't pay the bills. Creighton can't rest on its overachievements or it could get buried. CU ranks in the middle of the pack in the Valley in facilities. That's not good enough. It needs to get its women's teams out of the high school gyms, get its men's hoops team in the new Omaha arena, finish the baseball stadium and, above all, build Simon a first-class downtown soccer complex. If not, then, as Rasmussen says, "We should drop soccer."

— **DECEMBER 12, 2000**

Creighton celebrates a three-overtime victory over Indiana that sent the Bluejays to the NCAA soccer championship game in Charlotte, N.C. Connecticut defeated the Jays 2-0 for the title.

LEISE LIFTS NEBRASKA TO SERIES | GREATEST DAY EVER AT CWS | HONORING AMERICA

2001

> "I can't tell you how many times I got in a car at night to get to see a prospect play. It's 30-below, there's a ground blizzard and you spin out and end up in a ditch. This is before cellphones. But you felt like you always had to get an edge."
>
> — UNO HOCKEY COACH MIKE KEMP

Nebraska beat Iowa State 16-8 to win its first conference baseball title in 51 years. The Huskers acted like they beat Peru State. Who can blame them? The Big Red players have been programmed like machines to treat every game the same, like W's to be gobbled up as if by some enraged Pac-Men. Funny, but none of the Huskers, including coach Dave Van Horn, were alive the last time Nebraska won a league baseball title. Forget the CWS. Nebraska's season is already special. Rare. Historic. "For a team to do this, especially in this part of the country, it means more," Van Horn said.

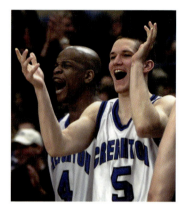

If you're tired of the endless reel of dunks and preening every night on "SportsCenter" and yearn for the good old days, when players did the little things, did them quietly and did them right, you owe it to yourself to come watch Ben Walker (left) and Ryan Sears. Don't worry, you won't need a program. You'll know who they are. They'll be the ones doing everything but trying to sell you the program. "People who haven't seen them play are missing a unique chance," Creighton coach Dana Altman said. "No question, they play the game the way you'd want to play it. Their competitiveness, unselfishness, their focus, without showboating, the way they handle themselves, never gotten a technical. Those are the qualities you want players to have." There will be a lot of debate on where the dynamic duo fit into Creighton history books. Best guards ever? Most influential teammates? Top 10 all-time players? Top five? Who knows? What can be documented, in the skin marks burned into the hardwood of the old gym at Creighton, is that nobody ever left more on the floor.

The Huskers beat Creighton 8-4 at Rosenblatt Stadium, but the score and the game were so inconsequential. This was all about a dress rehearsal. Nebraska in the CWS, take one. There were 13,862 (though it seemed like more), the vast majority in big red. There was so much red last night you would have thought it was Notre Dame Stadium.

158 • 20 YEARS WITH TOM SHATEL

HUSKER MAGIC BEATS OU | A HAMMERING IN BOULDER | ERIC CROUCH'S HEISMAN TROPHY

Ted Baer never wore a sweater or took a hip-check, but the Lancers owner is the most influential man in Nebraska hockey. Besides forming the Lancers and Tri-City Storm, Baer helped pave the way for the Lincoln Stars to exist. He's a deserving Omaha Hockey Hall of Famer.

Nebraska's tradition of cheering opponents has received media recognition. First, Tim Prister, editor of Notre Dame's Blue and Gold, wrote, "I've never seen anything like this. You are the most incredible fans I've ever seen." Next, Jacksonville, Fla., columnist Mark Woods implored Jaguar fans to cheer for the visiting Tennessee Titans "like Nebraska fans" and their "wonderful tradition."

What if the College World Series left Omaha? OK, there might not be people lined up on the I-80 bridge, ready to take a dip in the Missouri River. But there would definitely be a June-sized hole in our city's heart. It's too depressing to think about. So now you have an idea what Oklahoma City folks are going through this week. The Big 12 Conference baseball tournament (and before that the Big Eight tourney) is Oklahoma City's CWS. It's been played there every May since 1976. It's supported by the community, from the corporate types to the moms and dads whose moms and dads brought them to games. It has a loyal, knowledgeable following, folks who remember when Turner Gill played here. It's a slice of Americana. The state fair. It's corn dogs, funnel cakes, country music and homers over the Marlboro Man at All-Sports Stadium. It's families sitting on a blanket watching Oklahoma vs. Oklahoma State for the championship. Now, in the thoroughly modern Bricktown Ballpark, it's dinner at Mickey Mantle's restaurant and then a walk across the street to the left-field bleachers to watch Nebraska play Baylor for the Big 12 championship. It's tradition so thick you need a fork. But after this year — after all these years — the fair's leaving town. Guess where it's going? Dallas, of course. Next year's Big 12 tourney will be staged at The Ballpark in Arlington, home of the Texas Rangers and Alex Rodriguez. You can see why Ranger fans would want the Big 12 tourney. They crave the chance to see some good pitching.

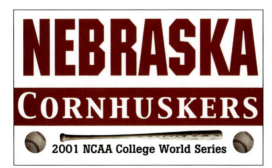

What lies behind the goalie's mask? You want to know. Because UNO freshman Dan Ellis does not act or play like any freshman you've ever seen. Ellis plays the most insane position in sports, and he plays it with a grace, and calm, that is almost eerie at times. He is an uncommon rock for a team doing uncommon things in its second season in the CCHA. Ellis is going to be UNO's first big-time star in the National Hockey League. You can see that. But all you see is the mask. What's behind it? You call up Jack Stark, the team psychologist for UNO hockey. Stark is like a kid in a candy store with these hockey players, and his No. 1 case study sits in front of the goal. You ask one question. What's behind the mask? "He's an unbelievable kid," Stark said. "He's only 20, but you think of him as being 25 or 30 years old. If there was one guy on the team I would let date my daughter, it would be him. I'm learning. I'm trying to study goalies. I'm reading books, trying to figure them out. There's nobody else like them. They're loners. They win and lose games. John Fletcher, who coaches the goalies, says that if you can figure out their minds, you could be a millionaire. Dan has every angle down. In that way, he's kind of like Bill Russell. Before the game, he knew how many rebounds, how many shots he was going to get. He studied every opponent. Ellis is like that. He's got all the angles down."

MARCH 16, 2001 • CREIGHTON BASKETBALL

A Chilly Day for CU Gunner

UNIONDALE, N.Y.

ONE DAY, KYLE Korver will be able to look back on this day without the pain in his heart. He'll remember that something good came of it. He might even laugh.

But all he could do was cry.

The Creighton sophomore sharpshooter sat, head in hands, in his locker stall at Nassau Coliseum. His eyes were glazed. You could see he was trying to hold back the dam, trying not to break. But as Korver sat there, answering questions like a champ about his 2-for-13 shooting day in CU's 69-56 loss to Iowa in the first round of the NCAA East Regional, his voice started to quake.

You knew it wouldn't be long before the dam broke.

"I really thought they were going in," Korver said. "I feel really bad. There's a lot of seniors on this team who don't deserve to go out this way. . . ."

And then the dam broke.

Sometimes you forget. You see these college athletes soar and do the incredible time and again. They seem so old. But then you witness their pain, and it reminds you that these are still just kids.

Korver is the fifth-rated 3-point shooter in college hoops. But he looked like some poor guy at the state fair, trying to win his girl a teddy bear. Clang, clang, clang. The game was rigged. Was this some cruel joke?

It was the worst of all possible times for cool-hand Kyle to go ice cold. You work all season to get here, and when the lights come on and the nation's watching, you want to play your best. And when you're a kid from Pella, Iowa, and you grew up shooting hoops in your backyard pretending you're playing for the Hawks, and you find yourself facing the Hawks, the dream becomes larger. So, too, does the nightmare.

"It's not like I was saying, 'I'm playing Iowa, I better force it up,' " Korver said. "They were all wide open. They all felt good. I'd shoot it, and say 'That one's going in, now we'll get going.'

"I was just so surprised. I mean, right before I left the floor during warmups, I made 10 (3s) in a row. I was like, 'These guys (Iowa) are in trouble.' "

Kyle Korver could manage only 2-of-13 shooting against his home-state Iowa Hawkeyes.

They'll analyze this one for a long time, and nobody more than Korver. But he's too hard on himself. This wasn't his doing. How many games has he won in two years? Too many to count. Korver's a big reason CU got here in the first place. One day he'll know that. But not now.

"I'll be hard on myself," Korver said. "I'll learn from this. Be a better person. Be a better player. We'll be good next year. But right now, it hurts."

Korver broke up again, and teammate Brett Angner couldn't stand it. Angner came up to Korver, locked his arms around him, hugged him long and hard and whispered in his ear, "It's going to be OK, Kyle."

Leise Delivers the Hit Heard 'Round the State

THIS IS FICTION. This is a movie. This can't be real. Only a boy could dream this up. A Nebraska boy.

Bob Leise knows. He was once that boy. He once had this dream. Leise grew up in Omaha, patrolled center field for Creighton Prep and later Creighton University. He grew up going to the College World Series. He always wondered what it would be like to play in the CWS. But he never got to find out.

His son will.

Bob stood in his superstitious rally spot, down the first-base line behind the Nebraska dugout, when his boy, Jeff, got the game-winning RBI to send Nebraska to its first CWS.

"I was stunned," Bob said. "I'm still numb. It's unbelievable. This is every kid's dream."

Nebraska. In the College World Series. It's every Nebraskan's dream.

A dream come true.

This can't be real. This must be a movie. After so many years, decades, of waiting, praying and dreaming — 10 years after Creighton gave the CWS its first home team — the CWS is about to be painted Big Red.

The wait was so long. And the moment came so fast. Nebraska trailed the entire game against Rice. The Huskers couldn't touch starter Kenny Baugh. There would be a Game 3, another sleepless night.

But then they broke through. They scored three runs in the ninth, and then three more in the 10th, and suddenly Nebraska was up, 9-6, and it was all right here. Finally here. Before you knew it shortstop Will Bolt smothered the last out and the dam holding back all the emotions, all those boyish dreams, came tumbling down.

The boys in red met in center field, in a joyous dogpile for the ages. And then it was time for a victory lap after a last game at Buck Beltzer Stadium that no one will ever forget.

Jeff Leise led them.

The center fielder is the quietest Husker. But euphoria does something to the brain. You can forget who you are. Little Jeff Leise, the kid in the back of the class, led his conga line around the fences and it looked like they might dance all the way to Omaha.

Omaha boy. Omaha bound.

Leise bounced. He yelled. He high-fived every kid and his mom and dad and sister around the park. He led a cheer and then held his hand to his ear as if to say, "I can't hear you." He had a smile from Alliance to Rosenblatt Stadium.

"That's not like him at all," Bob said.

This is not like anything at all.

"This is the happiest I've ever been," Jeff explained. "This is the best moment of my life."

Much of that life has been around baseball. Like most boys, Jeff learned the game from his father. They are so much alike it must give the old man goose bumps.

Bob is left-handed. Jeff plays left-handed. He's actually a righty, but he learned to throw left-handed because, as a young tot, he refused to play with anything but his father's mitt.

Just like his dad, Jeff grew up to be a Creighton Prep center fielder. Unlike his dad, he played for Nebraska, not Creighton. But he and his father, like most boys and their dads, grew up on the CWS. The Leises have had tickets for 18 years.

"He's been going to it since he was 3 years old," Bob said of Jeff. "When he was 5, he brought his glove to get a foul ball."

Jeff gets to bring his glove again this week.

"I've always gone to the World Series," Jeff said. "You can't believe the dream it is. When I was in high school, I used to go watch them practice when they came to town. I just remember being awed by those guys. Now, we're going to be the guys out there."

Jeff Leise's game-winning RBI sent Nebraska to its first appearance in the College World Series.

Greatest Day Ever at CWS

"HEY, GRANDPA, what are you watching?"

"An old College World Series tape, from 2001."

"Why are you watching that?"

"Well, the College World Series starts tomorrow. I was just trying to get in the mood. And that was the greatest day ever at the College World Series."

"Better than the day you took me and we caught a foul ball?"

"Well, no. But this was a special day. It was the day that the president of the United States came to the College World Series. And, later that very same day, the Nebraska baseball team played its first game in the World Series."

"You mean the Huskers didn't go to the series every year, like they do now?"

"Heavens, no. They weren't as good as they are now. The fans went to World Series games for years and years and never got to cheer for their team. Then one year, they hired a good coach, named Dave Van Horn, and they finally made it, in 2001. And it was the biggest thing that ever happened to the World Series."

"Is that why the president went to the game?"

"No. President Bush was a big baseball fan. He just wanted to say he'd been to the World Series. He didn't even stay around for the Husker game. He threw out the first pitch for the Stanford-Tulane game and left after a few innings."

"Was he a good player?"

"He had a good arm, for a president. He hummed in a strike, then shook the hands of both teams, even the umpires. As he walked off, he waved to the crowd and the crowd roared and waved back. As I recall, I got goose bumps.

"It was an amazing day. There was an energy to that day, like nobody had ever felt before. It was like someone plugged in the whole city. Some fans spent the night before at the stadium, waiting to get into general admission. There were cars and people everywhere, as early as 8 a.m.

"The College World Series has always been like a state fair. But that day, it was louder, brighter, faster. It just felt better. There were police cars everywhere, the Secret Service men talking into their cellphones, everyone waiting for the president to arrive. And all the Nebraska fans. Red, everywhere.

"It seemed like all 22,000 were in red. Red hats. Red shirts. Red pants. They painted their faces and chests red. Everyone had red beads. But mostly I remember the sound. Especially the sound after the first game ended."

"What was it, Grandpa?"

"The crowd started buzzing. And then, slowly, it built into cheering, louder and louder. The Huskers had arrived! They were out there in their red uniforms, running onto the field. I can still see them, jogging in the outfield, with the fans in the bleachers, leaning over, pounding the side of the wall.

"Then, when the team ran out for introductions, there was this thunderous roar. And everyone stood and chanted, 'Go Big Red! Go Big Red!' Some people said they had never heard it so loud at Rosenblatt, not even when Creighton played there in 1991. I remember I started crying. And other people around me were wiping tears, too."

"Did Nebraska win?"

"Well, no, they didn't. I don't remember the score, but they lost to Cal State Fullerton. I don't remember much else about the game. Shane Komine, the great Nebraska pitcher, gave up three runs early but stayed in and pitched a whale of a game. The Huskers were nervous early, but they fought back. John Cole hit two home runs to dead center. It was a close game.

"But what I remember most about the night was the crowd. The atmosphere. The electricity. The noise. It was just a madhouse. Fullerton showed a lot of guts.

"Nebraska didn't win, but it was hard to walk away from that game without smiling. It was just so much fun. The whole day was fun. Just seeing Nebraska out on that field, finally, after all those years. And the president, too. It was a day I always want to remember. Which is why I got the video!"

"Grandpa, how did Nebraska do in that series? Did they come back to win it?"

"That's a story for another day."

President George W. Bush meets Husker coach Dave Van Horn in the locker room before the game.

JUNE 9, 2001 • COLLEGE WORLD SERIES

The sea of red moved to Rosenblatt Stadium for Nebraska's first appearance at the College World Series.

2011 INSIGHT *Some of my best memories of the past 20 years happened during this era of Nebraska baseball. There were some great characters on this team, Will Bolt and Jeff Leise and Shane Komine. Dave Van Horn was a straight shooter and a hoot to cover. In 2000 and 2001, every game felt like history. This first day of the 2001 CWS was over-the-top history. I mean, George W. Bush and Nebraska's first game in the College World Series on the same day? It's a columnist's dream and nightmare. Easy to write. Easy to screw up, too. I thought this imaginary grandfather angle, looking back on the day years later, would be something people would relate to. I think anyone who was there will remember that day, for Bush throwing out the first pitch, the fans banging on the outfield wall as Nebraska ran onto the field, the flashbulbs. I thought the column needed to reflect the immensity of the day. I remember well after the game, people were still tailgating and hanging out. I went down to see some friends at Row J. People were trying to put the whole day into perspective. It was that kind of day.*

AUGUST 3, 2001 • GOLF

Vermeer, Dad Share Dream

AS HIS SON walked up the 18th fairway, with the name "Vermeer" flashing on the leader board, there was no mistaking the stuff on Bob Vermeer's face.

Sweat. And pride.

They had both been here before, father and son, in their dreams. They both had taken that Sunday walk up the 18th, waving to the thunderous cheers, knocking home that winning bird. The dream will never happen for the father.

It's still alive for the son. And so Bob sits on the hill at Champions Club and watches, with wife Laura, and they all dare to wonder: What if Ryan, the Omaha boy, could make that victorious walk this Sunday? Wouldn't that be something if his first win could be the Hometown Classic?

"I've thought about it," said Ryan after shooting a first-round 68 in the Omaha Classic. "This is the tournament I'd love to do well in. It's so cool to look up at the 18th and see all those skyboxes and know that they want me to do well."

Bob chuckles out loud when he's asked how the kid is handling the pressure of playing in front of the home crowd. He loves it, Bob says. He's thriving on it. So, too, is dear old dad.

Bob Vermeer has been the head pro at Oak Hills Country Club for 14 years. He's been a club pro his whole career. The one time it might have been different was in the mid-1970s, when he had just begun as head pro at Spencer (Iowa) Country Club. He had always wanted to be a tour pro, chase Arnie and Jack and all that.

He had a wife. And kids. But one time he decided to try, just to see. He went to the Qualifying School. Missed getting his tour card by three lousy strokes.

But he got to keep his husband and father card.

"You have to give something up," Vermeer said. "I decided to make a career, raise my family. You can't do that and be gone all the time. It doesn't work."

Instead, he passed on a love for the game to Ryan. By age 2, Ryan had learned to hit a wiffle golf ball off a shag-carpet lie in the living room. One time, the course superintendent spent the night on the couch and woke up at 6:30 a.m. to the sound of Ryan hitting flop shots off the drapes.

Ryan was hitting real balls on the range by age 3 and won the Iowa Pee-Wee Open at age 6, with a score of 113. Soon, Bob was footing the bill for Ryan to play the national junior circuits. By sixth grade, Ryan played only golf. He went on to play at Millard South. Then, at Kansas University.

"I told my son, 'There's a part of me that's a little envious of what you're doing,' " Bob said. " 'You've got an opportunity to pursue dreams. You need to take advantage of it.'

"He has the tools. He has all the shots. He has the length. He has the heart. Does he have the head? That's a work in progress, but that's something you learn your whole life. This is the toughest game there is to master. The mind set ... it's just amazing at this level."

Now, father and son will have something good to talk about.

"He's as frustrated as I am because he knows how good I can be," Ryan said. "It's hard calling home after a bad day. He feels the same way."

On this day, they were both gushing.

"He's digging it," Bob said. "He knows this is what it's all about."

Ryan Vermeer's caddie and father, Bob, offers help at the 2008 tournament. Ryan tied for 18th in 2001.

Not the Game but the Glory

THEY PLAYED A football game here on a Thursday night, but I really can't remember the score.

I'll never forget what happened before the game.

When the only drama of the evening was played out. When we met the real hero and gave him a long, standing ovation. When the turning point of the game, of the evening, occurred.

It happened during the pre-game ceremonies of Nebraska's game against Rice at Memorial Stadium. It was one of the first two football games, college or pro, since the terrorists' attacks on our country last week. You knew there would be something special, perhaps understated, but something appropriate from the folks who bring you Husker football.

But nobody had any idea how special.

It was after Congressman Tom Osborne told us everything would be all right, after the crowd sang "God Bless America" and "The Star-Spangled Banner" and paused for a moment of reflection and the two teams walked, not ran, onto the field. It seemed like that was the end of it.

But then, that familiar note rang out over the stadium speakers, that first chord of the Alan Parsons "Tunnel Walk" song that every Husker fan could get after two notes in a "Name That Tune" contest.

And then the "Tunnel Walk" video popped up on the video screens. Tunnel Walk? Huh? The Huskers were on the field already. What Tunnel Walk?

And then the video played out, from the cornfields of Nebraska to Chimney Rock to the Henry Doorly Zoo to the sower raising the roof. And then the doors opened. And there IT was.

Old Glory. Oh, my God.

A capacity crowd of 77,000 said as much, in its stunned silence, before it broke into a thunderous, stadium-rocking cheer, the kind usually reserved for Jim Pillen falling on a Billy Sims fumble.

They stood and cheered, and tough old farmers were bawling like babies, and the place was covered with red goose bumps, on top of red goose bumps, all because of what Butch Hug thought up in between his own tears.

Hug, the University of Nebraska director of events, had this idea: Instead of coach Frank Solich and the Huskers coming out of the "tunnel," a trio of Army ROTC officers would come out carrying the American flag.

And behind them would be five officers, one each from the Lincoln Fire Department, Lincoln Police Department, UNL Police Department, Nebraska State Patrol and Lancaster County Sheriff's Office.

They marched, slowly, out of the locker room doors and through the tunnel. And the closer they came, the louder the people were cheering, stomping, crying, until the ROTC trio arrived at the opening into the stadium. The flag had to be lowered just a tad to make it under the overhang.

And then it popped up, on cue eliciting the biggest, loudest noise of the night.

It was the coolest thing you'll ever see in this stadium, maybe anywhere.

"That was unbelievable," said Officer Mark Eberspacher of the Lincoln Fire Department Honor Guard, who carried a smaller flag onto the field. "That crowd. That noise. All of those people standing and cheering. You can tell everyone is behind our country.

"I've still got goose bumps."

He wasn't alone.

This sort of poignant, spine-tingling patriotic scene seemed right at home in Memorial Stadium, which was built in honor of Nebraska's World War I veterans. Each of the four cornerstones is engraved with a few lines, written by former NU professor of philosophy Hartley Burr Alexander, the most famous of which reads: "Not the victory but the action. Not the goal but the game. In the deed the glory."

With apologies to Professor Alexander, the words of this night were: "Not the game but the glory."

Old Glory.

Dave Volk (58), Eric Crouch (7) and teammates during the national anthem before the Rice game.

OCTOBER 28, 2001 • NEBRASKA FOOTBALL

NU-OU Does It Again

OKLAHOMA-NEBRASKA DID it again. Put these two legends of the fall on the same stage, throw a conference title and national championship on the pile on the table, and it never fails. Somebody gets validated. Somebody gets a legacy. Somebody becomes a hero for life.

Well, it happened again in a 20-10 Husker victory at Memorial Stadium that turned on one play that will go immediately up on the shelf next to the other Nebraska-Oklahoma classics.

It came with just more than six minutes left and the Huskers clinging to a 13-10 lead. They were trying to score, or at least run out some clock, because the Sooner defense had been awfully stingy about letting them do either on this crisp October day.

First and 10. At the NU 37. Eric Crouch took the snap and handed to Thunder Collins on the "flash reverse," one in which Collins ran for a 39-yard gain earlier in the game. Only this time, Collins flipped the ball to Mike Stuntz, the freshman split end from Council Bluffs St. Albert.

Wait. It gets better.

So here's Stuntz, a lefty, going to his left, as if he's running a reverse. Only right there in front of Tom Osborne, Barry Switzer and all of America . . . he throws, on the run, a perfect spiral to Crouch, who acted as if he was blocking or doing nothing at all, and somehow had sneaked behind the defense. Crouch caught the ball at the Oklahoma 39 and ran untouched for a touchdown, despite the earth moving beneath him.

Officially, the play is called "Black 41 Flash Reverse Pass." Get me rewrite. Plays like these need glorious, colorful names, aliases that send up immediate snapshots whenever you hear them.

How about "Croucharooski"? Or "Stuntzarooski"?

To be sure, these Nebraska-Oklahoma, No. 1-vs.-No. 2 endeavors are always team wins and losses. But this series has never failed in randomly selecting anonymous bit players and lifting them to instant stardom, the kind that lasts a lifetime.

It sure seemed that way for Stuntz, as he stood up at the lectern, explaining himself and cracking one-liners for the national news media.

"Look at him," Nebraska left tackle Dave Volk said. "If he never does anything else at Nebraska, he'll always be up on that video screen."

Eric Crouch races for a score on "Black 41 Flash Reverse Pass."

2011 INSIGHT *Ask Husker fans what they remember about the 2001 season. They'll start with the debacle at Colorado. The controversy around making the national title game in the Rose Bowl. Most of the memories of that season are painful ones, because you tend to remember the end. That's too bad, in the sense that this Oklahoma game gets lost in history. This day was as good as the others were bad. Frank Solich hadn't had that signature moment yet. This was it. Can anyone forget how the old stadium shook as Eric Crouch took the pass from Mike Stuntz? Solich eventually got fired, and there was a great debate about that and his legacy. But for one day, Solich was on top of the world. It would be short-lived, but this game validated Fearless Frankie as a coach who could make the gutsy call and win the high-stakes game. That was the clear sentiment among those at the press conference after that game. Solich stood tall. Nobody could have known what was around the corner in Boulder, Colo., or even the drop off the cliff in 2002. In a way, this day was the end of the innocence, or the last day of innocence, for the Camelot that was Nebraska football.*

NU Was the Nail in Hammering

BOULDER, COLO.

FIRST OF ALL, before we get started here, let's just say upfront that what you saw was not an aberration. Do not call your cable guy to complain. Unless, of course, you threw your shoe through the TV set.

Colorado 62, Nebraska 36 was not a dream.

OK, maybe a really, really bad dream.

Nebraska football has just about seen it all. There have been days of glory, national championships, a Game of the Century and a million nine-win seasons and bowl games. There have been wins that bounced off a player's foot and into another's arms. And there have been all of those days when Nebraska played the hammer.

But there has never been a day, a defeat, like this one, when the Huskers finally got the nail's point of view. Now they know. It hurts. It really, really hurts. This was the worst defeat in the history of Big Red football, or, if you will, since 1962, when the Bob Devaney era began.

Oh sure, there have been wider margins than 26, like 45-10 at OU in 1990 or 38-7 at OU in 1977. There was the 35-31 loss to Missouri that ruined a shot at No. 1. There have been gut-wrenchers and Sooner Magic and daggers to the heart on late November afternoons. But there was nothing fancy or magical about this one.

There have been Orange Bowl nights when Miami outclassed the Huskers, but those Hurricane teams had more talent, more speed. Colorado does not have more talent than Nebraska.

But CU ran and ran and scored and scored. The Buffs scored the most points ever against a Nebraska team, more than Minnesota (61) in 1945 or Bud Wilkinson's Sooners (55 in 1954 and 49 in 1956). But that was before Nebraska discovered winning, discovered football. That was different.

This was really different. This was Colorado going up 35-3 before the Huskers even knew what hit them.

This was Colorado lining up and beating the Big Red at its own punishing game. This was Colorado using basically three running plays to roll up 380 yards, including a delay trap play that worked over and over and over because, well, the holes were bigger than the Continental Divide.

This was Buffs coach Gary Barnett going for two with a 55-30 lead and Nebraska coach Frank Solich saying he had no problem with it.

This was Colorado's fourth-team back, Chris Brown, running for an obscene six touchdowns and saying the Husker safeties were "scared" to tackle him.

This was Colorado leaving starters in and trying to run up the score, to 70 points, on Nebraska.

How could an undefeated season go into a free fall so quickly? How in the name of Lincoln, Neb., could this happen? There were no easy answers. And there was a very simple answer. Nebraska was outplayed, out-tackled, outrun, out-passed, out-turnovered, out-coached, out-prepared, out-desired and flat-out Buffaloed.

These two teams could play 10 times, and Nebraska would win, maybe, seven. But on this day, Colorado had the better coaches, players and game plan. The Buffs, who had a Big 12 North title and shot at a Bowl Championship Series bowl at stake, wanted it more.

How could this happen? How could Nebraska get Nebraska-ed? The answer is as complicated as human nature and as simple as five Colorado linemen blowing five white-jerseyed defenders onto their backs.

These things happen. They just aren't supposed to happen to Nebraska. But they did. This was no dream. But it was definitely a nightmare.

Colorado's Chris Brown breaks past Nebraska's Jamie Burrow (48) and Scott Shanle (43) on his way to one of his six touchdowns.

DECEMBER 9, 2001 • HEISMAN TROPHY

A Wild December Night

YES, NEBRASKA, THERE is a Santa Claus.

And this year Christmas came early, on a Saturday night in early December, a night when the presents kept unwrapping themselves in bigger and more stunning ways and Husker football fans all got what they wanted.

Oh, what a night. A night no one in this football-mad state will soon forget, a night not even the greediest die-hards could dare ask for because it could never, ever happen.

But on this great night of Nebraska football, it did.

Eric Crouch wins the Heisman? And Nebraska gets first in line to play Miami in the Rose Bowl for the national championship? All on the same night? Are you kidding me?

No. Talk about four hours of frantic football-frenzied fever.

It started out on cue. Just before 7 p.m., the most dramatic Heisman race in decades ended with the name "Eric Crouch" breaking the unbearable silence and Nebraska's newest legend striding up to accept the third Heisman in Big Red football history. Could it get any better than this?

Before Crouch could even sit down and catch his breath, it was heart-pounding time again. LSU was lining up to play No. 2 Tennessee in the Southeastern Conference championship game. If the Tigers could pull off the upset, the Huskers were next in line to fill the other Rose Bowl spot, barring some wild and crazy happenings in the polls overnight.

But how wild and crazy can this season get, anyway? Even this was too much to hope for, after Nebraska, Oklahoma, Florida and Texas going down — the jinx of the No. 2 ranking — the past two weeks. It couldn't happen, could it?

LSU 31, Tennessee 20. Merry Christmas.

The wackiest college football season in recent memory just went over the top, and Nebraska has a front-row seat. And is no doubt enjoying the view.

The thing is, even if Tennessee had won, the night would have been a rousing success. That's because

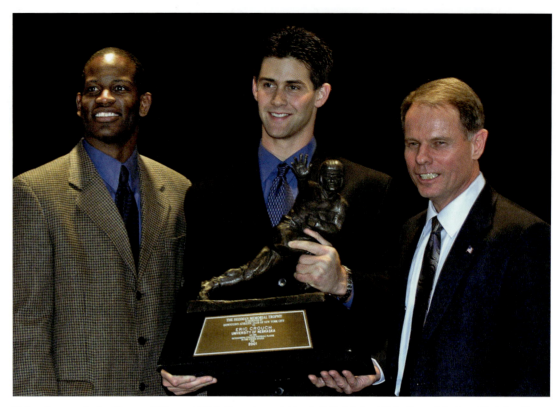

Nebraska quarterbacks coach Turner Gill, left, and coach Frank Solich joined Eric Crouch in New York for the Heisman Trophy presentation.

Crouch had his gifted hands wrapped around the most famous trophy in sports.

And, make no mistake, the Heisman is coming home. To Omaha.

Crouch is the third Omaha boy to join the Heisman fraternity. It started in 1939, with Nile Kinnick, who will always be known first as an Iowa Hawkeye but who was groomed here at Benson High School. Our modern-day Mr. Heisman was Johnny "The Jet" Rodgers, who perfected his instinctive genius at Omaha Tech.

Now, with Crouch, Omaha has three Heismans.

This was for Omaha. This was for Nebraska. This was for all of us.

This was for Omaha kids and boys and girls across Nebraska. Pay attention to that kid in your backyard, or the one next door. You never know. Maybe someday.

Crouch grew up in our midst. He played at Millard North High School. How many of us saw Crouch play on Friday nights? But how many of us were saying to ourselves, "I'm watching a future Heisman Trophy winner"?

We will from now on.

DECEMBER 20, 2001 • SPORTS AND FAMILY

Life's Miracle Is a Girl

"OH, MY GOD, look at this head."

I describe things for a living. I watch events and try to put them into words, try to take their colors and sounds and actions and describe them in a way that has some meaning to you, the reader. I try to make you feel as if you were there, that you could see it, hear it, feel it, too. Well, I'm sorry, but I'm going to have to ask for the day off. I can't possibly do it today.

"Look at how big this one is."

Fathers today are lucky. We get to see the miracle. When children of my generation were born, our fathers didn't get to watch. They sat in the waiting room. They had cigars ready to go. They sat and sat and sat, like they were waiting at the deli for their number to be called, and finally some nurse walked out and said, "It's a boy." Which was fine with my father. It's the old Shatel squeamish stomach. We can't stand the sight of blood, especially when it's our own. Or somebody very near and dear to us.

So there was some major trepidation rolling around my insides as I sat next to my lovely, courageous wife, Jennifer, at Methodist Hospital. Doctors Michelle Knolla and Craig Bassett were about to perform a C-section. The sheet was pulled up so Jen (and I) couldn't see. When the baby pops out, they hold it up for you. Good concept.

Well, part of me wanted to look, and part of me said, "Stay where you are, don't pass out." So I stayed. I'm the Mack Brown of Lamaze coaches. I talk a great game, but when it comes to the big game, I've got the ol' deer-in-the-headlights look pasted on my face. My wife was telling ME to breathe.

Then somebody said, "Look at this," and, well, it was instinct. I've never seen anything so mind-bending, heart-thumping, wonderfully amazing and head-shaking incredible as watching a baby — my baby — being born.

The first thing you say is, "Look at that! I helped create that!" Then they're cutting the umbilical cord and they're saying, "It's a girl" and your jaw has dropped and everything is suspended and you wonder: "How does this miracle happen? How does God do this?" And your heart is pumped up with so much pride and love, it could explode. Instead, your tear ducts do.

Welcome, Sarah Suzanne Shatel. Yes, her initials are S.S.S. I thought about the names Bridget Chandler, so the initials would be B.C.S., but given how wildly popular the bowl system is right now, that probably wasn't a good idea.

Sarah is so stunningly beautiful, with her blue eyes and sandy blond hair with the curl on top. She's got her mommy's looks and her daddy's, well, snoring, although I did hear her mom say that she was cooing in her sleep. Next time Mom complains about my snoring, I'll just say, "I'm cooing."

Sarah is 9 pounds, 14 ounces. That is a power forward. Or perhaps an outside hitter, coach John Cook. She'll be able to drive the green from the red tees. She'll play any sport she wants. Yes, even soccer. Does this mean I finally have to watch a soccer match? Somebody said this is God's way of getting back at me for not covering as many women's sporting events as I should have.

I don't take pictures. But I had no problem with my wife posing our first born, Sarah, with props to commemorate her birth around the time of Nebraska's 2001 Rose Bowl berth. She was a Rose Bowl baby.

Sarah, I can't wait to read to you, rock you to sleep, change your diapers at 2 a.m., take you for walks, watch cartoons on Saturdays and football on Sundays (please, do not throw your baby bottles onto the playing field or you will be ejected). I said, boy or girl, we're going to play catch, and we will. But you can also take piano lessons or ballet. You can have a pet, but you'll probably want a cellphone first.

Sarah, you will be photographed and camcorded a thousand times over by your new family. Your Aunt Allie took the video of you in the delivery room, meeting the world for the first time. But I won't have to watch it. The memory of meeting you, the greatest day of my life, will always be fresh in my mind.

Some moments are better than others. This one was the best.

2011 INSIGHT *This is one of my favorite columns, for obvious reasons. It was extremely selfish. I wrote it for me. I wrote it for Sarah, so she could read it one day. I always thought it was a small abuse of my position. I mean, not every dad gets to put his kids' name in the paper when they're born or brag about them to the world. But what I found was that most readers didn't care about that abuse. They loved it. This got a ton of response, from both men and women. I remember hearing from many female readers, in later years, who specifically recalled this column and said that was when they started reading me. But I was surprised to hear from the men who loved it as well, the fathers who said welcome to the club. I considered myself a journalist first and a sports fan second. But I've always thought of myself as just a regular guy. This column, in many ways, put me in that regular guy fraternity, which is a real elite club. It helped me connect with a lot of readers on a deeper level. I just hope Sarah doesn't read the part about the cellphone. That's not happening any time soon.*

TOM'S TAKE
REFLECTIONS ON

Painful Cut First of Many?

IT'S JUST BUSINESS. Nothing personal.

Tell it to the swimmers who had their team drained by the University of Nebraska. Look them in the eye and tell them that they're just a number.

Nebraska Athletic Director Bill Byrne tried to on a day as dark as the black suit Byrne wore to a press conference, where members of the men's and women's swim teams waited. How fitting. This, after all, was a funeral.

This was the day men's swimming passed, the first time for a men's sport at NU and probably not the last. A big piece of these young men died, too. These are sportsmen, no different from football or basketball players. Their passion is a lonely one, full of grueling sacrifice, up each day at 5 a.m. to jump in the water and swim countless laps. It's certainly no less a sport than football. But it's most certainly less a business.

"I've been downsized by Bill Byrne."

— THE MESSAGE ON A T-SHIRT WORN BY A NEBRASKA SWIMMER

One swimmer's T-shirt read, "I've been downsized by Bill Byrne." Athletes as numbers to be crunched? Welcome to college athletics. Welcome to reality.

People love to paint Byrne as "Dollar Bill," the miserly Scrooge who takes joy in emptying locker rooms. He doesn't. Byrne loves athletes, loves watching them compete, loves to win. But his job isn't ordering sweat socks. He's the CEO of a business. Huskers Inc. He has to meet a bottom line, 100 yards long.

In a perfect world, Byrne would save the swim team by going into the football cash cow, hacking the recruiting budget or downsizing the weight room. Anybody here in favor of that? Can we see a show of hands?

Football is and always will be the chairman of the board of Huskers Inc. But now it's time for Byrne and anyone in red to face another cold, hard truth. Football can't carry this corporation anymore. Huskers Inc. is too big.

Nebraska has the smallest population of any state in the Big 12 but insists on carrying the most sports (23). In Texas, they call that "fuzzy math."

Why? Why does NU have to support so many sports? What is it they are trying to prove? Who needs the Sears Cup, the all-sports trophy? Let's face it: Husker fans would rather cradle the Sears Trophy, for the national football championship.

Byrne's $39 million budget is $250,000 in the red, thanks to asbestos found in the Devaney Center roof. Those surprise maintenance expenses are going to pop up every year with NU's aging facilities, along with coaching salaries, tuition and the normal inflation of college sports' arms race. Byrne says you have to generate $1.2 million annually just to stay out of the big red.

Don't even think about cutting one of the 13 women's sports. Women deserve every opportunity, too. They'll also see you in court. It's about comparing opportunities and scholarships, not number of sports. The flaw in Title IX is that football's not a separate entity. There's no female equivalent in number of scholarships.

So as belts get tightened, who's going to pay? Sorry, guys. Not track, which is getting new facilities. Not baseball, the new golden boys, whose shiny palace opens soon. But everyone else has fair warning: His or her program could be next.

Is Nebraska biting off more than it can chew? Should Huskers Inc. concentrate on being competitive nationally in a handful of sports? At the very least, every sport should have to cut back, including travel. But if some sports are cut back so much they can't compete, what's the point?

"Those are questions we have to ask ourselves," Byrne said.

You can ask yourself next time the bill for football tickets comes in the mail. Husker fans are going to be asked to contribute more to the cause. That will help stem the tide of cutting sports. But how much money is there in this state?

Here's some irony for you: Last week, just days before cutting men's swimming, Nebraska vaulted into first place in the Sears Cup standings. Get ready for a party. Better bring paper plates and cups.

— MARCH 27, 2001

THE CHANGING SPORTS LANDSCAPE 2001

Omaha Proves Itself Again

THE SUN CAME up Saturday morning on the College World Series. The parking lots were back in Mardi Gras form. The T-shirt tents were in full bloom. The bleachers were packed early. High cholesterol was in the air.

Then Miami and Stanford played for the national championship before 24,070, many of whom didn't know the Cardinal from the Cardinals. And the Air Force band played on.

There was so much hand-wringing about the 2001 CWS. So much uncertainty. So much anxiety. Would this be the year the music died?

This was the Nebraska College World Series. Nobody knew how that would work. Would the Husker fans stomp on the purity of the event? Would Nebraska ruin it? Could the CWS survive the arrival of the Huskers?

Could it survive their departure? And then some. This was a CWS unlike any in memory. George W. Bush and his army of Secret Service literally turned the CWS upside down. Hundreds of fans fumed outside the gates, locked out until the First Right-hander hummed the First Strike.

Would they come back? In force. A new voice led us through the week. There was a beer garden at Zesto's. A Nebraska team taking infield. It was so different. Could it ever be the same?

Same as it ever was.

Sure, this didn't always look or feel like the CWS, not like mom used to make. Of all the College World Series ever played, this was certainly one of them.

There wasn't a whole lot to latch onto here. Not a lot of classic games. No underdog to hug for the week. No LSU. Not even that big Cajun chef with the beard and white hat turning the parking lot into his personal French Quarter.

But what this CWS lacked in style, it made up for in substance. This year was a litmus test for the CWS. For Omaha. This year, we would see how sturdy, how tough, this old June tradition really was. It's solid.

To be sure, Nebraska transformed the place. For two days, all of Rosenblatt Stadium was doused in red. The CWS wasn't itself at all. It was a giant Husker home game. It was a little awkward. Tulane fans had better cheers.

The Huskers were as good as Tulane or Georgia or Tennessee. They could have stuck around. Purists were glad they didn't. The CWS got to return to normal.

It wasn't easy. The two or three days after Nebraska left felt like a letdown. There was no emotion, no aura, no passion at the CWS. It felt like the crowd was going through the motions. There were empty seats. Attendance was down 4,000 this year. Those dratted Nebraska fans who bought CWS tickets only to see their team play were the culprits.

The atmosphere was down for the count early. But this isn't single-elimination.

The CWS rebounded nicely. The weather cooperated. The fans got back into the old routine. And the baseball got better.

After those two early football scores, the four-hour heavy metal concerts, everyone was ripping college baseball. But as the week went on, we saw terrific pitching, great defense, strategy and baserunning, the whole nine innings.

College baseball will survive. The CWS will survive.

We saw that on a sun-splashed championship Saturday, when everything — the tailgating, the sweet sounds of the organ, the familiar rush of adrenaline — was just like old times.

No, we didn't get a classic game. But we got a classy champion. So much for the ghost of Ron Fraser. Coach Jim Morris just equaled his predecessor's national championship count.

Stanford's terrific run ended abruptly. The Cardinal lost this one in the sun, that brilliant sun that filled the day and event with warmth. Stanford will be back. So will the College World Series.

— JUNE 17, 2001

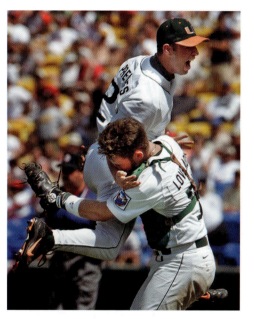

Miami pitcher Alex Prends jumps into the arms of catcher Greg Lovelady as the Hurricanes claim the College World Series championship.

RED FACES AT ROSE BOWL | TERRELL TAYLOR'S MAGICAL SHOT | AK-SAR-BEN COLISEUM CLOSES

2002

"It's like we told our players the first day we got here. Why not Iowa State? You should have the opportunity to experience these things. Why does it have to be Nebraska, Texas, Ohio State and Miami? Why not Iowa State?"

— ISU FOOTBALL COACH DAN MCCARNEY

Awesome. Charming. Gorgeous. Unreal. Inspiring. Mind-boggling. Stunning. Worth the price of hooky or scalpers. I'd come up with other descriptions of Haymarket Park, but I'm too busy gawking. There can't be a more beautiful or perfect ballpark in college baseball than the new digs finally christened by the Nebraska baseball team. The Huskers cracked the bottle of champagne against the Kearney pitching staff. There isn't a bad seat in the house, not to mention the yard outside the fences. The grassy knoll seats are the ones you can still buy. From the box seats close to the field, to the picnic tables down the first-base side, to convenient parking and reasonable concession lines, this park is so fan-friendly it does everything but drive you home. And for those midweek blowouts, there's always a terrific view of the Lincoln skyline, the State Capitol and that place where they play football.

Eight years ago, Mike Hastings was in the fast lane, with all green lights. He was in his first year as head coach of the Omaha Lancers when the call came. A friend was taking over the hockey program at Colorado College. Would Hastings be interested in joining up? For some reason, Hastings hit the brake. "I remember sitting in my apartment, thinking, 'I've only been in Omaha a year,'" he said. "That's not long enough to be a head coach and leave." So he stayed. And the rest is Lancers history. Since then, Hastings has done everything a man can do in junior hockey.

The door to Connie Yori's office is open and so you walk inside. There are questions to ask of a Creighton women's hoops coach having her best season. I really had no idea that we would end up talking about Yori's, uh, pipes. Please, an explanation. Yori is 38. She and husband Kirk Helms want to be parents someday. She spent the first several minutes of our talk asking how my future power forward is doing. Anyway, Yori's biological shot clock is winding down and, as one gentleman so eloquently put it, she's out of timeouts. "I was at a function last year and I ran into this old guy," Yori says. "He's asking me all kinds of stuff. Are you married? How old are you? Do you have any kids? Then he says, 'Your pipes are getting rusty. You better get moving.'"

172 • 20 YEARS WITH TOM SHATEL

GARRIDO IS REDEEMED | END OF NU'S NINE-WIN SEASON STREAK | HIRING OF STEVE PEDERSON

Nebraska was rolling along pretty good last season until the Buffs cold-cocked them, 62-36. The Huskers have not been the same since. Remember Barrett Ruud's line before the Penn State game? About the little slice of doubt about the Colorado game happening again? We scoffed. We should have listened. It was a cry for help.

Maybe the Royals' new "Big O" will grow on us. Or maybe we'll throw some sprinkles on it and ask for a dozen to go. The new doughnut logo is less than inspiring. It's O-so-boring. But think of the promotions. How about a "Homer Simpson Night?" There's a new look on the field, too. Manager Bucky Dent is more than just a historic autograph for your dad.

The end is near for Ak-Sar-Ben Coliseum. There's a generation out there that understands. There's one that doesn't get it. To those of us who didn't grow up in Omaha, who showed up here in the past 10 years, Ak Coliseum is an old barn where Lancers skated and Racers played. And why in the wide world of sports were they doing it next to a horse track? The older generation knows. For as long as they can remember, when Omaha Knights turned into racetrack days, this was the place to be. Ak-Sar-Ben was Omaha. For busloads of Midwest gamblers, Ak-Sar-Ben was the front porch of Omaha. It's where Gordie Howe played, where Sinatra crooned and Cosby entertained and the rodeo lived. FDR spoke at Ak Coliseum. During World War II, it was used as a transportation depot. There were three NHL regular-season games there. One NBA game. The point is, there was a time when you didn't need a big, fancy arena or a convention center.

St. Louis Cardinal baseball. Denver Bronco football. Kentucky basketball. These teams are more religion than sports. They are a lifestyle for their fanatical fandom. Nebraska football is one of those. Bob Devaney built this dynasty, and then Husker fans grabbed the wheel. They are the Jeff Gordon behind this Big Red Machine. Their bottomless passion works like a security system, making sure Nebraska football is always clicking. The same fans who almost drove Tom Osborne to Colorado in 1979 worked like the tide, bringing their coach back home. And not just because Osborne loved the attention. The best recruiting tool you can offer is a place where people care. It's the fanaticism that makes this thing work. Let fans log on and call in. Let them vent. Just don't let them go away. Forget the offense and the defensive coordinator. The first time you hear silence in Memorial Stadium? There's your sign of trouble.

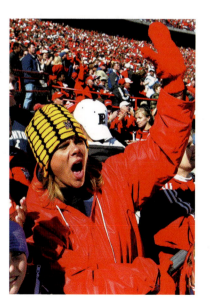

Thank you, Terry Pettit. The former Nebraska volleyball coach's sales pitch may have been the most important in securing the 2006 NCAA volleyball final four, the first major sporting event for the Big O's new arena. Pettit played a crucial role for two reasons. One, having him speak to the Division I Volleyball Committee is like having Mike Krzyzewski talk to the men's hoops committee. When he speaks, they listen. But it also speaks to cooperation between Omaha and Lincoln. If the NCAA senses a community force behind getting events here, especially a community with more than 1 million people, it's going to be impressed.

Humans, Not Computers, Smarter This Time

PASADENA, CALIF.

THEY CAME, THEY saw and they conquered the Rose Bowl on Thursday night. They were everywhere, at every flank. They threw a red blanket around ol' Granddaddy and practically smothered him. In Nebraska's first Rose Bowl appearance since 1941, they were downright overwhelming.

Yes, Nebraska fans are definitely No. 1.

Their favorite team, however, wasn't even in the ballpark, not to mention the Rose Bowl.

Miami defeated the Huskers 37-14 in a national championship game that wasn't as close as the score indicated but was certainly uglier.

It began as such a glorious night. What a sight. More than 60,000 rabid Herbies in red had turned the Rose Bowl into a Husker home game. Memorial Stadium West. If Nebraska had a chance against mighty Miami, it was all that red. The night began with such promise, anticipation.

It ended with 60,000 shuffling out slowly and all of them had to be saying, "This couldn't have happened again." But it did.

Never have so many traveled so far and paid so much to see so little.

It will be a long drive home, long flight home, long winter after the Huskers lost consecutive games for the first time since 1990. But even in 1990, when Nebraska was accused of quitting after losses to Colorado, Oklahoma and Georgia Tech, things weren't as ugly as the losses to CU and Miami by a combined score of 99-50.

For the first time since that 1990-92 era, Nebraska looked overmatched on the biggest stage in college football, and it made you wonder if they should have been in this game at all.

In hindsight, they shouldn't have been.

That was painfully obvious in the first quarter, after a 49-yard touchdown pass from Ken Dorsey to a wide-open Andre Johnson. NU corner Keyuo Craver slipped at the line of scrimmage. But even then, you got the feeling Miami was toying with the Huskers and this thing could break open if the Huskers didn't keep up.

It was obvious on a 39-yard touchdown run by Clinton Portis, who stepped in and out of a highlight reel of missed tackles.

And when James Lewis returned an interception 47 yards for a touchdown after cradling a pass that bounced off Tracey Wistrom's hands.

And the 66-yard, two-play scoring drive that was so easy it was ridiculous.

Miami's Ed Reed, on the ground, and Philip Buchanan bring down Heisman Trophy winner Eric Crouch.

JANUARY 4, 2002 • NEBRASKA FOOTBALL

And when Miami fans mockingly cheered when the Huskers finally got a first down in the second quarter.

And when Oregon coach Mike Bellotti, who was flown to the game by ABC in case there was a Husker upset and a split title, stepped into the press box and told reporters he thought the wrong team was playing Miami.

There wasn't much to say about this one, except that, well, humans are obviously smarter than computers. Humans had Oregon ranked No. 2 in both polls. Again, in hindsight, the Pac-10 champs would have given Miami a better game, though there's no guarantee the result would have been different.

Nebraska should have been in the Sugar Bowl or the Holiday Bowl and, frankly, a game against Illinois or Washington would have been a preferred matchup. At least then the Huskers would have had a better chance to rinse out the bad taste from the Colorado debacle.

But how do you refuse a shot at the national title? You don't. It's not Nebraska's fault that it had the winning BCS lottery ticket dumped in its lap. The Huskers won 11 games. They beat the defending national champ in Oklahoma. This is a proud program that lives for No. 1. Of course they were game.

For the past four weeks, they've said all the right things. They said they wouldn't waste their reprieve. They said the Colorado game wasn't them. They said this time they would show up. Then all you heard out of the Husker camp was how intense, and physical, and focused those December practices were.

I'd hate to have seen what would have happened if they had been out of focus.

It's just too bad it had to end this way, with the game over at halftime, with Eric Crouch not showing his stuff, with everyone wondering if the right team was here, and 60,000 who never got to join in and make their awesome presence known.

They went to Disneyland, Universal Studios, Sunset Boulevard, Venice Beach and the Granddaddy of them all. The Rose Bowl will never forget them. The game, they will all try to forget.

20 YEARS WITH TOM SHATEL • 175

Knight Steals Show, Not Win

FOR ONE NIGHT, one snowy night, the Devaney Center was the place to be. The place to see and be seen.

To see Bob Knight and be seen by Bob Knight.

That's the only possible explanation for Nick Sorrell. The University of Nebraska freshman obviously had heard Knight, the Texas Tech basketball coach, had a penchant for fishing. Sorrell showed up as bait.

There he stood, dressed in a red basketball jersey (a UNO jersey, by the way). He wore a pair of bright red Indiana University basketball shorts, purchased earlier in the day at a Lincoln mall. His face, on the other hand, was a mess.

Sorrell had red "choke" marks (drawn) all over his neck. He had a (penciled-in) black left eye. If this was the Husker Hoops version of Halloween, Sorrell came as Neil Reed, the former IU player who was caught on tape being choked by Knight.

Sorrell wanted to see if he could make it two-for-two.

"I want him to come choke me," said Sorrell, from Plattsmouth, Neb. "My whole goal tonight is to get him to throw a chair."

Sorry, Nick. Sorry, Red Zone student section. Sorry, Husker fans. No chair. No love seat. No sale. Your final score: Nebraska 80, Texas Tech 69, and zero incidents to make Nebraska part of the Knight Horror and Hoops Show.

Instead, a sellout crowd had to settle for a ton of goose bumps, smiles and memories, courtesy of a coaching legend who still made it a night to remember, even with his chair stationary.

This in spite of the plea from a student sign that read, "Bobby Knight Furniture Special — Buy a Sofa, I'll Throw in a Chair."

Or the student holding a metal chair with the sign, "Throw me." Or the guy who flashed a sign toward the Tech bench that showed a photo of Knight and Reed, with a caption from Reed saying, "No Tolerance Means No Choking."

Husker basketball fans braved bad winter weather to get in their digs at Texas Tech coach Bob Knight.

And certainly in spite of the industrious young men in the front row of the Red Zone, who, in full view of Knight, wore bright orange hunting gear with bull's-eyes on their bull's-ends, in honor of Knight's notorious hunting accident.

At one point, the Red Zone hunters rolled up some newspaper into huge "balloons," then burst them to make a "pop" noise. They dived onto the ground, as if someone had just shot a gun, then got up to say, "We're OK, Bobby."

Sigh. The General wasn't looking.

Why? What made them do it? What made 13,500 Nebraskans trudge out in a snowstorm to see Texas Tech even though a game against a real top 20 team, Oklahoma, drew half as many? Why was everyone but the E! Network covering this game?

Why, after the 80-69 Nebraska victory, did the student section storm the court like the Huskers had just beaten Duke?

Because this was not so much a game as an event. Because while Knight has been on his best behavior since finding Lubbock, Texas, the man is still a time bomb long overdue for an explosion. And what better place to implode than Lincoln, Neb.

Because some people go to Knight games the way some go to watch NASCAR: to look for a wreck.

Because there's something that draws one to a man who says, "When my time is gone, they should bury me with my face down, so my critics can kiss my . . ."

Because, as the Red Zone chanted toward the end of the game, "We beat Bobby."

All Wet? No, They're Dedicated

HIS FRIEND THE alarm clock screams in his ear at 4:40 a.m. Every day.

And Jon Enenbach hops out of bed, gets into his car and drives across town to Mockingbird Pool. By 5:30, when most high school kids are still sawing logs, Enenbach jumps into the water and starts his day with an 80-minute workout.

Think about the Omaha Creighton Prep senior captain this weekend, when the Nebraska state high school swimming and diving meet takes place. Think about all of these swimmers, the most dedicated and unheralded athletes in our midst. And wonder why.

Why do they do it?

There must be a very good reason for this lunacy. It must be because kids today just love getting up at 4:40 a.m. and working out in a pool.

OK, forget that.

Maybe it's because swimmers get all the girls (or in the girls' case, the guys). Could be, except for that schedule. Look at Enenbach. He's different; he swims and dives. But his schedule is typical for these nautical nuts.

After his workout ends at 6:50 a.m., he has to make it to class at Creighton Prep by 7:30. He's in school until 2:20 p.m., then back in the water from 3 until 5. Then he has diving practice from 5:30 until 7. Then he goes home, has a quick dinner and studies until 11 p.m. or until he passes out, whichever comes first.

He doesn't need to borrow the car. He needs to borrow a pillow.

Obviously, it's because swimmers get all the attention and, everywhere they go, people can't wait to talk swimming.

"At school, people ask, 'Are you guys going to win again?' and that's the extent of the conversation," Enenbach said.

"Every once in a while, I have my letter jacket on, and I'll hear somebody behind me say, 'Oh, it's just swimming.' I feel like turning around and saying, 'Let's see you get out here and do this every day and see what happens.' Sometimes I wish I could throw a football around all day."

Maybe it's because they get to wear those really cool haircuts. Prep swimmers got together and took turns shaving each other's heads, all in the name of grabbing that extra nanosecond.

Later they go home and shave their bodies.

"Privately," Enenbach said.

If not the haircut, it must be the exciting lure of big-time college recruiting. What's that? You say swimmers have to sell themselves, sending their times to college coaches? You say a lot of Division I schools, such as Nebraska, are cutting off the incentive by chopping swimming programs?

"That affects us," said Enenbach, who is being recruited by Yale, Notre Dame and Georgetown. "What future do we have in the sport? When Nebraska did that, it was like men's swimming completely died in this state."

So if it isn't the girls, the glory, the hair or the recruiting, what is it?

"We all talk about it," Enenbach said. "We love to compete. We love to push ourselves, to see how fast we can go, how far we can take it. That's our fun."

Why do they do it? You don't have to understand swimming. Just respect it.

Omaha Creighton Prep's Jon Enenbach explained swimmers' devotion to their sport: "We love to push ourselves, to see how fast we can go, how far we can take it. That's our fun."

Transition Complete, Tradition Upheld

ST. LOUIS

FORGET THE BLEWJAYS. Forget the transition year after Ryan Sears and Ben Walker. Forget the NIT.

Remember the Creighton BLUEjays? They're back. Back on top of the ladder at the Savvis Center, cutting down nets and wearing Missouri Valley Champions T-shirts. Back in the NCAA tournament, for the fourth straight year.

They reintroduced themselves to the world of college hoops on a wild, wonderful night in the Valley tournament title bout. The Creighton program, the tradition, remains in good hands after the Jays' 84-76 victory over Southern Illinois.

And those would be the hands of the players.

This was their game, their week, their championship. Oh sure, Creighton coach Dana Altman, who is the Valley coach of the year every year, knows his way around a chalkboard. Altman did a superb coaching job this season.

This week, the Jays did a superb playing job.

As the blue Mardi Gras of players, families and fans engulfed one basket to cut down some nets, Altman stood at the opposite end of the court, alone, arms crossed, watching like a proud parent. Why?

"It's all them," Altman said. "They really got focused this week. This was their tournament."

Who let the Jays out? Who knows? Altman was out of answers with this group. He's pushed every button all season, and while a co-league title is no small achievement, he knew there was more there. They couldn't finish off teams. They stopped playing.

It got to the point where Altman finally stopped begging for toughness and focus. In fact, his pregame talk consisted of the coach saying, "If you guys can't compete, if you can't get up for this, you don't belong here."

The Jays proved they belong with the Sears-Walker teams that set the bar for this program. But this standard isn't just about an NCAA tourney streak. It's more about a tradition of work ethic, defense, unselfish play and floor burns.

The tradition was alive and well this week. The Jays came to play 120 minutes and didn't cheat themselves. Sears and Walker would be proud. But this was no two-man show. This was a 12-man wrecking crew and there were too many heroes, too many big plays to count. Down by three at the half with a rocking SIU crowd smelling blood, the Jays went to work.

They came out and knocked the Salukis in the mouth. The so-called soft Jays outmuscled and outrebounded SIU's bruisers. Defense? There were eight blocks and seven steals. They back-doored SIU to death.

Terrell Taylor was focused and athletic. Ismael Caro, the forgotten point guard, ran the show like a champ. Kyle Korver was Kyle Korver. Brody Deren was the force everyone was waiting for. This was the team everyone was waiting for.

Why now? Why not? Deren called it a sense of urgency, and that was as good an answer as any. Maybe they felt as if they were letting down the program. Maybe it was unfair to expect them to uphold those standards with so many new faces.

"No, it wasn't," Altman said. "If you're going to establish a tradition, you've got to have those standards of unselfish team basketball. There has to be a way of doing things around here. That has to be our tradition."

The torch has been passed. The Bluejays are back.

Creighton center Brody Deren had 13 points in the Missouri Valley championship game.

MARCH 16, 2002 • CREIGHTON BASKETBALL

Like Mike, CU's Taylor Is Walking on Air

CHICAGO

SO THE KID wearing No. 23, the kid who grew up wanting to be like Mike, gets to play on his court in his city. And the kid is wearing his Michael Jordan tattoo, with the Jordan socks and armband and Washington Wizards No. 23 T-shirt with you-know-who's name on the back.

And this is after the kid was so nervous about seeing the statue of his idol that he wouldn't even look at it as the team bus drove past. He had to go back later, after practice, and walk backward toward the statue until the moment was just right to turn around and gawk.

And then, coming out of the locker room, the kid runs past the Chicago Bulls locker room and out the tunnel, past the six NBA championship trophies emblazoned on the wall. Just like Mike used to do.

And there's his team, Creighton, overmatched in talent but not heart, clawing for the kind of NCAA tournament upset that the good folks of Omaha will be able to recite shot by shot 30 tournaments from now. And there are his teammates Kyle Korver and Brody Deren on the bench with foul trouble.

And here's the kid, having the game of his life. He's going up against Florida, a team with five dudes who will play in the NBA, but all eyes are on the kid.

The kid makes a 3. Then another 3. He feels it. So does the crowd. The United Center is full of Illinois fans, full of Chicagoans, folks who saw Michael play. They're on their feet, cheering for Creighton, cheering for the upset, cheering for another No. 23.

And now the Jays are down by six and there are two minutes left. No problem for the kid. He swishes a 21-footer, and the crowd roars and everyone believes again. Here comes the kid again. He takes a pass from Korver at the top of the circle. He launches a sweet arc from — what else? — 23 feet.

And of course it goes in. Tie score. Overtime. Just like Mike used to do. But now it's the second overtime, and things don't look so good because Korver's fouled out. There are 45.2 seconds left, and Florida's up four. Who will Creighton turn to now? Who else? The kid hits one to cut it to two.

With 29 seconds left, Florida turns it over on a five-second call trying to inbound the ball. CU runs down the clock, but a Gator tips the ball away and it looks like it goes off of the kid out of bounds. The officials say it's Creighton ball with 4.5 seconds left. This can't be happening. This must be somebody's dream. Where's that kid, by the way?

He's taking the inbounds pass. His team's down by two. He fakes a drive. The kid steps back. He fires a 3-pointer, with a strikingly familiar fade as he releases, with two-tenths of a seconds left. Swish. Just like Mike used to do.

"It's like a fairy tale," the kid says. "Doing the things Jordan did, hitting the big shots down the stretch, hitting the shot to win the game, and doing them here, where he used to do them. It's a dream come true."

And then you wonder, was this whole thing an actual NCAA tournament game? Or just Terrell Taylor dreaming? Both.

Terrell Taylor's shot with 0.2 of a second left on the clock beat Florida at the United Center in Chicago.

2011 INSIGHT *Two of my all-time favorite road trips weren't football games. One was the 2000 NCAA super regional for baseball, with Nebraska at Stanford. Then there was this little stop, the NCAA first-round regional at the United Center in Chicago. NCAA hoops. Rush Street. St. Patrick's Day weekend. You do the math. The only way it could get better was if Creighton would upset Florida and there was a great story attached to it. Voilà. Terrell Taylor, a good kid who lived and played outside of the Dana Altman mold, hits the winning shot in double overtime. Taylor also had another anti-Altman trait: He loved attention. So when he went flying around the court after the shot, it was game on for the Omaha columnist. Taylor was in fantasy land doing the post-game interviews, and since it was one of the early games, the national and regional columnists and TV guys all flocked to Taylor's locker afterward. When we found out that Taylor grew up worshipping Michael Jordan, even down to his No. 23, it was game, set, match. I decided to try something I did with Eric Piatkowski at that 1994 Big Eight tourney, and that was follow him around afterward and take notes on what he was asked and what he said. I remember going to the ESPN Zone after we finished writing and meeting some Creightonians I knew. One friend of mine had run up a $500 bar tab by the time I got there. It was wild. That night, Altman tagged along with his buddy, Oklahoma football coach Bob Stoops, in a limo on the way to dinner. That next day, CU beat writer Rich Kaipust and I tried to get Taylor to pose by the Jordan statue outside the United Center, but Altman shot down the idea. He didn't want Taylor to lose any more focus than he already had. CU lost the next game, to Illinois, and Taylor would leave the program soon after. But it was a weekend, and a story, nobody at Creighton will ever forget.*

MAY 13, 2002 • LANCER HOCKEY

Curtain Lowered on Ak's Tradition

TURN OUT THE lights. The party's over.

But this was no way to end an Omaha hockey shindig. This was the last sporting event at the grand old Ak-Sar-Ben Coliseum. The Omaha Lancers were going to win the Clark Cup. That was the one and only ending to the "Final Ak."

Obviously, Ryan Geris and the Sioux City Musketeers didn't get the script.

Ryan who? Geris is now the painful answer to the trivia question, "Who scored the last goal at Ak-Sar-Ben Coliseum?" He did it just 3:41 into overtime as the Musketeers overcame a 3-1 deficit to win 4-3 and unleash a bizarre end to an era.

This is how it ended for Ak-Sar-Ben: With 5,000 Lancer fans slowly shuffling out of the building with blank faces, fathers' arms over their sons' shoulders, girls in Lancer jerseys crying, old men in orange jackets shaking their heads.

Meanwhile, inside the arena, there were the faint sounds of the visitors, the strangers, getting the last laughs out of an Omaha institution.

A bitter ending to a sweet night.

Backstage, maybe on the spot where Frank Sinatra once crooned, a shocked coach Mike Hastings was singing the blues: "It's going to leave a mark, hurt for a while. We had a chance to send off the building the way it should be sent off."

Instead, the remaining Lancer fans gave it a shot, serenading the devastated team off the ice with one last rendition of "The Heat Is On." Years from now, the ghosts of Ak-Sar-Ben will be whistling that tune in the hallways of an office building where the old barn used to be.

Omaha Lancer Yale Lewis watches Sioux City celebrate its victory in the final hockey game at the Ak-Sar-Ben Coliseum.

JUNE 23, 2002 • COLLEGE WORLD SERIES

Garrido Redeemed in Eyes of Texans

PHILOSOPHER. LEFT-COAST DUDE. Zen master. Jet-setting pal of Kevin Costner. College baseball coaching legend.

Texan?

Augie Garrido has been called many things in his long and storied career, but "podnah" has never been one of them. Well, maybe until now.

Garrido delivered the University of Texas its first national championship baseball trophy since 1983. Time for a Texas baptism. But, please, be gentle.

"Am I an honorary Texan? I hope so," Garrido said. "I don't want to be branded. A light spanking would be enough."

It's time for the demanding Longhorn fans to give it up, literally, to their baseball coach of six years. He won his fourth national title. He moves alone into third place on the all-time list behind Southern California's Rod Dedeaux (10) and LSU's Skip Bertman (five), but even the begrudgingest Horn out there would have to admit what Garrido has done is not only special, it may be harder than what Dedeaux and Bertman did.

Garrido's won at two schools. In this day and age of scholarship limits and major league poaching, that's Texas tough. He's also done it in two settings as opposite as the North and South Poles: Texas and So-Cal.

Cal State Fullerton? Nice little school in suburban L.A. High on the celebrity elbow-rubbing meter. Very low on the facilities and pressure meter.

Texas? Off the charts on the money and pressure meter. They love you, win or win. You fit into the culture and bring home a national championship. Then they'll want to know how long before there's seconds.

Which is why it was doubly hard for any Horn fan to warm up to the cosmic Garrido. When he was hired in 1996, fresh off a national championship at Fullerton, Garrido was about as welcome as an Oklahoman on the second Saturday of October.

Why? Three reasons. He wasn't Cliff Gustafson. He was too California cool. He wasn't Cliff Gustafson.

Texas Athletic Director DeLoss Dodds replaced a legendary coach with another one, but that was beside the point for Texas fans. Coach "Gus" didn't go out the way he wanted, and here was Garrido, not only in Gustafson's shoes and office but climbing up the all-time victory list, trying to pass "Gus" at the top.

"I understand where the bar was set when I took the job," Garrido said. "The fans are passionate. They love their school, they love their team. I just wish it hadn't taken so long. But it was time I needed to learn the environment.

"I'm just pleased DeLoss and the administration gave me time to find my way."

It has taken him six years to find his way back to this place, on top, and the view is considerably better this time. Consider that the last time we saw Garrido on this field celebrating a national title, he was scooting around Rosenblatt Stadium's turf in a motorized chair after being laid up for the 1995 CWS with back surgery.

This time he stood tall, even in the eyes of Texas legends.

"Augie's a philosopher," said James Street, the father of Texas closer Huston Street, the quarterback of UT's 1969 national championship team and a pitcher on three CWS teams. "He's a mentor for these kids. You listen to what he says, and after you think about it, it makes sense. He's pretty good."

Augie Garrido won national titles at Cal State Fullerton in 1979, 1984 and 1995 before moving to Texas.

NOVEMBER 30, 2002 • NEBRASKA FOOTBALL

Remember, Huskers Only Human

WELL, IT WAS one heck of a run. And we're not talking about Brian Calhoun.

A moment of silence, please. The most impressive streak in college sports — or any other, for that matter — is over. One of the truly amazing chapters in college football history — or any other kind — is closed and ready for binding.

Nebraska lost to Colorado 28-13. The Huskers have won seven games. They can win eight by conquering the Independence Bowl.

They cannot, however, win nine.

For the first time since 1968, the Huskers will not have a nine-win season. For 33 straight seasons, they won at least nine games. Think about it. That's three decades. That's a lot of winning.

Has there ever been a better, more durable streak? There was a man on the moon and Watergate and disco and Title IX and scholarship limits and Cyndi Lauper and Dick Vitale and Barry Switzer leaving Oklahoma and Kansas State winning 11 games and rap music. The Streak went through more history than "Forrest Gump."

It included five national championships. Three head coaches. Three Heisman Trophies. Countless All-Americans. Skyboxes. HuskerVision. White pants on the road.

It included wins over Northern Illinois, Pacific and Middle Tennessee State. But it's also built on victories over Miami, Florida State and UCLA. Joe Paterno, Bear Bryant, Barry Switzer and Bobby Bowden all fell victim to the Streak.

And then there were two. Nebraska still has 40 consecutive winning seasons, a streak that will be on the line in this year's bowl tilt. This will be the 34th straight bowl trip, too.

But it takes just six wins for a winning record and bowl season. Nine? That's an entirely different story. That's heavier lifting.

Too much, it appears, for Nebraska these days.

Maybe it was bound to happen. All of the great empires, starting with Ming and Rome, flamed out eventually. UCLA in basketball. Alabama, USC, Oklahoma, Miami, Penn State and Texas in football. Even in the fertile fields of Florida and Florida State, the soil dries up on occasion.

Look at North Carolina. The Tar Heels have been winning in basketball since James Naismith first emptied a peach basket. Last year, the Heels not only didn't make the NCAA tournament, they won just eight games. If it can happen there, it can happen anywhere.

It has happened here.

Kiss your wife. Hug your kids. Pet the dog. Take a deep breath. This isn't the end of the world. Just the end of an era.

Husker assistant Dan Young leaves the field after his final game coaching at Memorial Stadium. The Huskers won nine or more games in every one of the 20 seasons he was in Lincoln, except the last one.

Bo Pelini came from the Green Bay Packers to join Frank Solich's staff for the 2003 football season.

Pelini Will Stoke Huskers' Fire

DOES BO KNOW college defense? Pelini has never been a defensive coordinator and hasn't been in college football for more than a decade. It's a bit of a risk for Frank Solich, whose margin for error gets slimmer by the season.

Still, there's something about this hire that looks absolutely brilliant.

Maybe it's his pedigree. Pelini's from Youngstown, Ohio, home of the Stoops brothers (maybe there's something in the water). He groomed under Hayden Fry at Iowa for two years. When it came to assistants, Fry had the magic touch.

Or maybe it's that the body of Pelini's coaching work has been in the NFL. Perfect. I can't remember the last time Nebraska had an assistant coach with NFL experience. Recruits' mothers care about academics. The kids want to know about getting to the NFL.

It might be that Pelini has a no-nonsense reputation and a two-alarm fire in his belly. He won an award at Ohio State for inspirational play. There's a story going around that he once yelled at Will McDonough, the famous Boston Globe NFL writer, in the press box.

Passion and fire are two things the Blackshirts could use a little of these days. It doesn't matter if Pelini knows college trends or not. Just tap a little of that flame out of his belly and pass it on.

After watching NU's Blackshirts scurrying like mice to get in the right formation before the snap, it's obvious the Huskers need to get away from rocket science and back to basic physics. Line up. Find the ball. Tackle.

If nothing else, Pelini needs to teach the Blackshirts how to tackle again.

Ball carriers, not sportswriters.

TOM'S TAKE | REFLECTIONS ON

Two Sports Giants Emerge From the Shadows

HUSKER FOOTBALL IS the big dog. But what happens when Brutus has to see the vet?

It gives us a chance to pause to pay tribute, and attention, to the other worthy members of the sports kingdom.

Creighton is in the College Cup, soccer's version of the final four. Nebraska volleyball plays for a third straight trip to the final four and a shot at a second national title in three years.

Their timing couldn't be more therapeutic, at the end of the worst Husker football season in four decades. But the thing is, Jays soccer and NU volleyball are there every year.

We think of Big Red football as our national champion. Perhaps it's time to rethink that. As Frank Solich retools his ailing program, Nebraska volleyball and CU soccer look like the real sports machines in Nebraska.

Forgive us for overlooking the obvious. Volleyball and soccer take place in football's autumn shadow. And these are niche sports that live outside the mainstream, attractive to a loyal following that hangs through thick and thin.

Mostly thick.

How do they do it? Hard work. Ingenuity. Attitude over budget and facilities. Mostly, great management. CU soccer and NU volleyball thrive in their non-revenue cocoons because of impeccable hires.

Both underwent change at the top that would devastate others. Both survived because the head coach knew a thing or two about choosing a successor.

Terry Pettit hand-picked loyal assistant John Cook to take care of NU volleyball. Bob Warming recommended Bret Simon to replace him, and Simon made the job so good that Warming came back to replace him.

Creighton is a basketball school and hosts the College World Series. But soccer is CU's best chance to compete for a national title.

The pool of soccer schools is smaller than basketball or baseball. That doesn't make the challenge less deep. The Jays travel eight and 14 hours on bus trips. And they couldn't host an NCAA tournament game last month when the field — which they've outgrown — was too sloppy two days after snow hit.

The job gets easier next year when the CU soccer stadium and state-of-the-art field opens. But it won't necessarily be more satisfying.

Nebraska is the big dog in volleyball trying to fend off challengers and NCAA-legislated parity.

In that way, Cook is like Tom Osborne or Frank Solich, trying to feed a monster and survive the self-imposed pressures.

"This year was more enjoyable because we weren't favored," Cook said. "But the pressure is still there. Every time you step on the floor, you get somebody's best shot. That's what makes what our seniors have done so remarkable.

"Some days it does feel like (football pressure). I watch what's happened to them and it makes you wonder, 'What if that happened here?' "

We won't stop watching football. We may not understand soccer or volleyball. But we understand, and appreciate, winning and doing it with class.

— DECEMBER 13, 2002

THE CHANGING SPORTS LANDSCAPE 2002

Nebraska Gets Just What It Wanted in Steve Pederson

GIVE ME A "P." Give me an "E." Give me a "D." Give me another "E." Give me an "R." Give me an "S." Give me an "O." Give me an "N." What's that spell?

Hope. It arrived at the University of Nebraska like a surprise package on Christmas morning. Steve Pederson, the only person for the job, was introduced as athletic director at a press conference that was more like a pep rally. Merry Christmas. There's good news under the tree. And who needed it more than the good folks in Huskerville?

For so long, this place has been Downersville. Start with a 7-6 football season. Three defensive coaches fired. A head football coach who appears to be stumbling around in the dark getting his staff reorganized. A vacancy at athletic director and no apparent urgency to fill it. And a man at the top, Chancellor Harvey Perlman, who had given no indication that he had any clue how to run the athletic machine on campus. Would Perlman run it off the road? Could he woo Pederson home from Pittsburgh? Would Frank Solich have new nameplates on his coaches' doors by next year's opener? Ten years from now, would folks from Miami to Pasadena say, "Whatever happened to Nebraska? I hear they have a good chemistry department."

These were nervous days to be a Husker. For years, Nebraska was the model of stability. Now, suddenly, it looked like a good time to dump the stock.

There's a billboard in Lincoln for Nebraska basketball. It shows the slogan "Believe." Well, forget hoops. That slogan could apply to the entire NU athletic family. They needed someone to believe in.

He has arrived. Perlman was absolutely correct when he said the school, and state, need a healer. A rallying cry from a rally leader. Pederson would appear to have that charisma. Put it this way: He calls himself a friend of both Bill Byrne and Tom

Steve Pederson leads cheers after he was introduced as athletic director at halftime of the Nebraska-Creighton basketball game.

Osborne. There aren't many who can say that.

Only one thing can spoil this perfect marriage.

Pederson will only be as popular as his football coach. And, it's important to note, Solich is not his coach.

To be sure, the men are friends. They spent a lot of time together during Pederson's two stints with NU football. But business is business. And, right now, Nebraska football business is not good.

Do not assume that because Pederson used to work with Solich that the coach now has a long leash to "get it done." Or that because Pederson and Osborne are close, and Solich is Osborne's legacy, that Solich is safe. Assume only that, unless Solich shows big improvement next season, this will be a sticky wicket for Pederson.

For now, it's enough to know that there's a leader in the building. Speaking of which, how about that Harvey Perlman? Who knew? This was a bold stroke of leadership, cutting through the red tape and hitting a home run when most folks were afraid the chancellor would get caught looking. Indeed, when Pederson said, "How lucky are we to have Chancellor Perlman running our university?" our response was, "We had no idea."

— DECEMBER 21, 2002

2011 INSIGHT *If only we knew then what we know now. Most people in Nebraska knew that December 2002 was a critical crossroads for the program. Frank Solich's program was broken, and there was a vacancy in the athletic director's office. I wrote that Nebraska needed to hire a football guy, and a Nebraska football guy, if possible. I think most were in agreement that that guy was Steve Pederson. I'll never forget driving down to Lincoln for the press conference the day that Harvey Perlman hired Pederson. Everyone thought they had died and gone to Husker Heaven. The press conference was played live on Omaha radio. The room was packed with staff, boosters, coaches. The mood was upbeat. Pederson talked about the Husker way and how everyone else was going to have to bring their "A game" to beat Nebraska. The general feeling was that things were all right now. Pederson was here to save the day, take care of football, paint the town red again. Nobody – and I mean nobody – argued with this hire. Nobody could have imagined that Pederson's vision of Nebraska was drastically different from what Nebraskans wanted. Nobody dared think that Pederson would bumble and stumble over the football firing and hiring a year later, and that he would slowly alienate the state. Or that, five years later, he would be banished with the same unanimous passion that he was welcomed back in 2002. The Pederson Legacy is engraved in Nebraska history. But it's worth noting that, once upon a time, he had arrived as a hero.*

KYLE KORVER'S A BIG SHOT | A PEACH OF A SOFTBALL PITCHER | RICE CAPTURES THE CWS

2003

> "I'm not a golfer. I'm not a fisherman. I'm a football coach who loves his work and respects his profession. And I'm a Lexington, Nebraska, boy who grew up in that town of 5,000 people in a state where there is only flatlands and football."
>
> — MONTE KIFFIN, TAMPA BAY BUCS DEFENSIVE COORDINATOR

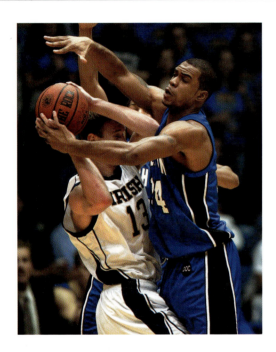

If ever there was a Valley lock for The Tournament, it's the boys in blue. Barring any major injuries, the Jays are playing for a seed. An NCAA seed. They're in the rankings, which doesn't put you in the NCAA Dance but does put you in the highlights and score crawls and the minds of the committee all winter. Creighton is No. 1 in the Sagarin ratings, which also doesn't tip the scale with the committee, but provides a tip as to how high the Jays are in the real RPI. The wins over Notre Dame and BYU. The "good" loss at Xavier. Those will go a long way toward a fifth NCAA berth as the Jays go through their Valley exercises this winter and, basically, try not to screw things up.

She's been called a traitor. Her Nebraska women's basketball program has been compared to the men and, at last check, that wasn't a compliment. She's down to 10 players, and that includes three walk-ons and two volleyball stars. The roster's so shallow that a handful of frat rats fill in at practice, when there isn't a big foosball tournament back at the house. Meanwhile, her former team is playing for first place in the Missouri Valley Conference and in line for a return trip to the NCAA tournament. So this is probably a bad time to ask Connie Yori if she has any regrets about leaving Creighton for Nebraska. Actually, it's a perfect time. "No regrets, not at all," Yori said. "I'm totally confident we can get it done here. This is an unbelievable challenge, the challenge of my life. But it's a challenge I look forward to."

The honeymoon's over for Barry Collier. When he was hired, Collier was one of the "hot" basketball coaches, a guy with a clean image who got players to work hard, play smart and eat all their vegetables. He spoke Nebraskans' language. He's finding out that the most popular word in the Nebraska vocabulary is winning.

186 • 20 YEARS WITH TOM SHATEL

BO'S BLACKSHIRTS CORRAL COWBOYS | FIRING OF COACH FRANK SOLICH | ARENA OPENING

Oh, Bob Warming. That crazy romantic. The Creighton men's soccer coach decided to surprise his wife, Cindy, for their 26th wedding anniversary — with a trip downtown to CU's unfinished soccer complex. On a clear, hot Aug. 13 night, Bob and Cindy sat on a blanket on a tall mound of dirt. Bottle of wine. Under the stars. Looking east, beyond the field where Warming wants Creighton to celebrate its first athletic national championship, to a much bigger picture. And Warming fell in love all over again. "It was so awesome," he said. "You should see downtown at night. I never knew it was so beautiful. The buildings. The new arena. People will love it."

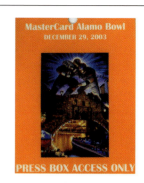

Hi, Bo? Er, um, coach Pelini? Hello, Mr. Pelini. Nice to meet you, and did I mention what an honor it was to finally make your acquaintance? I have a confession to make: I was downright knee-knocking, sweaty-palm nervous about meeting Nebraska's new defensive coordinator the other day. OK, nervous is not the right word. Let's say anxious. Job-interview, meet-the-parents anxious. What's the fuss over a football coach? You know, it could be the eyes. That stare, glare, whatever. We're talking laser beams. Don't mess up, son. But if you do, absolutely do not look into the man's eyes. It's like having Coach Medusa. Those who gaze into his eyes turn to stone.

The Matt Hopper Story could be a book. Something nice and succinct, like "War and Peace." There's no truth to the rumor that Hopper played with Buck Beltzer. It just seems that way. After five years at Nebraska, here's what we know about Hopper: He's one whale of a player. And he hangs around school more than "The Fonz." "I'm 23," Hopper said, sheepishly. "Most of my teammates are 18. But they have really taken me in."

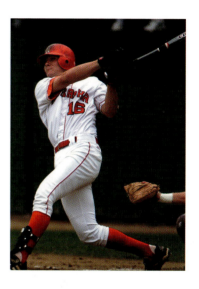

It's not just a phrase in hockey, it's a way of life. It's understood. You lose half your bridgework, take a hot stick to the eye, watch your dreams get run over by a Zamboni, you pick yourself up, dust off the ice chips and play on. That's what we love about hockey players. It's part of their charm. Maybe that's the wrong word to describe what UNO's Greg Zanon has gone through this season. Actually, there are hockey words to describe Zanon's senior year, but this is, after all, a family newspaper. Zanon expected to be deep in the midst of his coolest winter by now. Instead, he spent much of his senior year performing unusual stunts. "For most of the season, Greg played on one leg," UNO coach Mike Kemp said. It's hard to tell which was wounded more, Zanon's knee or his pride.

20 YEARS WITH TOM SHATEL • 187

Korver Becomes Jays' Big Shot

THERE'S NO TRUTH to the rumor that Kyle Korver arrived in this world with knees bent, shoulders square and wrist slightly cocked.

It just looks like he was born with the perfect jump shot. Perfect? When he catches, stops, turns, squares up, cocks, releases, follows through and then swishes, even the ball applauds.

Korver has a jump shot so beautiful it belongs on the cover of Cosmopolitan. It's so fundamentally sound it looks like it was built by NASA. It's a timeless piece of hoop art, something that should be on display down the street from the Civic Auditorium, at the Joslyn Art Museum.

Korver's jumper is so sweet and pure that, when he misses, it's the basket's fault.

You'd never know that the shot used to be a clunker, an absolute mess, and that the Creighton senior forward still has to take it into the gym every day for fine-tuning and maintenance.

Indeed, the Pella, Iowa, boy was a hoop project, not prodigy.

"My shot has been through everything," Korver says. "I was left-handed in the third grade. And my uncle said, 'You need to change to the right.'

"When I was a sophomore in high school, I used to sling it from my shoulder. It would take off and spin like a helicopter to the basket. It was ugly. Finally, I got strong enough to hold it up and shoot it correctly, release and follow through. Then I started to get help."

Help? His father, Kevin, played basketball at Central College in Pella. So did uncles Karl, Keith and Ken. Uncle Kris played at Northwestern College. They all took turns taking young Kyle into their shot lab.

The result was what you would get if you took a golfer to five different teachers. In other words, a basket case.

"It was hard," Korver said. "They would tell me to do this with my elbow, that with legs, this with my wrist. They all meant well. But I was a mess. My shot was so horrible. It was my fault because I was misunderstanding them.

"It's taken a lot of practice, a lot of shots, a lot of time in the gym."

Some things never change.

Korver has made himself into a wonderful all-around player. He came to Creighton three years ago as the young marksman. When coach Dana Altman challenged him to do more, his pride kicked in. He hated the label of having one dimension.

Now Korver does it all. He rebounds. He passes. He defends. He drives for the foul when the jumper isn't there. But, like any great shooter, Korver cannot forget his roots, his first love. A boy, a ball and a basket. Does it get any better than that?

No. That's why whenever Altman hears a sound in the old gym at night, he knows it's his favorite gym rat, preparing for a game in therapeutic bliss.

"The night before a game, or if I'm shooting bad, I'll head up there by myself," Korver said. "I'll

turn out all the lights, except for that row above the basket. All you can see is the basket, and the light reflecting on the "Creighton Bluejays" painted on the wall behind it.

"It's where I go to get away from everything. Everywhere you go, somebody wants to talk basketball. Don't get me wrong, I love it. It's great that everyone's excited around the school and around the city. But it's good to have time to yourself. Shooting by yourself is relaxing. It's fun."

It's to the point now where his prowess is legendary around Creighton. He's taken down Kevin McKenna, long regarded as the school's greatest shooter, in H-O-R-S-E. He's the Tiger Woods of a free-throw game at practice, where participants take 18 shots (or holes) and get a birdie for a swish, a par for a ball that hits the rim but goes in and a bogey for a miss.

"I have the record, 14 under," Korver says with pride.

Korver is like a golfer, always tinkering, always looking for the perfect swing. He'll watch other players, work on his fundamentals, tweak his own shot. But mostly, the science of shooting is in the feel.

"When I'm out there, I don't have a plan. I'm shooting to find a rhythm. That's all shooting is to me, rhythm and confidence."

That's what you see during a Creighton game, when Korver's on one of those mind-bending tears. That's what Korver is doing when he's locking and loading from the Jaybacker Room.

"I really don't pay attention to where I am," Korver said. "We used to have X's on the court at the Civic, from where we shot at practice. But now they're gone. So I really have no idea where I am.

"You get into a zone. You aren't really thinking about it. You're just kind of reacting. It's very instinctive. It's the kind of feeling you want to be in."

Kyle Korver's shooting touch carried Creighton to four NCAA tournament appearances.

MARCH 11, 2003 • CREIGHTON BASKETBALL

Salukis Bark, Then Get Bitten

ST. LOUIS

CR8N IS STILL GR8. That's the most plausible explanation for what happened, the only plot line that works.

Creighton whipped, stomped, smashed, pummeled and otherwise muzzled the Southern Illinois Egyptian dogs. The final margin was 80-56, but the score ceased to matter after halftime. The Jays didn't just win their fourth Missouri Valley Conference tourney title in five years. They devoured it.

This was Creighton as we remembered, way back in December and January, when the Jays were the flavor of this college hoops season. Before the night at SIU that made the taste of success not quite as sweet.

This was Creighton, fresh with new Energizer batteries, flying around, making plays on both ends, passing with that old radar, the extreme chemistry overflowing into the ESPN lens. This was Creighton, back and still accounted for and ready for business.

So where did they come from?

Maybe it was some good old-fashioned Jesuit emotion, a cauldron of anger, frustration and even a little embarrassment bubbling over the top.

Maybe it was the obnoxious way SIU has turned this series and "rivalry" into a goofy grudge match.

Maybe it was the way SIU coach Bruce "Whiner" Weber appeared to rub it in to CU coach Dana Altman as Weber accepted the Valley coach of the year award, calling it the "Dana Altman Trophy" and saying that some folks in Carbondale, Ill., thought

Creighton's Larry House shoots over Brad Korn of Southern Illinois in the Valley championship game.

Weber should have won it last year, too.

Maybe it was how, for dessert, Weber called out Creighton at the lunch, saying he hoped SIU could play the Jays for the title.

Lesson No. 1: Be careful what you wish for.

Maybe it was those wacky T-shirts. The "I H8 CR8N" shirts, worn by students and adults alike, few of whom have been within 100 miles of 24th and Burt. Or the obscene chants at Kyle Korver.

Lesson No. 2: This is still the Creighton Invitational, for the fourth time in five years. There's a legacy there. A standard. And, even with the record number of wins and ESPN mentions for Creighton this year, it was a standard that had yet to be met.

Maybe that's what Altman was referring to when he grabbed his three seniors at halftime of the Wichita State game and asked them if a semifinal loss to the Shockers was how they wanted to go down in local history. "We wanted to put 'Champions' behind something," Korver said.

Lesson No. 3: Don't taunt a champion, don't bait a winner, don't rustle a team that has struggled with the pressure of being the heavy favorite and is searching madly for incentive.

"The energy was there tonight, and it came from anger," said senior Larry House. "We've been reading everything they were saying, that they wanted us again, that they wanted to win the tournament real badly. What everyone forgot was that we wanted to win it bad, too."

Lesson No. 4: Korver is more than just another Omaha sex symbol. The nation saw No. 25 at his best, grabbing 10 rebounds, making six assists, including a one-handed bounce pass on the fast break to Joe Dabbert that Jason Kidd would have framed.

This became a scene that even the most optimistic Creighton fan couldn't have imagined. The SIU crowd with nothing to say. The Salukis walking to timeout huddles with heads down. Creighton showing who the real champ was and finding its groove all at the same time. And just in time. It's March. Just another night at the Creighton Invitational.

2011 INSIGHT *You can make the argument that the time between 1999 and 2007 was the greatest era in Creighton basketball history. No game defined that era more than the 2003 Valley title. SIU was Creighton's chief hated rival in that era. Salukis coach Bruce Weber was a smirky Darth Vader for Creighton fans. The 2003 team was Dana Altman's crown jewel, his best group. And yet, it finished second to SIU in the regular season. You had all of those emotions, and subplots, going on when the two teams took the floor that Monday night in St. Louis. In my opinion, this was Altman's finest moment. Nobody saw a blowout coming. The CU coaches were focused, but worried about how they would stop SIU forward Jermaine Dearman. The answer was Kyle Korver. This may have been Korver's finest moment, too. For me, the signature moment was Korver's one-handed bounce pass downcourt to Joe Dabbert for a fast-break dunk. I don't usually get personal with players or coaches, but Weber always rubbed me the wrong way. It was kind of fun to see him sit there and squirm the entire game.*

NU's James Is a Peach of a Pitcher

OK, MEAT. SHOW me what you got. Throw me the cheese. Don't mess around with any fancy stuff. Come right at me. Show me the freight train. Come on. Bring it.

"Whiifffff."

OK, that's one. No big deal. I gave you one. Now I've got your speed down. Think you can do it again? Try it. I dare you. Go ahead, put one inside. I'm digging in. Bring it, meat. Bring the heater. Bring the bad boy.

"Ping."

Owww! Time out, ump. There you go. Got a piece of it. You can't blow it by me. I've got you now. Yeah, see, I'm staring you down. Don't look away. Look in my eyes. I'm not afraid of you, meat. Bring it. I own you.

"Whiifffff."

OK, Peaches. Thanks. Yeah, that was great. No, that's really all right. That's enough research for today. Besides, I don't want to wear out your arm before the big NCAA regional this weekend.

What compels a sportswriter to shove a batting helmet over his big head and stand 43 feet away from one of the biggest, baddest and, let me say, nicest softball pitchers in the country? Why take cuts with an aluminum toothpick against a softball roaring in at 65 miles an hour — which affords the same reaction time as a baseball fastball in the upper 90s thrown from 60 feet, 6 inches away? And, by the way, there is nothing soft about a softball.

Let's use intrigue as a euphemism for stupidity. There's something about softball pitchers. Actually, there are a lot of things that make the position extraordinary.

Maybe it's because most of us played slow-pitch at some point in our lives — usually before we grew up — complete with the roving fourth outfielder and keg of beer on the bench dressed up as the coach. You can enjoy slow-pitch. But you really can't respect it. It's more recreation than sport.

Keep your eye on the pitcher when the NCAA regional begins at Nebraska's Haymarket Park in Lincoln. Why? She's the centerpiece. The Show. The game master. Everything flows through her. She controls the board, as they say, and she can run the table day after day. If she wants to turn a regional into a four-day game of catch between her and the catcher, who's going to stop her?

There's a power to that position, an influence unlike any other position in team sports, unless it would be a hockey goalie. Maybe that's the whole fuss. Maybe it's why a girl from Papillion who could play any sport goes for the big yellow ball.

"It's kind of weird, in a way," says Peaches James, Nebraska's ace pitcher. "The pitcher is the center of attention out there. I'm not used to being the center of attention. I don't like all that attention. It's not like being an outfielder, where you're overlooked. I'd like to be an outfielder sometimes.

"But I've grown to love it."

Peaches — named by her grandmother because she said she "looked like a little peach" — has grown into one of her sport's best.

"I used to get behind and give in to hitters," she said. "Not now.

"But I wouldn't say I intimidate them. I don't even look at them. I don't want to see them staring back. I try not to make eye contact."

Perfect. Then, just between you and me, Peaches, I had my eyes open.

An inside pitch from Peaches James was an eye-opening experience.

Score One for Houston, Honor

HOUSTON, WE HAVE a champion.

Move over, Rockets. There's a new great sports moment in town. The Astros have never played in a World Series. The Oilers couldn't beat the Steelers and blew the big lead at Buffalo. And Houston still remembers the U of H Cougars, on the wrong end of one of the most stunning upsets in NCAA Final Four history, in 1983.

Maybe the national champion Rice Owls can help them forget.

Thanks, Rice. Houston needed it. Heck, we all needed that.

Never mind that the Owls won the College World Series championship 14-2 over Stanford on June 23 with all the drama of a Feb. 23 game. Never mind that the dreadfully dull game, along with the crowd of 18,494, was a letdown.

Mind only that the Owls and their Casey Stengel-esque coach, Wayne Graham, are the coolest thing to happen to college sports in a long time.

It's been a brutal spring for us college types. Wild coaches on the loose. Reality TV, starring Larry Eustachy, Mike Price and Rick Neuheisel. Sex, booze and gambling. The only thing missing was Hunter S. Thompson.

Thank goodness, then, for the Owls of Rice.

Here's a school that has been a bit of an athletic stepchild, left out of the Big 12 by the other Texas schools, with no national championships, no signature teams or athletes to speak of. Until now.

Here's a school with an enrollment of just 2,700, lower than many high schools in Texas. Here's a school that has led the nation in National Merit Scholars becoming No. 1 in a sport. Here's a school whose baseball guide devotes four pages to areas of study and dignitaries who visited the Rice campus.

Henry Kissinger, Kurt Vonnegut, Norman Mailer, Margaret Mead, Bill Cosby and Margaret Thatcher can now say they've been to the home of the CWS champs.

Here's a school in a league (WAC) that doesn't have a BCS bid and gets no love from the college basketball RPI computer. But in college baseball, a school like Rice can still recruit three hosses on the mound and win it all.

And here's a head coach who won big on the junior-college level, who couldn't get hired at the major level until later in life, who still gets passed over for so-called better jobs, sipping from the holy grail at age 67.

Even here in the land of make-believe, at the college event that maintains a purity and innocence, it doesn't get much better than this.

Sure, the championship game could have been better, or at least been a game. But that's baseball. The trade-off for the anticlimactic ending was getting to witness 25 kids who care as much about SATs as RBIs and a wise old Owl of a coach who's as good as any of them.

"There are a lot of passionate people at Rice, and they wanted this and needed this," Graham said. "The city of Houston has always been proud of the university because of its academics and sense of honor. That's why I went to Rice. There's a quest by everyone to maintain honor and do the right thing."

Honor in college sports? Thanks, Owls, for the reminder.

Rice coach Wayne Graham is carried off the field after the Owls' victory over Stanford.

AUGUST 31, 2003 • NEBRASKA FOOTBALL

Huskers' Bo-Shirts Pass First Test

AS HE WALKED back from his postgame radio show through the tunnel to his locker room, Frank Solich did not look any different. But this clearly is not the same old Frank Solich.

The head Husker had his IQ raised. And he's more secure. Why? Two reasons.

(1) Bo. (2) Pelini.

Coaches always say it's the players, the chess pieces, who win and lose games. And most of the time, they speak the truth.

But you don't win games, and championships, without someone to line them up right and turn on their motors.

This is what we saw on the biggest Saturday at Memorial Stadium in many moons. It was a Saturday of confirmation, whichever way the oblong ball bounced. Beat Oklahoma State, and the newly named Husker Nation could breathe a sigh of relief. Lose, and it's the end of the world. Film at 10.

It was a win, 17-7, and the exhale was deafening. Nebraska fans stood and roared at the end, like they haven't in a long time. The venerable Husker palace was filled with old pride and faces — more than 800 former players were in attendance — and everyone wanted to feel the old feelings. They wanted hope.

They got it from the Bo-Shirts.

Hope was delivered in the form of a blitz, a forearm shiver, two fumble recoveries and one returned for a touchdown.

It was delivered by Pelini, the intense new defensive coordinator who had captivated Husker Nation even though he had never been a coordinator and hadn't coached a college football game in over a decade.

Pelini was worth the hype. Guess what? Oklahoma State was not.

Pelini's Bo-Shirts ransacked quarterback Josh Fields, stuffed running back Tatum Bell and threw a wet blanket all over Rashaun Woods (five catches, 47 yards), not to mention his All-America campaign.

This is why head coaches make changes. This is why coaching is not overrated. A year ago, the same Cowboy outfit made fools of Solich and his former coordinator, Craig Bohl. This year, Solich got the last laugh.

"We had players on defense who could run," Solich said. "We needed a philosophy that the players could believe in. A philosophy that would enable them to make plays."

They believe. We believe.

Defensive coordinator Bo Pelini congratulates Trevor Johnson as he comes off the field.

Huskers Slip to Sad State Against KSU

RED ALERT. NEBRASKA football reached a new low. This is getting to the danger level. Kansas State came in and beat the Huskers at home like nobody has since 1958, 38-9, but the embarrassment and hopelessness were worse than the score indicated.

How bad was it? It was so bad that, by the middle of the fourth quarter, as K-State kept scoring with ease, nearly half of the faithful at Memorial Stadium had left.

It was so bad that, as coach Bill Snyder put up another finishing-touch score late, the sounds of the Wildcat band playing "Happy Trails" could be heard throughout the home field.

It was so bad that Nebraska defensive coordinator Bo Pelini got in the face of Snyder afterward for leaving his starters in against NU's defensive walk-ons. The Huskers complaining about K-State running up the score? At home?

This was bad, folks. Worse, this was sad.

It is sad what is happening to a proud program and its beleaguered head coach, who has given a lifetime to Husker football but who appears to be capable of giving no more.

It would be one thing if you could write this off as one bad game, one wacky second half in which all the planets aligned and Kansas State just happened to outscore NU 31-0 and outyard the Huskers 313-77 and it was just K-State's turn.

But this was no fluke. Kansas State is now beating Nebraska every year and doing it the way the Huskers used to do it to the Wildcats.

The Huskers are now middle of the pack in their division and, worse, they look like they belong there. Nebraska isn't even competitive in the biggest games in its own league. And that's what will hurt Frank Solich.

The speculation on Solich's future will reach a new level this week. The coach would be advised not to read the paper, listen to the radio or answer the phone. Can Solich recover from this? It will be hard. I don't see how.

Kansas State defenders smother Husker running back Cory Ross.

2011 INSIGHT *2003 was a strange season, maybe the weirdest in Nebraska football history. It started with optimism, with Bo Pelini's Blackshirts storming Oklahoma State. It ended with a 10th win in the Alamo Bowl. Somewhere in the middle, it was apparent that NU was going to fire a football coach for the first time in 40 years. It became apparent to me a few weeks before this K-State game. NU Athletic Director Steve Pederson had just announced a major football complex project and he did so without inviting head coach Frank Solich to the party. During that time, Pederson made some comments to me that led me to believe he wasn't exactly a big fan of Solich. It became all but official after this bizarro game. K-State winning at Memorial Stadium for the first time since 1968. Bo Pelini cursing at Bill Snyder. The K-State band playing to an empty Memorial Stadium. I remember seeing Bill Doleman, an NU grad and a local TV and radio guy at the time, in the interview area. We both said, simultaneously, "It's over." We didn't see any way Solich would survive. But firing Nebraska football coaches didn't exactly happen every year. So nobody really knew what might happen.*

Solich Deserves Another Year

BOULDER, COLO.

A SOURCE NOT close to the Nebraska football program says that Frank Solich should be retained as head Husker.

The source says it doesn't matter that Solich didn't win his final three games or that he and Athletic Director Steve Pederson don't have hot cocoa together every Wednesday afternoon. The source says Solich should be in.

Of course, you may take it for what it's worth that this source is an over-carbed sports columnist for an Omaha daily newspaper who has been known to flip as well as flop and does not write big checks to anyone except the bank.

Nebraska's 31-22 victory over Colorado was worth a lot more.

After two weeks of speculation and rumors, innuendo and no comments and a whole lot of guessing by a whole lot of people, some hard evidence was finally presented in the case of Solich.

A team playing to win. A team that didn't get down. A comeback. A call to go for it on fourth-and-goal. A goal-line stand.

And the finest moment in the six years of Solich.

With his job on the line, and distractions lined up from the Flatiron mountains to the Flatiron Cafe in Omaha, Solich came, saw and kicked Buff.

He called an aggressive game. He coached with guts. He threw caution to the Rocky Mountain wind. He inspired his troops to rise above the rumors and make courageous play after play. In short, Solich did what you want your head coach to do.

The question is, will he still be the head coach next week? Better question: How do you fire a guy who wins nine games?

How do you get rid of a coach who, faced with impending doom and the biggest game of his career, shows up with one of his better games, if not his best?

How do you give the ziggy to a coach who has done things the right way, who is not hated or despised, whose biggest failing has been failing in the biggest games but then shows you what you wanted to see at the exact moment you wanted to see it?

You don't.

It's time for Athletic Director Steve Pederson to come out of the woodwork and say something. What that something should be is that Solich is his man, at least for another year.

Give Fearless Frankie and his staff another year, a chance to recruit and build on the incredible karma they found in a most unlikely place.

Whether that happens is still anybody's guess. Pederson was conspicuous by his absence again, disappearing into the thin Colorado air after the game. Pederson did not show up in the locker room or at Solich's postgame press conference.

What to make of it? Perhaps not much. Pederson has been uncannily consistent in his policy not to make any statements, symbolic or otherwise.

Here's Pederson's dilemma, if that's what you want to call it. He's thinking big picture. He's thinking long-term. He's asking himself who is the best man to lead this program into the future.

This has nothing to do with records. This has everything to do with an athletic director wanting his own guy.

A third straight loss to CU would have made it easier on Pederson. Now, the athletic director is faced with looking ruthless and unreasonable, and making NU look foolish, nationally, if he goes ahead with the ax. Tonight on SportsCenter: Outrage at Nebraska.

That doesn't mean he won't still do it. Pederson used to be at Ohio State, and the Buckeyes jettisoned John Cooper, who could beat everyone except Michigan. OSU took the PR hits and won a national championship.

But even those critics who say Solich is not the answer long-term have to admit that winning nine games should always be enough at Nebraska. Especially when the ninth win is done so emphatically that it becomes a tiebreaker of whether or not to roll the dice.

Solich just made it very interesting. He just made it harder. There will be no resignation, although you could hardly blame Solich if he has had it up to here with the pressure and the critics. If he went out on this high, it would not be a bad way to go out.

Forget it. When asked about resigning, Solich laughed and said he expected to show up on Monday and meet with the team until he heard otherwise.

If Solich does get the call, Pederson had better be right. He'd better hit a home run. You don't fire a coach unless you already have your man.

Rumor has it, he already does. His name is Solich.

Nebraska football coach Frank Solich went out a winner with a 31-22 victory over Colorado.

Firing Solich Is Right Move

ONE MAN. ONE DECISION. Let there be no doubt, no question, who is running the Nebraska football franchise these days. It is one man. His name is Steve Pederson.

It used to be the power in the family was with the man on the sidelines. Bob Devaney. Then Tom Osborne. Now, it's an athletic director who calls the shots.

Devaney. Osborne. Pederson.

Pederson, in his first year as NU's athletic director, made the first move that will shape his tenure and legacy at Nebraska. He fired Frank Solich as head coach.

It was the right thing to do.

Understand, this is not your average, everyday occurrence in Big Red land. Football coaches don't get fired at Nebraska. They just win. And win. The last guy to get a Big Pink slip was Bill Jennings, back in 1961, before Husker football as we know it was born.

So Pederson, a son of Nebraska football, did not make this decision hastily or easily.

In fact, there's every reason to believe Pederson had this in mind ever since he set foot back on campus last December and declared a revival of Husker Nation. If the football program is the porch to a university, then the football coach is the face on the porch, greeting all.

Pederson knew he needed a strong face to lead this program, the Nebraska football in his vision, which is the only vision that counts. If you buy that Solich was never going to be that man, that Pederson was going to replace him sooner or later, then the sooner the better.

Solich is a great man. A class act. But he has never shown the leadership skills, or the recruiting, for that matter, to be a great head coach. He took leadership counseling from David Sokol, a successful Omaha CEO, last year.

But even Sokol can tell you that the great CEOs are not taught. They either have that thing or they don't. Leaders are born, not made.

It appeared that Solich hired several promising young assistants. But it was all for naught. Solich got only one year to be that CEO.

Pederson never promised him a rose garden. Bill Byrne was the one who allowed Solich to survive a 7-7 season and make the changes on his staff. Had Pederson been here at the time, he may have made this change a year ago.

Why? Because Pederson, a former recruiting coordinator at Nebraska, Tennessee and Ohio State, knows recruiting. He's got a vision of what it takes to recruit to win national championships. Solich wasn't going to fit that mold. I'll never forget hearing Solich speak at a Christ the King banquet in Omaha a few years ago. Afterward, somebody in the audience said to a buddy, "Geez, how does he recruit?"

So Solich was never going to be Pederson's guy, so it might as well have happened now, no matter what happened in Boulder. It was easy to write that Solich deserves another season after going 9-3, even though I've known all along that Pederson's decision was never about a record or number of wins. It was about "direction" and "improvement."

Let's be honest. It was never going to include Frank Solich.

With that in mind, this is absolutely the right move. Why bring Solich back if you are just going to make a change next year, which does not look particularly promising with games at Pittsburgh, Oklahoma, Kansas State and Texas Tech? Nebraska football needs to move forward.

I believe Pederson is right. This program has tradition and passion, but it's stuck in the middle of the country. In this age of parity and everyone on TV and 85 scholarships, you'd better have the best possible coach. You'd better have a salesman. You'd better have someone who knows personnel and how to motivate it.

Solich, from his indecisiveness to the way he played favorites to how he turned NU's offense into a one-dimensional quarterback-runs-the-ball scheme, was not that guy.

I believe Pederson had better be right. You don't fire a coach unless you have the next guy on your speed dial, waiting to accept. Pederson needs to hit a home run.

2011 INSIGHT *In 20 years, I don't have a lot of signature moments or columns. There might be two. And here they are. The flip and the flop. I still get razzed about this from my friends, and I deserve every razz. How did it happen? Good question. Easy answer. I write with my emotions on my keyboard. It's who I am. It's not a particularly proud journalistic trait, but I can get caught up in the moment. It's happened more than once. It happened on Friday, Nov. 28, 2003. NU's win was an upset. And after the way the K-State game had ended two weeks before, who knew Nebraska would rise up and beat the Buffs? The way Solich was carried off the field. The fact that Steve Pederson wasn't there to congratulate him. The signs were everywhere for a firing. I was actually in favor of it. But when I sat down to write, the emotions of the moment began to drip on the keyboard. Give him one more year. Give this staff a year to recruit. As soon as I got home the next day and read it, I immediately said, "Oh, nooooo. I didn't." When the firing was announced that night, I sat down and wrote the column I had expected to write all along – supporting the move. It was a brutal flip-flop. I see now that I actually tried to explain it in the second column. Nice try. Heck, that just watered it down even more. Soon, I became known as the "flip-flop" guy. Hey, I earned it. I had to wear it. And I forgot about it. When a fan or reader brings it up, to this day, I'll joke about it. And explain what happened for those who want to know. Mainly, I just wanted to have both bases covered so I was right either way. You're buying that, right?*

TOM'S TAKE
REFLECTIONS ON

'Old Barn' Magical at the End

CAN AN ARENA get goose bumps? If it was ever going to happen, then it was at the Civic Auditorium, with 12:52 left in the Creighton-Wichita State game. That's when Kyle Korver stopped, popped, and hit a 3-pointer on the fast break.

And, well, if only I could type the noise it made. It was loud, the kind of loud that only a college basketball game can make, when it's March and it's Senior Night and it's the last game in a building that hasn't always felt the love but certainly had to feel it this special night.

Feel? Yes, if you believe in the power and magic of old stadiums, arenas and venerable old barns — that they have a personality and charm all their own — then you had to believe the old Civic was getting all warm and fuzzy inside.

Civic? Warm? Fuzzy? Charming? I would not have believed it if I hadn't seen it, heard it, felt it. And, of course, we saw it, heard it, felt it, all season.

The Jays are moving east next season, toward the river, toward progress. But this was no time to debate the future, whether there will be empty seats or higher taxes or how people can't wait to leave this old barn. This moment was all about saying goodbye to an old friend.

Say this for our friend: It went out in style.

For those of us who weren't here for Rick Apke at the buzzer or Coach Red beating Coach Wooden or the days when Harstad-Gallagher turned the Civic into their personal tag-team ring, this season has been pure heaven. Hoop heaven.

And even for the fortunate who were, this had to be grand fun.

I'm not exactly sure what constitutes a sellout at the Civic, but this season there were 14 nights of 8,000 or more. If that's not a sellout, well, it sounded like one.

There were more than a few games with people standing in the aisles. The people stood. They cheered. They screamed. It was like one nonstop winter party. Amazing that the roof held up.

There have been special moments in this building, big events, memorable nights and games. But there has never been a better season for the Civic Auditorium than this one.

It was the place to see and be seen. The lines at ticket windows went out the front door. There was a buzz in the concourse. The roars were endless. There was a home-court advantage, and there's no greater compliment for an old barn.

For one season, this was our Madison Square Garden. Our Palestra. Our Cameron Indoor. Our Allen Field House.

And even though most of the sentiment was aimed toward three seniors graduating from Dana Altman's School of Hoop, you knew that everyone was aware there was another graduation at work here, too.

There are those who haven't had the kindest words for the old barn. Guilty. But even the harshest critic of a building falling behind the times had to admit: It's always a little sad to witness the end of an era. And yet, with everyone standing and cheering and feeling good, there was a satisfaction here, too.

"Since the renovation, the Civic has been a good place to play," Altman said. "Before that, that wasn't the case. I think it still has a place. For a city our size, there are a lot of activities that can go on here.

"It's over 50 years old. It's time to make the next step. It's an exciting time for the city, our university and our basketball team."

Every barn, new or old, deserves that much. It deserves to have a night when the people stood and yelled and they didn't want to leave and the noise stayed with you all the way out on the walk to the car.

That's how I will remember the Civic.

— MARCH 4, 2003

DeAnthony Bowden lets out a howl after being introduced to the Civic Auditorium crowd.

THE CHANGING SPORTS LANDSCAPE — 2003

Arena Ups the Ante for Teams and City

WE'VE HAD THE tireless campaigning, the leap of faith by voters, the raising of money and the building of steel and brick. Now, Omaha's new arena opens for its first official sporting event, the UNO hockey Maverick Stampede.

Now what? Now the fun part. Now the hard part.

This won't be easy. There has been, and will be, much trepidation. Omahans, and Nebraskans, don't embrace change. It's scary. Change is jumping off the cliff not knowing if there's a safety net.

Change can mean more taxes.

This change is going to be worth it. But it's up to us to make it so.

This new building is going to be one of the cornerstones of our community. This is going to be one of those grand meeting places. It will bring us together.

But mostly, it's going to make us change how we think about ourselves. It's going to force us to up the ante. It's going to force us to grow, to stretch our imaginations and self-image beyond all of our small-town boundaries.

We've signed up, as taxpayers and tenants. Creighton and UNO have decided that the Civic Auditorium fit their past but not their future. They have taken the leap. So have Omahans, who have never needed anything this big but wanted it anyway. But signing up is only the beginning. Now we have to get in the game.

It's going to transform UNO. For years, UNO was the nice little Division II commuter school in midtown. Then came Division I hockey in 1997, and UNO delved into the world of big-time money and boosters and revenue streams. It's been an uneasy mix. You get the feeling UNO still isn't quite comfortable balancing its old friendly status with its demanding new one.

Well, strap it on, Durango. You ain't seen nothin' yet.

UNO wakes up today with the third-largest arena in college hockey, behind only Ohio State and Wisconsin. With that comes the responsibility of filling those seats.

That means UNO will have to upgrade its current marketing of hockey, probably at the expense of its other sports. That also means that when the big crowds do come, UNO will have to keep them happy.

Good morning, Mike Kemp. With one of the brightest facilities in

UNO's Maverick Stampede was the first official sporting event at the new Omaha arena.

college hockey, and seats to fill, the UNO coach will now be expected to raise the bar he's set.

Now we'll watch UNO grow. As it strives to recruit Hobey Bakers, sell its sport and host NCAA hockey events, UNO will become a player in Omaha like it never could have imagined. That will be fun to watch.

Now we'll watch CU grow. The Jays already dominate the Missouri Valley Conference, and Dana Altman has helped Creighton basketball sell more than 8,000 season tickets. What else is there?

Plenty. The new arena will allow CU to host NCAA regionals. With the biggest gym in their league, the Jays have a recruiting edge that should keep the machine rolling and move up to Sweet 16 and Final Four status.

Why not? This is the time to think big, bigger, biggest. It's up to UNO and Creighton to do their parts. Up to the Metropolitan Entertainment and Convention Authority to provide appealing games and events and upgrade the arena, including adding seats in the upper end, if that's what it takes to get NCAA events.

Last, but not least, it's up to us to get off our duffs and drive downtown and be consistent spectators and not just big-event bandwagoneers. There's no turning back now. This is going to be great.

— OCTOBER 10, 2003

BASKETBALL WIN OVER JAYHAWKS | LUNCH WITH BILL CALLAHAN | LAMBASTED IN LUBBOCK

2004

> "I'm not a politician. I don't change my mind with the wind. I make decisions that are best for the university. If I make good decisions, those that don't understand will understand."
>
> — NEBRASKA ATHLETIC DIRECTOR STEVE PEDERSON

You know what hurts Tyler McKinney the most? His heart. The Creighton junior point guard sits on the Bluejay bench in street clothes, nursing the mother of all eye infections and a bit of a guilt complex. Even with just one good eye, McKinney sees a Creighton offense that is hard to watch, tentative, out of sync. It beats wondering when he will regain full sight in his right eye or whether he will need a cornea transplant. "Sitting out and watching is the hardest thing," he said. "Losing three games, when you think you could have helped. I feel bad for the seniors, especially. This is their last year. I wish I could be out there to help them."

Kevin McKenna doesn't remember exactly when he knew he wanted to coach. It wasn't one of those magical moments. It wasn't in the quiet solitude of a gym, with sunlight bursting onto a hardwood floor, as McKenna knocked down jumpers. It may have been the time some nerdy stock runner elbowed him in the face as they jostled for position. To sell pork bellies. This was 1989. McKenna had finished a career as an NBA journeyman. Now what? He called a friend who had a job on Chicago's Board of Trade. The next thing he knew, McKenna was in the eye of chaos: a trading floor. "I was in the middle of it all, flipping signals, placing orders," McKenna said. "It was intense and competitive, like basketball. My size helped. You could block out or post up. Actually, I posted up there better than I did in the NBA. I was starting to get good at it when a coaching opportunity came up. I missed the game. I missed being around a team, the locker room, the camaraderie." The rest is UNO history.

To paraphrase another Bay area guy named Callahan, Dirty Harry: Steve Pederson, are you feeling lucky? One of the longest and strangest coaching searches in recent college football history has produced perhaps an equally bizarre result for the University of Nebraska: Bill Callahan, the former Oakland Raiders coach. So the guy who led the Hell's Angels of football is coming to the white-bread capital of college football. Holy culture clash. This is like the old movie "The Wild One," where Marlon Brando and the biker gang take over the rural town.

END OF THE BOWL STREAK | LUNCH WITH DANA ALTMAN | TURNER GILL LEAVES NEBRASKA

When I grow up, I want to be Augie Garrido. Yes, he is the head baseball coach at the University of Texas. Sure, he's the winningest coach in college baseball history. Four national titles. Blah, blah, blah. But that's not it. It's the way Garrido does what he does that fascinates me. He's terminally hip. He's the coolest coach on the planet. Definitely my all-time favorite. I admire Bob Knight for his knowledge of basketball. I love Mike Krzyzewski for his passion for student-athletes. Tom Osborne had both. Barry Switzer loved to have a good time and made the game fun. Garrido is the first coach I've known who was the trifecta: brilliant, passionate about kids and worlds of fun. I'm not a coach (an admission bound to stun thousands), but if I were, Garrido would be my model.

Ten years later, Damon Benning can still see him. He can still hear that voice. He can feel the embers burning in his own belly, still, after all these autumn Saturdays, like coals that won't ever extinguish. "I remember when it was 17-9," says Benning, his eyes lighting up and voice quickening the way you do when you're telling a good story. "Tommie (Frazier) was on the sidelines. He hadn't gone back in yet. He had his helmet in his hand. He was pacing. I remember he started yelling at people, 'We are going to win this game. You either believe it or you don't. If you don't, get off the sideline.' And he was going eyeball to eyeball with everyone, almost like he was checking your temperature. And then everyone started getting animated. Cory Schlesinger started getting hot. Donta Jones almost blew a gasket. It was unbelievable." Ten years later, that 1995 Orange Bowl night lives on for the sportswriter and Benning, the former Nebraska running back, reminiscing in an Omaha restaurant.

Nebraska fans may not understand the new offense yet. But they understand scoring. And winning.

It was Zack Greinke Night at Rosenblatt. That's not an O-Royals promotion, but maybe it should be. Greinke was on the mound for the blue and white on this chilly Omaha baseball night. He's 20 years old. He has four pitches he throws like magnets in the strike zone. He's going places. Greinke is what is known as a Phenom. Remember them? It's been a while since we've seen a member of this baseball species. Years ago, they used to frequent our ballpark on the hill. When the Kansas City Royals had the best farm system in baseball, the Road to the Show went through the Big O. The future of baseball was down the street. For whatever reason, the well dried up. And the Road to the Show went south. The best and brightest leapfrogged from Class AA Wichita to Kauffman Stadium. Omaha became an outpost on the road to nowhere, a place to put struggling careers on hold, a place for players never to be named later.

20 YEARS WITH TOM SHATEL • 199

Osborne Shows Loyalty to the End

HE CAME DOWN from the mountaintop. Actually, it was an escalator at the Cornhusker Hotel.

He stood before us again. He bared his soul. He showed his anger. He nearly wept. He offered forgiveness. He was wishy-washy. He was human.

Tom Osborne held a press conference like no other he has ever given, to give his side of things, to speak to the people. No sooner did he take the last question than some folks were questioning his methods. Why does a congressman take time out to talk football? Why do we need to hear his take?

He should do it more often. Osborne is a world away from football now, in Washington, D.C., in a different game. But he will always be the coach, the man, the pope of all that is Big Red.

For all that Osborne has done for Nebraska, the man has earned a lifetime pass to give his opinion or keep quiet, use his larger-than-life name to sell buildings or keep his name to himself, stay involved or stay out.

Legends should be made to feel welcome around the program, but make sure they know they won't always understand or agree with policy. Is that what is happening with Nebraska and Osborne? You have to wonder.

Osborne gave the press conference because he had been besieged with interview requests. There were rumors. Would he pull his name off the $50 million football facility project? Was he mad at Athletic Director Steve Pederson? On and on.

Personally, I have wanted to know since the fateful night Frank Solich was fired what was going on inside Osborne's head, heart and soul. Finally, he spoke. Here's what we learned:

1. The coach has taken the changes in Nebraska football hard, harder than almost anyone. 2. Pederson is not nearly as smart as I thought.

There is no easy way to fire a lifetime Husker like Solich. But the absolute wrong way to do it is not consult the man who basically hired Solich, and built much of what is Nebraska football tradition today. All Pederson had to do was meet with Osborne, face to face, explain what he was going to do, get Tom's side of things and say, sorry, this is how it is. Maybe Osborne is still angry. But you at least involve him in it.

Here's what you don't want: to have a tearful Osborne get up at a press conference one day and say how disappointed he was that he wasn't told first. To have the Godfather basically say: "You have shown me no respect."

Maybe Pederson was afraid of the reaction.

That was the most amazing thing about Osborne. In 25 years on the sideline, he was as stoic as an old oak tree. He never raised a voice or shed a tear. Even the day he retired, he was more together than he was on this day.

That's when you knew. This thing has really gotten to the coach. Not just the firing of his guy Frank. Not the changing of the offense, his offense. It was more how the change happened. It was the people.

The crux of the matter, the stake through his broken heart, was the assistant coaches and what they went through, how they stayed through the bowl game, putting their careers on hold for dear ol' NU, and got dismissed like that.

Well, watching Osborne was like watching King Arthur realize that Camelot was no more. It has hit him that everything he built, and lived for, has changed. That press conference was his way of venting, his way of announcing to the world: Nebraska football as we knew it, as he knew it, is over.

The thing Osborne has to realize, and he does, is that football programs change coaches and offenses and systems. Nothing lasts forever.

But maybe this was Osborne's way of showing his loyalty, to the end, even in a futile press conference with words that perhaps would never reach an ear. And maybe, just maybe, Osborne was talking about a loyalty that was not shown to him by the current administration.

This was an opportunity for Pederson to mend a big fence. Maybe his presence at the press conference would have made it a circus. But at least acknowledge Osborne's comments about the process, about being hurt for not being consulted.

Instead, Pederson released a short statement that came off sounding smug, about how this has caused him pain, too, and that we should follow Osborne's lead and move on. Like they are on the same page.

In fact, even in his statement, you still feel that Pederson is not acknowledging Osborne's reluctance to put his name on the building. You still get the feeling that this is Pederson's idea, which it was, and he secured T.O.'s approval before firing Solich, knowing Osborne never would have done it had he known what would happen.

The whole Osborne complex thing is a mess, and the coach didn't help things by saying he would keep his name on it but take it off, please, if you find a money name.

Right or wrong, Osborne is still about principles and loyalty and character.

Nebraska needs more, not less, of that right now.

Tom Osborne held a press conference in Lincoln to explain his feelings about the firing of Frank Solich.

FEBRUARY 16, 2004 • NEBRASKA BASKETBALL

Husker fans storm the court at the Devaney Center after the rout of Kansas.

Huskers Finally Get Day in the Sun

SO HOW ABOUT that Nebraska coaching staff?

No, not the football staff that took its first bows at halftime at the Devaney Center. Their day will come soon enough. The best work by Husker coaches on this day was during the basketball game.

To paraphrase football coach Bill Callahan's notes, there is no place like Nebraska when the Kansas Jayhawks come to town.

Nebraska 74, KU 55. Just like old times.

It was wild. It was crazy. It was a blast from Nebraska basketball's past, when the Big Red would bring its "A" game out for KU and the crowd would roar like a freight train and the floor would shake and Goliath would fall and you would swear Nebraska was a basketball school.

Finally, this was a day for basketball. It was one of those days you wished they could bottle, a day that made you wonder why they don't do this more often, a day that Barry Collier had yet to have in four years here.

Oh sure, KU is always the bull's-eye game for NU. This is the day Husker fans come out of the woodwork to see if Nebraska still has a basketball program.

So the place was jumping, the electricity was on, the Jayhawks have struggled and the stage was set. But nobody could have predicted what would happen.

The biggest win over Kansas since 1982? That was the crazy part.

It began after a 12-6 KU start. A spark. A basket inside by John Turek. Then another. A jumper by Jake Muhleisen. A 3-pointer by Nate Johnson. The Huskers had an 11-0 run and a 20-15 lead. And Nebraska-Kansas had a ballgame.

KU regained the lead at halftime. But instead of sanity, we got insanity.

Nebraska took the lead and kept adding to it. It was nuts. Turek, going against All-America candidate Wayne Simien, played out of his mind. Andrew Drevo, the former Morningside player, was shaking and baking and knocking down everything. Brian Conklin was raining 3-pointers. Tony Wilbrand blocked a shot.

But maybe the craziest thing of all was how Nebraska outplayed, outcoached and out-toughed a Bill Self team.

It was so simple, so devastatingly easy, that Kansas dribbled out the final seconds and the students' rush to the court was anticlimactic.

Or maybe not. Players celebrated with students. Coaches hugged. Even Mr. Stoic, Collier, broke out a smile. Why not? A ton of frustration and losses had built up. The fans needed this emotional release. Collier, too.

'Gooch' Loves Hometown Boost

Let's be honest here. It's only the first round of the Cox Classic. Plenty of birdies to find in the lush hills of Champions Run. But who's kidding whom?

Anybody look at the name on the leader board Thursday and not fast-forward to Sunday?

Not the red-clad fans who call themselves "Gooch's Gang," who would like nothing better than to turn the 18th green into a Sunday sea of red.

Not the hard-working chaps in the news media room, always suckers for a great story. Give them a local boy winning his hometown trophy, and that's a story that writes and proofreads itself.

Not the Cox Classic folks, who would need an extra party tent if the local boy makes good.

Not even the local hero himself, Scott Gutschewski, could deny sneaking a peek at a leaderboard fantasy where he's walking up a native 18th fairway and waving to the homeboys while he hoists a check big enough to hold his name.

Gooch winning the Cox Classic is the scene we all dare to dream.

"It would be awesome," Gutschewski said. "I'm not going to lie to you and say I haven't thought about winning this tournament. I've thought about it since the first year of the tournament."

"Gooch" put himself in fantasy's way with a 5-under 67 in the first round, four shots behind leader Doug Barron. It could have been better. He bogeyed the par-5 10th. Missed the green on the par-3 eighth and didn't get up and down.

Oh, well. It was a good start for a young pro with a high recognition factor and a high expectation bar among the army of red tromping after him.

"The gallery is about the same," said Amy Gutschewski, Scott's wife. "But now I'm starting to hear other people say, 'There goes Scott Gutschewski.'"

Where did he come from? He's a Cinderella story, and it started here, a year ago, when he jump-started his career with a special exemption. By the time Omaha had figured out it had a guy on the Nationwide Tour, Gooch had won a tournament, played the Pebble Beach Pro-Am and was on his way this season to making the top 20 on the money list and earning a spot on the PGA Tour.

The thing has been so whirlwind that eventually Gooch had to catch his breath. He's tumbled down the money list in recent weeks, to 38th. It feels like a disappointment. But that's just how far he's come in one year.

"If you had told me coming into this week I'd be 38th, that would have been fine with me," Gutschewski said. "Only one week matters, the end of the year."

This week might matter a ton. Gooch is home. Here we go again?

The karma is there. He and Amy and infant son Luke are home, not in their RV. A Cleveland golf rep made a change in how Gooch's irons were lining upright, and he started hitting it straight. He knows the course well enough that when he made bogey on the first hole, he quickly calmed himself.

Then there are the red Gooch's Gang shirts and applause on every hole. Talk about home cooking.

"You want to play well for them," Gutschewski said.

"It's great. I love it. That's what everyone wants to do out here, play for big money in front of big crowds. If you can't handle it, you shouldn't be out here."

The guy with the long name and big game has proved he can handle it, that he wasn't a one-week wonder. He bombs it. He's got touch. He's got patience. And he has that infectious toothy grin, like he's just heard a good joke, that hints he may know something nobody else does this week.

"It's good to be home," the homeboy said.

Scott Gutschewski gave his hometown fans a thrill with his first-round 67. He finished tied for 21st at the 2004 Cox Classic.

AUGUST 8, 2004 • NEBRASKA FOOTBALL

Lunch With Nebraska Coach Bill Callahan

▶ **Q:** Why coaching?

▶ **A:** I've always wanted to be a coach, ever since I was in grammar school. I remember in eighth grade, the teacher gave out an assignment. You had to guess where everyone in class would be when they would be 40 years old. The gal that had me talked about me being the coach for the Chicago Bears when I was 40. Little did she know I would be with Philadelphia then. In Chicago, they had a great after-school program in the public schools system. You competed in just about every sport known to man. Ping pong, wrestling, horseshoes, volleyball, softball, relays. I grew up playing sports.

▶ **Q:** Every coach has influences who shape them. Who is your biggest influence?

▶ **A:** There is so much I took from 'Gru' (Tampa Bay coach Jon Gruden). A system, how to teach it, how to present it in a professional manner. We shared a lot of experiences, collaborated on everything. It was a two-man show. We tried to do a lot of things technically to push the envelope. In pro ball, it's a laboratory. You have the best players, best facilities, best equipment, and all you do is coach football all day long.

▶ **Q:** Where does your passion for organization come from?

▶ **A:** (Former Illinois coach) Mike White was an extremely organized coach. Being around him at a very early age, as a 23-year-old grad assistant at U of I. Watching Mike put the systems together, in terms of practice planning, recruiting, all the organization.

▶ **Q:** How many plays are in your playbook?

▶ **A:** We were talking about that today. In the passing game, we have 35 principles, OK? It's endless in terms of what you can create off that. We are more into principles than we are plays. In the running game, there is a core package of 15 principles, and we work around that. We could have more, but we have to work within this framework, be able to execute and have technique.

▶ **Q:** How often do you come up with plays?

▶ **A:** (Takes out a thick notebook.) This is my little summer study. I think about things now and then, as I go along, I just start writing things (flipping the pages), start writing and start writing and start writing. I keep a notebook and just scratch it down.

▶ **Q:** It's third-and-goal at the 5. Run or pass?

▶ **A:** Who are we playing? What are they in? What are their tendencies? What hash are we on? What's the personnel? What's the situation? Is it early? Is it late? You have to define it for me. I'm into situational football.

▶ **Q:** Are you a go-for-fourth-down guy?

▶ **A:** I saw last year where the guy from Texas Tech went for fourth down 38 times, 48 times, something like that. Incredible. I'm going to look at the situation, see where we're at. A lot of those decisions, what time of year it is, where you are at, on the road, at home, hostile environment, pretty good fourth-down play, am I ahead, behind?

▶ **Q:** You became available when Steve Pederson desperately needed a candidate. You fell into each other's laps. Do you believe in fate?

▶ **A:** Absolutely. In some respects, I thought it was like divine intervention that I was here at Nebraska. The chain of events happened so quick. I never even thought Nebraska. I remember Steve called, the Monday after New Year's, I was ready to head down to Tampa Bay for an interview, then New York with Tom Coughlin. I told Steve, in the NFL it's like musical chairs, and if you don't have a chair when the music stops, you're out. I started doing my 48-hour research. I was here on Thursday.

▶ **Q:** Do you have the NFL out of your system? Do you feel like you have something to prove, the way it ended in Oakland?

▶ **A:** I don't feel that way. I have enough confidence that I know what went on. I know I could be successful anywhere. I'm not being cocky. I have confidence in what we've done, what our system has done, our approach. It was a great experience for me. I learned a lot, gained a lot of valuable insight into personnel. If you have the right personnel for your system, you're going to have success. I don't think I'll be back in the NFL. I want to finish my career here.

▶ **Q:** Describe the talent on your roster. Project or win now?

▶ **A:** I believe we can win now. Made great strides in the spring. I see the improvement, not only in system, but also guys working with Dave Kennedy. Like Al Davis said, ask me in January and I'll let you know.

▶ **Q:** Last question. How do you feel about columnists calling plays?

▶ **A:** You mean, Red Right F Short 22 Flanker Drop Halfback Burst? Or do you want to go with 24 Dragon? Never mind.

2011 INSIGHT *I liked Bill Callahan. That said, I didn't really know him. I found Callahan to be a good guy, but not a media guy. He wasn't looking to talk. He did one-on-one interviews sparingly, if not grudgingly. I don't think anyone in the Nebraska media really got to know Callahan other than as a football coach who spoke at the weekly press conference. But this was one of those rare occasions I got some quality time with the coach. I remember it was strange seeing him in the same office where I used to talk to Tom Osborne. He had a Tommy Bahama-style shirt. He looked like he was going to a cocktail party on a boat. He was very friendly and chatty. Most of the time Callahan had a corporate feel to his quotes. He was very much into the technicalities of football. But he warmed up talking about growing up in Chicago and the White Sox. He came off as very smart and confident about what he was going to do. I honestly don't think failure or the idea that he was a bad fit was even a remote possibility to him when we did this interview.*

OCTOBER 11, 2004 • NEBRASKA FOOTBALL

Husker Pride Lost in Texas

LUBBOCK, TEXAS

DIARY OF A NU Era. Game Five: Whatever happened to Nebraska football?

It is a question worth asking today, hangover day, after a brutal 70-10 loss to Texas Tech that was as unthinkable as anything that has happened in the last two zany years of this program.

Can you lose more than a game? It seemed that way on a rock-bottom night. It seemed that, as the Huskers slumped off into the night and put Lubbock in their rearview mirror, they needed to take a good look in that mirror.

It sure seemed that some Nebraska tradition, and pride, died out here in the West Texas prairie.

Of course, you consider Nebraska's fragile state of transition. But consider the opponent, a mid-level Red Raider outfit that might not even qualify for a bowl this season, and I give you the worst, most embarrassing defeat in this observer's 13 years of watching Big Red.

Worse than 2001 at Colorado, a Big 12 champion. Worse than Kansas State last year. Worse than anything Miami or Florida State used to do.

Worst ever? Perhaps. The history books say so. But does that really matter?

What matters now is that Bill Callahan has other issues on his first-year plate besides teaching a program how to pass. Like fundamentals. And effort.

Did this Nebraska team quit on its coaching staff? I don't know. I'm not wearing a helmet or pads. All I know is it was hard to tell which was worse late in the game, the fact that the first-team Blackshirts were still in the game or the fact that they couldn't help giving up the most points in school history.

How bad was it? Texas Tech coach Mike Leach, who never met a touchdown he didn't like, either became sympathetic or bored (and apparently had enough revenge for the 56-3 loss to NU here in 2000, Leach's worst) and punted on a fourth-and-one with the score 70-10.

Don't blame Mad Mike. His team was just scoring

Texas Tech's Jarrett Hicks beats Nebraska's Fabian Washington for a second-quarter touchdown.

(49 points in the second half) off its base offense with all the ease of a lay-up drill.

Don't blame Frank Solich, the newest member of the Oklahoma Sooner sideline. Yes, the former coaching staff's recruiting has NU in its current quarterback and talent predicament, but this one isn't on Solich's tab.

This one goes to coach Bill Callahan and Co. If the honeymoon isn't over, we're about to have our first squabble.

Granted, this is one whacked-out Twilight Zone place to play. Granted, Leach's offense is one

whacked-out Twilight Zone offense to prepare for.

But the Huskers couldn't score more than one touchdown against a Red Raider defense that has allowed 27 points or more in four games — to New Mexico, TCU and Kansas.

And the Blackshirts gave up an outrageous 44 completions and 436 yards with only one sack of Sonny Cumbie, who is a nice enough Texas Tech quarterback but will never be confused with Matt Leinart or even Matt Lauer.

The point is, in a season full of excuses, there appeared to be none for this debacle.

NOVEMBER 27, 2004 • NEBRASKA FOOTBALL

Nebraska defensive end Benard Thomas can't hold on to Colorado back Lawrence Vickers.

This Husker Fall Wasn't Necessary

DIARY OF A NU era. Game Eleven: I'll be home for Christmas.

Now what? There is no bowl game for Nebraska. Lock up the helmets and the pads and the footballs. There is no practice until late March. There is no more Nebraska football to watch, cheer, analyze and agonize over until next September.

In other words, every Christmas light should be hung on time and every garage cleaned in the state. Merry Christmas, Bill Callahan.

Nebraska lost to Colorado 26-20, and the season was history. Literally. Is this it? Is this rock bottom?

This was the end of an era, the first losing season since 1961. The first December at home since 1968. And the landslide that began in Boulder three years ago has buried a former heavyweight.

There is no bowl at Nebraska. The Huskers finished 5-6 in football. Those are two sentences I thought I would never have to write. I thought I had seen it all last year when Kansas State won a football championship. Not even close.

That's the way the Champs Sports Bowl crumbles. Stuff happens. With two uncanny streaks like that, maybe this was bound to happen.

The shame of it was, it didn't have to happen.

That's the way the first year of the Callahan Era at Nebraska should be remembered. A crash that could have been avoided. Unnecessary roughness.

For sure, there were obstacles. There were new systems on both sides of the ball. And players learning their third system in three years. And players the new coach didn't recruit. And injuries to key players. A quarterback who struggled to complete any pass.

Yes, there were all those things. But the bottom line to 2004 is that Nebraska underachieved. The coaches. The players. The athletic director. It was an underachievement of historic proportions.

This didn't have to happen. This was not a 5-6 team. The Huskers lost a quarterback and a big-time linebacker off a 10-3 team. That doesn't translate to a swing of four or five losses. This team was better than it played, better than it was coached.

Sure, there are talent questions. This is not championship-level talent. That's why A.D. Steve Pederson fired Frank Solich a year ago this weekend and went out and hired a recruiter. But did he hire a coach? It's too soon to tell. Callahan coached in a Super Bowl, and you don't do that with mirrors. He deserves to be judged with his own players. He and his staff deserve time to figure out where they are and what to do. (Hint: Beat Iowa State.)

Even so, with this shocking result, the honeymoon is over for Callahan. In fact, we're going to have to ask him to return the blender, too.

These are nervous times around Nebraska, and the thing that should make people shiver this winter is the constant insistence from Callahan that recruiting is the answer to the question.

"I'm big on personnel," Callahan said. "It's going to take time. It all depends on how many high-caliber recruits you can sign."

High-caliber recruits can make an average coach look good. Yes, it may be an amazing transformation when NU has a quarterback who can thread a 15-yard pass or a big, fast running back who can hit the corner and scoot. But thoroughbreds still need a trainer. You won't bring in a stable of five-star studs and wave a wand and win the national championship.

Can Callahan and his staff coach? Can they motivate? Is there substance to go with the style? We won't know for a few years. But this year gave us an indication. And it wasn't good.

DECEMBER 10, 2004 • CREIGHTON BASKETBALL

Lunch With Creighton Coach Dana Altman

▶ **Q:** Is the game against Nebraska different for you?

▶ **A:** Nebraska can say whatever they want, but no one can argue the fact that interest is higher for this game. The players sense it. The fans sense it. The media. But I try not to, just to stay balanced. We've got 18 conference games.

▶ **Q:** If you were king of college basketball for a day, and you could change anything, what would it be?

▶ **A:** We ought to be able to spend a little time with our athletes in the off-season. I know a lot of them probably wouldn't want to spend time with us, but if a young man wants to develop his fundamentals and skills in the summer, we ought to be able to work with him. That's where the Euros have caught us and developed some players. They spend more time on the fundamentals and work. I'd like to see less time playing pick-up games and more time on individual workouts and working on the fundamentals of the game.

▶ **Q:** Do you keep in touch with Kyle Korver?

▶ **A:** Yes. He was back here all summer, which was great, because he could have been anywhere, and he was here. He's still tight with a lot of the fellas. I always hope he knows, as well as all our players, they can always come back here and the university will always take care of them for what they've done for us.

▶ **Q:** There was a rumor that he is stashing away all his money and living on the daily per diem.

▶ **A:** He bought himself a BMW. But as far as clothes, he's not spending much money there. He's smart. He's conservative with his money.

▶ **Q:** Did you ever think back in 1994 you'd be here 10 years later?

▶ **A:** I never looked at it that way. You move to a place when you're 35, and you just want to coach. You hope that things happen and they want to keep you, but if not you can always find another job to coach. I just wanted to coach.

▶ **Q:** Would you like to go somewhere where you can go to the Final Four and win a national championship, if you can't do it here?

▶ **A:** Everybody wants to win, and everyone would like to win at the national level. But there are so many variables that go in. If that was my only goal, then chasing jobs would be a lot easier. But that is only a very small part of the equation. Is it right for my family? Will you get an opportunity to truly build a program the way you want it? It's different for different coaches. To some, it's the most important thing. For me, it's one variable.

▶ **Q:** How do you like the Qwest Center?

▶ **A:** When we were building it, it didn't help us. But now I see the look on the kids' faces when they first walk in. I think it will pay dividends. It's a great place to watch basketball. It's fan friendly. If anything, it's too nice. It's not noisy enough. The acoustics are too good. It's like a pro arena. The old buildings are still some of the best places to play.

▶ **Q:** If you could take a year off to follow a coach, who would it be?

▶ **A:** Eddie Sutton has always been someone I liked, just the discipline his teams showed, they rarely beat themselves. He's always intrigued me. Rick Majerus is another guy. His teaching, his attention to detail, I think a guy could learn so much from him. There would be some coaches I'd want to see their recruiting techniques. Some have different schemes. That's an interesting question.

▶ **Q:** How did you get to know Bob Stoops?

▶ **A:** He was an assistant football coach at Kansas State when I was there. We were the same age. I used to have a party for the football coaches after the first game. You'd see him in the weight room, in the cafeteria. We'd work out together. He kicked my butt running.

▶ **Q:** Did you grow up a Husker fan in Wilber, Neb.?

▶ **A:** I used to sell those seats in the stadium from 1970 to 1975. You'd sell the seats before the games, and then you'd get to watch the game, and then you'd have to pick them all up. They paid you $5. I used to go to the old Coliseum and watch basketball games. Joe Cipriano and Moe Iba. I remember Jerry Fort, Norm Stewart, Al Eberhard, Fat Jack (Hartman). I remember how dark it got during games. The lights were only on the court.

2011 INSIGHT *We're not supposed to be friends with the people we cover. I've broken that sportswriting rule a few times in my career. One of those was with Altman. As I mentioned earlier in this book, Dana and I went back to when I covered Kansas State basketball in 1987-89 and Dana was on Lon Kruger's staff. When he was hired at Creighton, I was thrilled. He gave me all the time I needed, and I really felt like I was in on the ground floor of the program he created on the Hilltop. A couple of times I invited him to my annual football party in August and he showed up. When I wrote something he didn't like or disagreed with, he'd call me and scold me in that Tom Osborne/ Ward Cleaver manner. Something changed the day he went to Arkansas at the 2007 Final Four. We were both in Atlanta. When reports were pretty heavy that Dana was talking with Arkansas, I went to his hotel to try to talk to him. He wouldn't even confirm that he was talking to them. That didn't make me very happy, and I was less excited when I talked to a friend of mine, Arkansas Democrat columnist Wally Hall, who said he and Dana had been talking about Arkansas all weekend, about where to live, Frank Broyles, etc. I wish I had confronted him about that, but I never did. When Dana came back to Creighton, our relationship wasn't the same. When he left for Oregon in 2010, I left a message on his cellphone to call me back sometime. He never did.*

DECEMBER 18, 2004 • CREIGHTON WOMEN'S BASKETBALL

Dads: Let Kids Watch 'Spanny'

GOOD NEWS, SARAH. Just because daddy couldn't race a snail across the street or beat a snake in the high jump, doesn't mean you can't play some ball.

For exhibit A, I give you Laura Spanheimer.

I take my 3-year-old daughter Sarah to sporting events. She likes the cotton candy. She likes the mascot. She also likes to watch the ball and the players.

We like to watch Spanheimer and her Creighton Bluejays.

What's not to like? Spanheimer, the senior point guard, is a role model for girls and boys alike.

It's not just that Spanheimer has been Missouri Valley Conference defensive player of the year two straight seasons or was All-MVC or has been MVC player of the week twice already this season.

It's her effort. It's her motor. Spanheimer never, ever stops on the basketball court. She's always running, either on defense, for a rebound or to set up the offense. She's played more than 30 minutes in each of her seven games and twice played the entire game, including all 45 minutes of an overtime loss to Iowa.

She's not the tallest or the fastest on the court. But she's the smartest. She knows how to get position, how to use screens, how to make plays on defense. She knows how to play the game, period.

Laura is the second Spanheimer to grace the Jays' court; her sister Krissie was a Creighton star who scored more than 1,000 points in her career. That's more than 2,000 points in one family.

Naturally, being the father that I am, I assumed Mr. Spanheimer must have led the New York Knicks in rebounding or shut down Larry Bird at the Civic Auditorium or led Omaha Creighton Prep to state title glory back in the day.

Good news, Sarah. I was wrong.

Dick Spanheimer has three girls, but he's more likely to be in the Lowe's Hall of Fame than in Creighton's. He owns a siding and window business. His wife, Mary, is a nurse. Neither of them played the game, at least for very long.

Laura Spanheimer, the youngest of three sisters, said, "I've always felt that if I've played my hardest, I can be satisfied with how things come out."

"I love sports," Dick said. "I was never very good at them. I was the kind of kid who tried out for the team at Creighton Prep and then you go to see if your name is on the list and it's not and your career is pretty much over.

"But I loved to play and I remember when the girls were real young, I put up a hoop in the driveway. They would see me out there shooting, and they would come out and join in. That's how they started."

And Laura has never stopped. Literally.

"To me, she has an incredible ability to focus," Creighton women's coach Jim Flanery says. "Someone once said she's not obsessed, but very dedicated.

"That's true. She knows what she has to do to get better. She's very focused on that. More than anything, she's about being the best."

Her motor may come from the most logical of places: being the youngest of three girls. Jenny played at Marian before Krissie went to Creighton.

"As long as I can remember, I've always felt that if I've played my hardest, I can be satisfied with how things come out," Laura said. "I think I got it from following my sister around. I followed her everywhere. She had a great work ethic, to be the best, and so that's what I was going to be, too.

"I've seen the payoff in our victories and championships and accomplishments."

Spanheimer is a natural runner, a former cross-country and track star at Marian, who made herself into a top hoopster.

Her relentless, all-out effort is still the main attraction, along with the cotton candy, for any father who wants to show his kid how the game is played.

"Start them out young," Dick Spanheimer says. "I know some parents want to wait until they are in seventh or eighth grade. But the younger you get them out there playing, the better chance they'll have to succeed."

The hoop goes up on the driveway tomorrow.

TOM'S TAKE REFLECTIONS ON

The Ties That Bind Are No More at Nebraska

IT WAS A bittersweet day, the day the music died in Big Red Land. Turner Gill stepped to the podium, but not for the reason some had always envisioned. Gill ascending to the throne of Nebraska football, standing at its helm, seemed as inevitable, and natural, as one of his patented smooth option plays.

Turner Gill announces that he is leaving Nebraska.

But there were more tears than smiles at this press conference. Number 12 is no longer a Husker. As he said his goodbyes, and resigned to take a "leap of faith" and go after that head coaching job somewhere else, Gill started to talk about his players.

He stopped. He fought back the tears. He finally had to turn his back and gulp a few times before continuing. And it struck you that it wasn't just the thought of leaving his players that punched Gill in the gut. It was the reality, sinking home, that he was leaving. He was leaving Lincoln. Turner Gill, the classic Husker, was leaving Nebraska football.

Change happens in college football. Coaches are hired to be fired and land on some other campus. Assistant coaches don't hold press conferences when they fly away. But this was no ordinary assistant coach. And this was no ordinary press conference. The room was packed, with everyone from former quarterbacks to football secretaries in the back of the room, all looking solemn, all brushing back the tears.

They were saying goodbye to more than just a friend, a coach, a legend. In some ways, this seemed like a press conference to say goodbye to the past.

Gill was the last link to the Bob Devaney/Tom Osborne era. Now they're all gone. This is the clean break, for Gill and Husker fans. For the past year, Husker fans had their world turned upside down, with the West Coast offense and new faces on the coaching staff and a 5-6 season that felt like the end of an era. Through it all, Gill was there, looking like a security blanket. A reminder that the world had not gone completely mad.

Gill could have left a year ago when Frank Solich and Co. were fired. He looked out of place. He didn't know anybody on that new staff. But he stayed, and it looked like a smart career move, because a year of coaching receivers in the WCO doesn't look bad on the résumé. But you wonder, too, if Gill stayed as sort of a protector, an older brother, to look after the old house and make sure nobody messed with it.

Gill was a Husker Hero, tried and true. He remains a standard for Nebraska quarterbacks, and Huskers, period, on and off the field.

He was the first big-time recruit Osborne ever stole from Barry Switzer at Oklahoma, and he started an era of big-time players and big-time winning for T.O. He was the consummate leader, a field general, calm, cool and collected. He was Osborne's extension, his coach on the field. People used to joke about how much they were alike. Turner Gill is Nebraska royalty. If Osborne was king, Gill was prince.

But a funny thing happened on the way to the throne. The plan was never spoken, but it was understood. Osborne was going to pick Solich, his loyal lieutenant, to succeed him. But you knew Osborne would have loved to see Gill standing next in line to Solich.

The funny thing is, Gill always seemed like a reluctant head coach or coordinator, always saying he would go if it was God's plan for him. Finally, Gill made a forthright statement that he has his own plan and he's ready to carry it out.

The irony is that Gill is leaving Nebraska to go off and become a head coach. As Gill left the room with his family, the irony was running down his cheeks.

— DECEMBER 5, 2004

2011 INSIGHT The day Turner Gill left Nebraska came one week exactly after NU's historic loss to Colorado and the end of the bowl streak. It was the end of an era, and a symbolic cutting of old ties, and I could tell Bill Callahan wasn't exactly broken up about it. Those of us who knew Gill were happy that he had made a decision to go pursue a coaching career, because he had always seemed wishy-washy about that commitment. After the press conference, I drove to Kansas City to cover the Big 12 championship game. On the way down, there was some great radio on. Caller after caller to the Omaha ESPN show ripped into Callahan and Steve Pederson. The state was pretty much in red alert panic mode. Scott Frost called in to the show and got after it pretty good. Frost talked about how Callahan and Pederson were "systematically killing off Nebraska football person by person." There was so much history and soap opera going on that it made your head spin.

THE CHANGING SPORTS LANDSCAPE | 2004

Mav A.D. Should Be Thinking About Division I

MEMO TO DAVID HERBSTER: Think big.

Herbster was named athletic director at UNO, and the move left you wondering which path the athletic department will take.

The University of North Dakota has announced a committee to study the possibility of moving to Division I. Hint: UND is outta here. Hint: The North Central Conference looks like a future ghost town.

Where will UNO end up? Looking at Herbster's background, it could go either way.

Herbster comes from Concordia University in St. Paul, Minn., a Division II school in the Northern Sun Conference. Concordia has won five league titles in various sports the past two years.

But Herbster also worked as a marketing director at North Dakota State, which is now Division I (1994-95), and was marketing man at Pittsburg State (1995-98).

Let's hope his vision leans toward the latter. Can UNO make it as a Division I school? Would the political climate in this state allow that to happen? Don't know, but the possibility should be investigated.

At the very least, UNO should be pounding on the door of the Mid-America Intercollegiate Athletics Association to see if it can join in the near future.

The Northern Sun would not be a desirable option, especially for UNO football. Mav football needs to be in a league with schools that think and spend alike. For UNO attendance's sake, the MIAA makes sense. The Northern Sun doesn't.

Welcome to a challenging job in a challenging time, David.

— DECEMBER 8, 2004

At 6-foot-8, UNO Athletic Director David Herbster was literally the big man on campus. With him are staff members, from left, Ron Higdon, Katie Ryan, Sandy Higdon and Kenya Crandell.

ANOTHER VALLEY TITLE FOR JAYS | MEASURING ALEX GORDON | JOBA BEATS THE HURRICANES

2005

> "I'm not into the Southern Cal thing. I'm not trying to get to the next level. This is my hometown. My ego doesn't require that I manage in the big leagues or coach in the Big 12 or Big Ten."
>
> — UNO BASEBALL COACH BOB HEROLD, A FORMER MINOR LEAGUE MANAGER

June is now Mardi Gras in Lincoln. The state's diamonds have never shined brighter. They are Borsheims quality. A total of 33,713 attended the NCAA regional in Lincoln and watched 30 home-grown players in major roles on the national stage. Thirty, for two teams, Nebraska and Creighton. Think about it. At this rate, the baseball will soon replace the football as the state bird.

It's Opening Knight. And Gary Anderson is ready. Has been, for that matter, since 1975, the last time the team of his youth, the Omaha Knights, skated off the ice and into his memory. Anderson is no longer a youth. His hair is gray. His mind is sharp. He remembers that night like it was, well, 30 years ago. "It was in the playoffs, against Salt Lake City," Anderson says. "It was April 19, 1975. It was a Saturday night. We lost, 4-3. There were some indications that the Knights were going to leave. I remember I clipped out the last two game accounts from The World-Herald. I still have them. That next decade or so, until the Lancers came, was rough on hockey fans here. There was a lot of withdrawal." But tonight, that withdrawal ends for Omahans who missed their winter Knights, who have wanted their pro hockey fix. The Omaha Ak-Sar-Ben Knights are back.

It was a day for history at grand old Memorial Stadium. All the ghosts were on hand. Tom and Barry. Christian and Aaron and the rest of the 1995 national champion Nebraska Cornhuskers. It was a day for dreams for a kid like Zac Taylor, the Nebraska junior quarterback. His dad played for Oklahoma in the 1970s. Taylor grew up on the Sooners' doorstep in Norman. He grew up wanting to play for Oklahoma. And now, here he was, looking across the line at the red helmets with the "OU." The kid with a Sooner legacy was given the job of beating his dream team. What a nightmare. Oklahoma beat Nebraska, 31-24. And Memorial Stadium became Taylor's personal house of horrors. Whatever boyish heroics Taylor had drawn up in his dream game plan, they were quickly scattered and blown to South Dakota like most of the debris caught in a strong, almost spooky, south wind.

STREAK ENDS IN LAWRENCE | RECORD VOLLEYBALL CROWD | ALAMO BOWL WIN OVER MICHIGAN

He's a good man. That's what the people say about Barry Collier. It should count for something, in a profession with its share of slimeballs and money-grabbers and bad actors. A college basketball coach who is a good man should count for a lot. Then again, it's kind of like the blind date "who has a great personality." But people will tell you the Nebraska men's basketball coach is a gentleman, a stand-up guy, the kind of guy you'd want your kids to be. Maybe that's all they can say about a coach who is on his way to four losing seasons out of five, has been to one NIT, has a half-empty building and keeps piling up embarrassing losses.

Welcome to the CWS, Nebraska. This grand old event is full of all the great things in sports, but it's got a dark side, too. College World Series Boulevard is also the Boulevard of Broken Dreams. The place is littered with broken hearts. And now the Huskers leave one, too. Nebraska and Arizona State staged one of the greatest CWS games of all time, an elimination game with one of the cruelest twists ever: The loser didn't deserve to go home. In fact, both teams should be allowed to stay. This was the greatest CWS game I have witnessed in my 14 years in the Rosenblatt Stadium press box. Yes, better than the 1996 Miami-LSU final, the Warren Morris game, because, in its own way, as much or more was at stake. For one, this was an elimination game, in a year as wide open to the title as any ever played, with each of the eight teams feeling it had a chance at June glory. For another, there was the Nebraska factor. A home team playing to fight its way back to the title. Legions in red cheering and moaning, living and dying, with each incredible play. I didn't see the 1991 Creighton-Wichita State classic, but more than one local observer in the press box said this was the best game since that one and, in fact, reminded them of it. So Nebraska has had its Creighton moment, its heart broken, true indoctrination in Omaha.

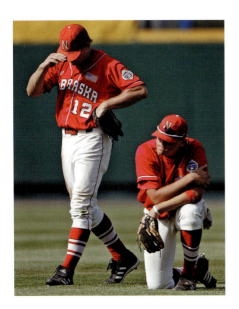

The Cox Classic should have given itself a trophy. Our local golf tournament was the big, big winner here. Our baby is growing up. It's been 10 years now since a guy named Rocky Walcher won the first Omaha Classic, back in 1996. How long ago was that? Dana Altman hadn't coached a postseason game for Creighton. Nebraska hadn't lost a football game in two seasons. Now we have skybox suites and beer tents and galleries so big that the players say it's just like a PGA Tour event, minus Tiger. Which, come to think of it, makes us like a lot of stops on the big-boy tour. The Cox Classic is getting older. And better. Year No. 10 was the best ever, by a couple of strokes a side. Look at the crowd on Sunday, 32,000 — so huge that PGA Tour officials watched with mouths agape. For the week, the tally was 82,250. Yes, the third-largest city in Nebraska.

Lunch With UNO Wrestling Coach Mike Denney

Q: Here you go again, another run to another title. Does this ever get old?

A: No, I still love it. I still love preparing the team for competition. I enjoy the competition. Putting together a team, organizing them and then preparing them for battle, I love that. Wrestling, the one-on-one, for a young man, is just huge. It's kind of an old warrior thing. One-on-one combat, like street fighting with rules. It's a great vehicle for learning and teaching.

In this day and age, for a young man to compete and fight and have one hand go up at the end of it, that's huge. It's an old warrior thing. I love that."

Q: What do you mean?

A: I think we all have that warrior inside us. One of the rewarding things about my job is to bring it out of a young man. But it's not just men. Women are warriors, too.

For instance, my mother. She raised my brother and I. She came from a home with an alcoholic father. She worked all those years on that farm, up at 5 every day, never complaining. She's my definition of a warrior.

My wife (Bonnie) is a warrior. She has MS. In 1991, she was in bad shape. She was in the hospital for weeks. We had said our goodbyes.

The doctors had a new medicine. They gave it to her, and it started working. Now she's out there working out, walking around. She can't run. But she does weights. She's a warrior.

Q: Where did you grow up?

A: I grew up on a little farm near Neligh, between Norfolk and O'Neill.

We used to go to a one-room schoolhouse until eighth grade. I always tell people I graduated at the top of my class; there were eight students in it. The teachers there didn't have college degrees. It was a country school. They had a high school degree and a certificate from taking a six-week class. We used to ride horses to school. They had a barn out back where you tied them up.

Q: How did you get into wrestling?

A: A lot of country kids wrestled. But it wasn't like we wrestle now. It was just grabbing each other and trying to put somebody on the ground. Some of my friends went to high school and joined the wrestling team. When they came back to wrestle, they were way better than I was. I wanted to get better, like them. So when I got to high school, I joined the wrestling team.

Q: Do you have a favorite team? Wrestler?

A: All of them. That's the truth. But 1991 was a different year. That was the year we won our first national championship, up in Fargo. All that season, my wife was in the hospital. Then, in October, we lost Ryan Kaufman. He was a former wrestler, he was 32, he worked for me. He was killed in a car accident, had a wife and two little girls. That year was a blur.

Q: Have you ever thought about coaching at the Division I level?

A: Yes. I used to have an A.D. here named Bobby Thompson. He was from Oklahoma. He smoked cigars. He called women 'Darling.' You get the picture.

Well, I think it was 1988, I was making $25,000 and we had three scholarships. I was offered the job at Wyoming. I had never asked for a raise. But this time, I felt like I had some leverage. I wanted more money for myself, more scholarships and more money in the budget. I was going to say, 'I want two of those three, or I'm gone.'

I was nervous. Bobby was sitting at his desk, with his feet up, smoking a cigar. I told him what I wanted or else. He took a puff of the cigar and said, 'I tell you what. If you go to Wyoming, I'm dropping the program.' Well (laughing), I just slumped out of that office. That was the end of it.

Q: Did you ever consider leaving any other time?

A: I've had other opportunities. I just felt like this was where I was supposed to be. In Division II, we still have that balance between sports and academics. In Division I, it seems like it's more about winning, money. I like that balance here.

Q: How did you get from coaching and teaching at Omaha Bryan in 1979 to UNO?

A: I was playing for the (semi-pro) Omaha Mustangs at the time, and Don Leahy was our offensive coordinator. He knew me, liked my work ethic. He took a chance.

I loved football. I played at Dakota Wesleyan, but I wasn't good enough to get drafted. And back then, there weren't a lot of free-agent opportunities; there weren't that many scouts.

Q: Do you take on your wrestlers at practice?

A: Not much anymore. It's my knees. I do judo workouts (he's a third-degree black belt) every day. I'm into the ultimate fighting now, where they put you in a cage and anything goes. I'm coaching a guy in that.

Q: Have you ever used judo, like, in real life, in a fight? Ever hurt anyone?

A: Yes. Yes. (silence)

Q: OK, on to another topic. How much longer do you want to coach?

A: The thing that would chase me out is if I don't have that burning desire to do this. I still do. I still love every day.

2011 INSIGHT *One of the things I wish I'd done over 20 years was get to know Mike Denney. He wasn't just a great wrestling coach. He was one of those people who transcended coaching. I think he had a lot of wisdom and great lessons to teach. He's one of those coaches I think could have won in other sports. I would have liked to have sat in his office more and talked about life, sports, people, history, etc. This was one of my favorite lunch interviews. It took place at the Venice Inn, where all my UNO interviews seemingly took place. Listening to him talk about being a warrior was fascinating. It also kind of scared the heck out of me.*

Jays' NCAA Ride Is Hollywood Stuff

ST. LOUIS

SWEETHEART, GET ME Hollywood. OK, make that ESPN. Got an idea for a movie. It's about a little basketball team from a little Jesuit school in the Midwest. Their season's going nowhere. They win eight straight games. They win a tournament championship. They cut down nets. They make the NCAA tournament.

Yes, it gets better. They have a kid named Jimmy Motz. He looks good. He's got a pretty shot.

Unfortunately, that's all he can do, and it doesn't always go in. The fans rag him. One game, when Motz happened to hit a shot, an opposing coach turned to his assistant and exclaimed, "We're going to get beat by Jimmy (expletive) Motz."

Cut to scene where Motz is getting carried off the Savvis Center floor by the students after turning three-point assassin in the championship game.

This team also has a kid named Anthony Tolliver. Three weeks ago, he couldn't pull down a rebound, much less hold one. His coach called him into the office. They had a heart-to-heart talk. The message: Keep it simple, Anthony. Just bend your knees.

Cut to scene where Tolliver has a net draped around his neck and is signing autographs after scoring eight points, pulling down seven boards, blocking two shots and bending his knees more than anyone.

There's also a guy named Tyler McKinney. Get out your handkerchief. McKinney is the point guard who lost the sight in his right eye and a year ago had cornea surgery that didn't work. During last year's Missouri Valley Conference tournament, McKinney was wondering if he would ever play basketball again.

Cut to scene where McKinney hugs his parents and feasts his eyes — both of them — on an MVC tournament trophy. There's not a dry eye, right or left, in the house.

What do you think? Oscar material, right?

Well, if nothing else, the Creighton basketball team that won the Valley tournament, and an improbable trip to the NCAA tournament, will make the school's highlight film. That, apparently, is an honor.

The Jays' 75-57 victory over Southwest Missouri State — and the sixth NCAA bid in the past seven years — was won back on Valentine's Day, when coach Dana Altman took his team on a date to the movies. No roses were given.

The team was 15-10 then, after a 7-0 start that included wins over Missouri, Ohio State and Xavier. The Jays were 7-7 in the Valley. They were one-dimensional, soft in the middle and inconsistent. They looked like a candidate to make history — the wrong kind: staying home from postseason. So Altman showed the team a highlight tape of Creighton's run from 1999 to 2002, which included four Valley tournament titles and five NCAA tournament games. History class was in session.

"We talked about the tradition," Altman said. "I got an old highlight film out, and we talked about all the things the program had done, all the streaks we had going: 10-win seasons in the conference, 20-win seasons, eight years of going to postseason play.

"I asked them, 'Do you want to be the team that's remembered for breaking them?'"

Tradition makes heroes out of young men.

"He's living a dream," Jerry Motz said of son Jimmy.

"He's had a few years of ups and downs, taken some crap from the fans for being slow or this and that. After the game, I asked him, 'Was it all worth the hard work and tears?' He said, 'Yeah.'"

You'll see it all on the next highlight tape.

"If you had told me we would have done this a few weeks ago, I don't know if I would have believed it," Jimmy Motz said. "It came out of the blue."

Sounds like a good title.

Jimmy Motz said Creighton's Missouri Valley championship run "came out of the blue."

Viewing Title IX in a New Light

I HAVE PROOF God exists. It's there in my beautiful daughter Sarah's sweet smile, and on Monday afternoon, it was there in the first twinkle of an eye in the life of Katherine Paige (as in sports page) Shatel.

I also now have proof that He (or is it She?) has a sense of humor.

As the proud father of two little girls, I can probably forget about being the doting dad of the next John Elway or Roger Clemens. I say "probably," because Lord knows what women athletes will be accomplishing 20 years from now.

However, with a little luck, and mommy's athletic genes, a volleyball or basketball or soccer star is not out of the question.

Therein lies the irony, which is most delicious for those who know this crusty old chauvinist of a sportswriter. In a career that's spanned more than 20 years, I've tried to avoid women's sports as much as possible.

Now, I may be spending the next two decades watching hours upon hours of girls' practices and games. Sounds like an old episode of "The Twilight Zone."

Sounds good. From what I know about women's college sports in this area — and what little I have seen — this could be a very good thing.

There's something refreshing about the female side of the field. There's a lot for an old-schooler to appreciate. The girls are more into fundamentals, and while some games are not necessarily aesthetically pleasing, it's often due to lack of physical ability, not lack of teaching.

To the contrary, the women's coaches I've met and seen at NU, Creighton, UNO and College of St. Mary are as technically sound, if not more so, as their male counterparts. Most women's coaches are not recruiting hucksters, or there to preen for the cameras (there aren't many) or earn top dollars (there aren't many). They are there to coach and teach.

There also seems to be a lot of sportsmanship, shaking hands and perspective in women's sports. Another good thing.

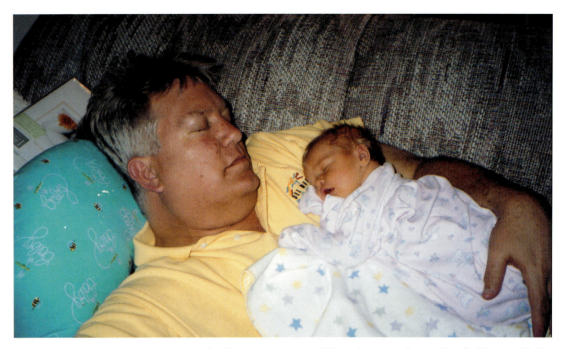

No props here, just a proud dad. If there had been props, it would have been a Nebraska baseball hat and ball. Katherine Paige was born May 2, 2005, right about the time of the Huskers' last CWS berth.

Put a "former" in front of this Title IX critic. Title IX is the best thing to come out of the Nixon administration. It's enabled a father to have girls and still have a catch, go one-on-one in the driveway and, yes, swing a golf club. There you go.

Who knows? Maybe in the process, a guy who once rooted for Bobby Riggs to blast Billy Jean King off the tennis court will take a liking to these games and soon begin writing about them on a regular basis.

Now THAT would be one of God's miracles.

A quick story: If Kate has half of her mother's focus, she'll be OK.

My wife, Jennifer, is to the Discovery Health channel what I am to "SportsCenter." In fact, when "Make Room for Baby" comes on — or any show where babies come popping out to greet the world — that's daddy's cue to leave the room and go find the channel where only Jeff Van Gundy cries.

So there I was on Monday afternoon, on the ninth floor at Methodist Hospital, holding my wife's hand, as we prepared for a C-section. They put up a sheet between the procedure and the mother's eyes, which is a good thing, so the husband there to support her doesn't pass out.

Anyway, the doctors are doing their thing, and the anesthesiologist sees that I'm turning white as a baseball, so he tries to distract me: "Hey, Tom, how about that Johnny Dorn?" Meanwhile, Jen is looking up at the ceiling, and in the light fixture, she can see a reflection of the birth taking place below.

"COOOOOLLLL!" she exclaimed. "Honey, I can see it."

Yeah, cool. How about that Johnny Dorn?

Gordon Shares Erstad's Drive

HE DID IT AGAIN. He was Superman. Flash Gordon. Alexander the Great.

No, Alex Gordon didn't hit one to downtown Beatrice. Didn't start a fireworks show with a shot off the scoreboard. Didn't execute an unassisted triple play. None of that mundane stuff.

No, this time Gordon made news with four simple swings of the bat. Four singles. Three sharp ground balls that had legs, one drive up the middle. Nebraska beat Missouri 7-5. Thank you and sit in traffic on the way home safely.

Alex the Amazing has been an All-American and Big 12 Player of the Year and hit 39 home runs and driven in 165 runs and had 213 hits. And walked a lot. But until this game, the NU third baseman had never, ever had a four-hit game. Amazing, huh?

It is and it isn't. Because even though we know there is something special going on here, Gordon has done it so often for so long it's easy to shrug. Gordon will be one of the top five picks, if not the No. 1 pick, in the major league free agent draft. And he makes it look as easy as falling out of bed.

In a month, Gordon will be a millionaire. He will be The Future for some franchise. A city will pin its baseball hopes and dreams on his sweet swing.

It's hard to project college baseball players into the major leagues. Gordon could have a nice little career. Or he could be an All-Star who becomes a household name on a world championship team.

Like a guy named Erstad. Darin Erstad left Nebraska in 1995. He was the first overall pick of that year's draft. He's been a two-time All-Star, a three-time Gold Glove winner, a household name for the world champion Los Angeles Angels of Anaheim, or wherever. The thing is, Darin Ballgame has grown in stature since he left. He's a legend, larger than life. You see him on TV now, and you swell with pride. Remember when he played in Lincoln? Do you?

The images of Erstad in Husker red are blurry, at least in this fog-filled head. You knew he was special. He was an All-American and co-Big Eight player of the year and held several records. He was clutch and a gamer and all that jazz. But I, for one, took Erstad for granted, probably for a couple of reasons.

First, NU baseball was a different world 10 years ago. The Huskers weren't going to regionals. On a sunny day, maybe 1,000 would stumble onto Buck Beltzer Field. A lot of folks in this state never saw Erstad take a swing. Heck, more people saw him punt.

Then there was the history. Nebraska has had Bob Cerv. And Stan Bahnsen. But the list of accomplished major leaguers from Big Red is not long. One reason you didn't look at Erstad at NU and say, "There's the next major league star," is that just didn't happen to former Huskers.

Then came Darin. He set the bar for the current generation of Huskers.

Now comes Alex. The comparisons are inevitable.

"It's an honor," Gordon said. "Darin is such a great player. To be compared to him is unbelievable. Hopefully, I can follow in his footsteps."

You can't predict how he'll do on that path. But Gordon looks the part. He's got matinee-idol looks. He's got the air. The swagger. The swing. He attacks, and punishes, a pitch. When he's up, everyone watches. Gordon is a Nebraska classic.

His uniform's always dirty. He grew up driving to Kansas City to watch George Brett, and the comparisons are there, too. As you watch Gordon man third base, hitting from the left side, how he releases the bat, you can see a lot of Brett in Gordon.

"It's (the draft) going to happen, so I'm not thinking about it," Gordon said. "I'm trying to go out the right way. Winning championships. A lot of them."

This guy's going to be something someday. Already is.

Alex Gordon was the No. 2 draft pick overall by the Kansas City Royals in 2005.

Joba Spins His Own Legend

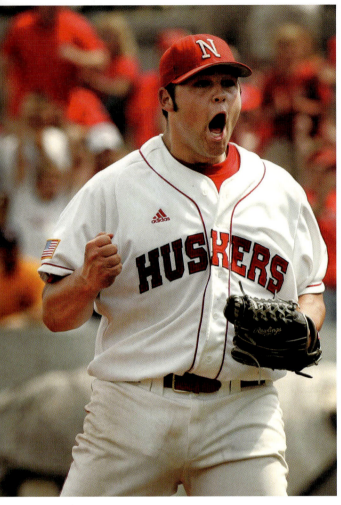

Joba Chamberlain celebrates a strikeout in his victory over the Miami Hurricanes.

SO NOW WE have it, on paper, the baseball dream for the Nebraska boy as he throws in his backyard, sits on a tractor or watches a ballgame with his father at Haymarket Park.

Who does he want to be when he grows up?

He wants to be Joba Chamberlain, who, with his steely eyes and stocky build and cocksure swagger, looks like the poster boy for dirt-stained, hard-nosed, small-town Nebraska baseball.

He wants to be No. 44, the Cinderella Man, the long-shot story, who took up baseball late and gutted his way through a 3-6 record at Division II Nebraska-Kearney and somehow found himself pitching at Nebraska on ESPN.

He wants to be that guy, facing the Miami Hurricanes, in the NCAA super regional with a trip to the College World Series in the balance and 8,308 in the stands and many more watching at home or in their offices or at the town coffee shop.

He wants to go against Miami's best, Cesar Carrillo, who never loses, and who will be throwing strikes in the big leagues one day soon.

He wants the ball first, in the important first game of the two-out-of-three series, with everyone picking Carrillo and Miami and saying the Huskers will have to come back and win on Saturday and Sunday.

And he doesn't want anyone to catch him dreaming, like the day before the game, when the press and the TV guys are asking if you grew up watching Miami play in the CWS. And so you say what Joba said:

"I can't say I've ever watched them. I can't say I've ever been a fan of theirs. You may not like them, but you have to respect the things that they've done. But that's about all they're going to get from me, to be honest with you."

And then you go out and prove it.

The dream is good, but you make it better, saying you have to take a summer school sociology quiz the morning of the game. Then you warm up and swagger in from the bullpen, but the rains come and they pull a two-hour delay on you.

No matter. This is your day. The skies clear, and the game starts, and you strike out the leadoff man, looking.

You give up a single in the top of the ninth. But it's OK. You have a 3-1 lead. Coach Mike Anderson comes out to take you out and slaps you on the back. The crowd is on its feet. The roar is deafening.

People are shaking your father's hand. He shakes his fist and claps his hands and looks like he's going to cry.

You are asked how many times you've been to the CWS and you say, once, a few years ago, but it's not over yet. And then you are asked what it's like to live this dream, the dream Nebraska boys dream, to be the guy they want to be.

"It's just an honor," you say. "It's a blessing to be pitching here."

And then, and only then, if your name is Joba Chamberlain, you realize the perfect ending to the perfect day in the perfect dream.

You're really awake.

2011 INSIGHT *I remember this day more than the column. I'll never forget it. After the rain delay, it turned into an absolutely spotless spring day, a Friday, with the Miami Hurricanes finally in Lincoln, Neb., to play for something. It was like the quintessential day for Nebraska baseball, a day you would put in a frame and hang on a wall in your Husker den. NU had been to the CWS twice before. But this was even better, because it was with a new coach, and at the time it looked significant, making you think the dynasty could go on forever. Now we know better. But on that day, two Lincoln kids, Joba Chamberlain and Alex Gordon, played big-time roles in the Huskers beating Miami on ESPN. I remember watching the last inning with Joba's dad, Harlan Chamberlain, who was sitting in his wheelchair on the concourse. When I think about those Nebraska baseball days, this is one that will always come to mind.*

The Ghosts Are Gone: NU's for Real

THERE HAVE BEEN 55 College World Series played in Omaha, but there has never been a CWS like this one.

Nebraska is in the winners' bracket.

Oh sure, Creighton won here in 1991. That was the first time a local nine graced our baseball stage. The Jays beat Clemson, and the old stadium on the hill rocked. Then the Bluejays lost a classic to Wichita State. Creighton went 2-2 in that CWS. The Jays didn't make it to the last out. But they will always be the first.

This time is different. Nebraska is different.

If you didn't see that in 2001 or 2002, then you got an eyeful at 10 a.m. Friday — three hours before the Florida-Tennessee game — when 13th Street and Bob Gibson Boulevard looked like a Husker football Saturday, with all the traffic and trimmings.

Or maybe you caught the zoo while the SEC rivals were having at it, and we don't mean Omaha's world-famous lair. This was the one with the animals, er, people in red grazing on the side of the hill, below the left-field wall. Just hanging out. Some would get in the game. Some would not. It didn't matter.

You could certainly feel it in the hours before Nebraska's game with Arizona State, with the rows upon rows of red tents and red flags and red people in the main parking lot at Rosenblatt Stadium. Invasion of the CWS Snatchers.

You could definitely hear it in the stadium, during the game, when the chants of "Husker" and "Power" bounced around the old ballpark. And, then again, in the top of the ninth, when 24,000-plus erupted after the last out and NU's first CWS victory was in the books.

Yes, it's different when the Huskers visit the CWS.

The Huskers broke through, finally, at the CWS. After going two-and-barbecue in 2001 and 2002, the Big Red put down their forks and beat the Sun Devils 5-3. With enough expectations and hype and crowd to put an exhibit full of monkeys on their backs, NU made it look like a Friday night in April

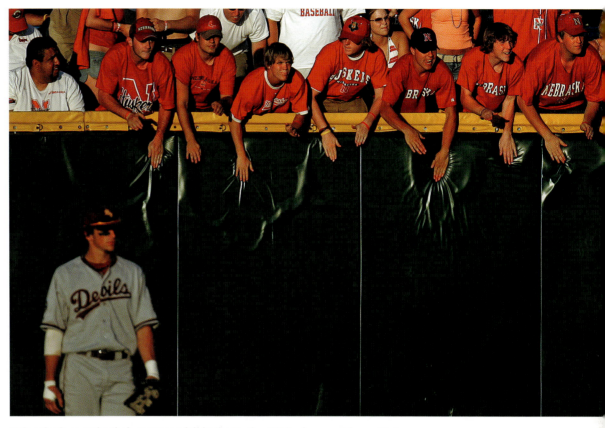

Nebraska fans make their presence felt in the Huskers' 5-3 win over Arizona State.

against Oklahoma State.

The historic first win had all the elements of a season that is developing into a classic.

The first punch: A Joe Simokaitis single, an Alex Gordon walk (what else?) and a Curtis Ledbetter single made it 1-0. An Arizona State error gave NU its second run. But that's what this team does. The offense isn't always pretty. But the Huskers take what you give them and then make you pay.

The pitching: Joba Chamberlain shined in his CWS debut. With everyone wondering when the clock will strike midnight on this fairy tale, the Cinderella Man went seven innings, allowing five hits and three runs. And the most impressive thing about his night was how he shrugged off a two-run double in the sixth, got the last out and moved on.

The defense: Hometown hero Ryan Wehrle's relay throw to the plate nailed ASU's Colin Curtis, who had been waved home as the Sun Devils tried to squeeze three runs out of Tuffy Gosewisch's double. Big risk, no reward. Again, NU caught a break and took advantage.

The heart: NU had every reason to fold, to start thinking about ghosts, to start figuring out ways to lose at Rosenblatt again. Not this time. Not this team.

Jaworski Is Pride of Prep

THE CLOCK STRIKES 2:30 p.m. and the bell rings. School is out at Omaha Creighton Prep. Class is in session.

You meet Tom Jaworski in the front office. Practice starts in 45 minutes. He suggests we talk in a conference room upstairs. No way. A tour of the football office, please.

Jaworski agrees, and you figure this is going to be something. After 33 years, Jaworski is more than just the head football coach at Prep. He is the Pride of Prep. He's a legend. He's an institution. He is Nebraska high school football. He's just Tom Jaworski. That's a good thing.

Jaworski leads you downstairs to his office, and this should be a treat. The man has won more high school football games than anyone in Nebraska history. His next win will be No. 300. That's a lot of Friday nights.

So you figure his office will be a walk through a hall of fame. The walls will be covered with photos of state titles and guys who went to college or the NFL autographing one for Coach. A man's life, on display.

There are four blank walls. There are two big stuffed couches. Two desks and a table. And one chalkboard with several plays written in grease.

"This isn't my office," Jaworski explains. "It's the coaches' office. It belongs to a lot of people."

Perfect. If you walked into this room, you would say this is a football coach's office. That, pure and simple, is Tom Jaworski. What will win No. 300 mean? Another chance to get goose bumps on a Friday night.

"It means you've been around a long time," Jaworski said. "It does give you a sense of pride and accomplishment. Not the number, but it makes you feel like you've done things the right way, for the most part, for a long time.

"Prep has been a labor of love. I've been here all my life. I get to coach great kids, study film, go to practice and try to figure out the game of football."

It's been some quest. Jaworski will be 62 in November. He started this gig in 1972, taking over for Don Leahy. He has coached kids through Vietnam and disco and MTV and the Internet and cellphones. And yet he still has a handle on this job, and kids in society. He still commands respect. That's a tough chore.

"That's always been my concern: Could I still relate?" Jaworski says. "The culture has changed so much. Kids today live in a tougher world, with more distractions that can get you off course. But they're really no different. They still want to work hard and have fun."

How does a 61-year-old relate in today's punked-out world? The answer is all over Jaworski's face, before another practice on another Westside week.

Jaworski is talking about how the routines haven't changed over the years. Postgame get-together at a coach's house. Up early Saturday for coaches' film session. Sunday morning: church with the team, go over the film. On and on.

Joy fills his face.

"I love the camaraderie," Jaworski said. "I've always been a sports nut. I like figuring things out, watching film, the time you spend arguing as a staff."

It has been this way since his childhood in Omaha. Jaworski's parents took him to Omaha Cardinals games, Prep games, any games. His mom would coach baseball practice when his father, an executive at Mutual of Omaha, couldn't be there.

Leonard Jaworski, now 89, still goes to Prep games, but now it's to watch his son coach.

His son the coach was once a backup guard for Prep from 1957 to 1960. He played against the great Gale Sayers, a running back/linebacker at Omaha Central, at Creighton Stadium and Rosenblatt Stadium.

Back then, Prep coaches recruited former players to help coach. Former Prep basketball coach Tom Brosnihan asked Jaworski to volunteer coach while he went to school at CU. Ten years, one Creighton degree, one UNO teaching certificate and one teaching job at St. Bernard grade school later, Jaworski was back at Prep as head wrestling coach and top assistant to Leahy. A year later, a legendary run began.

"I followed two of the all-time greats, in Broz and Don, and that's all-time greats anywhere in the country," Jaworski said. "The biggest thing I learned from them was loyalty.

"I still look forward to every day. And you talk about coaching the kids, going to practice, watching film, I still get fired up about it."

Us, too.

Omaha Creighton Prep's Tom Jaworski celebrated his 300th coaching victory in 2005 with a win over rival Omaha Westside.

NOVEMBER 6, 2005 • NEBRASKA FOOTBALL

Kansas fans celebrate their first football victory over Nebraska since 1968.

2011 INSIGHT *This loss to Kansas felt like a turning point for Nebraska football. The Jayhawks were like the final straw for a lot of Husker fans. If you lost to them, it really was over. But this came out of nowhere. And it came in a flurry. The way it happened, the lack of response from Bill Callahan afterward, it felt momentous. That was a slap in the face for Husker fans who suddenly began to think Callahan would be a bust. It was a code-red situation. On the drive home from Lawrence that Saturday night, three of my golf buddies – one of whom had been at the game – called from Omaha and said, "Emergency Meeting." We sat up all night drinking beer and lamenting what felt like the end of an era. These guys were hard-core Husker fans who were wiped out emotionally. They hadn't seen days like this. They were scared about where it was going. Strangely, this KU game would be the last loss of the season. Nebraska would rally to beat K-State with Harrison Beck, upset Colorado in Boulder and beat Michigan in the Alamo Bowl. Then, win the Big 12 North the next year. Still, if anyone trusted Callahan, that was over after this Kansas game. In many ways, it was like the beginning of the end.*

Is NU's Home Sellout Streak Next to Go?

LAWRENCE, KAN.

NOW I'VE SEEN everything. Kansas State in 1998. Oklahoma State in 2002. Iowa State in 2002. Missouri in 2003. And now this, the biggest stunner of all, Kansas 40, Nebraska 15.

No, folks, that is not a halftime score of Jayhawk-Husker Hoops. That's the final tally of one of the most incredible, unthinkable afternoons of Big Red football you've ever seen, and, thankfully, most Nebraskans didn't see it. Perhaps the one positive of the day.

Are there any goal posts left? Everybody had his turn at the piñata? Everybody had a kick at the bully while he's down?

The end of Nebraska's proud dynasty in the old Big Eight is now officially complete. It ended, appropriately, with an embarrassment at the hands of the old doormat, the anti-football, KU.

The last history-book, decades-stretching Nebraska winning streak over a conference opponent is now officially history. NU had beaten Kansas 36 straight years, which is remarkable, anyway. Nothing lasts forever.

But what happened here was not about fate or the odds catching up.

This was not about the cyclical nature of college football and scholarship limits and parity. This was not about one play or two plays, about how the Huskers would be 7-1 if they hold onto the interception against Texas Tech or get the holding call. This was not about Steve Octavien or Matt Herian. This was not about recruiting or four-star players. In fact, NU was so bad that a couple of its five-star players were down to two stars by the end of the game.

This was rock bottom. This was lower than anything that happened during 7-7 or 5-6. This was Kansas dominating Nebraska, without Raef LaFrentz or Kirk Hinrich. This was the Jayhawks physically pushing the Huskers around, breaking through the NU offensive line like a paper banner, chopping up the middle of the defense with delay run after delay run with no adjustment or linebacker in sight.

This was the Kansas offense, ranked last in the Big 12 and 106th nationally, going for 428 total yards. This was a Nebraska Blackshirt defense admitting that it didn't show up, that it took plays off, that it didn't play with its normal passion and fight. This was Nebraska getting out-coached, outplayed and out-passioned by Rock, Chalk, Jayhawk.

This, ladies and germs, is not acceptable for Nebraska football.

Finally, the man in charge, coach Bill Callahan, seems to agree. He used the words "frustrating," "really disappointing" and "God-awful" over and over. He didn't say anything about being proud of his team's effort. Actually, quite the opposite.

The good news is, Callahan's face is red. The bad news is, he doesn't have any answers.

"We just have to get better," Callahan said. "We have to go back to work."

That's what a coach says when he doesn't know what to do.

DECEMBER 12, 2005 • NEBRASKA VOLLEYBALL

Husker Heroines Make History

ONE DYNASTY REBUILDS in Lincoln. Another keeps rolling along, crushing whatever is in its way and plowing through the national landscape on the way to San Antonio. And history.

Nebraska volleyball won the Omaha regional, disposing of the Florida Gators in 90 minutes and letting the crowd out of the Qwest Center Omaha in time for dinner in the Old Market. Hooray for NU volleyball.

Hooray for the dynasty with ponytails.

John Cook's ladies are taking their coach back to the NCAA volleyball final four, his third appearance. Cook will go for his second national championship next weekend and the third in school history.

What the heck. It's time. Terry Pettit won the school's first NCAA crown in 1995. Five years later, in his first season taking over for Pettit, Cook won the NCAA title. Every five years, they win it all.

Every five years, the machine cranks up. Sane observers get out of the way.

"Coach Pettit told me we're like a Hummer," Cook said. "We crush everything and plow along. We'll be the last car running. We're not like a Porsche. We just keep coming."

The Hummer had company. An NCAA volleyball record crowd of 15,119 hopped aboard the express. Together, they sounded like a locomotive.

"That was history tonight," said Florida coach Mary Wise.

Nebraska volleyball is all about history, making it and leaving opponents in its wake.

From left, Nebraska's Melissa Elmer, Christina Houghtelling and Maggie Griffin celebrate a point against Florida in Omaha.

NU Defines Season With Bowl Triumph

SAN ANTONIO

REMEMBER THE ALAMO Bowl? They will never forget this one. In a football season that has been a wild and crazy ride, Nebraska saved the best for last. The Huskers beat Michigan 32-28 in an Alamo Bowl that looked just like their season.

There were some ups, some downs. Things looked bleak. But the Huskers never, ever gave up.

In fact, it was a masterpiece, a portrait of what this team was and what coach Bill Callahan's program is after two seasons. Tough. Resilient. Full of character.

This should go down as one of the great bowl wins in Nebraska's long and proud football history. Yes, there have been championships and heroics and wins that meant more on paper. But considering the opponent, and its own circumstances, there cannot have been a more valiant Big Red bowl victory.

Michigan finished with a 7-5 record, losing five games for the first time since 1984, when it went 6-6 and lost the Holiday Bowl to national champion Brigham Young. But Michigan is still Michigan.

Underachieving or no, the Wolverines began the season ranked in the top five. And, personnel-wise, they are ahead of Nebraska's reclamation project.

Throw in NU's patchwork line, and undermanned secondary, and the linebackers in street clothes and other assorted bodies with slings on arms, and you had an NU team that was down to the nub.

This wasn't the dream matchup we begged for eight years ago, at the end of a controversial 1997 season. But in so many ways, it turned out to be a classic. To be sure, a Husker classic.

To win, the Huskers handed the ball to their heart and soul, Cory Ross. The senior running back had success early in the ballgame. But in the third quarter, Callahan went away from the running game. During the TV broadcast, ESPN's Kirk Herbstreit chastised him for it. And, meanwhile, quarterback Zac Taylor was paying for it, getting pounded harder than he had all season.

So, finally, Callahan went back to Ross. And he took the ball left and sprinted 31 yards for a touchdown. A two-point conversion pulled NU within three points, 28-25.

Then came controversy.

On Michigan's next possession, with 5:56 left in the game, Nebraska's Blake Tiedtke appeared to knock the ball out of quarterback Chad Henne's hand. Nebraska's Ola Dagunduro scooped it up and ran to the Michigan 16.

TV replays hinted that the referees on the field should have called it an incomplete pass, not a fumble. Michigan coach Lloyd Carr called his last timeout, hoping that the fumble would be overturned.

But the call wasn't changed. And a few plays later, Taylor passed to Terrence Nunn for the winning score with 4:29 left.

It was the perfect wild and crazy capper to this season, which began with folks wondering about Callahan and his struggling team. Forget about talent. Did they have heart? Would they fight?

The last two games came with resounding answers. First, the 30-3 victory at Colorado was not a fluke; it may have been just the beginning.

And now Michigan. Who could forget it?

Nebraska running back Cory Ross rushed for 161 yards and a touchdown against Michigan.

TOM'S TAKE — REFLECTIONS ON

Omaha Dips Its Toes Into the Water of Olympic Sports

SO HOW FAST do you think Michael Phelps can swim across the Missouri River?

Major kudos to the Omaha Sports Commission for its bid to host the 2008 U.S. Olympic Swim Trials — in the Qwest Center, not that rolling body of water adjacent to it.

This bid is nothing to Spitz at.

This is a natural for our River City. That is, as natural as putting two 50-meter pools inside an arena and convention center can be.

Dan Morrissey and the members of the Sports Commission have recognized that the Qwest Center cannot live on Big 12, Missouri Valley and NCAA events alone. We need to think bigger. We need to think global.

Olympic trials are perfect. Swimming. Gymnastics. Wrestling. Fencing. And if bowling ever becomes an Olympic sport, trust me, we'll be all over it.

The U.S. Olympic Trials are evolving. They are not the mere competitions they used to be. No, in today's world of Opening Ceremonies on Broadway, the trials themselves have become a big event, eight days of corporate tents, games, food, music and, yes, shuttle services.

What makes Omaha so sure it can deliver? Isn't there a 10-day sporting event that takes place here every year in June? Give me a minute. I'll think of it.

Lo and behold, the head of USA Swimming, the body that will select the 2008 Swim Trials, has been to the College World Series. And was wowed. What a shock.

Sure, there's going to be stiff competition, but Omaha has a shot. The facility is superb and, oh by the way, the swimming venue for 2008 in Beijing, China, is indoors. Like the pool at Creighton Prep, only bigger.

Maybe it's just me, but I see fans from all corners of Nebraska, Iowa, Missouri, Kansas and Minnesota driving down for this poolapalooza. I see a mini-fan village that would go from the Qwest Center to the Old Market and wind around downtown. I see 12,000 fans a day, all holding stopwatches.

The Sports Commission sees it, too. What a grand statement this will make to the rest of the country, a statement that says Omaha is serious about getting into the game, all kinds of games. Even if we don't get it, it's a message to the U.S. Olympic Committee that we are serious about hosting future five-ring events.

Let's hope USA Swimming gives us a shot. The water's fine in Omaha.

— JANUARY 9, 2005

Dan Morrissey and the Omaha Sports Commission secured a bid for the 2008 U.S. Olympic Swim Trials.

THE CHANGING SPORTS LANDSCAPE | 2005

Downtown Ballpark Would Elevate Omaha Sports Scene

THE 37TH FLOOR OF THE FIRST NATIONAL TOWER

EVEN ON A cloudy day, you can see forever. The view from high atop our city is spectacular. I was visiting a friend this week in the First National Tower and sneaked a peek at the north side of town. At "NoDo."

Denver has its "LoDo," its "Lower Downtown" area, rows of shops, bars and restaurants that lead you to Coors Field, a crown jewel of a ballpark. Looking down at our north end, the natural corridor that goes from the Creighton campus and soccer stadium to the Qwest Center Omaha, it's easy to envision a dynamic northern downtown. Or "NoDo."

Where there are pawnshops and empty lots and vacant buildings, there could be a thriving business and entertainment district, complete with condos and, yes, a new ballpark. Haymarket Park East.

Imagine parking at the Qwest Center and walking two blocks to 14th and Cuming for a baseball game. You have dinner. Take a trolley to the new Holland Performing Arts Center.

Maybe you're going to a Creighton game. Or a concert. You park in "NoDo." Walk or trolley it to the Qwest Center. Hit a sports bar on the way back to the car.

Imagine this type of attraction for an NCAA or U.S. Olympic Committee looking for a place to set up a sports carnival. Imagine what Omaha will look like to visitors driving in from Eppley Airfield, as they see the giant convention center/arena on one side and a renovated neighborhood and new ballpark on another.

Talk about Extreme City Makeover.

Developers, city officials and Creightonians are salivating over the possibilities of a "NoDo" area. The anchor that could set it in motion is apparently the new Omaha Royals/Creighton ballpark. Yes, another ballpark.

It should make for an interesting next year or two. Let the poker game begin.

— APRIL 29, 2005

Parking areas northwest of Qwest Center Omaha became the site for TD Ameritrade Park.

AMATEUR SPORTS CAPITAL | OREGON STATE WINS CWS | ANOTHER TOUGH LOSS TO LONGHORNS

2006

> "I didn't know anything about volleyball. I coached them like I coached football players. That first year, there was a lot of crying. But I went to a lot of clinics, studied the game, and grew to love it."
>
> — NEBRASKA'S JOHN COOK, DESCRIBING HIS FIRST VOLLEYBALL COACHING JOB

So I'm walking through the parking lot at Hy-Vee when a car pulls up. The window rolls down. The driver, a middle-aged woman, leans over and yells: "Is this finally it for Collier?" "Don't know," I said, a little stunned. "We'll see." Next thing I know, I'm in the produce section (OK, OK, it's the cookie aisle). And a guy says, "So, are they going to get rid of Collier?" Good question. Better question: Where are the Double Stuf Oreos? Husker Hoops is all the rage. Finally, Barry Collier is the talk of the town. I don't think this is quite what he had in mind.

One of my favorite parts of the CWS is watching friends in the news media the first time they witness the event. For years, I have tried to get Joe Posnanski of the Kansas City Star, a friend and fellow columnist, to make it up to Omaha. Last year, he finally made it. I gave him the full tour, through the parking lots and T-shirt booths. We stopped by Greg Pivovar's card shop across the street. We had a Zesto shake. I told him stories, the lore, stuff I'd written about years before. I introduced him to some of the CWS's colorful characters. Every time I do this, I watch people's eyes. Sportswriters are a hardened, cynical bunch. Not much impresses them. They are numbed by most big events. But when they come here, their eyes become wide and bright. Like they're kids again. Joe wrote one of his best columns the next day. The CWS always delivers.

So you want to improve the lousy officiating that's permeated the NFL playoffs, college football, college basketball and probably even the X Games? Here's a 100 percent, sure-fire, foolproof way: Get rid of instant replay. We see too much. The replays are hammered over and over. These bang-bang calls are easy to make from a couch when seen over and over. They're a little harder to make when they happen in a split second. Maybe even harder when you are worried about Big Brother always looking over your shoulder. What I'd like to see is the officials hold a press conference after games and maybe even a day later. Officials are no more or less human than players or coaches. Let them explain their calls and answer critics.

HUSKER HOOPS WIN OVER JAYS | BIG 12 HONORS ZAC TAYLOR | NU VOLLEYBALL TITLE IN OMAHA

Nebraska pitching ace Joba Chamberlain showed up for media day 20 pounds lighter, at 225. He said he did it to "set an example," and I know he was talking about his teammates, and not the news media. Chamberlain said he watched what he ate and when he ate and "made running fun." So much for selling that diet on the market. Nobody will ever buy the last part.

Nebraskans have a way of charming you to death with their honesty, sincerity, values and passion. Yes, passion for sports. I've been at newspapers in Kansas City, St. Louis and Dallas. I've done pro sports. Give me college sports. Give me passion for college sports. There is no place like Nebraska. There is no better place to write college sports than Nebraska. Sure, there are moments when it's over the top. We have squeezed all of the water out of the rock this week analyzing the game plan for USC. The intensity here can leave you breathless. But that's the passion. Don't ever lose that passion — or you become Los Angeles, where they arrive late and leave early, to beat the traffic.

Somewhere, Rod Dedeaux likely rests in peace. Denny Walker, an Omaha businessman and sports fan, spoke to the former USC baseball coach's son, Terry, the day after the old mentor passed away. Dedeaux, a master storyteller, was good for one last story. "Rod passed away at 3 a.m. last Thursday," Walker said. "He was in the hospital, watching the Rose Bowl. I was so afraid he had died of a broken heart. Rod had a stroke last month. He couldn't speak. His body was half-paralyzed. He had written a note to someone saying he was going to go to the Rose Bowl. He really wanted USC to win. I was afraid he had seen the ending and it broke his heart. Terry said that, with two minutes left in the game (and USC still ahead of Texas) Rod fell asleep. And he never woke up. He went off into another world thinking his Trojans won."

The entrance of the interview room was clogged. Media members were huddled four-deep around a Rose Bowl celebrity. Matt Leinart? Reggie Bush? Vince Young? Will Ferrell? Nope. It was the granddaddy of them all, Keith Jackson. The college football icon dropped in on media day, and his mere presence stopped traffic. Jackson is now the game's historian. Folks want to know what he thinks. About the greatest-team-of-all-time debate: "The 1972 USC team is the greatest team I ever saw. But then came the '95 Nebraska team. Whoa, now. My word. That was a team. They averaged 556 yards per game (he was right!). That was a team that dominated every game they played."

Amateur Sports Capital of the Midwest?

I WISH THERE were something to do in this town.

They said it couldn't be done. They said nobody would come. They said the building would be a waste of time, space and money. The rest of us argued.

But not even we dreamers had imaginations as big as today in Omaha.

If you like wrestling, we've got the Nebraska state championships at the Qwest Center.

If you like hockey, we've got Meesh-i-gan and UNO at the Civic Auditorium.

If you like hoops, and ESPN, we've got both. Fresno State vs. Creighton in the BracketBusters, at 11 p.m. Presented by No-Doz.

If you like volleyball, we've got the top young players in the nation, 312 teams, ages 10 to 18, on 39 courts in the convention center, auditioning for the top college coaches in the land.

Now all we need is a parking space.

Today is Amateur Sports Day in Omaha. Throw in Bob Knight, whose Texas Tech Red Raiders play Nebraska in Lincoln, and this area feels like the amateur sports capital of the Midwest.

If the College World Series is Omaha at its best, then today is the winter wonderland version. Between state wrestling in the afternoon, UNO-Michigan at 7 and Creighton at 11, there figure to be around 30,000 sports fans downtown today. What does that tell you?

That we love our college and high school sports. In 2008, we will learn to love Olympic swimmers.

That doesn't mean pro sports need not apply. But if the Knights didn't know before, they do now: Amateur sports are Omaha's passion. Minor-league teams must try harder. Ask the Royals.

It also says the Qwest Center is a good thing. Were there actually sports fans against building this?

The Qwest Center is the door to our sports future, to our wildest imaginations. We can be a hub for NCAA championships and Olympic Trials. We can make days like today happen all the time. And then some.

"We have the makings of a great amateur sports hub," UNO hockey coach Mike Kemp said. "If we can fit them all in."

The Qwest Center was host to the state wrestling tournament during the day and a Creighton basketball game late at night.

Sports Hall Says It All for Omaha

GALE SAYERS IS in town to appear at a special showing of "Brian's Song" at Omaha Central's auditorium, the proceeds of which will benefit the Wesley House. He will return in June to host his golf tournament at the Players Club.

Welcome home, Gale. Good to see you. We don't see nearly enough of you, it seems.

Why don't we bring the Central High graduate home for good?

No, this is not a plea for Sayers to move back to Omaha. Rather, it's a thought that we should see the old Chicago Bear more often. In fact, we should be able to look him up whenever we want. Isn't it time for an Omaha Sports Hall of Fame?

Seriously. How many Omahans know that Sayers learned his ESPN Classic moves in Omaha's neighborhoods and sandlots before moving to the University of Kansas and the Monsters of the Midway?

Is there a generation that knows Bob Gibson was the greatest pitcher of his time, and a Harlem Globetrotter to boot?

How many in our burg remember when Bob Boozer played with the giants of the NBA and was a member of the first U.S. Olympic "Dream Team" in 1960?

A generation or two still remain that can answer most of the above questions. But 10, 20 years from now, will that be the case? When the last person who saw their greatness in person is gone, how will future generations know?

Shane Bradford is not a sports legend. He is a local sports fan. He's also a guy with an idea. Not the first guy with this idea, but the first guy to take action.

Bradford and Leo Smith, executive director of the Durham Museum, are putting together an Omaha Sports Hall of Fame.

I'm a big fan of this idea. Then again, I love history. I love plaques and statues and buildings and fields that honor the past.

Bradford said the committee is still working on the criteria for membership. Does Andy Roddick, who lived here for several years but didn't make his name here, qualify? What of high school or college stars who never made it big after here?

"These are people who are being honored because they enriched our city, and our state, made a difference, enhanced the image of Omaha," Smith said.

It's an ongoing process. But, finally, it's a process.

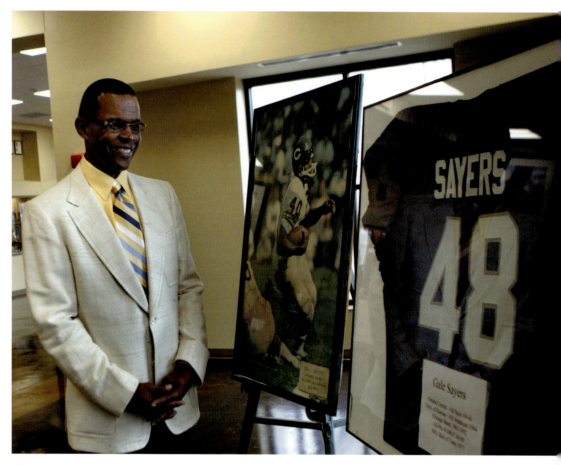

Gale Sayers, above, was joined in the first class of the Omaha Sports Hall of Fame in 2007 by Bob Boozer, Marlin Briscoe, Connie Claussen, Eric Crouch, Bob Gibson, Nile Kinnick, Dave Rimington, Johnny Rodgers and Roger Sayers, Gale's brother.

A Fickle Flip of Fate Favors OSU

BEAVER BELIEVER? NAH.

To borrow from Jack Buck, not Dallas Buck, I don't believe what I just saw.

Oregon State loses its first game at the College World Series, 11-1 to Miami, and wins the national championship? No way.

The Beavers trot out Jonah Nickerson, the rubber-band man himself, and he goes 100 pitches Monday night, on three days' rest? And Nickerson throws 323 pitches in three starts in one week? And holds North Carolina to two runs, neither earned? Forget about it.

North Carolina attempts to steal home and the play fails because the batter ends the inning with a strikeout? You must be joking.

Oregon State's starter on Saturday night, Dallas Buck, comes in with two on and no outs in the eighth and the score tied 2-2 and gets out of the jam, including striking out the last two batters? You must be kidding.

The Beavers score the winning run in the bottom of the eighth when Bryan Steed, the Tar Heels' backup second baseman, takes a routine grounder and throws the ball wide of first base, where Tim Federowicz — the all-CWS catcher — can't make the catch? Unbelievable.

And Kevin Gunderson, the little warrior, comes back from throwing 5-plus innings of relief the night before to record the final two outs? OK, maybe we believe that one.

And, finally, Oregon State wins its first national championship in a major sport at the CWS?

It was our pleasure to witness it.

Oregon State's Kevin Gunderson leaps into his teammates' arms after getting the final out against North Carolina.

OCTOBER 22, 2006 • NEBRASKA FOOTBALL

Tough Ending Part of Growing Pains

IT WAS THROWBACK day at Memorial Stadium. What a beautiful sight.

The sky was that eerie battleship gray, the wind was dancing like Johnny Rodgers on a punt return, the temperature was bone-chilling and the linebackers were bone-crunching.

ABC was in the house, sending the action to more than 80 percent of the nation's houses. The Texas Longhorns were on one sideline, and from their all-white uniforms to their strutting playmakers to their cheerleader coach, they looked for all the world like another old adversary.

This looked and felt like one of those big, big, big Nebraska-Oklahoma games we used to know.

All the way to the heartbreak ending.

Terrence Nunn caught a short pass for a first down, but a Texas defensive back knocked the ball out. Texas recovered with 2:17 left, just when it looked like NU was going to ice a significant 20-19 victory.

Then a walk-on by the name of Ryan Bailey made a 22-yard field goal with 23 seconds left to give the Longhorns a 22-20 great-escape victory.

A breathless, edge-of-your-seat football game came down to those two twists of fate, like twists of the knife in the gut.

What can you say? No pain, no gain. Or, the bigger the game, the bigger the pain.

Marcus Griffin of Texas dives for a fumble by Terrence Nunn with just over two minutes left in the game.

NOVEMBER 19, 2006 • NEBRASKA BASKETBALL

Huskers Have an Identity

JUST WHAT THE Doc ordered.

An identity. Self-esteem. Toughness. A big win. And, most of all, bragging rights. Husker Hoops has been floating at sea, searching for land, looking for all those things.

Nebraska found them, especially the last one, in a 73-61 victory over Creighton at the Devaney Center.

There's a season of hoops left. But this one could not be overplayed from the red standpoint.

At the end, the "Red Zone" rushed the floor. It felt appropriate. The Jays were ranked 20th. It had been eight years since the Huskers beat Creighton in the regular season. Danny Nee was still the coach at NU. Dana Altman had yet to take CU to the NCAA tournament.

Eight years. In that time, the Huskers have had it tough in the Big 12. But their measuring stick, their reminder of how down they were, always seemed to be 50 miles to the east.

That's what this was all about. This was for the message board junkies, the folks in red who have to listen to the ones in blue, the Nebraska fans floating out of the Devaney Center, the players who have to listen to those people all year.

This was for the big brother school who has been relegated to little brother during the winter.

This was good medicine from the Doc, first-year coach Doc Sadler, the guy who arrived here in August from El Paso, Texas, and seemed to grasp it better than anyone.

"Dana and I talked about this this afternoon," Sadler said. "There's a lot more big games ahead for both of us. But I do understand that Creighton has built a tremendous program. We've got some catching up to do.

"Creighton has a classy program. But we've got some class, too."

Nebraska's Ryan Anderson drives past Creighton's Dane Watts.

Storybook Career Reaching Final Chapter

OK, SO LET ME get this straight.

A kid grows up in Norman, Okla. The kid's dad played football for the University of Oklahoma. They live four miles from Owen Field.

The kid is a BIG Sooner fan. There are autographs and photos on his walls. Brian Bosworth. Barry Switzer. You hit the doorbell, it plays "Boomer Sooner." When the kid scrapes his knee, he bleeds crimson.

Or something like that.

One year, when he is in high school, the kid goes to an OU football game. The Sooners are playing No. 1-ranked Nebraska. Oklahoma wins. The Sooner fans drive around and around the campus, honking their horns and howling at the moon until after midnight.

The kid is in one of those cars, screaming for his Sooners. The police stop their car and ticket a friend riding on the outside of the car.

Anyway, the kid grows up to be a quarterback. He imagines himself playing college football. He imagines himself playing for you-know-who.

Got it so far?

OK, so the kid is good, he's got the bloodlines, but he's not THAT good. He's not Oklahoma good. He's not bitter. He commits to play at Oklahoma State.

But then, one day, he sees that OSU already has a quarterback, a freshman, who isn't going away. The kid decides to sign with the only other school that wants his services, Wake Forest. He plays there a couple of years. It doesn't work out. He leaves and goes to Butler Community College, in The Middle Of Nowhere, Kan.

It's right about this time that fate intervenes again. He's getting ready to move on and try Division I football again. He goes to another Nebraska-OU game in Norman. He walks into the stadium. They are carrying out one of the student pep squad "Ruf/Neks" on a stretcher.

The kid watches the game. He's not very impressed with the Huskers, who run the ball all night.

He reads a story the next day. The Nebraska coach had called the OU fans "hillbillies."

A few weeks later, the kid is meeting with that coach. The coach needs a quarterback. Now. Four months later, he is in Lincoln, Neb., wearing a white helmet with a red "N."

But the kid is not a big deal. Nebraska has recruited a five-star blue-chip quarterback from Florida. Another one from Kansas City will soon be on the way. The kid will start the 2005 season for the Huskers, though he's just keeping the spot warm for one season.

But then a funny thing happens. The kid turns out to be pretty good. Smart. Tough. He sticks to the depth chart like gum on a shoe. The two young guns fade away.

Suddenly, the kid is the glue holding the Nebraska program together. He has a big senior year, hands the ball off a lot, manages the offense well, makes the calls for the linemen at times, makes big throws. He leads a two-minute drill winning touchdown drive at Texas A&M. His team wins the Big 12 North. The Oklahoma kid is going to play Texas in K.C.

Then it happens. The Longhorns are stunned by A&M. Oklahoma wins the South.

Get me rewrite. The kid will play the Sooners for the Big 12 championship.

Got that? Press conference day in Lincoln. The kid is walking around like he always does, with a Nebraska shirt and jeans, doing interviews, smiling, saying all the right things. But then there is a buzz. And then comes the news.

The journeyman kid, who kicked around at Wake Forest and at a juco and came here almost by accident, is named All-Big 12 quarterback and Big 12 offensive player of the year by the league's coaches. A half-hour later, your narrator calls up the kid's dad, Sherwood Taylor, and asks if he's heard the news.

"Yep," says Sherwood, who played defensive back for OU from 1977 to '79. "Zac just called me and told me. That's the most excited I've ever heard the kid.

"This is the biggest award he's ever won," the dad says. "He wasn't even all-state."

The kid is back in front of the press conference cameras again. He's happy but says the Big 12 title would mean more. He tries to say Oklahoma is just another team, but nobody believes him. We all saw his dejected face a year ago, when he fell short of beating OU and it looked like he would never get another chance to play his boyhood team.

"The funny thing is, Zac grew up following Oklahoma football in the '90s, when it wasn't very good," says the dad. "To him, the 2000 season was amazing. Those were the glory years to him. To the rest of us, that's how it always was.

"That's what is so cool about this. Zac witnessed Oklahoma's resurgence. Now he's helping bring Nebraska back on its own resurgence."

This would be one heck of a story to write. Too bad nobody would ever believe it.

Zac Taylor was named Big 12 offensive player of the year in 2006.

DECEMBER 18, 2006 • NEBRASKA VOLLEYBALL

Huskers, Omaha Celebrate Success

WE'RE NO. 1. There has never been an NCAA women's volleyball championship like this week, these two nights, this one match. There has never been a party like this one. There is no place like Omaha to host the annual convention of kills, digs, sets and blocks. We're the best.

OK, we had a little help.

Nebraska's volleyball team isn't so bad itself.

We threw one heck of a shin-pad shindig. With apologies to the great Stanford team, this historic occasion — our first volleyball final four, and certainly not our last — had the absolute perfect ending.

Nebraska 3, Stanford 1.

For the second straight night, more than 17,000 people paid money to watch women's college volleyball. The majority were in red, from football jerseys to Volleyball Santa. They made history. They were here to see history. Could a Nebraska team win a national championship in its home state? The Huskers don't get many chances.

They didn't waste this one.

The answer came when NU sophomore Jordan Larson pounded a kill down the pipe of the Stanford defense, flipping the switch on a roar they could hear all the way to the farms — the ones around Larson's hometown of Hooper and the one in Palo Alto, Calif.

It was absolute madness. Coach John Cook celebrated his second national title by thrusting his arms into the air and looking for an assistant to hug. The Huskers stormed the court. The players danced to the standard "Celebration" song.

There was a lot here to celebrate. Start with the match. Take Kirk Herbstreit off ESPN Classic and put this match on, pronto. This was incredible.

On women's volleyball's biggest stage, we saw the sport's best, its finest two hours and 12 minutes. The level of play was astoundingly high. More than that, it was just relentless. Back and forth, both teams feeding off each other, trying to top each other. It was one of those games where the players and fans had to stop to catch their breath.

The Cardinal won the first game. Nebraska won a tight second game, a game it had to have or this party was over. The Huskers took games three and four with more muscle, more hustle and a nice little coaching gamble by Cook.

The heroes in this one will be the arms of Sarah Pavan and Larson, who hit for a dominant .378 percentage. Here's a layman's way to put it: They beat the you-know-what out of the ball. They hammered and hammered and hammered until the final nail went in on Stanford's season.

Pavan, in particular, delivered. All eyes were on NU's national player of the year to do something special, to carry this team. And that started way back in August, when last year's national player of the year, Christina Houghtelling, was lost for the season. That was when Pavan said she would not let this team lose. She kept her promise.

The crowd was enthralled with Pavan and Larson, but the play of the game might have come from Cook, who put reserve Amanda Gates in the match late in the third game. Gates was in on two blocks to help win the game and had a kill to open the decisive fourth. Coaches' intuition? It worked.

By the fourth game, the crowd was louder than ever, going up a level with each Husker point. It was the most electric, most unusual atmosphere for an NCAA championship you'll ever see. Or hear.

Was it fair? No. But who was to know when Omaha was awarded this championship that Nebraska would do this? Sure, the Huskers have been known to play in a final four or three. But the nucleus of this team hadn't yet arrived on campus.

The NCAA knew that Nebraskans will come out to watch Long Beach State play Clemson in mid-June. So it was a pretty good bet they would show up to watch volleyball, a sport with roots already deep in the fertile Nebraska ground.

In a sense, it was fair. The NCAA was attracted to the interest level in volleyball in our state, which the Husker program was responsible for. So in a roundabout way, Nebraska earned this home court.

It was also all in the name of progress. Even Stanford coach John Dunning said, on the eve of this tournament, that he felt this weekend would be some sort of launching point for the sport.

But how could Dunning have known his team would get caught in the jet stream?

"This was the biggest match in (women's college volleyball) history, in some scope," Dunning said afterward.

Nebraska's Cook agreed: "I think this will produce the biggest impact our sport has had in a long, long time."

What happened here had to open eyes, national as well as local. The Huskers' timing was impeccable. But so was the quality of play by all four teams. Fans had to leave this building wanting to see, feel and even hear more.

The Huskers got the trophy. But the real winner was women's college volleyball.

So was Omaha. It's hard to imagine we will not be in a regular rotation to host this event. After this week, we should be in the front line.

DECEMBER 18, 2006 • NEBRASKA VOLLEYBALL

A third Nebraska national volleyball championship is a reason to jump for joy.

2011 INSIGHT *I can't think of too many cities where women's college volleyball sells out the arena. Or gets a special section in the paper. I can't think of any sports columnists I know who have covered a women's volleyball match. They're all missing out. One of the charms of this place is that every once in a while, we give certain nonrevenue sports the New York Yankees treatment. College baseball, hockey, too. The athletes deserve it and, even better, appreciate it. Weekends like this NCAA volleyball final four in Omaha are a reason I'm glad I'm in a college sports town. It had a big-time feel, yet with the wide-eyed innocence of female athletes that gives the event a freshness. I even wrote the championship game column on deadline. But I cheated. I didn't point out any technicalities or strategy. I don't think anyone cared.*

TOM'S TAKE — REFLECTIONS ON

Hopefully, Osborne Won't Stop Serving Nebraska

TOM OSBORNE HAD lost a big one. And now, on cue, is the second-guessing.

A Nebraska football chat board that offers refuge from political talk was lit up, right as the results of the Nebraska Republican primary for governor were coming in.

These chaps were all pulling for Osborne to be their guy. Alas, the old coach couldn't pull through. The attempt was wide, political right.

The election night quarterbacks took turns explaining how this political upset could happen.

One said the Osborne campaign had gotten off to a slow start, speculating that Osborne may have assumed his icon status would carry him through at the end.

On and on they went. He came off as too moderate. He was betrayed by his staff.

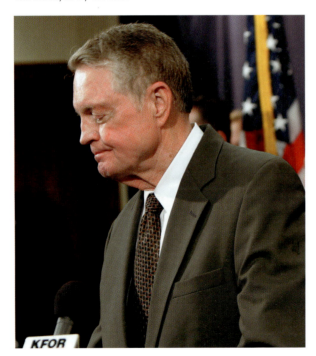

Where's Charlie McBride when you need him?

When Osborne leaves Congress seven months from now, Nebraska will be without him in a coaching or leadership position for the first time in a long time.

Selfishly, I wish Osborne had never left coaching. The man was just hitting his stride in 1997. Who knows how many national titles he would have won? He was born to coach. Yes, he looked and sounded tired, and talked of his health, but then he jumped right back on the train to Washington.

I understand why he left. But this is why a man should never make promises to his wife or his best friend.

I hope Osborne doesn't leave us now. He's 69. But he has so much more to give, more to do.

His TeamMates mentoring program will take up time, no doubt. But if I were Harvey Perlman or Steve Pederson, I would call Osborne and get him on their team, pronto.

This will not be easy. Osborne was upset about the way Frank Solich was fired, that he wasn't consulted. Should NU consult Osborne about everything that happens? Better question: Shouldn't they always consult Osborne?

Here is a fountain of wisdom and experience, a man who can raise money and bring a splintered Husker Nation together. Why wouldn't Pederson want to make sure Osborne has an office and a pass to football practice for life, just like what Oklahoma State had for Henry Iba?

Then again, some people might rather give Pederson's office to Osborne.

He's off to the fishing hole now. I hope NU keeps his number handy. He's not our governor. But he will always be The Man.

— **MAY 11, 2006**

When Tom Osborne left Congress and lost his bid for governor, Nebraska was without him in a coaching or leadership position for the first time in a long time.

THE CHANGING SPORTS LANDSCAPE 2006

Cuts Show UNO Isn't Ready for Big Time

THIS IS GOING to get ugly at UNO. This looks like a train wreck in progress. If you have a love for Maverick athletics, or a squeamish stomach, look away.

When UNO decided to add Division I men's hockey in 1997, it was tantamount to jumping off a cliff. It required a change in commitment, a change in mentality. There was no turning back now.

Apparently, the folks in charge at UNO want to turn back. That's not how it works.

When the University of North Dakota announced it was moving up to Division I, that was the final nail in the coffin of the North Central Conference as we knew it. RIP, NCC.

It leaves the other members scrambling for cover. It's sad. The NCC was once a proud power in Division II sports. But that's life in today's college athletics. It's every school for itself. The strong and aggressive survive. The rest play glorified intramurals.

Will UNO move up or move down? Play ball or intramurals? An answer came, coincidentally, when UNO announced it was cutting five positions from athletics: an assistant athletic director; an assistant coach in both men's and women's basketball; a sports information director for hockey; and a secretary. All to save $444,000.

Maverick athletics are at a crossroads. This is the most important time in UNO athletics history. Frankly, some of the most powerful UNO boosters are scared to death to watch.

This is a school with a small-time Division II mentality. It's a place in conflict with itself. An administration in over its Division I head.

UNO dived into Division I sports. Then it moved into the Qwest Center. Unlike Creighton, UNO has no idea what to do with it. It has treated hockey like wrestling or basketball. It has never aggressively marketed the sport in town. It refuses to separate hockey and treat it special.

The result was, when season tickets fell during the move to the Qwest Center, UNO had no clue how to get them back. The result showed up in the unemployment line this week.

What happened was unconscionable and unnecessary. I spoke with a Division I athletic director this week. I told him of the UNO situation. He said it was shocking.

Most universities and athletic directors, he said, have a contingency plan to avoid those kinds of cuts. A reserve. He said, at the very least, an athletic director should exhaust all donor avenues to make sure jobs don't get lost and the department can get back on its feet.

— JUNE 23, 2006

COTTON BOWL LOSS TO AUBURN | ANOTHER VALLEY CHAMPIONSHIP | NEWCOMERS AT THE SERIES

2007

"Every one of those (Cox Classic) champions is on the PGA Tour. So it's not just the guy who gets a hot putter. The winner here can play."

— ORLANDO POPE, THE PGA TOUR'S DIRECTOR OF OMAHA'S COX CLASSIC TOURNAMENT

Catch, turn, shoot. Catch, turn, shoot. Catch, turn, shoot. It's Thursday afternoon, 30 minutes before Nebraska basketball practice. Aleks Maric and assistant coach David Anwar are the lone figures on the Devaney Center floor. Maric shoots. Anwar rebounds and passes. Catch, shoot. Over and over, they repeat the drill. Jump hooks from the baseline. Jumpers from 10 feet. Then 15 feet, from each wing and corner. Then out behind the 3-point line. Anwar grabs a broom. They go down to the low block. Maric turns and shoots over Anwar and the broom. After practice, Maric will be back, alone again, shooting over and over. He does this every day, before and after each practice, working on his game, perfecting his trade for the future, for whatever next season brings.

I don't remember what I wrote last week. Apparently, some people keep track of these things. Apparently in December, when Nebraska volleyball was taking over Omaha, I might have mentioned that volleyball was more appealing to watch than women's basketball, and volleyball players were better athletes. "That's your opinion," Nebraska women's basketball coach Connie Yori said. "I think we have a great game, and it's getting better all the time. All I know is that our game has a beauty to it, the passing, the running and shooting."

It was Wednesday afternoon, just before 1 p.m., at the Creighton athletic offices. There was a line outside Athletic Director Bruce Rasmussen's door. But Rasmussen was out of town. Who were these people waiting to see? The pope? Close. They had come from all corners of the CU campus to be here. The man they had come to see, the man who was taking appointments and granting audiences, came to the door. It was Tom Osborne. Yes, that Tom Osborne. He comes to this campus, to these offices, every Wednesday. He meets with Creighton coaches and athletes, from Dana Altman to the crew captain. Professors. Secretaries. Fundraisers. Even the men in those white collars. Anyone seeking some advice when it comes to leadership, integrity, ethics and, yes, winning. But why Creighton? "They asked me," Osborne said.

OSBORNE RETURNS TO NEBRASKA | A NEW BALLPARK DOWNTOWN | A RED-LETTER YEAR FOR SPORTS

The Korver Legacy continues to grow. The problem is, it's not just about the points or the rings or the awards. It's the way Kyle Korver continues to touch his former school and basketball program. It's the fact that he's here, in frigid, gray and white Omaha, and not shooting 3-pointers among the bright lights in sunny Las Vegas on NBA All-Star weekend. It's the fact that, four years after leaving CU, he's selling Kyle Korver bobblehead dolls for $20, with the proceeds going to his new Kyle Korver Foundation, to benefit underprivileged kids in Omaha and Philadelphia. It's the fact that, everywhere he goes in the NBA, he is still the poster boy of Creighton basketball. "It's amazing," Korver says. "I could be in Dallas or Seattle or Miami, and there are Creighton sweatshirts and shirts in the stands."

Creighton baseball has the look and feel of a program in transformation. What we've witnessed is a coach and his program quickly moving toward their potential. And toward respect. Ed Servais has craved it since he took over in 2004. He wasn't affiliated with the 1991 CWS team. He couldn't schmooze like Jim Hendry or Jack Dahm. He was the guy who got the job because CU either couldn't afford anyone else or couldn't find anyone else who would take the job. In four seasons, Servais has delivered the school's first Valley regular-season title and first Valley tournament title. Any questions? No, not after the phone calls Servais has received the past few days — including a long voice message from Hendry, who told Servais how proud he was of him and the program.

It's the end of an error. Steve Pederson, the man who would rewrite Nebraska football history, became a footnote when he was exiled from the ivory tower. And, in many corners of the state, the people rejoiced. They raised glasses. Some suddenly found their wallets. They danced like the munchkins in "The Wizard of Oz" after Harvey Perlman dropped a house on Pederson. It became a day of celebration. All this over an athletic director. Oh, the irony. Pederson came home vowing to unite "Husker Nation." In the end, he had done just that.

Is Sarah Pavan, the senior right-side hitter for Nebraska's volleyball team, the greatest Husker student-athlete, in any sport, ever? It's an interesting question, one that was posed to me by a Husker fan. At first I was taken aback. Pavan over Johnny Rodgers, Eric Crouch, Dave Rimington, Tommie Frazier, Erick Strickland, Alex Gordon and Jim Hartung? What about Merlene Ottey or, closer to the NU Coliseum, Allison

Weston or Nancy Metcalf? See how the field stacks up against Pavan. She literally led the Huskers to the 2006 NCAA title. She's looking to be only the fourth four-time All-American in college volleyball history. She was last year's national player of the year, an award that is volleyball's Heisman. She was the first Nebraska winner of the Honda-Broderick Cup, for the top women's athlete in any college sport. Last, but not least, she was named Academic All-American of the Year this summer, joining former NU tackle Rob Zatechka as the only Huskers ever to achieve the lofty honor. Name a former Husker, any sport, who's got that résumé. Time's up.

Callahan's Program Missing Something

DALLAS

HAPPY NEXT YEAR! The Nebraska football team returns all of its running backs in 2007. All of its receivers. Most of its offensive line. Three linebackers. A big-time corner. It has a big-name quarterback with an NFL arm. And this will be the fourth year in the vaunted "system."

So it should be a big year, right? This will be the year to cash in, the return to the top of the Big 12 heap and national spotlight, right?

Right?

It's hard to say. It's hard to trust Bill Callahan's program. Reasons for optimism abound. But something is missing.

We saw it, yet again, in the Cotton Bowl. Nebraska played with, and at times outplayed, ninth-ranked Auburn. The Huskers, at times, looked like a top 10-caliber team.

Did we mention Auburn won the actual game, 17-14?

If Callahan were a car salesman, he would go hungry. He can't close the big game. His teams can't finish. They are so close. But what matters is they are 9-5 when they easily could have been 11-3 and carting a Big 12 trophy home on the way to the desert.

It's always something. A fumble when they're trying to run out the clock to beat Texas. A fumble that sets up Oklahoma with a 7-0 lead and takes the wind out of their Big 12 title sails. It wasn't one play at USC, rather an attitude that playing it close was good enough.

Sometimes, like in the Cotton Bowl, Callahan gets in his own way. Callahan is a gambler. Gamblers go hungry, too.

Right now, this program is starving for a big win. The Huskers looked poised to get it early.

They pushed the Tigers and their SEC speed all over the turf on a beautiful opening-game touchdown drive. Auburn tied it after intercepting a Zac Taylor pass that was deflected. It happens. Early in the second quarter, NU still had the upper hand in this game. Auburn couldn't move.

So why, on fourth-and-one from his own 29, does Callahan attempt a fake punt? And not just any fake punt, but a reverse off a fake punt?

Where does he come up with these things?

The Tigers weren't fooled. They busted through the line, hit fullback Dane Todd, who had taken the snap and was poised to pitch the ball to Andrew Shanle. Yes, a safety.

Todd's pitch was off, Shanle never got it and Auburn recovered at the NU 14. Four plays later, the Tigers were up 14-7.

Ballgames are made up of many big plays, plays that change momentum. But this was an unnecessary self-inflicted shot in the foot.

Next year is huge. Callahan's fourth year.

"We're getting close," Callahan said. "We're getting there. It won't be long."

He said it like a man who's on the clock.

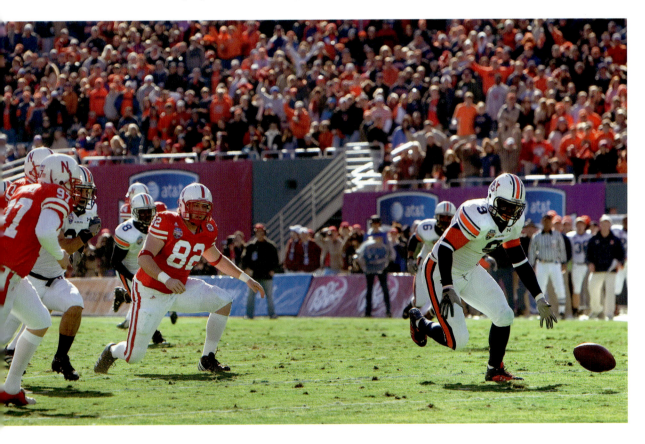

Auburn's Tristan Davis chases down a loose ball on a botched fake punt by Nebraska in the first half.

NU's Pederson Builds a Fortress

ALL I WANTED was a Nebraska baseball media guide. You know, roster, team bios, school records, a photo of Haymarket Park to get me through the winter. Shamus McKnight, the sports information baseball guru, puts out a terrific guide every year. And, as you can see by looking outside, it's baseball season.

So I walked through the front door of the Tom and Nancy Osborne Complex to go up to the media relations office. I reached for a second set of doors. Locked. Tight.

To the left, there is a security desk, behind a sliding window. Good grief. But there was no security guard. There was a sign pasted on the window that read, "Will be right back." I felt like I was at the gift shop at the Marriott.

So I stood there, waiting for someone to open the door to the athletic department of the public institution known as the University of Nebraska-Lincoln. Maybe they would emerge from the waterfall in the lobby.

Finally. What looked like a UNL worker came out of the weight room doors, saw me and hurried to the door. He opened it and growled, "CAN I HELP YOU?" (This reminded me of the scene in the "Wizard of Oz" when Dorothy and Co. knock on the palace door and a voice bellows out, "WHO GOES THERE?")

It is I, a sportswriter from Omaha, looking to get up to the media relations office of the public institution that is UNL.

"Who do you want to see?" asked the worker.

I've been around the college sports block a few times. Been to Oklahoma, Texas, Kansas, Duke, USC, Notre Dame, Ohio State, Michigan, etc. This is the first time a trip to a sports information department felt like going to the Pentagon.

"Shamus McKnight," I said.

"What do you want?" he said.

"A baseball media guide," I said, and I might have raised my voice. This was now officially frustrating.

"All right," the worker said. "Come on in. I'll take you up."

So the sportswriter and his escort got into the elevator to go fetch a media guide. The sportswriter says, "What's with all this security?"

The worker said, "We've had some people upstairs messing around."

I said, "Messing around? Who? Where?"

The worker said, "I don't know who. But they've been up there. Messing around."

I said, "How in the world did they get up there, past all this?"

The worker said, "I don't know. They just did."

Welcome to the Secret Society of Steve Pederson. The world of Nebraska athletics has officially become bizarre, over-the-top weird. Locked doors. Security guards.

And if you think getting in to get a baseball guide is tough, you should try the football offices. The plot for the next "Mission Impossible" movie will be getting in to see coach Bill Callahan.

This is college football, folks. Not the CIA. Not property taxes. Not annexation of cities. Not budgets for education.

Let me tell you about politics and education.

I decided to do my own research. For those keeping score at home: It was easier to reach the front doors of the governor's and UNL chancellor's offices than it was to get a baseball media guide.

Does any of this really matter?

In terms of wins and losses, no. But Nebraska has always been about more than winning. Nebraska football was like a family. This program didn't belong to any one person. It was accessible to everyone.

Those days are over. More and more, this is becoming Pederson's program, his way. Actions speak louder than words. And sometimes there are no words. Of course, Pederson will still take your money. Just drop it off at the guard's desk.

2011 INSIGHT

Steve Pederson's North Stadium structure had been up for a while, and I had gone through it a few times. But then one day I couldn't. For years, in the old South Stadium Nebraska athletic and football offices, anyone could walk right in. You could go down the hall to the athletic director's office. Or to sports information. Or walk up the stairs to the football offices. Generally, we writers didn't do that. The coaches and secretaries would give you the evil eye, like you were trespassing. Anyway, open access is how I've always seen things done, whether it was Notre Dame or USC or Duke.

So then, I tried to go up to sports information, on the third floor of Pederson's fortress, and was stopped. A guy who worked there, not even a security guard, told me I couldn't walk around by myself. We went round and round. Anyway, I was so upset about it I decided to write about how ridiculous this was.

There was definitely an attitude of paranoia, and one of trying to keep people away. I thought it would make a good column. But, to show how unusual this was, I went to the Nebraska governor's office and walked in unannounced. I kind of gambled there. I wasn't sure what the access would be at those places. I was surprised I was able to walk right into the governor's office. That was actually pretty cool. No, he wasn't in.

Pederson later sat down with me for a long Q and A that was the result of this column. Those were interesting, turbulent times around NU. There were two football alumni functions that spring, one that was seen as anti-Pederson. Nobody, and I mean nobody, could see what was coming just a few months away.

Altman Shows He Can Still Close

ST. LOUIS

A NATIONAL CBS audience and a crowd of 22,612, the largest to watch a basketball game at the Scottrade Center, saw Creighton make some sense of a long and crazy season, grab back some respect. The Jays did it in a way that made their tradition proud.

They delivered the first punch, made the plays, got the loose balls and never backed down. Southern Illinois admits it has tried to emulate Creighton's style. For the past four years, the Salukis have had the swagger.

The Jays took some of it back. Nate Funk and Nick Porter constantly pushed off SIU defenders as they dribbled. Finally, Creighton was pushing back at SIU.

"Today, they outfought us, period," the Salukis' Jamaal Tatum said. "The 50-50 plays, they beat us to all of them."

Crazy year. Choppy year. Injuries, illnesses and departures made it a weekly soap opera. There were times when Altman looked like he was slipping. He adjusted. Two weeks ago, he junked a matchup zone and went back to man defense. He's still got it.

Give the players credit, too. Funk, Porter and Anthony Tolliver carried this team to a Valley tourney title and an NCAA berth, the bar they are expected to reach. Two weeks ago, it looked like they were going to do the limbo. Their legacy was in limbo.

"This year was a little disappointing because the fans' expectations were so high," Altman said. "Our guys are all from the Midwest, they hear everybody talk, they had the weight of the world on them because they felt like they were letting everybody down."

The only thing that was heavy was that huge trophy that they wouldn't put down.

Creighton center Anthony Tolliver leads the celebration in St. Louis after the Jays beat Southern Illinois to win the Missouri Valley Conference championship.

Let's Hope Altman Is Back for Good

MEET THE NEW boss. Same as the old boss.

Get me rewrite. Former University of Arkansas basketball coach Dana Altman — sounds good, huh? — decided that he is more Nebraska than property taxes, more Omaha than fireworks and more Creighton than 24th Street.

He's staying. Or, rather, he's coming back. Coming home. For good, this time.

There is euphoria for Creightonians today. The emotions have swung 180 degrees in 24 hours. Panic to pandemonium.

Dana Altman is the coach at Creighton. Again. Still.

What happened? Who knows? This will go down as one of the most incredible, laughable, unthinkable sports stories in our city's history. But when your head stops spinning, the man who said goodbye to his players Monday was introducing himself to them again.

Hello, goodbye. I don't know why you say goodbye, I say hello.

There will be theories on this. And, as usual, only Altman will know the true answer. Family reasons? Did wife Reva say, 'No way I'm moving to Hogville'? Did Howard Hawks and David Sokol talk some $ense into Altman?

Or did Altman have a come-to-Creighton moment when he did that "Pig Sooey" thing at the press conference?

Is that when he said, "I'm not a call-the-pigs kind of guy; I'm a Creighton/Omaha/Nebraska kind of guy"? Or did he already know that?

And did it take him actually leaving, for however long (if you had 27 hours, 24 minutes in the pool, you win), for reality to smack him upside his hard head?

He's a Creighton guy. A Creighton coach. He's also human. But you know what? So are Creighton fans. And they deserve better than this.

Let the confetti fall. Creighton may or may not ever win the NCAA championship, but this was one shining moment, when CU beat the Southeastern Conference football school, when mid-major won over BCS, when it looked as if Altman had finally had enough of a good job, but a hard job, but then decided that it was the best job.

This was the day Altman chose Qwest Center Omaha over a legitimate shot at the Final Four, his current good life over a life in the fast lane to big things and who knows what else along the way.

When he chose a life with relatively no pressure over a big-time job with all the big-time pressures.

When he said, yes, he's always wanted to coach at a place where you could be like Billy Donovan and Thad Matta, for one night. But ultimately family, friends, relationships and, yes, personal comfort are more important.

Creightonians will soak up all the wonderful feelings of this moment. As they should.

But let this be the last one. This has to be the last time.

Creighton welcomes Altman back with open, forgiving arms. The school and Bluejays fans have rarely been hard on the man who has given them much recognition, pride and, yes, revenue.

But enough is enough. No more dances, Dana. No more hide and seek, and spy games, with Iowa, Arkansas, Tennessee, Illinois, Georgia, blah, blah, blah, blah, blah, blah.

No more hiding behind "no comment" when it comes to other job openings because your career is personal and you expect Creighton fans to understand.

If there should somehow be a phone call, Altman needs to answer the phone and say, "Dana Altman, Creighton basketball coach. Thanks, but no thanks."

For one thing, Jays fans deserve that.

For another, it's the honest truth.

Altman is the Creighton coach. Game, set, match. Who are we kidding? No more games, no more dances.

Altman has been through the wringer the past 48 hours. Arkansas Athletic Director Frank Broyles offered the job while Altman was still in Atlanta, and the coach slept on it. We assume he didn't sleep much. Even though he agreed, his body language and facial expressions the next day told another story.

He wasn't comfortable. He wasn't buying in. He didn't want to go.

But you know what? Creighton fans went through the same emotions, if not more. What a ride on Monday. Sadness. Fear. Anger. Depression. That's usually the first half of a Southern Illinois game. But this was worse.

Jays fans are jubilant today, and rightfully so. All is well in Camelot. Prince Valiant has come riding home to save the day.

He will be welcomed home. Now it's time for him to stay home.

2011 INSIGHT

Before I begin this story, let me state for the record that this never happened before and will never happen again. I'm still not sure how it happened this time.

The first week of April 2007, I was covering the NCAA Final Four in Atlanta. Two friends from Omaha, Bill Hargens and the late, great Dan Sims, tagged along. We had secured practice day badges for the Masters, two hours down the road, for Tuesday and Wednesday. I had never been to the Masters as a "patron." I was fired up.

This was the Final Four where Dana Altman left for Arkansas. Happened on Monday. I wrote the "Dana Leaves" column during the Florida-Ohio State championship game that night, got up the next day and drove to Augusta with Bill and Dan. So far, so good.

We had a glorious day. Walked the course. Sat in the bleachers at Amen Corner. Had a drink by the old oak tree. About 5 p.m., we decided to head out for dinner. Being the Augusta cuisine expert that I am, I suggested the Augusta Hooters, because it was fun, because they brought the waitresses in from all over the South and, well, never mind. My wife is reading this.

We were at Hooters from 5:30 on. A couple of groups of Omaha folks that we happened to know wandered in. It was a great night. Then, about 9 p.m., everything changed in a hurry. Dan's wife called his cellphone. He wasn't sure he wanted to answer, then he did. He said, "You're kidding me." He hung up and, with a wry smile said, "Dana's coming back."

I can't repeat what I said. Bill said, "What's wrong?" I said, "I have to write." My friends couldn't believe it. You're in no shape to write, they said. That's what I told my editor, Thad Livingston, when I called him that instant. His words: "Get yourself right. We need you."

So I dragged my posse back to our $200-a-night Super 8 motel – after a stop for wine (for them!). I had my computer with me, though I hadn't planned to write. There was no desk in my Norman Bates room. There was a phone line I could connect. So, at 10 p.m., I plopped my computer down on one twin bed and sat on the other and knocked out this column in 40 minutes.

When I was finished, I called Bill and said, "I need you to read this before I send it in," though looking back I'm not sure he was the best editor I could have employed at the time. He came over, with his cup of red wine, and read it. He said, "What's this word mean?" I said, "Good catch. Wrong usage." Don't ask what it was. I have no idea.

I sent the column in. Only a few people knew that story. Now, you do, too.

Postscript: I always enter the U.S. Basketball Writers Association writing contest. I sent in this column, just to see what would happen. I won third place.

CWS Old Guard Is Missed

HE WALKED OFF the elevator and into the press box looking like a ghost. A well-tanned ghost.

Skip Bertman was back in Omaha.

Too bad he didn't bring his team.

Where have you gone, Bayou Bengals? The College World Series has been overtaken by Beavers, Owls, Tar Heels, Cardinals and, well, Anteaters.

LSU. Stanford. Miami. Florida State. Remember them? It seems like a decade since they've been here. Actually, it was. Those schools, along with Cal State Fullerton, were the CWS in the '90s.

Whatever happened to Augie Garrido? Texas won the CWS in 2005 and hasn't been back since. It feels like a Texas-sized drought.

Fullerton made this year's CWS but was two-and-BBQ, or two-and-sushi-down-at-the-strip-mall. It is Orange County, after all.

Take off your hat and pay your respects. Old money has left the building.

New money has arrived, maybe for good.

Rice, Oregon State, North Carolina, UC Irvine and Louisville. Those are your new CWS regulars. Rice, with all of one national championship, is a sage veteran. Same for the Beavers, with their third straight CWS. Irvine and Louisville are newcomers. But they aren't flukes. They'll be back.

Just ask Wichita State and Oklahoma State. Remember them?

We are seeing a changing of the guard at the CWS. Is that a good thing?

Not necessarily. No offense to the cuddly Anteaters, the Louisville sluggers, Beaver Nation and Rice coach Wayne Graham, the Casey Stengel of college baseball, but I miss the old money.

I miss the LSU fans. The Cajun cook in the chef's hat. The endless strands of beads. Gorilla ball. I miss Miami's colorful uniforms, the Texas fans with the longhorns for hood ornaments. I even miss the brainiacs of Stanford, glove in one hand and BlackBerry in the other.

One of the comfort foods of the CWS was the presence of the traditional powers. It's one thing to

UC Irvine pitcher Tom Calahan throws in relief for the "Eaters," as in Anteaters.

have underdogs and goofy animals. It's another to have too many. Who's the underdog? The Beaver or the Anteater?

It's OK to have Louisville and Rutgers emerge in college football. But I still want USC and Ohio State and Florida playing for the national championship. The CWS this week is like Wisconsin and Texas A&M becoming Final Four regulars. The world is off its axis.

Get used to it, says our favorite ghost.

"The format to get here, and the result of having 11.7 scholarships (the per-team limit) makes baseball the poster sport for parity," Bertman said. "There used to be 12 teams that could win out here, and they were always here. And then there were 22. But now there's 60."

The super regional format, Bertman says, is one more step schools like LSU and Miami must take to get to Omaha. And they won't always host, because everyone is building on-campus ballparks these days. The scholarship limit means that more teams are good enough to host regionals.

"The NCAA, and most fans, want the Super Bowl," Bertman said. "What they like is that you can be 8-8 and win the Super Bowl the next year. They don't want anyone to have dominance. They want everybody to have an equal chance."

Writing's on the Wall for Pederson and Callahan

PLEASE, SOMEBODY STOP this nightmare. Harvey Perlman. J.B. Milliken. Howard Hawks. Anybody.

The fate of Nebraska football rests in their hands. It's not to be entrusted to Steve Pederson, Bill Callahan or the collective coaching staff at the program formerly known as Nebraska.

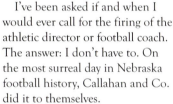

Steve Pederson

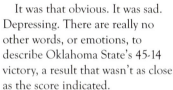

Bill Callahan

And yet, this is not a column about anger or calling for people's heads in the wake of what forever will be known around here as the day the music died. It's not necessary.

I've been asked if and when I would ever call for the firing of the athletic director or football coach. The answer: I don't have to. On the most surreal day in Nebraska football history, Callahan and Co. did it to themselves.

It was that obvious. It was sad. Depressing. There are really no other words, or emotions, to describe Oklahoma State's 45-14 victory, a result that wasn't as close as the score indicated.

It's not anger. It's just an utter feeling of sadness, like losing a best friend. Nebraska football, as we know it, the friend you grew up with, has left us.

OSU had not won in Lincoln since 1960, when NU was coached by Bill Jennings. That's appropriate. This was the lowest moment for Nebraska football since before Bob Devaney arrived.

The Cowboys, who were routed by Troy State last month, tromped all over Nebraska, before Nebraska fans, on Nebraska's turf.

They made it look easy. It was easy.

Oklahoma State scored on its first six possessions of the game before finally taking a knee with a minute left in the first half.

But it wasn't just how easily OSU was scoring. It was how Nebraska's defensive players — I refuse to call them Blackshirts — let them waltz down the field.

Unless you're in his shoes, you always have to be careful assuming what is inside a player's head or heart. But from my bird's-eye view, it looked like NU lost its heart, stopped playing — gave up — on OSU's 90-yard, six-play touchdown drive that made it 24-0 early in the second quarter.

This, a day after Tom Osborne gave the team a pep talk.

This, on the day honoring the 1997 national champions and after the '97 boys met the '07 team on the field with a fiery greeting. To play that kind of game, it was a slap in their face.

Tradition. Teamwork. Integrity. Pederson's catchphrase slogan for NU athletics was lost in the rubble of a rock-bottom day for Big Red football.

You have to feel for the players. They are hurting. They aren't trying to embarrass the program. Sam Keller spilled his heart and guts out in the interview room. It was powerful stuff.

But it's hard to buy this line that they are pressing or trying too hard. Hit somebody. Make a tackle or a block or a catch. It looks more like these players have lost their will to play the game. Is there any joy in Memorial Stadium? No, not in the stands or on the field.

It's been zapped by a group of coaches and a scheme that appears to be too complicated for the college game, too cerebral to get young talent on the field. When receivers coach Ted Gilmore said earlier that the staff was cutting back on what the players would be given this week, it was a glaring admission that this thing is way over everyone's heads.

A lot of good "scaling back" did, huh?

It's too late for that. Whether Callahan wanted to admit it or not, he's lost this team. Worse, he doesn't know how to get it back.

Asked repeatedly after the game how he was going to fix things, Callahan kept saying, "We'll go back to work tomorrow and do the best we can." Asked if he could fix it, he replied, "There's always hope." That should make Husker Nation feel better.

Callahan said his team was "gutted." Can he get them back this season? Don't hold your breath. For a man who took a team to the Super Bowl, Callahan sounds utterly clueless as to what to do.

This is Callahan's fourth year. Nebraska is a rebuilding dynasty. The fatal flaw that most dynasties make is trying to rush back too soon, getting on the impatience train and changing coaches every four years.

But at some point, there has to be progress shown. In four years, Callahan has had his moments. But he doesn't develop players. He can't get the talent on the field or the ball in their hands. And now his teams show a lack of fundamentals and fire. Other than that, he's doing a bang-up job.

This is no longer about defensive coordinator Kevin Cosgrove. It's a much bigger issue. Do you pink-slip Cosgrove and a few other assistants and let Callahan try again next year? Or do you just admit the mistake now and start over? Do you let Pederson make this decision? I don't see how.

Most athletic directors get a mulligan or two when it comes to football coaches. But Pederson is in a precarious position for three reasons.

One, he leveled the culture of the program in the name of his vision of football.

Two, given his track record, you can't trust him to hire another coach.

Three, he's made numerous enemies who no doubt will seize this opportunity to force him out. Saturday's game should have provided them that vehicle.

A lot of major decisions must be made in a short period of time. Interesting times, sad times.

Osborne Back Where He Belongs

LIFE BEGINS AT 70.

Tom Osborne, the king of Ak-Sar-Ben and Nebraska football, not necessarily in that order, arrived to save the day. Minus the cape.

The old coach leapt out of the history books and back into our lives, accepting the responsibility of interim athletic director at NU — at quite possibly the most important time in modern Husker football history.

Check that. The word "interim" doesn't do the man justice. When they build statues of you while you're still ticking, you can darn well stay as long as you want, and as long as you're needed. To that end, there's nothing "interim" about the task that lies ahead.

With apologies to Creighton soccer and basketball, the man belongs here.

There is football to fix, a coaching staff to evaluate and a future to weigh. The fate of Nebraska football rests on Osborne's shoulders. What a perfect place for it.

At a precarious time, with fans booing or leaving, players unable to tackle or fight and folks arguing over whether to keep the incoming recruiting class or the head coach, Osborne arrives like some wise old King Solomon. He is the right man at the right time.

With, finally, the right job.

Osborne will always be "the coach." He never looked right in Washington, D.C., surrounded by sharks in scandal-infested waters. He never got out of the gate in the governor's race. And while Osborne took that as a slap from "his" people, the fact is that people have always liked Osborne more in the football arena than the political one.

Now he's back. A reader called to suggest a headline, "The Second Coming." This is more like "Back to the Future."

This is the job many of us always envisioned him in. Has there been anyone whom anyone ever trusted more to make the smart, sound decisions for Nebraska football? Anyone else you'd want calling the plays with the fate of Husker football facing third-and-goal inside a minute left?

Who better to understand the culture than the man who wrote the book on the "Nebraska way"?

Forget the complexities faced by the modern athletic director. This isn't rocket science. An effective A.D. at a football school makes the right hire for football and raises money. Osborne is in position to do that. He can hire any number of bright young minds to run the website or make sure volleyball gets a TV commercial.

Of the utmost urgency is the fate of Bill Callahan and his staff and a decision that could jump-start Big Red football or send it further down the football food chain so it is looking up at Kansas, Kansas State, Missouri and Colorado, not just Oklahoma and Texas.

Chancellor Harvey Perlman could have hired a big name from the noted football school Louisville, or somewhere else, and that would be peachy. But if he had passed on enlisting the resource that is Tom Osborne, wouldn't we always be wondering "what if?"

This is the sort of mission that Osborne was made to tackle, and it comes with a bonus. Osborne gets a chance at a glorious send-off, into the sunset with his fishing tackle.

Of course, they say Osborne isn't perfect, that he started this whole mess when he handpicked Frank Solich. I have no problem with Osborne being allowed to make that call. His biggest failing was handcuffing Solich into keeping a terrific — but aging and tired — staff.

Then again, maybe people are just mad at Osborne because he retired.

Well, he's back, with a shot at redemption. Careful what you wish for. Osborne is risking his legacy. But he's no stranger to risk — he had the guts to go for two with the national title on the line.

Osborne has always been about what he thought was right for Nebraska. Don't look now, but integrity and credibility just re-entered the building.

Two weeks ago, Osborne's old Big Eight chum Barry Switzer turned 70. Switzer did it the Switzer way, paying big money to close down a popular Dallas chophouse on the eve of the Oklahoma-Texas game. Switzer, drink and cigar in hand, told old war stories until the gang left at 4 a.m.

For Osborne, being 70 means making new stories and writing more history.

The "interim" was removed in 2009 from Tom Osborne's athletic director title.

Plenty of Role Models for Girls

ONCE AGAIN, I have proof that God has a sense of humor. In fact, now I know that She is a woman.

Stunningly beautiful Annamarie Jean Shatel entered my life about 7:32 a.m. Tuesday, all 10 pounds and 22 inches of her. It was love at first sight.

First, I'd better give all credit to my lovely wife, Jennifer, who is the real hero in this story. Not to mention doctors Michelle Knolla and Craig Bassett, who, unlike some coaches I know, never fail to deliver.

"Here comes a Husker libero," said Bassett, the mega-Husker fan, referring to a position on the volleyball team. At first, I thought he said libido. No, Doc, that's what got me in this delivery room in the first place.

Anyway, I sat on the sidelines and helplessly cheered, although, by Bill Callahan's standards, I did an excellent job of helping, if I say so myself.

That makes three girls in six years, but who's counting? My friend Steve Hayes says, "You're either paying for weddings or bail bonds. Bail bonds are cheaper."

I just turned 49. By the time Anna gets hitched, she's going to have to walk me down the aisle. By the time my daughters get married, we're going to have to put in a wheelchair section for my friends. The good Lord willing, I'll be there. I'm sure She will make sure I last that long.

How do I know God is a She? For as long as I can remember, I've been a male sports chauvinist. I don't resent girls sports, don't deny them. Just don't make me watch them.

Guess what I get to do the next 20 years? These girls will be athletic, because they will take after their mother, a three-sport athlete at Valley High School. They aren't allowed to take after their dad.

So I will take them to soccer practice, and I will sit and watch volleyball practice, and play taxi driver to all points of the Midwest for basketball or softball or golf. Yes, especially golf.

Know what? I can't wait. This is the role I've always dreamed of playing, though it comes with a twist.

My wife the mad photographer was at it again. Anna was actually born about four weeks before Bill Callahan was dismissed. But her mother was so excited about the news that she figured it was a good time stamp. If you look closely, Anna is saying "Hire Bo."

I'm not going to lie to you. The thought crossed my mind of having a son. Most men, if not all men, think about having sons. It's not because they look forward to shelling out bail bond money. It's because they can't wait to buy that first baseball glove, ball and bat, that first pee-wee football or miniature basketball.

They dream about sitting under the Friday Night Lights and, as the star quarterback races down the sidelines, elbowing the guy next to him and saying, "That's my son!"

They dream, too, even bigger dreams, of that son wearing Nebraska football red and white, of playing shortstop for the Cardinals, of teeing it up at the Masters. These dreams are as inherent a part of being male as the father and son "catch" scene in "Field of Dreams" that made every hard-boiled male weep like a baby.

You did cry during "Field of Dreams," didn't you?

My father used to take me to the baseball field at the local high school every Saturday morning, where he would reach into a bucket of baseballs and pitch. I would hit. We would both chase. And repeat and so forth. That's how fathers and sons bond, or used to.

What am I supposed to do, have a catch with my daughter? Why not? And I'm supposed to go to the high school volleyball match and elbow the guy next to me and say, "That's my girl"? Absolutely.

What am I supposed to do, dream of them playing in the WNBA or LPGA? With any luck, yes. But I would be just as proud, if not prouder, if my daughters could turn out to be Sarah Pavan or any of the well-balanced female athletes at UNL, Creighton, UNO and UNK and on down the line.

I've never met a female athlete who wasn't smart, classy, nice, polite, good people. Maybe it's because the pro sports dream isn't there for them, at least not like it is for men. But the women have a better perspective, are more likely to have fun, more likely to get more out of it.

Who's to say my girls will even play sports? Maybe they'll play piano or go into finance or become doctors. Hey, somebody's got to pay for those college educations and weddings.

The point here is, I'm about to embark on a journey, a welcome journey. I've spent my entire life with my head in the sports page, the men's sports page. I have a feeling the second half of my life is going to be a refresher course on what life, love and a father's pride are really all about.

The other night, at a concert, my 5-year-old stood on her seat and yelled to the Jonas Brothers, "I love you." As I turned to look back at her, she quickly pushed my head back around as if to say, "You weren't supposed to hear that, Dad." That's a bonding moment I never dreamed of having.

There may be a thousand or so dads out there who can relate, to dreaming of the boy, and finding something unexpected, something even better, in the eyes of Daddy's girl.

By the way, can you take a cooler to girls soccer practice?

TOM'S TAKE
REFLECTIONS ON

New Park Reflects New Times

IF WE BUILD IT, they will stay. That's the bottom line. That's it. If you want to know why this is happening, if your friends in Los Angeles and Kalamazoo and Atlanta want to know why Omaha would tear down a historic relic like Rosenblatt Stadium and build a new downtown baseball park, this is what you tell them: Because the College World Series lives in a city, not a stadium.

The owners of the CWS (the NCAA) gave the host of the CWS (us) a clear direction on what it would take to lock up the event that, in so many ways, is the reflection we see in the mirror. To think that we could keep Rosenblatt Stadium, fix it up with some makeup and a few new trees and skyboxes, and keep the NCAA happy is terribly naive.

The "Save Rosenblatt" people have honorable intentions. But if we kept the status quo, Omaha would be part of a CWS rotation with other cities within five to 10 years.

If we build it, they will stay. There's a line of thinking that we have a better shot of keeping the CWS if we keep Rosenblatt, because it's unique. Build a cookie-cutter park and you run the risk of being like Indianapolis and all the others. You lose that thing that made you different, the history, ghosts, etc.

Times change. Sports change. The NCAA has changed. The NCAA now is very much into corporate hospitality, fan-fests, giving fans the opportunity to walk from the game to a hotel room, a restaurant and a place to shop. Crazy, huh?

We like to say that we want the CWS here forever. Well, forever means you'd better change with the times, and with the NCAA's times.

The beauty of this is that the NCAA didn't have to tell us anything. The NCAA could have remained mum and let us guess. The NCAA could have had an agenda to open this up to other cities and start the rotation process, ASAP.

But the NCAA has told us exactly what to do to keep our summer baseball gem. That happened because there are a few sentimental bones in the NCAA's body when it comes to Omaha and the CWS, and most of them belong to Dennis Poppe, the NCAA's managing director for football and basketball.

The NCAA gives 20-year extensions like it gives pardons to Jerry Tarkanian. Never. But this is that moment. This is our moment.

In case you haven't noticed, the CWS is evolving before our eyes. It's more corporate. And now ESPN is starting to call some shots. The new format, which pushes the championship series into midweek, could mean many empty seats. It won't look good on TV. It will look like Omaha has hit the wall and is ready to give it up.

If we get 20 years, none of that matters. By the time 20 years is over, the list of suitors for this thing will have moved on to super bowls or ultimate fighting.

This is a no-brainer. Except for the side of the brain where emotions and sentimentality and chocolate syrup reside. This is hard. Rosenblatt is the house we grew up in. But we all eventually leave that house and pack the memories, then make more somewhere else.

What opponents should do is follow the lead of Jack Diesing Jr. The CWS would not be what it is today without the Diesings' love for the CWS and that diamond on the hill. But there was Diesing, ever the loyal soldier, pledging his support for the new stadium. He did it with a heavy heart. But like the man said, it's the road to Omaha, not the road to Rosenblatt.

— SEPTEMBER 22, 2007

The view looking out from behind what would become home plate at TD Ameritrade Park. Omaha ended up with a 25-year CWS contract.

THE CHANGING SPORTS LANDSCAPE | 2007

Red-Letter Sports Year

It was the craziest, mind-blowingest, biggest sports year this little corner of the sports world has seen in many, many moons. Let's look back and assess the stress and account the history. — DECEMBER 30, 2007

▶ **1. STEVE PEDERSON GETS FIRED.** It's tempting to throw the entire Extreme Makeover, Husker Edition into one story. But these four stories are so big, so individually far-reaching in impact, that I gave them their own designations. Richard Nixon had Watergate. Pederson had the resignation of fundraiser and Husker loyalist Paul Meyers, an event so shocking it set off alarm bells that something was amiss in Pederson's fortress. The combination of that and eye-opening football losses did in Pederson. Even though Chancellor Harvey Perlman seemed to be the last to know, a lot of folks were gunning for Pederson. The moral to the story seemed to be that Nebraskans care more about how things are done and how people are treated than they do big buildings and scoreboards. Oh, and they care about winning, too.

▶ **2. TOM OSBORNE BECOMES ATHLETIC DIRECTOR.** The old legend came riding back in the middle of a lost football season to instill hope and take the job he wanted 10 years ago.

▶ **3. BILL CALLAHAN IS FIRED.** Callahan's NFL system was not built on belief or confidence, and when USC trashed it, it collapsed. In the end, Callahan was not treated with disdain. Most folks will recall him as the wrong guy in the wrong place at the wrong time, if they recall him at all.

▶ **4. BO PELINI COMES BACK.** With Pederson and Callahan gone, and Osborne and Pelini in, it seemed like somebody hit a reset button from 2003. In many ways, 2007 will be remembered for that.

▶ **5. THE DOWNTOWN BALLPARK.** When Mayor Mike Fahey released his plan for a downtown ballpark that would save the CWS legacy in Omaha, it sparked a debate that touched the very souls of every sports and baseball fan in Omaha and Nebraska. The story has many layers, and it isn't over yet. It became about at what point, and at what price, do you let go of all you know and embrace the unknown?

▶ **6. DANA ALTMAN STAYS AT CREIGHTON.** Altman didn't just surprise CU fans, he probably surprised himself, too. He chose family — as in all of Creighton and Omaha — over money and ambition. He supplanted his legacy, no matter how many wins he has left, and there are a bunch left.

▶ **7. NEBRASKA VOLLEYBALL FALLS SHORT.** John Cook's perfect team proved just less than perfect. But the legacy these classy ladies left was bigger than any championship banner you can hang. They did it right and, along the way, showed the male chauvinist world of sports that ladies can be sports rock stars, too.

▶ **8. JOBA CHAMBERLAIN PITCHES FOR THE YANKEES.** It still seems surreal that this kid who is from here is doing those things there.

▶ **9. DANNY WOODHEAD SETS THE NCAA CAREER RUSHING MARK.** This story is what Nebraska and college football are all about. Small-town hero forgoes the spotlight, and the national spotlight still follows him to Chadron State. This state loves its native-son legends. I can't imagine Woodhead will have to buy a dinner or drink the rest of his life. Then again, he'll probably be able to afford it.

▶ **10. THE USC GAME.** It was the most-hyped football game this state had seen in decades and it was expected to have a huge impact on the program and coach. In that respect, it didn't disappoint.

▶ **11. UNO'S COMEBACK SEASON.** Pat Behrns and his football team put UNO on the front sports page with their first undefeated regular season since 1954.

▶ **12. THE OMAHA KNIGHTS LEAVE.** It's never good to lose a sports team, because you rarely get one back. But three hockey clubs was a crowd in this metro area. The Calgary owners didn't have the patience to wait.

▶ **13. OMAHA CENTRAL'S THREE-FEAT.** State titles in basketball, track and field and football. The sleeping giant of Nebraska high school sports woke with a vengeance this year.

Danny Woodhead of Chadron State ended his college career with an NCAA-record 7,962 rushing yards.

NCAA BASKETBALL | MICHAEL PHELPS IN OMAHA | OLYMPIC SWIM TRIALS | PELINI'S FIRST GAME

2008

> "I know who has walked on this field before me, and I know how I should play. I want to make my own history here. It's pretty cool just to be one of them now, knowing that some kid could look up to me one day."
>
> — NEBRASKA QUARTERBACK JOE GANZ

I believe if he had his druthers, Omaha Royals President Alan Stein would prefer to have his own stadium, somewhere in Omaha, or somewhere else, than to share with the NCAA and Creighton. But he will listen. "I don't have any doubts that if we stay here we will increase our value to the community," Stein said. "That's our job to do that. This is a big community, 800,000 people. We don't need 800,000 people to love us. We need 4-, 5-, 6,000 people to come out on a regular basis. Our group sales people will bring in another 200,000 people a year on a one- or two-time basis. That's good for us. But in order for us to do those things, we need certain things in a facility to help us do that."

A few months ago, an old World-Herald newspaper clipping showed up on my desk, mysteriously. I saved it for a rainy, or a snowy, day. It's a column from Floyd Olds, a former World-Herald sports editor. The only date on the article is 1945. The headline reads, "Harmony Is Needed — Now!" Whoever put it on my desk obviously thought that the topic pertained to Omaha, 60 years later. I agree. The column begins:

"The time has come for everyone to work together toward giving Omaha the best possible all-purpose Municipal Stadium at Thirteenth Street and Deer Park Boulevard. Bickering must cease at once and be replaced by harmony. Despite the many unfortunate things which have happened in regard to stadium planning, everyone's goal is the same. But trouble is brewing."

History will show that Omaha did produce a stadium, Rosenblatt Stadium, and a few years later, an event called the College World Series would show up at our door looking for a home. The rest is history. Now it seems that history is repeating itself. Which way to go? We're waiting for the titans to stop arguing and figure it out.

Creighton extended three pretty incredible streaks. That's 10 straight years of at least 20 wins, 12 straight years of at least 10 Missouri Valley wins and 11 straight years of postseason. But is it enough? No way. Coach Dana Altman must sense that it's time to find the door to the next level. With Altman, you know what you are going to get. But there's a sense now that Creightonians, and the news media, are going to start asking for more.

'GAME OF THE CENTURY' REUNION | ALEX HENERY'S BIG KICK | NU VOLLEYBALL GALLANT IN DEFEAT

In 17 years here, I had never met Warren Buffett. Of course, I don't spend much time in his neck of the woods, unless it's Dairy Queen. But he was on my turf and had a few minutes to talk. On how often he goes to CWS games: "Not that often. The games take too long. It's a factor, you know. I used to go to games at Griffith Stadium (Washington, D.C.) and watch doubleheaders. You could watch a doubleheader in the same amount of time it takes to play one here." On the CWS moving downtown: "I think the love affair is going to continue. For a little while, it kind of looked like we were going to have trouble. But it all worked out. Now, with 25 years, the city can relax."

Retired UNO sports information director Gary Anderson:

▶ **Q:** If you were in charge of UNO's future, what would you do?

▶ **A:** I think you have to look at going up (to Division I). You have to step back and decide who your peers are going to be as an institution in 10 years. The reason Northern Colorado and South Dakota moved up was because their presidents felt their peers were going to be different. They didn't want to be peers with certain schools anymore, and I won't mention any names. They felt a higher level would help them academically, with enrollment and in the community. That's what UNO needs to decide. Is it in the MIAA? Or is it with Northern Iowa, Iowa State, Kansas State, UMKC?

▶ **Q:** Will the regents in this state ever approve UNO going Division I?

▶ **A:** Someday, but I don't know that you and I will be sitting here talking to each other.

Hope is where you find it. The Huskers found it in a 79-yard, eight-play touchdown drive in the final two minutes. And they found it in a coach who so believed in them that he passed on a two-point conversion with 29 seconds left that could have sealed an upset over Texas Tech. Instead, Bo Pelini chose overtime, because he believed. Nebraska's 37-31 overtime loss to the overrated seventh-ranked Red Raiders offered that kind of belief and revived hope for the second half of the season.

I'm not an expert on the subject of divorce, nor do I ever plan to be, but sometimes the "D word" is just inevitable. That's the case with the "Royals vs. City of Omaha." Draw up the papers. This was a marriage never meant to last. Neither the Royals nor MECA wanted this to work. It's nobody's fault. It's not 1973 or 1985 anymore. Times change. Minor-league baseball has changed. The Royals require a certain stadium size, dates, financial model and, above all, control of their own fate. I suppose if the City of Omaha really saw the Royals as a tourist attraction,  it would have found a way to get the Royals their own miniature stadium, complete with water slides and bartenders. Or shrunk the capacity of the new stadium to accommodate the Royals. No chance, Lance. And we all know why. Omaha has always made the College World Series its first choice. The new stadium was just the right excuse to break away.

Omaha Shines, but Games Don't

ALL WE CAN DO is provide a grand NCAA stage. That, we did.

The players and coaches — and sometimes the officials, to our chagrin — are in charge of the theatrics and dramatic endings. There wasn't nearly enough of either for our first NCAA tournament games in 30 years.

But the week was a huge success at the Qwest Center Omaha, and surrounding brick streets. Just ask Kansas. Or Wisconsin. Or the NCAA.

It was a workmanlike effort by the winners here, in a working man's town. The games were solid, not flashy, just like us.

As if being the host of the College World Series for more than five decades isn't enough reason for love, we cemented our legend with the NCAA this week. There may have been a few ice cubes missing in a drink or an official NCAA sign somewhere tilted just to the left. But overall, the reviews were smashing.

First, the building. Everyone — fans, teams, media, NCAA — loved the Qwest Center. The close proximity to hotels and restaurants was duly noted by all. Fans and media like things that are easy. This tournament was, in a word, convenient.

But the biggest hit, for the teams, NCAA and CBS, was the convention center. The coaches and school officials raved on and on about being able to drive their team bus into the cover of the convention center and walk right to their locker room. They were downright giddy about that.

The building was one thing. You still have to execute. But Omaha's CWS plan fit right into the NCAA basketball format. Creighton's Kevin Sarver, the tournament director, led a team effort that had NCAA and visiting school officials alike saying Omaha should get another bid — as soon as possible.

I'll make this prediction: Omaha will fall into a rotation with Kansas City and Oklahoma City for this event and get it every three or four years. The possibility of an NCAA regional final isn't out of the question, either.

"They've done a terrific job in every way," said Mike Slive, the commissioner of the Southeastern Conference and the Division I Basketball Committee representative at this week's tournament. Slive will file a report with the committee. It will be positive.

"It's a wonderful facility," he said. "Whenever we needed something or wanted something, they reacted immediately. And they have so many people."

Mario Chalmers of Kansas drives against Portland State's defense in a first-round game in Omaha.

Whatever You Do, Don't Take Away Kids' Play

DEAR ABBY — and Jim, Mick, Jean, Mike, Mark, Tina and Lindsay: Thanks for the advice.

This new "sports dad" asked for help. And I got it.

Concentrate on one sport. Play all the sports. It's all about having fun. It's not about fun, it's about getting enjoyment out of hard work. Definitely be a coach. Don't coach, stay out of the way.

Just as there are as many ideas on how to raise a child as there are parents, there are as many ideas on how to be a sports parent as there are sports parents.

One of the more intriguing responses came from Mick McCarthy, who has a son in basketball and soccer. Mick's advice: Spend more time on your marriage than your kid's sports. He has seen too many parents who are "married to their kids' activities. We don't want our kids thinking they have to do that when they are parents."

Something else Mick wrote really struck a chord: "What the kid really wants is not us at his games but us in the backyard actually playing basketball with him."

There was good, thoughtful stuff from Lindsay Blake, who wrote, "Allow your girls to pursue their dreams. Watch closely, discover with them what they love and let them pour themselves into it. Attend their games, meets and events but never allow your competitive nature to interfere. Your presence will speak loudly to their hearts, while outrageous comments will only build a wall."

Most folks know me as a guy with an opinion or two. But Jim Elworth says I should keep them to myself when it comes to my daughters' games.

"Don't critique," Elworth wrote. "The kid already has a coach. You're there for support. Always greet her with a postgame smile and a positive comment, even if she played so crappy there's not much to say beyond 'you gave it your best.'"

Mike Herman echoed that: "Don't rehash a game in the car on the drive home, unless your child starts that conversation. By the time the coach visits with them after the game and they walk to the car, the game is over for them and the last thing they want to do is return to the moment. They want to go on with their day and enjoy what's next — being a kid!"

Doug Thies, a golf pro at Champions Run, wrote about growing up on a farm in Iowa. His parents didn't have the time or money to follow him all over the Midwest. They steered him toward one sport. Thies recommends that highly, adding, "I was able to focus on what I needed to do to be the best I could be at that sport. And parents and kids get so tied up in four to six sports a year that I feel the family time goes south quickly."

Nils McConnell writes, "Let the coach coach. They will make mistakes. So what? Until middle school, probably until high school, it won't matter much." He adds, "If you coach, make sure everybody plays and that the rules in practice and games are the same for everyone. It's not as hard as people make it out to be. Be thick-skinned; listen to the parents but then do the right thing."

One of my favorite e-mails came from Kathleen Smith, who wrote that she and her husband were typical sports parents, driving their daughter, Jill, all over the Midwest to tournaments in golf and other sports. Eventually Jill picked golf, and she became good enough to earn a spot on the Kansas State University team.

One day, Jill called home, crying, begging to give up golf. She wanted to be a regular student. So she quit the team and joined the flag team. Today, she is a teacher in Omaha. As Kathleen writes: "My reward? Every Tuesday night May through September, I golf with my daughter in the local golf league."

The lesson here: Investing in a relationship now with your kid pays off with a relationship you keep your whole life.

Jim Miller, a sports parent, quoted a Golf Magazine article written by CBS golf analyst and funnyman David Feherty. When I read this, it was lump-in-the-throat time.

Feherty, referring to a tickling match with his daughter, wrote, "We both end up in tears, hers of laughter, mine of unsurpassable joy and indescribable love, mixed with an aching sadness, for I know she is only on loan to me, and I wish this moment would never end."

If you'll excuse me, I'm headed out to the backyard with a ball and glove.

There was no shortage of advice on how to be a good parent with kids in sports.

2011 INSIGHT *This is one of my favorite columns, and I hardly even wrote. That's not why. Ever since 1991, I've had a healthy relationship with my readers — some days healthier than others. Usually, the talk is Huskers, Jays or the controversy du jour. But this time, I wanted to seek their opinion on being a sports parent. I was in my late 40s when this ran. I'm slightly late to the party. No matter. I was a 49-year-old rookie asking for help. I got it and then some. This was one where I connected with the readers. You can't always plan those. But kids and kids' sports are topics most people can relate to. Next topic: how to get a kitchen pass to watch a big game.*

Is Phelps the Best Omaha Has Seen?

YOU DON'T HAVE to be an Olympics fan, or "ring head" as they are affectionately known. You don't have to be a swimming fan. Would that be a fin head? Nor do you need to be a teenage girl, hypnotized by a tall, dark, handsome swimmer with a mischievous grin.

The only requirement is that you be a fan of greatness, brilliance and genius. If you qualify, you owe it to yourself to be in the presence of Michael Phelps.

The amphibious kid from Baltimore has been called the greatest swimmer ever, the top American Olympian ever and the No. 1 athlete in the world as we speak, or until Tiger Woods' next tee time.

What about greatest athlete ever to come through Omaha? Or Nebraska?

I have a hard time finding anything quite like this in our sports history.

The starting point has to be Joe Frazier, who fought local pugilist Ron Stander in 1972. Frazier was the reigning heavyweight champ of the world when he beat Stander. But, alas, Frazier was also heading down the backside of his career in 1972. And Smokin' Joe was not the all-time lord of the ring.

The National Basketball Association came to town the same year, and you could state a case for Kareem Abdul-Jabbar, who was a young man when he visited Civic Auditorium with the Milwaukee Bucks to play the Kansas City-Omaha Kings. But was he the greatest player in his sport? No, that would be Michael Jordan.

Michael Beasley and O.J. Mayo played in the Qwest Center three months ago on a basketball court that's now at the bottom of the pool. Think they'll go on to break all of the NBA records?

Babe Ruth, Arnold Palmer and assorted others made their way to Omaha — for exhibitions. Bob Gibson pitched here — for Creighton and the Omaha Cardinals.

Down in Lincoln, we've seen college football greats on both sides of Memorial Stadium. Again, were any in their primes? Any considered the face of their sport?

College World Series? Almost all of our June heroes, from Dave Winfield to Barry Bonds to Roger Clemens, were on the early rungs of the developmental ladder when we saw them play.

Which brings us back to the exotic fish in our aquarium.

The Olympics don't spit out rock stars like they used to. Phelps is an exception. He's a worldwide phenomenon. There are more than 250 journalists in town, including foreign journalists covering the U.S. Swim Trials.

They aren't here to sample the international kitchens in the Old Market.

Phelps' reputation precedes him. He performs, on cue, almost like a superhero. He's Aquaman. This week, he's the Fish That Ate Omaha. The sports world, from Beatrice to Beijing, has its eyes on Omaha this week.

Mostly, though, we have the good fortune of timing. At 23, Phelps is near the peak of his career, if he's not there already. That's not to say, with technology and those skin suits they crawl into, that Phelps can't get faster.

But more than likely, we are witnessing a legend at the top of his game, mere weeks before he tries to etch his name atop Mount Olympus.

Michael Phelps dazzled Omaha before winning eight gold medals in Beijing.

JULY 7, 2008 • OLYMPICS

Omaha Has Lit the Torch for Future Olympic Trials

AS THE U.S. Olympic Swim Trials came to a close, I wondered what Mike Moran would think of this.

Moran, a former U.S. Olympic Committee media chief, is a graduate of Westside High and Omaha University. Back in 1992, at the close of the Summer Games in Barcelona, Spain, Moran and I got together and jokingly put together the "Omaha Olympics." Just for fun, we tried to decide where every event would be staged if the Olympics ever came to Omaha.

Mike Moran

The swimming venue, as I recall, would have been at UNO. It moved this past week.

What a week, huh? Great week. Unforgettable week. Historic week. Or, as Michael Phelps said about his own stay, "As a whole, it was a decent week." The only time all week that Phelps was understated.

It was a week like no other in Omaha, a week that forever changed our definition of a sporting event.

I was talking with some colleagues in the Omaha media about Omaha sports in 1991, my first year at The World-Herald.

We had the College World Series, of course. But after that? A Lancers game at the old Ak-Sar-Ben Coliseum was big stuff. The Racers, during the 1993 CBA championship series, packed them in.

Creighton? It drew flies. Martina Navratilova showed up and hit tennis balls in the Civic Auditorium. We had an NBA exhibition game between Seattle and Milwaukee. Seattle coach George Karl complained about the Old Market, saying it was "too artsy-craftsy" for him.

Back then, if you had told me that we would one day have a big-time arena, build an Olympic-sized swimming pool inside it and host an Olympic swimming event, I would have said you had too many 50-cent beers at the Racers game.

We've come a long way from the Ak-Sar-Ben Coliseum. And who knows where the future leads?

Our reputation with the NCAA is gold, as in $140 million. If the NCAA holds an event, we have a chance to host it. Perfect. Part of being the "Amateur Sports Capital" is being an NCAA hub. The other part of that lofty goal is the Olympics. And now, amazingly, Omaha has a foot in the door.

If they gave out medals for hosting Olympic Trials, Omaha would have won the gold. From the overall attendance of more than 160,000 to the accessibility of the venue for athletes and fans, acoustics, the pool, hospitality, the Old Market, etc., etc., we wowed them.

This entire week was an experiment by USA Swimming. I think we passed the audition. USA Swim officials gushed over the job by local officials, volunteers and fans. One official said he wanted to move to Omaha.

The competition was in the building. Sports commissions from St. Louis and San Antonio showed up to take notes. Other cities with NBA arenas will bid. But what many don't have is our secret weapon.

The convention center.

In landing events, it is a difference-maker. If the arena is the star, the convention center is the MVP. The NCAA loved it because the eight basketball teams could park their buses indoors and walk to the locker room. USA Swimming could put its warm-up pool in it, offering the swimmers an easy stroll to the competition.

We have the building. We have the organization. And we had the execution this week. Don't be surprised if other Olympic sports also took notice. Figure Skating Trials? Gymnastics? Who knows what we started here this week?

But it goes beyond that. There were fans and media here from all over the globe, many of them seeing Omaha for the first time. Several Olympic and national writers who spent the week here were pleasantly surprised by Omaha. Many fell for the Old Market. Who knows how many visitors will come back and bring an event or a business here?

It's hard to know the economic impact of the week. Were those Omahans in the seats? Or out-of-town fans? Probably a mix.

Mostly, it was a week of memories. I'll remember the first night, the first event out of the blocks, the 400 individual medley duel between Phelps and Ryan Lochte. One veteran swimming writer said it was the best race he'd ever seen.

We can always say Phelps slept and swam here, on his way to whatever history awaits in China. This is where the Dara Torres story took flight, and if it has the happy ending we hope for, it will be the all-time Olympic tale.

We saw fresh faces and gutsy performances and new superhero suits and world records and uncanny talent up close, stuff we usually witness every four years from our living rooms. It was all very cool for Omaha. And we gave the goose bumps right back to the swimmers and officials, with our Friday night crowd dressed in alternating red, white and blue.

Omaha grew up as a city in more ways than you can imagine this week. I'm proud of the way the city kept showing up, volunteering, working, cheering night after night after night.

2011 INSIGHT *This one could have served as a bookend to columns I had written in the 1990s, about what Omaha the sports town needed. Listening to the national writers the week of the Swim Trials gush about how great Omaha was, it sunk in. I thought a lot about the days of Racers at the Ak and Martina hitting tennis balls at the Civic. I took a lot of pride in this. Not that I had anything to do with it – I didn't. But as a resident of Omaha, showing off my town, it felt good.*

SEPTEMBER 1, 2008 • NEBRASKA FOOTBALL

Thrills, Chills Add to Win

CAN A VIDEO board get goose bumps? The evening began with the voice of God. No, not that God.

I'm talking about the unmistakable, legendary voice of John Facenda, the late, great voice of NFL Films. The "Frozen Tundra" guy.

Somewhere along the way, Facenda had narrated a film about Nebraska football. Several minutes before the 2008 season opener, the lights went down on the big screen. And then you heard Facenda saying the word "Nebraska."

And then all of these old film clips appeared. Rodgers juking. Devaney barking. Tagge diving up over the top. And it moved on to the next era of heroes. Gill. Rozier. Osborne. Frazier. On and on.

We've seen them before, but never like this. With Facenda calling the plays. With the Beatles' "Get Back" playing in the background. Get back to where you once belonged.

And then they came out. Bo Pelini and the Huskers. The stadium was rocking by then. Milt Tenopir and Charlie McBride followed the team out. Mike Rozier and Irving Fryar stood together on the sideline.

It was a surreal moment of nostalgia meeting passion, past colliding with present. This was one of the great moments in a stadium that collects them like a museum.

The game wasn't so bad itself.

Pelini's official head coaching debut was a success because, well, it was a win. Nebraska beat Western Michigan 47-24. Please excuse those who feared this could be a loss. After Ball State and some of the others, you just never know anymore.

By now, we know better than to read too much into a Nebraska debut. In 1973, Tom Osborne beat UCLA 40-13 en route to a 9-2-1 year. Frank Solich beat Louisiana Tech 56-27 to christen 1998 — a 9-4 year with rough spots. In 2004, Bill Callahan beat Western Illinois 56-17 — the first of five wins that season.

All were memorable only in the fact that the head coach finally got a good night's sleep afterward.

Coach Bo Pelini leads the Huskers from the tunnel in the season opener.

Likewise, it would be a mistake to buy or sell stock based on Pelini's first outing.

Here's what we know: Joe Ganz is a playmaker. But the Huskers can't, or won't, run the ball as promised.

On defense, Pelini's troops play hard and hit like a ton of bricks. But oh, those busted assignments.

It's hard to say why offensive coordinator Shawn Watson, who has talked of pounding the proverbial rock, backed off. It could be the game plan was to show off NU's ability to pass and catch. It could be that Western Michigan's defense was loading up on the run.

But here's the thing: Nebraska kept passing late, even when it looked like a good time to run clock. If NU is afraid to go after Western Michigan's middle, what's going to happen in the Big 12?

Once Again, 1971 Rivals Show How It's Done
NORMAN, OKLA.

THERE'S STILL ONLY one "Game of the Century."

The participants from Nebraska and Oklahoma who gathered in Norman on Nov. 25, 1971, set the standard for how to conduct a championship college football game. Those same participants gathered again, for the first time in 37 years, and set another standard.

This is how you have a reunion.

It took place on the second floor of the Barry Switzer Center, a three-story building adjacent to the south end zone at OU's Memorial Stadium. This is where Sooner football keeps its memories: trophies, memorabilia, programs, old helmets, videos of great moments, etc.

It was in this setting that an old piece of history came back to life. But this time, Johnny Rodgers had his breath taken away.

Rodgers arrived at the cocktail reception early and walked down to the field where he had left his footprints, in zigzag lines, 37 years ago. This was the first time he had been back to this field.

"And when I walked in, the first thing I see is the video screen," Rodgers said. "They were showing the (1971) game on the video screen."

But the players weren't watching the video board. They were too busy hugging, looking for name tags and watching the door to see who would walk in next.

There were some serious name tags at this reception.

In one corner, three generations of Oklahoma coaches — Chuck Fairbanks, Switzer and Bob Stoops — stood and told stories. Chuck Neinas, the commissioner of the Big Eight in 1971, was on hand, visiting with Steve Hatchell, the first Big 12 commissioner, who was an intern in the Big Eight office in 1971.

In another corner, Oklahoma receiver Jon Harrison and Nebraska defensive back Bill Kosch were in deep conversation. Hope Kosch didn't bring up that catch Harrison didn't make at the end.

Big John Dutton was there, still looming over the crowd. Tom Brahaney, the great OU center, walked around, maybe looking for Rich Glover, who wasn't there. Neither was the late Jack Mildren, whose death was an impetus for this great event.

"Everyone remembers where they were when that game took place," Johnny Rodgers said of the "Game of the Century."

Through the door walked Greg Pruitt, and he couldn't wait to find Rodgers and resume the trash-talking they had started during that 1971 season. The two most famous offensive players of their day hugged long and hard.

"Everybody still talks about Johnny's punt return," Pruitt said. "It shouldn't have happened.

"I was on the punt coverage team. Now, that previous year, Johnny and I had met at an all-star game and we hit it off and became friends. We kept in touch all that (1971) season and trash-talked about what we were going to do to each other when we met at the end of the season.

"My assignment on that punt return was that I was one of the first ones down, and I was to contain Johnny at the start. Well, I got caught up in our trash-talking and went after him. He made a move right by me. I actually caused three of our other guys to miss him."

Jeff Kinney, the workhorse from McCook, Neb., who scored the winning touchdown, looked like he could still drag a few Sooners on his back. Kinney, who lives in Overland Park, Kan., reminisced about how that game was one of the first in which tear-away jerseys were used.

Larry Jacobson, the defensive tackle who won NU's first Outland Trophy that season, was showing off four unused tickets from that game — in the original ticket envelope — listed at $6 apiece.

"For some reason, I got extra tickets for that game, and my dad tried to sell them outside the stadium before the game," Jacobson said. "He couldn't get any takers, even for $6."

The folks who gathered in Norman 37 years later will remember this night, too.

2011 INSIGHT *Owen Field in Oklahoma was one of my favorite places to watch a college football game. I covered a lot of bad OU vs. Missouri, Kansas and Kansas State blowouts there. Covered some fun Sooner-Husker tilts, too. I'm a sucker for the 1971 "Game of the Century." I remember watching that game, and to be in the stadium where that game was played always gave me chills as I tried to imagine where certain plays happened. When former OU quarterback Jack Mildren died, I was in Oklahoma City covering the Big 12 baseball tourney, and I drove down to Norman just to sit in the stadium that day. Well, this weekend in 2008 was my last official game at OU. The game wasn't memorable. Sam Bradford scored early and often and Bob Stoops romped easily over Bo Pelini. But this Friday night party was something I'll never, ever forget. The party took place in OU's Barry Switzer Center, connected to the end zone bleachers and with a view of the field. During the reception, they played the original "Game of the Century" on the big screens in an empty stadium. That blew me away to watch that replay in that stadium. I wasn't alone. Johnny Rodgers told me when he walked in that this was the first time he had been back to this great old stadium – and the first time he'd seen that replay. I find the latter hard to believe. But it sounded good at the time.*

NOVEMBER 29, 2008 • NEBRASKA FOOTBALL

Huskers Get a Kick in the Pants

WELL, BO PELINI'S first Nebraska regular season is in the books. And what have we learned?

No more fake field goals. Why? Exhibit A nearly tarnished a season and took Pelini from first-year genius to rookie coach.

Exhibit B bailed everyone out. With 85,000 holding their collective breath, Alex Henery kicked an improbable 57-yard field goal with 1:43 left that sailed all the way to Jacksonville, Fla.

The Huskers won an improbable game, 40-31, and survived Colorado. And themselves. And their coach.

The Bad News Buffs limped into Lincoln at 5-6, with an assortment of injuries. The Huskers were going to spend the day after Thanksgiving devouring Buffalo burgers. But somebody forgot to turn on the grill. The entree of the day was almost boiled Pelini.

An afternoon that was supposed to be a statement of Husker revival turned into a reminder that Bo doesn't always know. And this is 2008, not 1995.

After NU seized control, leading 24-17 late in the first half, the Huskers lined up for a 51-yard field goal. Rather than let Henery go for the 10-point lead, Pelini OK'd a fake field goal "toss" back to Henery that had worked three weeks ago against KU.

Colorado caught the film. CU's Jimmy Smith happened to be in the backfield at the time of the fake. And happened to catch the toss on the fly and ramble 58 yards for a game-tying touchdown.

"I almost screwed the game up," Pelini said. "I got greedy."

How so?

"It actually wasn't the same fake," Pelini said. "We were going to pass off it. But it was a bad decision. I knew we had a chance to go into the half up 10 and then come out and put it away. I wanted to put it away there. I got greedy.

"Dumb. Really, really dumb."

Hey, Coach. You're stealing my lines.

"I mean, that was stupid," Pelini said. "Bad, bad decision."

Now I'm starting to feel sorry for the coach.

Alex Henery watches as his 57-yard field goal puts the Huskers ahead.

It was a rookie mistake. It's allowed. It's easy to forget Pelini is still learning. Easy to forget he is, in fact, a rookie.

A lot of folks have hyped up Pelini. Guilty. It's easy. He's coached this team up. He's brought a blue-collar, smart-football approach back to Nebraska. He falls on the sword. He's human. Exactly. He doesn't wear a cape.

But because of the ever-present hype, you forget that there's a learning curve for the program and coach. Maybe that's the lesson on a harried day that no Husker fan will forget.

"We controlled the game," Pelini said. "Our execution and consistency hurt us. It's been that way all season. We still are learning that you have to show up every game and play every play."

On this wild and crazy day, Super Bo was saved by a Super Kick. And the tenor of his first season was saved, too.

All because of one improbable, breathless kick.

"If we had lost," Pelini said, "I'd have been kicking myself forever."

Despite Loss, Huskers Still Winners

WHO NEEDS A national title?

This was their finest moment. Sure, Nebraska lost to Penn State at the Qwest Center. On this night of nights, on women's college volleyball's biggest stage, the Nittany Lions survived a group of big-hearted Huskers in five sets. But this unforgettable night was as much about the Huskers as it was the advancement of the Penn State machine.

Nebraska has won three national championships. There have been too many All-Americans to count for the Duke of women's volleyball. But there has never been a Nebraska volleyball team like this. There has never been a match like this, with so many swings and end-of-the-world points, that stirred the emotions of 17,430 and so many more watching at home, in bars, restaurants, anywhere they could find a TV.

The record will show that the Huskers lost. But this was the finest moment for a program built on winning and with a library full of dominance and excellence.

Penn State moves on to the NCAA championship match tonight against Stanford. But the mighty Nittany Lions stagger to that destiny. They came to Omaha full of confidence and gumption. They woke up to a sigh of relief.

Russ Rose's excellent team had not lost a set. John Cook's plucky team was down 2-0. We should've known this would not be a walkover. After intermission, Nebraska won the first set against Penn State this season. Then, it won another.

Then, the Huskers led 10-8 in the fifth. They had Penn State on the run. The Lions hadn't been in this situation in a long, long time. It showed. They were rattled. Penn State could not handle Nebraska's savvy serves. The crowd, the seventh man, picked up steam.

My goodness, could the magic happen again? Here? Now?

No, no, no. Penn State showed its mettle. It won six straight points. Eventually, the fairy tale for Nebraska ended. But what a run. What a ride.

The eyes of Nebraska's Rachel Schwartz, left, and Sydney Anderson tell the outcome of the Penn State match.

The Huskers boarded a bus without a national championship trophy. But what they take back to Lincoln, and into the future, might be just as fulfilling.

Can you put a legacy in a trophy case?

This spellbinding match, on top of last week's breathless comeback at Washington, cements this team's status as one of Nebraska's all-time best.

Coach Cook called the game "mystical." But it was nothing of the sort.

In fact, had NU knocked off Penn State, it would have been called an upset, but not the greatest upset ever in volleyball.

That would have been an insult to the legacy that Terry Pettit created and Cook has perfected.

What we've seen the last seven days is exactly what Pettit and Cook have built.

A championship program. With the heart of a champion.

People have grown to love this team in the last week. Folks who have never been to the NU Coliseum in their lives are volleyball fans.

So now they will have new fans and a new look. Nebraska has always won so easily. We take it for granted. The players look less like people and more like machines.

This team has put a human face on the program, the steely eyes of Jordan Larson, the contagious smile of Rachel Schwartz. They are top-class players, to be sure, but they had to confront adversity, a rarity for Nebraska volleyball. The way they reacted, never quitting, always fighting, with the injured Kori Cooper over there in camouflage, was enough to tug at the heart.

In the end, Nebraska volleyball has opened a window to its soul and shown us what it's all about.

The heart of a champion.

No matter what the score said.

TOM'S TAKE

REFLECTIONS ON

Credit Diesing With the Save on the College World Series

ON A GOOD day for a campfire, they gathered to sing Kumbaya.

David Sokol and Mayor Mike Fahey did not join hands. But they did the symbolic equivalent, standing side by side at a press conference to tell the world they had reached a truce over the Qwest Center parking lots. Omaha's titans love their drama, but in the end, they are rich enough and powerful enough and smart enough to sit down and make progress happen.

It's a win-win-win-win. The mayor, MECA, College World Series fans and the NCAA, which is ecstatic over the news, all are winners.

A new downtown baseball stadium has been given the green light. If you build it, the NCAA will stay. How does 25 years grab you?

Let the road to Omaha's future begin. Let the long marriage between the city of Omaha and the NCAA continue. For that, you can thank our friendly neighborhood marriage counselor, Jack Diesing Jr.

"At all the talks and forums I've been to, I tell people, 'I'm the one who started this process,' " Diesing said. " 'So shoot me.' "

We should probably knight Diesing, the son of the father of Omaha's CWS, Jack Sr. He has long since taken the baton from his father. He is president of CWS Inc. But Diesing is more like the caretaker of the CWS and all of its traditions and nostalgia.

It's a job he takes seriously, 24/7/365, which is why, way back in December 2005, he called the NCAA with an idea. Our contract is coming up in a few years. Let's do some work on Rosenblatt Stadium.

Did the old park need it? Not at that point. Eventually? Yes.

There are various definitions of a good marriage. Here's mine: a husband who knows his wife well enough to know what she wants. In fact, he knows what she wants before she does. If she has to ask for it, he's done. In this case, the NCAA is the wife and Diesing plays the part of the insightful and thoughtful husband.

"It was like a wife," Diesing said, recalling the 2005 talks. "It was like, 'This is what I want, but you don't have to get it for me.' But you know you better get it.

"The NCAA had talked about new locker rooms, about fixing up the outside of the stadium, a new media compound. I just thought, instead of trying to piecemeal these things, why not come up with a master plan?"

The result was a $26 million renovation proposal. Soon, the mayor and city were involved. The wheels of renovation were in motion. But then, suddenly, Diesing's good intentions became a new downtown baseball stadium proposal.

"I forced myself to step outside and look at the future of the event," Diesing said. "I took a look at the finances and decided, in my little mind, that if you factor in the experiences of the student-athletes and the fans, and a very big contract that is unheard of, along with all the bells and whistles, and the money is the same, it's a no-brainer."

The "husband" in Diesing has helped him reason through the emotions tugging at his heart. The NCAA will never tell you what it wants, nor will it make demands. It makes you guess. And you'd better know it well enough to guess right.

As plans for the new downtown stadium took shape, Diesing could see this is what Omaha's partner would want, but never ask for.

"If you are a good partner, you know how to read the tea leaves," Diesing said. "I know the NCAA. I know what they like. Now, if we do this, we have to get 20-plus years. I suggested 25 years. We would have a very difficult time getting anything like that with Rosenblatt as the plan. That's just Jack talking. But I speak from experience, from knowing the NCAA."

— APRIL 2, 2008

Jack Diesing Jr., right, enjoys the moment as NCAA President Myles Brand signs a 25-year agreement with College World Series of Omaha Inc.

THE CHANGING SPORTS LANDSCAPE   2008

College Football Stadiums Were Built to Last

JOHN INGRAM ALMOST cried while watching the last game at Yankee Stadium with his two sons. But he's not a Yankee fan. Ingram, NU's assistant athletic director for facilities, is an old stadium fan.

"We were saying, if that was Memorial Stadium, we would be tied to a pillar, holding on for dear life," Ingram said.

Fortunately for Ingram, and fortunately for us college football fans, that won't happen anytime soon. Yankee Stadium, built in 1923, is 85 years old and has a date with a bulldozer. Memorial Stadium, built in 1923, is 85 years young and has the thumbs-up to live forever.

"We talk to engineers about the stadium every year," Ingram said. "They have all said, as long as we maintain it, we can have it as long as we want."

All I can say is, thank God for college football.

This is no country for old stadium lovers. All of the classic baseball venues are leaving us, save for Wrigley Field and Fenway Park. And who knows when the architectural bell will toll for them?

Time marches on, except in the land of Saturday's America.

The old venues are going away, but not because they're crumbling or can't be remodeled with a little duct tape. They're going away because the rules of the game have changed. Those are the rules of how we watch sports and how sports make money off of us.

The people who set those rules, the owners and general managers and marketing gurus and new-age sports architects, tell us you need an open concourse with flat screens by the ketchup machine, playground slides and a skybox suite with all the trimmings. We've been over all this before.

What's interesting, and very cool, is that these people can't touch college football. College football stadiums live forever. Literally. When's the last time you heard of a major conference school building a new football stadium? Iowa State in 1975?

According to the NCAA, there are 16 college football stadiums still around that were built before 1923. NU's Memorial Stadium was built two years after Kansas' Memorial Stadium, one year after the Rose Bowl and the same year as the L.A. Coliseum and Oklahoma's Memorial Stadium.

Why are these old, gray battleships untouchable?

Two reasons. First, economics. Building a new basketball arena is one thing. Building an 85,000-seat football stadium, with all the modern bells and whistles, is quite another. What would it cost? One hundred million? More?

Second reason: Geography. Almost all universities are landlocked. There isn't room on most campuses to dig a crater in the earth on behalf of the football team. Not unless you want to build it on the other side of town. Who wants to do that?

Ingram has a group of Chicago engineers come to Lincoln every spring to inspect the stadium, top to bottom, and make recommendations to preserve it. Mostly, the work entails concrete repairs and waterproofing. As long as NU continues to do that, Ingram says, the Huskers can play football on that spot for another 85 years.

Right about the time they'll need another Yankee Stadium.

— SEPTEMBER 25, 2008

JOE GANZ FINISHES STRONG | JAYS LOSE TO UK | ANOTHER LSU TITLE | COMEBACK IN COLUMBIA

2009

> "Coach (Bo) gave us a story this week about a situation that happened to him, where if he had done something different, he would have saved a touchdown. He says he wants to make sure we're always going hard and to the limit, because you never know what might happen."
>
> — NEBRASKA DEFENSIVE TACKLE NDAMUKONG SUH

Talk about growing pains. This one will hurt for a while. This was a punch in the gut, a self-imposed sucker punch, which made it worse. This one's going to leave a mark. Nebraska players trudged off the field at Lane Stadium. Some were in shock. Most looked angry. They should have been. They were just over a minute from celebrating the program's biggest victory in eight years. Instead, they rode off into the Virginia night wondering how they gave this one away. On the long trip home Saturday night, the in-flight movie would

be the horrific sight of Virginia Tech receiver Danny Coale streaking down the sidelines alone. Nobody said the program's comeback would be easy. Nobody said it would be this cruel, either. The lesson right in front of their teary eyes was this: Winning programs finish games. It was a tough philosophical pill to swallow, not that head coach Bo Pelini was in any mood for that. When asked what happened on the back-breaking 81-yard pass to Coale that set up the Hokies' improbable 16-15 win, Pelini said, "You saw it. It was obvious." Here's what is obvious about Pelini's Huskers: They are close. Very close.

The Mid-America Center expected the Lancers to draw more fans. The Lancers, who pay $3,000 per game and a share of concessions, have lost money and there have been scheduling conflicts with the MAC's other events. Frankly, I was skeptical that Omahans would follow the Lancers to Iowa in droves. Folks will cross the bridge to drop anchor at their favorite boat, but not necessarily for USHL hockey. In the Civic, the Lancers have a terrific hockey barn, filled with old ghosts in a sports town that loves its old ghosts. Will they fill up the 9,000 seats? No. But I could see them averaging 3,000 to 4,000 and maybe more on some nights. Some folks will go just to watch hockey in the Civic. Either way, it would seem to be the perfect home for the Lancers.

NEBRASKA-OKLAHOMA REBIRTH | NDAMUKONG SUH'S HUSKER LEGACY | UNO HIRES TREV ALBERTS

Remember when Kevin Costner was part of the "Save Rosenblatt" campaign last year? Well, Crash Davis came back to town last week with his guitar, not a baseball bat, to perform with his group at Slowdown. Costner brought up the College World Series and new stadium, telling the audience, "They may have moved your stadium, but they better never take (the CWS) away from your city. It's a really cool thing you guys have here." Costner added, "It wasn't the Civil War, but it practically was for you. Let's just move on and play ball." Agreed.

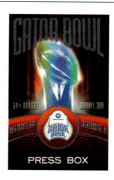

They are fun to watch, these Nebraska Hoosiers, Mighty Mites, Doc's Dwarfs, or whatever you want to call them. It's more fun to win, of course. As usual, Nebraska left it all out on the court at the Devaney Center against Kansas. Unfortunately, once again, they left victory on the court, too, in a puddle of sweat. This is getting old. In three straight games, NU has pushed Oklahoma, Oklahoma State and KU to the limit. Three straight games, the Mighty Mites came up, well, short.

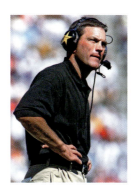

One Iowa columnist is calling for the U of I to give Kirk Ferentz a lifetime contract. I'm always intrigued by Iowa standards. At a lot of other schools, an Outback Bowl win and fourth-place finish wouldn't be a call for a lifetime deal; there would be heat on the coach to improve and clean up the off-the-field matters. But Iowa is different. That's not necessarily a bad thing.

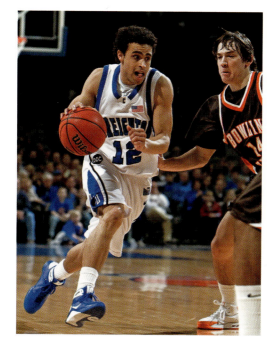

Three years later, Josh Dotzler can't recall the sound. I'll never forget it. It was the sound of a balloon popping. It was a glass vase falling off a table and landing on a hardwood floor. It was loud. It was disturbing. It made you wince. It was the sound of a cruel twist of fate. This was Feb. 11, 2006. Southern Illinois was at the Qwest Center. The SIU-Creighton rivalry was in full swing then, and it looked like these two terrific point guards, Dotzler and Bryan Mullins, might take the thing to warp speed. But then the kid from Omaha did what he did a lot of that year: He stole the ball. "I was headed down on a fast break," Dotzler recalled the other day. "And Jamaal Tatum (SIU guard) was running behind me and clipped one of my legs so when I fell, I fell directly on my knee. I don't remember a big sound. I remember I got up, took one dribble and felt something collapse." Like a storybook career.

JANUARY 2, 2009 • NEBRASKA FOOTBALL

Good Things Come to Joes Who Wait

JACKSONVILLE, FLA.

Nebraska quarterback Joe Ganz waves to fans after his final game as a Husker.

LISTEN UP, ALL you quarterbacks of Generation Xbox, who want the world and want it now or you'll find another game.

Pay attention, all you kids who are thinking about walking away from the long hours and the commitment and the team just because the depth chart says you're fourth-team, behind the team mascot.

Here's what happens when you stick it out:

The line in front of you leaves because guys graduate or they just get tired of waiting.

And then one day they hand you the ball.

And then, with one season to play, you set the school record for passing yards in a season and finish second on the all-time school career list. Yes, in one season.

And then, with everyone else who ever played ahead of you watching at home on their couches, you win the MVP award of the Gator Bowl, your last game.

And you're standing on a stage in the middle of the stadium, holding this impressive trophy, with thousands of fans standing and applauding.

And then you take off, holding the game ball, and start running around the border of the stadium, slapping hands with Nebraska fans, who are yelling, "You're the greatest" and "Thanks for staying."

And then as you leave the locker room, the media mob you, and ask you if there could ever be a better ending than this.

"No," said Joe Ganz.

The senior Nebraska quarterback stood outside the Huskers' locker room. He had led his team back from a 14-3 halftime deficit to a 26-21 victory over Clemson in the Gator Bowl. He was the MVP.

Joe Ganz, MVP.

It's the perfect ending to the perfect story of persistence, hard work, faith and belief, and all those other things that don't come with video games.

The only thing better would be if this had been for the national championship. Then again, this story isn't about championships.

"It's about good things happen to people who wait," said senior defensive end Zach Potter. "This was vintage Joe."

This was a vintage win for this nine-win Nebraska team, all about patience, adjustments and faith. The Huskers fell behind, they adjusted, they clawed back, they got a break (the overturned Clemson touchdown) and they eventually outplayed and outlasted the Tigers.

In the middle of it all was a guy named Joe.

That will be his legacy at Nebraska. It's not very sexy. You can't sell it on a video, along with Tommie Frazier's touchdown gallop. It won't go in a trophy case.

Ganz should be remembered. This is a tale — a most uncommon tale these days, sadly — that should be told in every gym class and locker room in every school in Nebraska.

Heck, there's a lesson in this story for anyone with a cubicle or a lunchbox or a bus route.

It comes straight from the horse's mouth, when he was asked what he would tell any kids out there who feel like giving up.

"Good things happen if you work hard and have patience," Ganz said. "I know everybody wants to play as a freshman and be all-world. But it's tough out there. You have to have faith in yourself and don't give up. Just shut up and work hard."

As he prepared to ride off into the sunset, the hero was asked what was next.

"I want to keep playing," Ganz said. "I don't want it to end."

A Special Night, but a Missed Opportunity

SOMETIMES YOU JUST have to get away. So Justin Carter left the silence of the Creighton locker room and started walking.

He slowly shuffled down the corridor, his head down and white Creighton jersey hanging out. He turned left out a tunnel, toward the court, where the score — "Wildcats 65, Bluejays 63" — was still stuck to the scoreboard.

Carter paused and took one last look around. Toward the free-throw line. Toward a dream that slipped through the Bluejays' grasp.

Finally, he turned back and ducked into a men's room, just off the court.

He was in there for several minutes, when finally, a visitor opened the door and saw Carter, just standing in front of a mirror, hands on his head.

This was the very reflection of gut-wrenching defeat.

"It just hurts, really bad," Carter would say later.

There was no escaping that. This was not just another NIT loss. The Jays had a chance to beat Kentucky, in their crib, then earn a shot at Notre Dame two nights later and the opportunity to take their program to the bright lights of New York City next week.

It was shaping up as Fantasy Week. But reality bit. Hard.

It cut like a dagger. For one last shot, Booker Woodfox had the dagger in his hand. He had an open 3 with three seconds left.

How many times has Woodfox made this shot? Catch, jump, shoot. How many times has Woodfox made this simple jumper in practice? In a game? In his dreams? Too many to count.

The ball bounced long off the rim, along with this dream finish.

"I thought he had it," CU coach Dana Altman said. "We set it up for him. He's made that shot so many times for us."

When the Wildcats rebounded and the buzzer went off, an entire arena was in disbelief — and that may have included the winners, too.

"We should have won that game," Altman said.

That's what they will remember most about this wild, loud and unforgettable night.

Missed opportunity. Kentucky comes to Omaha once every 69 years, this time because the NIT sent the bluebloods to a mid-major's den.

The Jays won't likely get another shot at UK — or any other major-conference opponent — at home for a long, long time.

They let the Cats escape with a victory that would have elevated Creighton's stature — at least in the Jays' own youthful minds.

This was their shot to show the world they could play with the big boys. They did. And then they didn't.

Creighton's Justin Carter reflects the Bluejays' distress after coming up short against Kentucky in an NIT game at the Qwest Center in Omaha.

2011 INSIGHT *This was a unique night, in many ways. For one, the specter of Kentucky basketball jerseys in Omaha, against Creighton, was one of those surreal moments around here. Second, I don't usually follow an athlete into a bathroom to see how he's doing. It was a great night for Creighton hoops, and maybe the last great night for Dana Altman here, but it had the wrong ending. Even though it was the NIT, you felt like beating a program like Kentucky would change things for Creighton. It didn't happen. When I hung around the locker room afterward, I saw Justin Carter exit the locker room and walk the other way. I wondered where he was going. So I followed him, like I did with Eric Piatkowski at the Big Eight tourney in 1994 and Joe Ganz after the Gator Bowl in 2009. Just for an interesting angle. Suddenly, I lost Justin. He was gone. Where did he go? I peeked inside a men's room, just off the court, and there he was, still in full uniform, leaning up against the mirror over the sink.*

I asked him how he was doing. That was my stupid question for the night.

LSU Is Back on Top

A MARDI GRAS parade had broken out in the left-field bleachers. There was a purple and gold dogpile on the pitcher's mound. And a conga line of revelers chanted, "L-S-U, L-S-U, L-S-U" as they marched out of Rosenblatt Stadium, down 13th Street and wherever the night would take them.

The sights and sounds of the College World Series came rushing back, like an old flashback. But the scene was so vivid you had to check the calendar.

Was this 1997 or 2009?

It was most certainly the latter. LSU won its sixth NCAA Division I baseball championship. It had been nine years since the last one.

Nine years? Really? Remember LSU?

Don't look now, but the Tigers are baaaaaack.

They made the declaration at this College World Series, and they finished it off with an exclamation point, pounding Texas 11-4.

How the Bayou Bengals did it — dropping a five-spot in the sixth to break a 4-4 tie, never letting go and making it look effortless — simply added to the retro theme of the night.

And while it all seemed too familiar, this was a rarity unfolding on the grand Rosenblatt stage.

This was a college baseball dynasty reinvigorated and reinvented, in the form of a national champion.

LSU won five CWS flags from 1991 to 2000. Now the Tigers are at it again, with a new coach and a team with more balance and more ways to win than the Gorilla Ball of yesteryear.

You would think that it's happened a lot. Even with college baseball awash in parity, we see so many of the same teams over and over. Don't they always do it again and again?

Not really. CWS dynasties don't usually come back to win it again with another coach, in another era.

There was Miami, with Ron Fraser and Jim Morris. Texas won two national titles each with Bibb Falk, Cliff Gustafson and Augie Garrido. Cal State Fullerton, with Garrido and George Horton.

And USC, winning 11 with Rod Dedeaux as the sport's John Wooden, but then going from 1978 until 1998 without one. But that '98 title has turned out to be an anomaly for the Trojans.

Is that how it will be for LSU? Or is this the beginning of a new championship era for the Paul Mainieri Tigers?

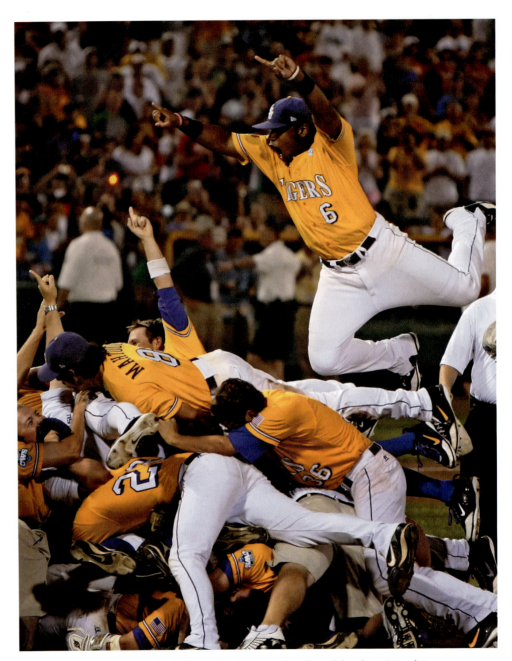

Leon Landry is about to put the finishing touches on a dogpile celebrating LSU's victory.

When You Least Expected It

COLUMBIA, MO.

HURRICANE SUH CRASHED into Faurot Field. Zac Lee had bailed out both himself and his offensive coordinator. Nebraska had seemingly turned an ugly night into a watercolor beauty.

And yet, with 5:24 left and Nebraska up on Mizzou 20-12, the thought crossed my mind.

How are the Huskers going to lose this one?

How will they have the rug pulled out this time? Will there be a turnover? Will Missouri run back a punt? Will Mizzou coach Gary Pinkel pull out the old throwback pass to the quarterback play, like he did to Bo Pelini in 2003?

Did the thought cross your mind, too? Did you trust this team to finish?

Nebraska had stopped Blaine Gabbert and the Tigers one more time, this time on fourth down, and the Huskers had the ball back with 5:24 left. Here we go again. Would this be Virginia Tech all over again?

No. In Blacksburg, the Huskers began celebrating on the sidelines in this situation and took their eye off the prize.

No. Missouri never got the chance to break Big Red hearts. On a crucial third-and-one with two minutes left, Lee sneaked three yards for the first down. A few plays later, Roy Helu burst around end and over the goal line, and it was finally here. Breakout night.

On the road. On national TV. In the loud and raucous den of the rival that has been a huge thorn in Nebraska's side the past two years.

You knew it was going to happen one day. But nobody could have known it would happen like this.

It happened in a flash, like the lightning over this soggy stadium. For three quarters, Nebraska could do little right on offense or special teams.

For three quarters, the Huskers couldn't catch a punt or get a first down or run a series without some sort of penalty.

For three quarters, this was a team that still couldn't get out of its own way, making so many little, sloppy mistakes.

For three quarters, offensive coordinator Shawn Watson inexplicably kept throwing the ball into a driving rain, with a quarterback who couldn't hit the broad side of a Knob Noster, Mo., barn.

It all turned on one play, one minute and four seconds into the fourth quarter. Lee dropped back and threw deep toward Niles Paul. But this time magic happened. This time, Paul caught the ball in stride and scored on a 56-yard touchdown pass.

The next thing you knew, the walls were caving in on Mizzou. Ndamukong Suh, dropping back behind the line in coverage, intercepted Gabbert. Then Dejon Gomes picked one off.

Then, before you could ask, "Whatever happened to the tight ends?" Watson pulled a wonderful play out of his hat, a little delay route against the flow to Mike McNeill, who caught Lee's pass wide open and scored. That's how it happened. Just like that.

One minute a Missouri writer in the press box is saying, "Just to let you know, the last time Missouri shut out Nebraska was 1961."

Nebraska's Niles Paul grabs his second of two fourth-quarter touchdown receptions, this one a 13-yard pass from Zac Lee.

The next minute, a Nebraska scribe is comparing this turnaround to the 1990 Colorado game in Lincoln, when NU was up 12-0 entering the fourth quarter and the Buffs stormed back on Husker turf to win 27-12.

Same score. Weird, huh?

2011 INSIGHT *It rained. It rained. It rained some more. It rained like the mother of all haunted house movies, like Bela Lugosi meets the Ghost and Mr. Chicken. It rained harder and harder all day, as we waited in Columbia, Mo., for the Nebraska-Missouri game on a Thursday night. With that kind of relentless rain, you could feel something different, maybe special, was about to happen. Very few suspected that it would be a Ndamukong Suh Coming Out Bash. Suh was a good player, but he had yet to dominate. This was where he would make his splash, pun intended. Moments like these are rare, when you know you are watching history, even as you watch it. The fourth-quarter heroics by Zac Lee and Niles Paul were lost in the Suh of it all. By the end, the stadium was half full of red and black ponchos, the rain kept falling, and Bo Pelini's first big win was here. I'll always remember Suh running off the field last, after an ESPN interview, as he held his helmet up to the Nebraska fans in salute. I'll also remember I never wanted to see rain again.*

NOVEMBER 8, 2009 • NEBRASKA FOOTBALL

A Glimpse of Past, and of the Future

THE CLOCK SAID there were 27 seconds left, but it felt more like eight years and 27 seconds.

There were 85,000 standing and waiting and holding their breath. They had waited all night, all season, and maybe even since 2001 for a moment like this. Nebraska was up on Oklahoma 10-3. The two had played a chess game with bloodstained pieces all night, and the longer it went, the longer the Huskers kept the lead, the more you could feel the tension. You could feel 85,000 waiting to exhale.

Just like old times. Just like Tom and Barry used to create. These Huskers were unranked and these Sooners were 24th, but they turned this into a heavyweight bout, trading body punches, waiting for someone to stagger. Nobody would.

The old legends were in street clothes at halftime, and Barry Switzer and Billy Sims were safely tucked in a suite somewhere, but the good folks with memories knew that as long as crimson and cream had one more shot in this stadium, it's never over.

Time and again, the Blackshirts had turned away Landry Jones and the Sooner offense. Five interceptions. Three missed field goals. It was an unreal effort.

But now it came down to this, with 27 seconds left, Jones in NU territory again and no timeouts. You wondered who was going to fall out of the sky and into the end zone this time for OU.

The answer was nobody. Jones threw a Hail Mary of sorts, deep near the end zone, and Matt O'Hanlon was there to catch it. And, yes, there is justice in this world.

A month and a half ago, the senior safety was seen chasing a Virginia Tech receiver down the sideline and got stuck with the tab for a huge missed opportunity. It's a long season, and you hoped O'Hanlon would get a shot at redemption.

O'Hanlon fell to the turf with his third interception, and the crowd roared. Memorial Stadium was like a bowl of popcorn with a lid, and finally the lid exploded. And on a day of crazy games and upsets in college football, in the Big 12 neighborhood there was a sense of normalcy that came with this one — at least to the good folks standing and screaming and going nuts.

Matt O'Hanlon intercepts his third pass of the game, a game-saving play in Nebraska's 10-3 victory over Oklahoma.

Suh's Legacy Is Beyond Awards

CONGRATULATIONS TO MARK INGRAM, this year's winner of the Heisman Trophy Offensive Player of the Year Award.

The most outstanding player in college football did not win the award for the most outstanding player in college football. But that's strictly an opinion, one that was outvoted by hundreds of other opinions.

Ndamukong Suh didn't win the Heisman. But, my, was he ever a winner all week.

It's a victory for a defensive tackle to merely be invited to this annual celebration of all things quarterbacks, running backs and receivers. For a mudder — even one as talented as Suh — to finish fourth in the voting, that's like winning.

That's the system, folks. But we're not here to lament what might have been.

We're here to celebrate this wonderful ride that Suh took us on in 2009. And to try to put into perspective what we just witnessed.

What a ride. Week by week, Suh kept pushing the envelope, upping the ante, breaking through offensive lines and barriers as he went. And now that the ride is about to end, it's safe to ask: What exactly did we just see?

Greatest defender in college football history? Greatest season by a defender ever? Greatest Nebraska defender?

I don't believe in "greatest ever" when it comes to athletes. There are too many inequities over eras. For me, the great ones are part of an overall conversation; on the top shelf, etc.

Well, Suh is a unique case. He might need his own shelf. He probably deserves his own branch on the NU family tree.

What's his legacy? I don't think we'll have a proper context on it for a while.

Did Suh jump-start Bo Pelini's program? Will he do for Pelini's defense what a great quarterback or running back could do for recruiting to an offense? He has the potential for a long, successful career in the NFL. Will he be known as the "greatest NFL player from NU," supplanting Roger Craig or Bob Brown or Will Shields?

Here's an early stab at finding a place for Suh in Nebraska history.

I think that there's a top shelf. The three Heisman winners — Johnny Rodgers, Mike Rozier and Eric Crouch — are on that shelf. So is Tommie Frazier, a Heismanesque player if we ever saw one, who set his own standard. And Rich Glover, an Outland-Lombardi winner who finished third in the Heisman voting in 1972.

I would put Suh on that shelf, ahead of Grant Wistrom, Dave Rimington and Dean Steinkuhler.

Suh vs. Glover is very close. But I'd give Suh the nod for three reasons: 1. His ability to change games with his hands (interceptions, blocked kicks). 2. He faced more double-teams and extra blocking than Glover, who played in the middle of a five-man front and saw more man-on-man blocking. 3. He did his damage on a 9-4 team.

Suh was surrounded by good, not great, players. Look at all of NU's elite players since the Bob Devaney era started; they were on great teams, championship teams. Suh is the only superstar-type player since 1962 to not be part of a conference champion.

He came within one second of that, but if it had happened, it would have cemented his status even more, considering the one-dimensional makeup of the 2009 Huskers.

That lack of championship pedigree makes what Suh accomplished this season even more astounding.

For now, Suh's immediate impact is clear. He'll leave without a championship ring, but his play no doubt will inspire a renaissance of great defense and teams at Nebraska. If and when the championships return to Lincoln, Suh will have been his own cornerstone. Heck, he might even be worth two.

You know what else he did? He turned the light back on. It had been too long since we'd seen true greatness on the Nebraska football field. We watched Suh in the rain and heat and under the brightest lights, making like a one-man wrecking crew and

Ndamukong Suh put his stamp upon the 2009 college football season with his treatment of opposing quarterbacks, such as Blaine Gabbert of Missouri.

throwing quarterbacks around and literally picking up this program and taking it with him. Along the way, he reminded us of the greatness that once was at NU — and can be there again.

There are countless numbers of trophies and awards in college football, and at Nebraska, for everyone but the team manager. There are too many, and yet there has to be room for one more, a new one. The Ndamukong Suh Award. Give it to "the player who impacts and inspires." Or to "the greatest player to not win the Heisman."

I think I know who gets the first one.

TOM'S TAKE — REFLECTIONS ON

UNO's New Team Has Much Work Ahead

ONE IS A former Nebraska football star, with a wife, kids and no meaningful career, who woke up one day at 38 and decided he wanted to become an athletic director.

The other is a chancellor at the University of Nebraska at Omaha who decided that he needed a splash hire, someone who could rebuild UNO's image, even if that person had zero experience as an administrator.

Trev Alberts and John Christensen needed each other.

Fate, timing and desperation brought them together. "In a way, it was a perfect positive storm," Christensen said.

Trev Alberts ? UNO athletic director?

Really?

This is so far out of left field that it will either be a home run or a mammoth whiff. There will be no in-between.

Can you run an athletic department without any experience?

Can you do it by being a cheerleader, fundraiser and "friendraiser" and hiring a right-hand man to do the rest? Will a college football hero take Division II volleyball seriously?

This is so crazy that it just might work.

The reason why was something you could see, and feel, at Alberts' announcement at UNO.

Alberts said all the right things. He looked sharp. He was smooth, polished, humble. That's what he does. That's what UNO is getting. That's what Christensen wanted.

But as I looked around the crowded room, at the student-athletes and coaches and boosters, I noticed something that I hadn't seen in a long, long time at UNO.

Smiles. Energy. Excitement.

Hope.

Alberts has never raised a dollar in his life, never managed a group of people, unless it was taking his kids out for ice cream.

Now you put him in charge of a Division II athletic department with one Division I sport and a $650,000 budget deficit. May his life preserver have air in it.

What he offers is the story of how a scrawny kid from Cedar Falls, Iowa, grew up to build a résumé that should reward him with induction into the College Football Hall of Fame.

"What I like about him is he made himself through hard work and a single focus on the job at hand," said David Sokol, a UNO booster of considerable passion and clout. "It's not that complicated of a job if you have those two skills. I think he brings a lot more to the table to do a good job than what we've had the last several years."

And that is hope. The past two athletic directors didn't bring hope. If Christensen had hired the flavor of the day in Division II athletics, there would not have been much hope.

And yet even without strong leadership, UNO has won, and won big. There are two hallways full of brilliant coaches at UNO.

They have won in spite of the chaos around them. Imagine what Pat Behrns and Mike Denney and Don Klosterman could do with an athletic director who provided them with better facilities and more money.

"Can you imagine?" Christensen said out loud.

Hope is what this hire is about. Credibility. Sanity. Making UNO a player in the city. Rebuilding old bridges torn down from the Nancy Belck/Jim Buck days.

Building new ones, paved with gold.

Hope is money. I know several UNO boosters who have told me that they have held back because they wanted proof that UNO was competent, credible. They have asked: Why invest in a hockey rink when we don't know what UNO wants to do with hockey?

UNO has a University Life Complex on the drawing board. There's a phase that would build baseball, softball and soccer fields for games and practices. A source in the NU Foundation told me that not one penny has been raised for the $18 million project. Why? He said donors want to see and hear from someone at UNO who has a plan, a vision.

Just what Alberts was saying.

There is a third phase to that project that involves ice. A hockey practice facility? A new rink for the Mavs? It's so far down the list you can't see it with a telescope. But someone with a vision can.

Maybe these things will never happen. But now, suddenly, they have hope.

They have hope because Alberts has one strong attribute: a clear understanding of who he is and what he can, and must, do. He will

THE CHANGING SPORTS LANDSCAPE 2009

consume every rubber chicken in town. He will play enough golf to turn pro. And every time he walks into a meeting or sports banquet or the post-golf dinner, heads will turn and someone will say, "There's Trev Alberts, the UNO A.D."

Fans don't buy tickets to see the athletic director. But UNO has not had the head-turning factor in forever. Bob Danenhauer is a great guy. He's not the celebrity No. 34 is. Alberts will get UNO inside doors that it has not been inside in a long time, if ever.

OK, so he's in the door. Can he close the deal?

In UNO athletics, Alberts has a very good product. But it's Division II. Can Alberts make people care about Division II sports? Can he sell them on the need to upgrade facilities because UNO is being passed left and right in the ultra-competitive MIAA?

More important, can he sell them on UNO hockey?

This is the area that has potential to be a disaster. As much hope as Alberts brings, he doesn't evoke much faith that he will transform Maverick hockey into a dominant force. He's never played the game, doesn't know the people, wouldn't know icing from frosting.

Here's what he said: He knows how important hockey is at UNO. He told UNO's coaches that hockey's success is "non-negotiable." He says he's going to surround himself with people in the community who know hockey and listen to them.

Knowing hockey is important, but knowing what to do about it is something else entirely. For instance, Alberts says Mike Kemp is his coach. But Kemp has one year left on his contract. You need to give Kemp at least a one-year extension to allow him to recruit. Or do you risk letting recruiting slide?

UNO hockey is stable. Christensen said it "made a little money the last couple years," but he's made it clear he's not happy with its direction. What is Alberts' vision for hockey? What could it possibly be?

This is the part where the cynics say, "It doesn't matter, because Alberts will be a puppet for the chancellor, just like the others." Alberts stated emphatically that Christensen has promised to let him run the show without interference. The chancellor echoed the sentiment.

"As of today," Christensen said, "I'm a fan."

He will be known as a genius if Alberts sparks a fire, UNO's student-athletes get great facilities and Maverick fans are happy. What's the worst that could happen? Hockey slides, starts to lose money and makes the regents take notice. That would not be good. Home run or whiff.

But here's why I think that Alberts will pay attention to hockey: If hockey fails, then Alberts fails as an athletic director. He tried to sound convincing, saying, "We're a hockey school. Is there anything wrong with that?"

Not at all, it just sounds strange coming from his mouth. Crazy? It might just work.

— APRIL 30, 2009

UNO Chancellor John Christensen welcomes Trev Alberts to the Mavericks' team.

NU WOMEN TO SWEET SIXTEEN | MCDERMOTT TO CREIGHTON | NEBRASKA MOVES TO BIG TEN

2010

> "I think any time you have success in a college sport, it helps the (high school) programs in the state. Volleyball helps volleyball, football helps football and now basketball is helping basketball. There are girls who are going to grow up wanting to be like Kelsey Griffin and Vonnie Turner."
>
> — KELLY FLYNN, SOUTH SIOUX CITY GIRLS BASKETBALL COACH

I've always thought that Dana Altman's best Jays teams were modeled after that 1988 K-State team: a balance of overachievers and role players with star power and, mostly, leadership. I say Altman has lost his way trying to upgrade the "talent." There's an inherent lack of fundamentals, passion and competitiveness in the program. The coach begs to differ. When I bring up overachievers doing the little things, he mentions Casey Harriman, Josh Jones, Antoine Young and Justin Carter. "To say the makeup of our team has drastically changed, I don't see it," he said. "Our biggest problem right now is a lack of leadership."

It was somewhere in the winter of my college hoops discontent that the lightning bolt struck. It came in the form of a voice, which made itself known as I was whining to myself that I've been here 19 years and all I've ever wanted to do was cover a college hoops team that was ranked in the top 10, was cruising to a Big 12 title and looked like a sure thing for a No. 1 seed with a legitimate shot at the Final Four. Just once. Will it ever happen? It was then that I heard the voice. Actually, the voice sounded a lot like Connie Yori's. "Wake up and smell the rankings, you moron. Take a look around. You have a team ranked No. 3 in the nation, with a player of the year, a team full of good people and better stories, in the driver's seat of the Big 12, and they look like a sure thing for a No. 1 seed in March. Oh, by the way, this team is undefeated on Feb. 11. Here, let me introduce you to the Nebraska women's basketball team."

It's been a tough year for us geniuses. That description belongs to yours truly, not Dana Altman or Doc Sadler. Lord knows that I've used up a few barrels of ink over the years touting the coaching prowess of Altman and Sadler, as if they invented James Naismith's game and then perfected it. This just in: Altman is not John Wooden. And Sadler is no Eddie Sutton. Heck, he's not even Scott Sutton. The bandwagons are in the shop. So are their coaching reputations (sadly, mine is beyond repair). Altman's Creighton team might miss the postseason for the first time in 13 years. Sadler's Huskers are so deep in last place they'd need a time machine to get to first.

270 • 20 YEARS WITH TOM SHATEL

ROSENBLATT'S BIG CWS FINISH | UFL NIGHTHAWKS' DEBUT | T-MAGIC TEARS UP MANHATTAN

NU's defensive coaches passed around a USA Today spread on Washington quarteback Jake Locker, saying he was ready for his breakthrough game. The only thing that broke was Locker's rep. He ended up 4 for 20 with two interceptions. And while you cut the guy some slack because NU's secondary didn't leave many men open, Locker was generally helpless against Bo Pelini's Flying Ninjas.

Red face around the world. Uncle. Enough already. In the words of Apollo Creed, "Ain't gonna be no rematch." Mercifully, thankfully, the eyes of Texas will no longer be upon Nebraska. Oklahoma never inflicted this kind of torture. Please, Mack Brown, take your whips and chains and leave the good folks of Nebraska alone. You could see it in them after a 20-13 loss to the Longhorns that won't be wiped off the Memorial Stadium scoreboard anytime soon. Husker fans were too beaten down to be polite. As the victorious Texas coaches and players left the field, Nebraska

fans in the southwest corner just stood and watched. Same with the fans who lined the path to the locker room. Typically, they give the opponent a hand. Barry Switzer, Warren Powers, Bobby Bowden and Bill McCartney have all gotten the "good game" treatment after breaking Husker hearts. Mack Brown gushes about it. I saw only a handful of fans in red clap. Several. Not many. They were frozen. They were in shock. They wanted this one, this one last, good shot at burnt orange. They wanted it badly. Really, really badly.

The big concern during the week was Missouri running on Nebraska's leaky run defense. What were we thinking? This was Gary Pinkel, after all. Mizzou came out in an empty backfield the first series and had just four rushes at the end of the first quarter. The Tigers never did try to establish the run. Then again, by the time they were down 24-0, it was a little late.

Arenas don't hang banners. They store them. It's the responsibility of the coach, and his staff, to do the honors. New arenas don't make phone calls to recruits. They can't charm a mother or father in the living room. And they can't develop the talent once it makes it to the new address. But the birth of an arena — the Lincoln Arena, Haymarket Arena or whatever it ends up having stamped on the outside — is a heck of a place to start for Nebraska basketball. Doc Sadler is ultimately in charge of selling Husker Hoops to the world. But first you need something to sell. Finally, Sadler has that something in this new arena — and a new practice

facility, which is set for a groundbreaking soon. The mere promise of the two structures makes them like two new ace recruiters for Doc's staff.

20 YEARS WITH TOM SHATEL • 271

MARCH 24, 2010 • NEBRASKA WOMEN'S BASKETBALL

Nebraska's Greatest Basketball Season

MINNEAPOLIS

YOUR TEAM. YOUR TIME. Rejoice, all ye long-suffering Husker Hoops die-hards. You have a Sweet 16 team to call your own.

Behold the ladies in red.

They came to Williams Arena with two choices: make history or be history. Nebraska 83, UCLA 70.

They have pushed the envelope and gone where no Nebraska man or woman in hightops has ever been before.

The classic moments in Nebraska basketball history have come in snapshots. Beat No. 1 here. Win a conference tourney there. It's always been short-term gratification, and it's always ended with Nebraska kids not knowing how to handle it, or with the basketball gods saying enough is enough for a school that celebrates football recruiting more than the winter game.

Not this team. Not this time.

Greatest Nebraska team ever? It's an apples and oranges thing when you compare men's and women's feats. But say this: The men have still never won one NCAA tourney game.

What Connie Yori's team has done and keeps doing now stands alone.

This is the greatest season in Nebraska basketball history. The top accomplishment. There's nothing even close.

Big 12 championship. Undefeated Big 12 season. Big 12 coach and player of the year. National coach of the year. National player of the year candidate. And now, the crown jewel: a Sweet 16.

It's an embarrassment of riches. A Halley's comet season. Check that. Will this be the last Big 12 champion for Yori? No, it doesn't have to be. Last Sweet 16? Nope again. Maybe this thing is just getting started.

But these kinds of total-package seasons happen with regularity only at places like Storrs, Conn., and Knoxville, Tenn. For NU, the stars and moon are aligned. The sky is the limit.

Enjoy the rocket ride. It's easy to do. Yori has assembled a team of hard-working, no-nonsense team players. The Huskers win on guts and chemistry. And there is no better feeling for a basketball coach or a fan.

This Nebraska team's legacy is already set. This is the team that will have the largest photo on the wall, in a frame. This is the kind of season you build a new trophy case for, with the spotlight on the balls and the nets and the photos.

Nebraska's Lindsey Moore beats UCLA's Rebekah Gardner to a loose ball.

Coach Connie Yori claimed national coaching honors, along with the Big 12 regular-season championship.

Time Out With Nebraska's Kelsey Griffin

DELIGHTFUL. REFRESHING. HONEST. In my time in Nebraska, Kelsey Griffin is on the short list of favorite athletes I've had the pleasure to cover on and off the court. A superstar with a handle on everything around her. What a concept.

▶ **Q:** How did you learn to play basketball?

▶ **A:** I was in the third grade when I started playing club basketball. My family was very active. I played soccer a lot when I was little, and I started playing basketball in the winter for something to do in Alaska (laughs). My soccer coach in middle school told me I was too slow to play soccer (laughs). That's when I started getting some good influences and started taking it seriously.

We had a hoop on our driveway. My brother would get out there and play with me. My dad, my mom, everybody. I don't remember anyone sitting down with me and showing me correct form or anything. It was always just fun, throwing the ball in the hoop. I really wasn't a gym rat. I liked hiking a lot more. I dated a guy in high school who played basketball. I played more then.

▶ **Q:** I have friends, all male, who say they enjoy watching you play because you play like a guy. How does that make you feel?

▶ **A:** I've heard that before. I didn't know how to take it at first. I didn't know what that really meant. Does that mean I'm talented? And if I'm talented, does that mean girls aren't talented? I take it because I know they mean it as a compliment, but I hope I can change the perception, so people know that girls can play at this level with this athleticism. And that it doesn't have to be that I play like a guy but play like a real aggressive girl.

▶ **Q:** Can you dunk?

▶ **A:** I've come very close. I can definitely get the ball up there, but I haven't done it yet. I definitely think I will.

▶ **Q:** There are still people out there who think that Nebraska has cowboys and Indians. Do you get the same questions about Alaska and Eskimos?

▶ **A:** That's one of the questions I got. Are there igloos? Are there polar bears walking around? Do you take dog sleds to school?

▶ **Q:** Did you?

▶ **A:** No!

▶ **Q:** Are you an outdoors person?

▶ **A:** I love mountain biking. Hiking. Fishing. Awesome. Deep-sea fishing is my favorite, going for halibut. But river fishing for salmon is great, too. Just chilling by a campfire is fun.

▶ **Q:** Ever seen a moose?

▶ **A:** I actually almost ran into one. We were playing tag when I was little, and I was running away from someone and turned the corner, and there was a moose eating out of a tree. You come in close contact with them all the time. But if you don't bother them, they won't bother you. A grizzly bear actually went into my neighbor's garage. That was the big deal in the cul-de-sac. It's like south Lincoln. That's where I live. And there was a grizzly bear.

▶ **Q:** Why Nebraska?

▶ **A:** Coach (Connie) Yori was the most blunt, honest, to-the-point coach who told me exactly what she thought I would become if I came here, whereas it seemed like a lot of smoke and mirrors everywhere else.

▶ **Q:** What should people know about Connie Yori?

▶ **A:** She told me once that she would rather be a good coach and a great mom than a great coach and a good mom. I thought that was really cool.

▶ **Q:** Anyone in sports you'd like to meet?

▶ **A:** Pat Summitt. Just to sit down and pick her brain about the game, what she's done over the years, the way the game changed, the players. What she thinks makes it a good game.

▶ **Q:** People like to say Pat Summitt could coach men. Could a woman play the men's game?

▶ **A:** I think it is case-specific. I know I couldn't. I really don't like playing with guys. I've played enough pick-up to know that I don't like it. I'm not a one-on-one player. I like team basketball. I know there are men's teams that are team basketball, but guys that I've played against aren't really into the team aspect of it.

One thing that is different is the personality aspect of it. You can get in a guy's face and tear him apart and you can be fine as soon as the game is over. But girls hold onto grudges.

▶ **Q:** Any similarities between Nebraska and Alaska?

▶ **A:** The "aska." That's about it. I tried doing some lake fishing here, but it was like, "Was that a bite?"

▶ **Q:** WNBA?

▶ **A:** I hope so. I've gotten a few questions about it, but I'm trying not to think about it too much right now.

▶ **Q:** What will Kelsey Griffin be doing in 10 years?

▶ **A:** Hopefully I'll be going back to medical school. I really like bones and muscles. The human body is an amazing, resilient thing and I want to learn more about it.

A fantasy of mine would be to be an orthopedic surgeon, but I'm not 100 percent sure of that. I'm not scared of blood and guts, you could say, growing up hunting and fishing. I don't really have a weak stomach.

Safe Choice Can Also Be Right Choice

BRUCE RASMUSSEN, THE wise athletic director and occasional stand-up comedian, once was asked if Dana Altman had a lifetime contract at Creighton.

"Yeah," Rasmussen quipped. "If he leaves, I'm dead."

Altman left. But Rasmussen and Creighton basketball are still very much alive. Make that double for Greg McDermott's career.

There's a faction in the audience that is less than impressed. They'll tell you that Rasmussen hiring McDermott has all the risk of a bachelor party where they serve only Dr Pepper. Mac made the safe move, booking out of Ames before a posse could be formed. Ras made the safe hire. They say Coach Mac is too much like Altman. More on that irony later.

For now, I'm going to venture out on this limb: Both Creighton and McDermott just made themselves better.

OK, it's hard to use the word "upgrade" when you look at Altman's complete body of work on 24th Street. Let's go with this: CU and McDermott did not take a step backward or sideways, as some would have you believe. They both took a step forward. CU's record is currently 2-0. This was a win-win.

McDermott just won big. You say he took a step down? No way. He left a Big 12 school for a better job — in the Missouri Valley.

Yes, Coach Mac is a better fit in this league. But it's not just about fit. Iowa State was once a very good job in the Big Eight/Big 12. It had one of the better arenas and fan bases. You could win the conference title there. And the Clones did.

Iowa State can and will win again. But it's a much tougher task. The Big 12 South schools have discovered basketball and are rolling in talent. Kansas State and Missouri are winning big.

When you get into a hole in the Big 12, no matter what sport, climbing out is hard work. Especially at a place that is not bathing in revenue.

Speaking of that, what conference will Iowa State be in five years from now? Good question. ISU has no power in a league that is as stable as a cardboard box in a tornado. The Cyclones might be competing for the Big Mountain West title one day.

There's a saying in coaching circles: Don't leave one of the top jobs in a league for one of the bottom jobs. McDermott just did the opposite. He's making BCS-type money, recruiting to a better facility than Hilton Coliseum and to a city that's thriving. Yes, he's in the Valley, where two NCAA bids in one year is cause for celebration.

But look at what just happened last month: Northern Iowa. Butler. These weren't flukes. They are the future. The gap is closing. In fact, there's a prevailing wisdom that it's better to be a "power" mid-major than at the bottom of a BCS league, stuck in the muck. You can make the Sweet 16 and Final Four from here.

And if you don't, who cares? ISU competes with Kansas and Texas; the expectation is to make the NCAAs and win. At Creighton, how you coach and how hard you play are just as important as winning.

In other words, it's a saner, more secure world — with a lot of the same perks. There's a lot to be said for that.

There's also a lot to be said for knowing your strengths and where you can succeed. That's the key to life. McDermott swears that he wanted to stay and fight at Iowa State, that this was a family decision. Well, part of that may have been long-term security. Look, no matter what anyone says, it wasn't going to end well at ISU. He may have parachuted away from a forced career change, but I honestly believe McDermott when he says he made the move because Creighton was the better fit for him and his family.

"I'm still the same person I was at Wayne State," McDermott said. "I'm never going to change. You adjust, but my values haven't changed, what you stand for. I'm not willing to take shortcuts and do things that could possibly embarrass the university to achieve success. I'm going to do it the way I know how, the way I was brought up."

Creighton fans may say they don't want another Altman, but Rasmussen knows better. He knows what worked. He knows Jays fans better than they know themselves. Why on earth would you go away from that formula?

And here's the beauty of it: McDermott is not an Altman clone. He's better at coaching big men. He'll go on the road and play a BCS school without the return game. He's on Twitter and he'll do a coach's show and he's more personable with boosters and fans. Altman left Omaha without saying a word. McDermott held a press conference from his driveway, telling Iowa State news media and fans what he was doing and why he was doing it.

If — when — McDermott wins here, he'll have Creightonians eating out of his hand.

The pressure, the challenge, will be chasing Altman's record. McDermott was 0-3 in the NCAAs at UNI. Again, what if he had stayed the past four years? If he can win two NCAA games, he would equal Altman's total. Two NCAA wins in one tournament? Make room for the statue.

Rasmussen and McDermott made the safe choice. But since when does safe have to be a bad thing?

Greg McDermott, like Dana Altman before him, came to mid-major Creighton from a school in a top league.

NU Stood at Center as Landscape Shifted

IF THIS WERE a football game, you'd want to keep the program. What a day. Whirlwind day. Important day. Historic day. Hell of a day. One of the biggest days, if not the biggest, in University of Nebraska history.

The historians can debate that one. What can't be denied is the unmistakable feeling that this day changed Nebraska. Within a breathless, mind-blowing four-hour span, Nebraska went from trying to beat out Missouri for a Big Ten invite to trying to play for the 2011 Big Ten championship.

The Board of Regents meeting. The overflow crowd. The application sent for Big Ten membership. Four hours later, Big Ten Commissioner Jim Delany strolled into the campus visitors center with the invite in hand and a red "N" pin on his suit lapel. The "N" logo and Big Ten logo appeared side by side on a projection screen.

Matt Davison, who helped define the Big 12 with his 1997 catch at Missouri, held a Big Ten Network microphone with a big grin on his face.

Finally, the nuptials. Do you, Nebraska, take this league to be your lawfully wedded home for the next 100 years? I can't believe it. College football will never be the same, and it all seemed to start right here, with Lincoln as the epicenter of change, on a day when Big Red football would never be the same.

Goodbye, Manhattan; hello, East Lansing. Goodbye, Boulder; hello, Columbus. Goodbye, Austin; hello, Iowa City.

It was a big day, the biggest day, and nobody was bigger than Harvey Perlman and Tom Osborne.

The chancellor and athletic director/legend-at-large put on a show at the regents meeting. They laid it all out. And while they were at it, they laid out Missouri and Texas. It was powerful. It was clinical. Nebraska, eerily quiet all these weeks, finally spoke up and turned up the volume for all the Big 12 to hear.

Perlman called out Mizzou for being the one to start the expansion circus. Osborne talked about schools in the Big 12 that were asking NU to stay and all the while selling themselves to not one, not two, but three other leagues.

Perlman said the Big 12 presidents wouldn't commit to staying in the league if Colorado and Missouri both left.

And then, in a downright delicious passage, Perlman talked about calling Texas' bluff. And how he asked Texas to commit its TV rights to the Big 12 if it was serious about the league, and how Texas declined. Brilliant, Harvey. The Steve Pederson years are now forgiven.

Then, finally, the money quote from Osborne: "One team leaving does not break up a conference. Two teams leaving does not break up a conference. Six teams leaving breaks up a conference."

Boom. They should engrave those words on a plaque, or on the side of Memorial Stadium. Maybe put them on the final Big 12 football trophy.

Osborne and Perlman were rolling, and, for many, it was like 14 years of frustration flowing out.

The lack of emotion toward the old Big Eight ties was the one downside to this day. It should not be taken lightly.

What happened here was the end of a 100-year relationship. Nebraska started the Missouri Valley Conference with Kansas, Missouri and Iowa State, Iowa and Washington U. of St. Louis. Kansas State, Oklahoma, Colorado and Oklahoma State would later make it the Big Six, Big Seven and Big Eight.

Nebraska cut the cord with all of that, in the name of loyalty. Loyalty to itself. In a world that changes like a Twitter post, Nebraska stood up for itself and secured a spot in this game of musical chairs. Even the master of understatement seemed to get the magnitude of the moment. Said Osborne: "This is a very important day for Nebraska."

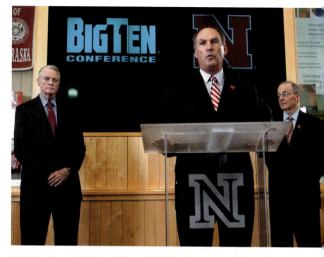

Big Ten Commissioner Jim Delany welcomes the University of Nebraska to the Big Ten at a press conference with Athletic Director Tom Osborne and Chancellor Harvey Perlman.

2011 INSIGHT *The end of the Big 12 for Nebraska and the beginning of the Big Ten was a whirlwind. In fact, my head is still spinning. One day, Texas is threatening to leave for the Pac-10. The next week, Big Ten Commish Jim Delany is walking into a press conference at the campus visitors center. For a Big Eight rogue such as myself, it was emotional. But there was no time for emotions. This was great history happening, and happening by the day, the hour. I wrote my column on a small table 15 feet from the press conference, crammed next to two old friends, Dennis Dodd of CBSsports.com and Blair Kerkhoff of the Kansas City Star. Blair occasionally got updates on his phone on the rest of the Big 12. Dennis brought out an old Big Eight Skywriters hat and put it on the table. Tom Osborne came by and commented on the hat. So did Delany. The whole day was like a dream, a fantasy. Driving back to Omaha, I wondered what just happened. I don't think it's hit a lot of us yet.*

JULY 1, 2010 • COLLEGE WORLD SERIES

Unforgettable Finish to Unforgettable 60 years

NOBODY WRITES AN ending like Rosenblatt Stadium. For days now, even weeks, people have tried to come up with the perfect crescendo for the College World Series at the diamond on the hill. They talked about walk-off homers, plays at the plate, last at-bat heroics. LSU vs. Texas. Zesto vs. Stadium View. You name it.

We should have known all along that this grand old yard, a stadium with a soul and an imagination, would give us the perfect ending.

Perfect? How could it get any better than what we were treated to on an unforgettable night at the CWS?

Extra innings. Eleven innings. People standing in all corners of the stadium. People sitting outside the stadium, refusing to leave, watching on a big screen. The "ping" of the bat. The roar of the crowd. The winning run scores. South Carolina 2, UCLA 1.

The Gamecocks won their first baseball national championship. But both teams, the fans, the CWS and Rosenblatt Stadium were all winners.

Greatest game ever? Who knows what that is? This one will be in the conversation as long as the CWS lives downtown and in this town.

Warren Morris spoiled us. The former LSU second baseman's walk-off homer to win the 1996 CWS is the moment that too often defines this event.

And as soon as South Carolina tied this game in the eighth, you could feel it in this sellout crowd: Everyone was waiting for the ghost of Warren to show up in Carolina garnet.

Exactly why, in the top of the ninth, I left the press box to go sit on the steps behind home plate: It's where I watched Morris swing the bat and change everything way back when, 14 years ago.

But there's only one Warren Morris. And there are many ways to write a perfect ending.

What's a perfect ending for a classic event in a classic stadium?

It's 11 innings of tight, taut, intense, every-pitch-counts baseball. UCLA, rebounding from an off night in game one of the championship series, gave us that with South Carolina. It was everything a CWS championship game should be and more.

It's a sellout crowd of nearly 25,000 sitting and wondering for three hours if they would see history.

It's the buzz of the crowd when South Carolina tied the game at 1 in the bottom of the eighth.

It's the silence before every late-inning pitch, a silence caused by an entire crowd holding its breath.

It's the sight of cameras flashing with every single pitch.

It's all but a handful of fans refusing to leave the game, and those who did congregating outside on the plaza, watching the action on a big screen.

It's people standing in back rows, along the bridge that connects to the bleachers and along the aisles down the left- and right-field lines. When people are standing and groaning for every pitch, there's no better atmosphere and no better way for a stadium to take its final bows.

2011 INSIGHT *How do you write history when you know going in that it's going to be history? That was the question on this last College World Series game at Rosenblatt Stadium. Actually, it was game two of the championship series, so there was no guarantee. Still, I tried to take notes of details, small or big, that happened that night. Just in case. At the end of the game, with the score tied, I decided to plop myself down on the spot where I saw Warren Morris make history 14 years earlier: on the steps behind home plate. One, it was a great vantage point. Two, that's where I wanted to be for the last CWS game at Rosenblatt. I'll remember the camera flashes, on every pitch. It gave it a surreal movie effect, like in "The Natural." When the game ended, I tried to take note of the moment, the roar of the crowd, the faces, etc. I ran outside the stadium, because I wanted to see the expressions on the faces of Omahans as they left. Looking back, I see I didn't use much of that. It must not have been memorable. I think I could relate. I think we were all a little beaten down by the emotions of the CWS, and the past few years, waiting and waiting for the end. In the end, it almost felt like relief that it was over.*

It's two pitchers, Matt Price of South Carolina and Dan Klein of UCLA, digging down deep and refusing to blink. Those two may have had to pitch all night, and they looked up to the task.

It's the double bonus of all this drama being for the national championship and the lasting memory of Rosenblatt.

It's the late-game cheers for South Carolina, and you didn't know whether the locals had adopted a new team or were cheering to witness the end or both.

It's Scott Wingo — a second baseman, like Morris — walking and advancing to second on a wild pitch to open the 11th. It's Wingo advancing to third on a sacrifice bunt.

It's the anticipation of the crowd that now is the time, right here at 10:55 p.m., with one out and a man on third and Whit Merrifield up.

It's the roar of the crowd when Merrifield dug low and lined a sinker to right field.

It's more flashes, the dogpile, and the realization that this was it. It's over.

It's those chants of "U-S-C, U-S-C." And what a cool thing, in a throwback sort of way, that South Carolina goes by the same initials as the Southern California program that put this event and stadium on the map long ago.

It's the streaker, sort of, who made an ill-timed appearance. Underwear? Understand, we're not complaining. On this night, modesty seemed not only appropriate, but necessary.

It's all of those history-witnessing folks filing out slowly with smiles on their faces.

That's how you close a great event at a great ballpark.

What made this the perfect ending for the CWS at Rosenblatt was how the entire evening was like a trip down memory lane. All of the elements that made us love this event, nurture it and ultimately protect it for 25 more years were on display, in four hours and 15 minutes of pure CWS baseball joy.

There were fireworks. They turned off the lights to show a terrific video of all the great moments and familiar faces. A trumpet player stood at home plate in the dark and belted out "Take Me Out to the Ball Game" in a slow rhythm that sounded somewhat like taps.

And South Carolina coach Ray Tanner complimented Omaha, saying, "You really know how to do it." Somewhere, Jack Diesing Sr. and Johnny Rosenblatt himself were nodding in approval. Down here on heaven on earth, Steve Rosenblatt stood behind home plate with a big smile on his face. Perfect ending, indeed.

"I just kept saying, 'It's going to happen tonight, it's going to happen,'" Rosenblatt said. "It's going to be over. I just wanted to see a great baseball game, and I think that's what most people wanted. I think the fans enjoyed it. It was thrilling."

There was relief on this night, and that comes with knowing we can finally put the emotions of the final CWS here to rest and turn to the north.

The diamond on the hill will be open for business again this weekend. But for many, this amazing, perfect ending is how they will remember it.

We'll never forget this game or this night. And we will never forget the College World Series at Rosenblatt Stadium.

Friday Night Lights, Rosenblatt Style

I'D LOVE TO see what the United Football League can do about property taxes.

Who are these people? They whisk into town, quietly and confidently sell their brand of football, create the cool logo and the must-have jerseys. They sign a four-time Pro Bowl quarterback and then the local running back legend.

They pack the home opener — 24,000. Then they arrange for the weather to be the best day of the year, 72 degrees, not a trace of wind.

Then they give us this dramatic, down-to-the-wire, last-gasp-from-the-old-gunslinger ending. Jeff Garcia to Robert Ferguson. Touchdown. Six seconds left. Omaha Nighthawks win.

If you were there at Rosenblatt Stadium, catch your breath. If you weren't, find a ticket to the next game.

I'm still trying to figure out what a UFL is. Here's a place to start: It's fun. Big fun. Crazy fun.

The football was good. The atmosphere was better. At times it was hard to tell if the Nighthawks' franchise debut against Hartford was a football game with a concert or the other way around. Or both.

I wasn't here for Creighton in the College World Series. I saw NU in the CWS. This was different. This was unlike anything anyone's ever seen at this historic ball yard.

Warren Morris' famous home run to right field to win the 1996 CWS was loud. This was louder.

By the way, Morris' home run, if hit last night to the same exact spot in right field, would have been wide right.

The Omaha Nighthawks' Robert Ferguson performs the Rosenblatt Leap after catching the game-winning touchdown pass.

OCTOBER 8, 2010 • NEBRASKA FOOTBALL

T-Magic Provides the Final Word

MANHATTAN, KAN.

K-STATE WANTED to send Nebraska off to the Big Ten in style, with a reminder that Little Brother would be just fine without Big Brother.

The Wildcats wanted to inflict some pain on an old foe that, in their minds, was turning its back on the prairie.

They were worked up, in a purple froth, and this last Nebraska vs. Kansas State game was more of a statement for K-State than a game. They brought signs, including one that said it all: "Trea$on."

This would be their statement that the Wildcats would be OK without the Huskers. But there was no revenge, unless you count the game in Lincoln in 2003, when Bo Pelini thought Bill Snyder was scoring a little too much on his backup defense.

In the end, what we saw was a history lesson for those who don't remember life before Snyder got here — and a familiar result for those who do.

Nebraska 48, Kansas State 13. Remember those?

The Huskers slowly and clinically dominated this one. By early in the third quarter, the ESPN national stage had turned from Snyder's last stand to the re-emergence of Nebraska as a power player.

And the introduction of a little thing called T-Magic.

Where did this kid come from? And where he is going? The Taylor Martinez story is the talk of college football now. The redshirt freshman quarterback has been a phenomenon in Lincoln the last several weeks. He opened the eyes that were watching the regional broadcast in Seattle a few weeks ago.

But he took it up a few notches in front of the college ball-watching nation.

Martinez ran 15 times for 241 yards and four touchdowns — a whopping 16.1 yards per carry. He was an efficient 5-for-7 passing for 128 yards and a touchdown.

But it was how he did it. Martinez doesn't run, he strikes. He turns broken plays into brilliant strokes. His TD runs were 14, 35, 80 and 41 yards. The 80-yard run was on a quarterback draw through a hole the size of Aggieville. If you blinked, you missed it.

Taylor Martinez ran for 241 yards and four touchdowns against the Wildcats.

NOVEMBER 21, 2010 • NEBRASKA FOOTBALL

Bo Must Rise Above Officiating

COLLEGE STATION, TEXAS

BO PELINI LOST his mind. The Huskers lost their composure. Nebraska lost a game 9-6 to Texas A&M.

Can they still hold on to this season?

Pelini will have a hard time living down this night. He screamed. He raged. Lip-readers in the television audience were covering their children's eyes. Pelini screamed at tight end Ben Cotton. He yelled at quarterback Taylor Martinez in a surprising scene. He even spewed some fire at reliable kicker Alex Henery.

Then there were the officials. Pelini saved his best fury for the zebras. There were a school-record 16 yellow flags against NU for 145 yards, only two against the Aggies. Pelini let them hear about it in no uncertain terms.

At one point, with his team backed up deep in its own territory in a 6-6 game with field position paramount, he got an unsportsmanlike conduct flag. That's like a hoops coach getting a technical foul late in a tie game.

Then, after the game's final play, Pelini immediately chased after referee Greg Burks to get a few more choice words in.

Pelini has worked hard on curbing his hotheadedness, but it came back in living color, overshadowing a valiant night from his defense and a gutsy performance by Martinez on one ankle in the most hostile environment you could imagine.

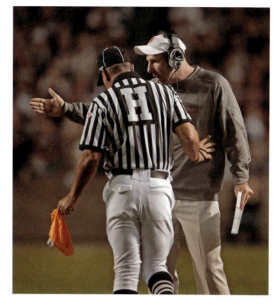

Did he have reason to chew on some zebra? You bet.

Look, the Big 12 officials have had a bad year. They've been uneven, inconsistent, just awful at times. It's gone both ways, though conspiracy theorists would beg to differ.

Those theorists seemed to get ammunition last week from an espn.com report that said NU ranked first in fewest penalty yards by opponents.

I'm guessing last night's ratio probably added to the margin.

Nebraska coach Bo Pelini voices displeasure over one of a school-record 16 infractions called by officials.

Although maybe the Huskers just forgot how to play football, the easy theory is to say there's some striped revenge going on. There was some weird science out there, stuff that officials never have to answer to. Courtney Osborne's personal foul after hitting Ryan Tannehill in the chest? Top of the list.

Honestly, I still have my doubts that this is some huge Big 12 conspiracy. I don't think Big 12 officials are good enough to collectively figure out a game plan and execute it.

The truth is, officials are human. They make mistakes — like coaches and players. And Nebraska's move to the Big Ten almost led to the Big 12's destruction. A lot of officials could have been out of jobs.

Would they hold a grudge? I don't know. We can't talk to the officials. We're all left guessing and hoping/assuming there's integrity there.

Here's this, though: How would the Huskers losing to Texas A&M help the Big 12? NU entered the game with an outside shot at the BCS title game and giving the league a second BCS bowl team. And if there's a conspiracy to keep Nebraska out of the Big 12 title game, it couldn't have ended last night. NU still has a shot.

But that's up to the Huskers, not the officials.

2011 INSIGHT *I'm not afraid to say it. I whiffed on this one. Whiffed bad. And you let me know it, the next morning, all 200,019 of you. It's not that Bo Pelini needed me to defend him. But the story on this wild and weird night in College Station wasn't how Nebraska should have risen above 16 penalties. It wasn't even necessarily scolding Pelini for putting on his werewolf mask. The story was why Bo went Lon Chaney on the zebras. He was clearly defending his players in a situation where he thought they were getting royally screwed by the Big 12 — with nothing to do about it. The story was also how the Big 12 could allow this to happen. I mean, it was just so extreme and so obvious. The league looked bush league. It looked as bad as Bo did. I can blame it on night deadlines. I don't have time to go downstairs and talk to the coaches or players after night games. I have to have the column in 30 minutes after a night game ends. But that wasn't it. Blaming losses on officials is a pet peeve of mine; there are 100 different plays in a game that a team could have done differently to win. But in this case, the 16 penalties were sitting up there on a tee, and I whiffed. Oh, and that "late" hit by Courtney Osborne? Not even close to a 50-50 call. I had a horrible angle on a replay TV for that one, and they showed the replay only once. I also never saw the below-the-belt foul against Ben Cotton. If this game did nothing else, it changed one thing: From now on, I'm moving my press-box seat next to a TV.*

TOM'S TAKE — REFLECTIONS ON

Is There a National Title on the Horizon for UNO?

LIKE A LOT of Omahans, I didn't know Dean Blais from Dean Martin.

He had won two NCAA hockey championships at North Dakota. He sounded like a good hire for Athletic Director Trev Alberts at UNO. But this is UNO we're talking about. What could he possibly do? Win a national championship?

Well, it's only the first year.

"When I took over at North Dakota, the first year we were .500," Blais said the other day. "The second year, we were about six, seven games above .500. The third year, we won the national championship. I could see the same thing here."

I'm sorry. Did he just say he thought that UNO could win the national championship in two years?

He did, in fact. And just a word to the wise: Don't bet your farm against him.

So far, Blais has delivered. And then some. If anything, he may be exceeding the hype as college hockey legend/savior.

It's the way he wields an unfailing confidence and the way he picks up believers like hitchhikers along the way. Blais has an aura about him, a swagger. He talks about greatness matter-of-factly, like it's to be expected. And that's just it: It is.

In that way, Blais is unique among coaches in this area. Tom Osborne delivered the goods, but he made it sound like his team would be lucky to win seven games every year.

Blais doesn't brag or make predictions. He's just making statements. National championship in year three? Why not? About his recruits on the way, he says, "We've got NHL-type players coming in."

It's refreshing, and a little bizarre, to have a coach like this at UNO. But that was the point of the hire.

"He has surpassed every expectation I have had, especially in creating an image and an energy for our department in this community," Alberts said. "I feel so fortunate. We have the best hockey coach in the country."

Alberts discovered that Blais reminded him of someone else.

"I was talking with one of our players, Nick Von Bokern, about this week's opponent," Alberts said. "He said he didn't know anything about them. He said, 'We don't pay attention to what the opponent does. We just worry about ourselves and what we run.' I found that amazing. That's just how much confidence he has in what they do. They expect to win every game. That's how we were at Nebraska. We expected to win every game, even as 17-point underdogs to Florida State. Dean has brought that same attitude."

Another story: "After we swept Michigan, I was in the locker room and there's loud music and the kids are hooting and hollering," Alberts said. "Dean looked at the room and said, 'Isn't that great? That's what it's all about.' A minute later, he walked into the room and everything stopped. No music. It was quiet. That's how much respect they have for him. It reminded me of when Coach Osborne would step into the elevator and everyone on there would go, boom, quiet."

— FEBRUARY 25, 2010

> "When I took over at North Dakota, the first year we were .500. The second year, we were about six, seven games above .500. The third year, we won the national championship. I could see the same thing here."
>
> — DEAN BLAIS, UNO HOCKEY COACH

THE CHANGING SPORTS LANDSCAPE 2010

NU-OU Series Didn't Have to Go Away

SOME NEBRASKA FANS will be carrying extra baggage down to Arlington, Texas, this week. All that anger toward Texas. Dan Beebe. The Big 12 in general.

But what about the school in crimson on the opposing sideline?

This week is a sentimental journey for a generation 35 and older. Those Nebraskans miss playing Oklahoma. They miss their best friend. They blame the Big 12, and even Texas, for ending the series that was like family. But that anger has been misdirected.

The fact is, it was Oklahoma that ended the series, Oklahoma that walked away from dear old friend Nebraska. It says here that if Oklahoma and Nebraska had continued their series on an annual basis, NU would not be leaving for the Big Ten.

Go back a few years. Oklahoma Athletic Director Donnie Duncan and Texas Athletic Director DeLoss Dodds got together and assembled the Big 12 — the Big Eight plus four SWC schools.

Where was NU Athletic Director Bill Byrne in this scenario? That may have been the first sign of things to come.

As divisions and schedule rotations were set up, Duncan made a decision that would change history. With OU and NU in separate divisions, he decided that Oklahoma would no longer play the Huskers annually. Duncan told this story last May while he attended the historic Big 12 meetings on Kansas City's Plaza. I asked him why he chose to end a meaningful rivalry like NU and OU. His reply: "Oklahoma already had a rival in Texas. There was no need to play both Nebraska and Texas every year."

As I recall, there was little uproar in Oklahoma about this. Most of the noise was coming from north of the Kansas border.

How could OU do this? The Sooners already had blood rivals in Oklahoma State and Texas, which would be annual games. And, as Duncan said, why should OU have to play Texas and Nebraska every year when nobody else in the Big 12 South would have to do that?

It's a lame excuse. Play Texas and NU in the same year? In the Southeastern Conference, they call that October.

Go back to the 1990s again. Nebraska had Tommie Frazier. OU had Howard Schnellenberger. Maybe that was part of the incentive. Texas wasn't a threat then. Neither was Oklahoma State. Did Duncan dump Nebraska while the getting was good?

The bottom line is, Oklahoma pulled the plug because it never cared as much about this "rivalry" as Nebraska. And, in hindsight, now we know: NU-OU was more of a classic series than a rivalry. True rivalries aren't allowed to end, no matter the conference structure. See Ohio State-Michigan.

Yes, there would be other reasons for NU to feel uncomfortable in the Big 12. But with OU-NU still intact, Nebraska would have been able to stomach Big 12 heartburn. There would have been something meaningful for NU to hold on to.

I don't think that Nebraska, especially with Tom Osborne at the helm, could have walked away from the Big 12 if it meant turning its back on the Oklahoma game. Without it, there was nothing historical or emotional to tie NU to the league.

I asked Osborne if Nebraska would have had a hard time leaving if the Sooners were still an annual staple on the schedule. And I asked if dropping the game got NU off on the wrong foot with the league.

Oklahoma got the last laugh in the series with a 23-20 victory over Nebraska in the Big 12 championship game.

"I would say that had Nebraska and Oklahoma played each other every year, it would have made it more difficult to leave the Big 12 Conference," Osborne wrote in a reply. "One thing the Big Ten made sure of in its realignment was to preserve the traditional rivalries, and I think those games tend to bind a conference together. I don't know that we had a sour mood going into the Big 12 because of the loss of the annual game with Oklahoma, but it did put a different complexion on things."

But it will end, and how ironic that Nebraska's dear old friend Oklahoma may have been the one to pull the plug.

— DECEMBER 2, 2010

NU UPSETS TEXAS IN BASKETBALL | MAVS MAKE MOVE TO DIVISION I | ALTMAN RETURNS TO OMAHA

2011

> "College hockey right now is pretty solid. Are we going to jeopardize that, as a body? Minnesota and Wisconsin probably make $4 million to $5 million a year in hockey … if you give them $7 million, does that matter? Is it worth the extra money to ruin college hockey?"
>
> — UNO HOCKEY COACH DEAN BLAIS ON PLANS FOR A BIG TEN HOCKEY LEAGUE

Did Creighton just hire its soccer version of Dean Blais? Athletic Director Bruce Rasmussen likes the comparison, though he points out CU soccer has had more success than UNO hockey over the years. That said, Rasmussen admits he was a little surprised to get North Carolina men's soccer legend Elmar Bolowich to move to Morrison Stadium next season. "I used to be on the (NCAA) soccer committee," Rasmussen said. "I know a lot of people and made a lot of calls. Someone told me I ought to give Elmar a call. I said, 'Who is he recommending?' They said, 'No, he's interested in the job.' My response was like everyone else: Why? My first take was surprise. It shouldn't have been. We feel our soccer program is in the top five in the country, with our facility, and our history of six elite eights, three final fours, and we don't share the spotlight with football." The latter is the big reason Bolowich stunned the college soccer world: He noted he was tired of running a national title program in the shadow of Tar Heel hoops and women's soccer. I hope he's OK with Nebraska football assistant coaching searches.

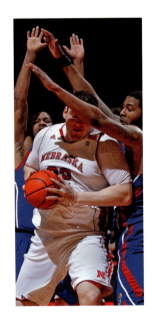

KU beat the Huskers 86-66 at a hopped-up Devaney Center. There were no keepsake memories for NU in this one, no buzzer beaters unless you count the fans leaving with five minutes to go.

In February 2007, Big Ten Commissioner Jim Delany released a letter to Big Ten fans in response to media criticism that the Big Ten looked old and slow in the dust of the sporty, up-to-date SEC. In the letter, Delany offered several bullet points comparing the Big Ten with the SEC in everything from NFL alumni to Heisman winners to head-to-head records. Everything but campus statues. What it all means, dear Husker fans, is that you are joining a conference whose leader is obsessed with the SEC. And while tradition and culture and national profile are all viable things, I think we now know the main reason NU was targeted by Big Ten expansionists last spring. Delany needs some muscle in the fight against the SEC bullies.

282 • 20 YEARS WITH TOM SHATEL

WERNER'S A WINNER | TD AMERITRADE PARK OPENS | NEW HOME FOR CWS | OSBORNE'S NEW LEGACY

There are accusations that Athletic Director Trev Alberts didn't want Division I wrestling to work at UNO. This would be a good time for a reminder that UNO coach Mike Denney, whose teams dominated Division II wrestling for years, has long been reluctant to move to Division I. In a column Sept. 2, 2010, World-Herald columnist Mike Kelly wrote that Alberts told him that his coaching staff was nearly unanimous about moving to Division I — the lone dissenter was Denney. Kelly also spoke with Denney and wrote, "Denney told me he doesn't want to be an anchor holding UNO down. But he said the move to Division I would include a transition period in which UNO athletes couldn't compete for NCAA championships, which would hurt recruiting." I'm sure Denney would prefer Division I wrestling to no wrestling. But that lends some perspective to this story.

Nebraska football attendance is mandatory, of course. But for anyone else trying to coax disposable income off the street and into their buildings, nothing spells interest like N-C-A-A. Look at Creighton basketball attendance. It's not about the suds. It's about the winning. It's about the hope and the buzz. The Jays went to seven NCAA tournaments from 1999-2007. CU earned its crowds of 15,000 to 17,000 by giving the people what they demand: a winner and a place to be seen. The season-ticket numbers are still up there, though the crowds aren't. Why? CU hasn't been dancing since 2007. Now look at UNO hockey. Dean Blais' teams are drawing record crowds. Why? Blais has brought a reputation of playing in NCAA tourneys and winning national championships. People believe. Same thing for Nebraska baseball. When the College World Series came into the conversation, Haymarket Park was standing room only. Remember the big crowds for Nebraska women's hoops last year? When Danny Nee's teams were an NCAA tourney and bubble regular back in the 1990s, Husker Hoops experienced the same buzz at the turnstiles. This is not just a football state. It's a winners state.

The poster boy of a bright blue future is Doug McDermott. You can close your eyes and see Creighton's Dougie Fresh with the strands of a net around his neck, the Valley Player-of-the-Year trophy in one hand and the league tourney MVP in another. Open your eyes and you see a 210-pound freshman with an off-season date in the weight room and Davis Diner. McDermott sent out a photo on his Twitter account of a plate of grease he was about to consume. It looked like the Mount Everest of calories. "Eggs, hash browns, toast and bacon," McDermott described his late-night meal. "And a chocolate shake."

Joe Ganz left us wanting more after his senior year in 2008. He became a starter too late in his career, and he left you thinking that if he could have had one more year, he would have gone down as one of the great NU quarterbacks. I feel the same way about Husker point guard Lance Jeter. With one more year, he would have put the team on his back and made the NCAA tournament — and he almost did that this season.

FEBRUARY 20, 2011 • NEBRASKA BASKETBALL

Huskers Mess With No. 3 Texas

HE STOOD ON the side of the court, on the edge of the madness, looking like a ghost. A friendly ghost with a crooked smile on his face.

"I've seen this before," Bruce Chubick said.

The students were rushing all around the new Nebraska Basketball Hall of Fame member, flooding the Devaney Center court. Husker players were hugging. Coach Doc Sadler had a tear in his eye as he hugged Assistant Athletic Director Marc Boehm, who already was sobbing. The place was up for grabs.

The Huskers had beaten No. 3 Texas, 70-67, and suddenly now everything was different. There really is nothing in sports like a college basketball upset. Three hours before, you were nothing. Now you're looking for a slide rule to figure out NCAA tournament bracketology.

The people with memories were saying this was the best win for Nebraska basketball since NU beat No. 3 Missouri in the 1994 Big Eight tournament, the day Danny Nee shouted down Norm Stewart. This was the biggest home win since NU beat No. 2 Oklahoma State and No. 3 Kansas in 1992.

Those were great days, glory days, days when the Huskers played big games in February and they were part of the NCAA conversation and it seemed anything was possible. What happened here, with the big plays and big shots and big noise, felt like those days all over again.

It felt good.

For today, what matters is that there's something to talk about, because there hasn't been something to talk about this late in the season in a long, long time.

"We're excited, right now," Sadler said. "You want to be in the situation to make the next day and the next game bigger than the last one. We're in that situation now."

Doc needed a big one. The program, the fans needed a big one.

Mostly, they needed proof.

It's about 6-foot-11, 340-pound Andre Almeida spinning around the paint like a dancing bear, block-

The clock runs out, and so do Husker basketball fans as No. 3 Texas falls in Lincoln.

ing shots, throwing the backdoor bounce pass while the Texas bigs watch in surprise. It's about another "Bear," Eshaunte Jones, throwing in a 3.

It's about Brandon Richardson taking advantage of a spread floor and driving to the hoop with no fear. It's about Nebraska holding Jordan Hamilton to 3-of-16 shooting, about owning the paint against a national title contender, about holding on when Texas erased an 11-point lead in a blink.

"We know how good we are," Toney McCray said. "We know how good we can be."

A lot of other folks know now, too. Enjoy the ride. It's been awhile since Nebraska has been down this road.

Bo's Blueprint Must Be His Own

TALK ABOUT UNDERWHELMING hires.

When Tom Osborne took over the wheel of college football power Nebraska in 1973, he immediately put his stamp on the program.

He hired a guy from San Jose State. Then, he hired the head coach at McCook High School.

Along the way, in 1977, he plucked a defensive coach out of Wisconsin, which was not exactly a Big Ten dynasty at the time.

Then came the head coach at Lincoln Southeast, an assistant coach from Brown University and the head coach at Westside High School.

Of course, you may know them, in order, as George Darlington, Milt Tenopir, Charlie McBride, Frank Solich, Ron Brown and Dan Young. They were the pillars of one of the greatest coaching staffs in college football history, responsible for helping Osborne win 255 games and three national championships over 25 years.

So Bo Pelini might be hiring a few no-names? So Pelini is putting together "his" staff with the weight of Nebraska football on his shoulders?

So the fourth-year head Husker is surrounding himself with an inner circle based on trust, relying on his still-developing instincts to roll the dice on people who don't have loaded résumés or star power?

For an old lion in winter, it sounds all too familiar. This was Osborne, the first 10 years or so of his brilliant career. Over the years, he changed assistants several times, remade his offense and defense. He was allowed to do so because his mentor was his athletic director, who worked just downstairs but seemed farther away.

He took the long way, but Osborne finally finds himself in Bob Devaney's shoes. He is Devaney for Pelini: the mentor and the standard who stays out of the way so the young guy can figure it out on his own.

"I'm staying out of it," Osborne said the other day. "Bo has a vision of what he wants and how he wants to do it."

Nebraska football coach Bo Pelini with his new offensive coordinator, Tim Beck.

Osborne knows as Devaney knew: Each coach must find his Ocean's Eleven. Osborne eventually found his in Tenopir, Darlington, Solich, McBride, Brown and Young. Just as Devaney had Jim Ross, John Melton, Mike Corgan, Cletus Fischer and Monte Kiffin.

Here's the big difference: Pelini never had to lead Osborne's men (save for Brown, who is on Bo's staff).

Osborne chuckled as he recalled his situation. Not only was he charged with keeping Devaney's Cadillac on the road, he had to do it with a staff of Devaney assistants, some of whom had wanted the job Osborne got and others who resented Osborne for, well, being young.

"It was a little bit awkward," Osborne said. "I was 35, and some of these guys were old enough to be my father."

Some, like Jim Walden and Carl Selmer, left on their own to become head coaches. So did Kiffin and Warren Powers. But, as Osborne said, "I was young, and they knew if they wanted to be a head coach, they were going to have to leave."

That left Osborne to figure out what to do with Fischer, Melton, Ross and Corgan. Fortunately, the mentor was there with a solution.

"The good thing was Devaney was athletic director," Osborne said.

The transformation started in the mid- to late 1970s, as Osborne was going through his Bluebonnet Bowl-Liberty Bowl phase and the heat was on to beat Oklahoma and get to an Orange Bowl.

"Tom didn't become a great coach until he was surrounded by his own people who were loyal to him," said Tom Ash, The World-Herald Nebraska football beat writer during that era. "There were some uncomfortable bunkmates in the early going, but I thought they all handled it with as little rancor as possible, thanks in no small part to Bob's presence. But Tom was not truly the captain of his own ship until all the assistants were his hires."

In 1997, Osborne recommended to his successor, Solich, that he keep some of Osborne's staff. And again, when Osborne hired Pelini in 2007, he was there to recommend that Shawn Watson stay around to run the offense.

Did Osborne hamstring Solich and Pelini? No. In the short term, it was the right call (keeping Watson with seniors Joe Ganz, Todd Peterson and Nate Swift made sense — for one season). Ultimately, it was up to Solich and Pelini to cut the cords with the past, as Osborne learned. And it took both several years to do that.

"Everybody has to figure out what's best for them," Osborne said.

Including Pelini.

"I'm not really involved in what Bo's doing," Osborne said. "That doesn't work. I try to be a resource. I try not to be intrusive."

Has Pelini shared his vision for the offense and coaching staff with Osborne?

"Not really," Osborne said. "He knows what he wants to do. And I'm here if he needs me."

Mavericks' Move Up Is Smart but Bittersweet

TODAY SHOULD BE a day of celebration at UNO. But it will feel like a wake.

The news on the front page heralds a day for which we've long waited. UNO intends to go Division I. But there won't be a parade or confetti.

I applaud the plan but do so with a heavy heart. The Mavericks will be growing up, but the powers that be are recommending that two great friends of Omaha, UNO football and Mav wrestling, be left behind.

It's all pending the approval of the NU Board of Regents, but finally, after years of indecision, UNO has announced its identity. Dodge Street High has decided what it wants to be when it grows up.

UNO will be a hockey school and a Division I basketball school. It will be a Summit League school, with a shot at the NCAA tournament, playing in an intriguing mix with former North Central Conference members and schools from Indianapolis, Tulsa and Kansas City.

UNO is not the state's school. UNO can never be UNL. It can't be North Dakota, which is the UNL of its state, with all the subsidized benefits of being the big dog.

For years, people — including myself — have wanted UNO to figure out what it wanted to be. Hockey was a brilliant idea in 1996. UNO had been the nice little Division II school down the street. But it was looking for an identity in Omaha, its slice of the pie. Creighton had basketball. UNO had hockey.

But the byproduct of hockey was having one foot in Division I and the other in Division II. For the most part, the hockey people and other coaches made nice. But the combination wore thin. The hockey people were competing against other Division I schools and budgets and wanted to raise the budgetary and marketing ante. But UNO had a Division II mentality, too. Eventually, you had a water-and-oil mix of treating hockey big-time — going into the Qwest Center — with a Division II athletic budget.

Through it all, UNO has had to deal with its own awkward growing pains: booming expansion, the dorms, the Ak-Sar-Ben move, and the scandal in the administration building. It was maddening to watch. How could UNO ever reach its full potential with incompetent leadership? You'd watch UNO and say, this could be so much better. If only they had a clue. If only they had a plan. A commitment to something, anything.

That commitment, that identity, comes today.

I applaud it. I applaud UNO deciding, once and for all, what it wants to be in this world. I don't applaud good men and teachers like Pat Behrns and Mike Denney losing their jobs or the programs they built. I don't applaud young men losing their chance to compete as champions. This is heartbreaking collateral damage for a move that could make UNO athletics financially viable and competitive in the bigger picture.

There's incredible irony here, too. For years, Behrns has quietly pushed for UNO to move up to Division I and play in the Football Championship Subdivision, formerly known as I-AA. Behrns has tangled with the administration at times, but it was all with good intentions and a vision in mind. Behrns felt UNO athletics had big potential in the city, with the money people and the casual fans. FCS football was part of that vision. It beat the alternative, which was staying in a Division II world that is becoming flooded with schools that are "lower-level" and "lower-commitment" football schools, those with 24 scholarships.

It's the sort of philosophy that says if you're not getting better, you're getting worse.

So UNO finally announced that it wants to be Division I and left Behrns behind.

This is a tough one. Al Caniglia. Sandy Buda. Behrns. Marlin Briscoe. Ed Thompson. Even in the mammoth shadow of Nebraska's Cornhuskers, UNO football made its own footprint in this community. The Mavericks may not have been good enough to play in Lincoln, but they were good enough to play championship football on gorgeous fall afternoons at Caniglia Field against the best competition in Division II.

But football, by virtue of its unwieldy size, is always the elephant in the room when it comes to athletic budgets. You either feed it or cut it. There's no in-between. Getting better or getting worse.

Trev Alberts says he can't afford to take UNO football along for the ride, and that's the honest truth. We're talking about going from 36 scholarships to 63. UNO football has its share of Omaha businessmen who love their Mavs, but not nearly enough who can step up and cover the difference. And that's not taking into account the added expenses in travel, stadium expansion, etc., of going to FCS. UNO also would have to add women's sports to balance the gender equity scales. UNO already is maxing out on subsidies. The State of Nebraska is not going to step up to save UNO football.

It's a nice pipe dream some of us had, UNO going FCS. But the brutal reality is, UNO was never in position to make that move financially. Why? The city. Count the larger cities that have competitive college football with a full-time commitment. Nebraska is a football state, but a Husker football state. Many of the Division II football powers are the thing to do in their town or area. UNO is one of many things to do around here.

At its best, Mav football is going to draw just under 10,000. Lately, and Behrns can take some of the blame here, attendance has dropped dramatically. Last year, UNO averaged 3,777 for seven games. Take away the big crowds for Nebraska-Kearney and Northwest Missouri State, and UNO averaged 2,446 fans.

It's unthinkable, but Maverick football — once the bell cow for UNO — became expendable.

College wrestling is a niche sport, but UNO wrestling made a national imprint — it won its third straight Division II national championship on Saturday. For years, Denney has been a hidden gem in Omaha, a coach's coach whom you could see thriving in any sport. His wrestlers have been a credit to UNO and the city, champions to the end. They deserve a better fate, but it's not about that. At some point, nonrevenue sports are all the same, interchangeable parts, soccer and golf for wrestling, in the grand scheme of gender equity compliance and the business of college sports. But if you care about good people, losing Mav wrestling is a punch in the gut, one that no doubt knocked the wind out of Chancellor John Christensen, a big wrestling fan.

In the end, this is about a bigger picture. That vision belongs to Christensen and Alberts. Who knew? When Christensen hired Alberts, the cynics cracked that he was hiring a figurehead, a cheerleader, someone to put a happy face on an athletic program stuck in the mud. Alberts has been a bull — who took the UNO bull by the horns.

Division I was Alberts' primary goal from day one. How he would get here would be interesting. But wow. This is incredibly creative, though certainly cruel. And it's flat-out full of guts. We all assume Alberts wants to eventually throw his hat in the ring to replace Tom Osborne at Nebraska one day. The primary duty of that job is to take care of Nebraska football, no questions asked. And so here comes Alberts, with a recommendation to cut UNO football. What will the Huskers think?

I know Alberts, and he did not take this lightly. He's a football guy and former player. If there's blood on his ax, it includes some of his own.

The bottom line is, Alberts is taking care of UNO's future, its best interests, just as Osborne would do for UNL. Hockey has become UNO's Husker football. And a financially fit UNO means a healthy hockey program.

There's another angle at work here. The one high hurdle folks thought Alberts might never clear is getting the Board of Regents to approve UNO going Division I. Why? Voting to create an in-state competitor for NU football would be widely frowned upon. Under this plan, that is no longer an issue.

What's indisputable is UNO is on the verge of deciding its own fate. The Mavs want to take on Creighton in this hoops market, and let the comparison of admission standards begin. They're going to feed the hockey machine. No longer will they have to worry about Division II dragging down hockey, or even what happens to Division II. They're not UNL. They're not UNK. They're the city school, bustling and growing and doing the city thing. It's a risk, but that's what bold people who aren't afraid to make changes do. Welcome to the new UNO.

This saga reminds me of a signature line from a classic movie, "The Shawshank Redemption." The line is, "Get busy livin' or get busy dyin.' "

Today, Maverick fans must feel like they're doing a little bit of both.

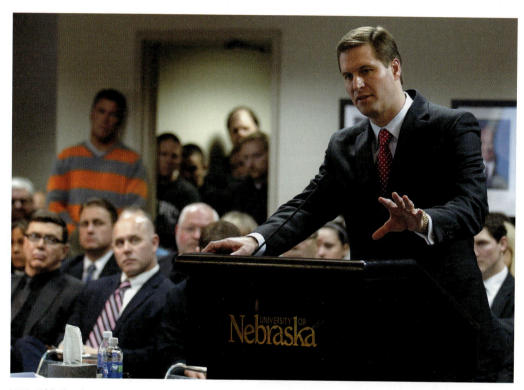

UNO Athletic Director Trev Alberts recommends the school's move to Division I to the Nebraska Board of Regents. Members of the Mavericks' national championship wrestling team were out in force.

Strange Night, but a Good One for CU

SAME LONG-SLEEVED white shirt. Same liberal use of timeouts. Same familiar walk off the court after a loss: quickly, head down.

Wait a minute. What's that? A security guard following Dana Altman? In Omaha? Really?

Next thing you know, Tom Osborne will need a police escort home from work.

It was a sign of the evening, a very strange evening, one of those nights where all 12,381 fans will have to go home and watch the film to make sure it happened. Dana Altman lost to Creighton 84-76 in the CBI finals, and there's a sentence nobody ever thought they'd read.

It was weird science, from Altman coaching on the opposite end to that security guard trailing him to the visitors' locker room.

Maybe the guard was there to show Altman where to dress.

"I've never been in here before," Altman said afterward.

No guard was necessary. That was a good thing.

Altman's return to Omaha, nearly one year after he left the Creighton job he had held for 16 years, went off without a negative vibe.

If there was a "boo" when Altman appeared before tipoff, it was drowned out by the applause as he entered the court.

Or the loud cheer when he was announced to the crowd as the head coach of Oregon.

Afterward, as he made his quick exit to the locker room, Creighton fans above the tunnel stood and clapped and cheered, and the only sound like "boo" was some students yelling "C-U! C-U!"

That doesn't mean everyone was happy. I saw several longtime Creighton fans stand with their arms folded — not cheering — when Altman was introduced.

What's the old saying? If you can't say something nice about someone, don't say anything at all.

Even the dissidents were polite on Altman Homecoming Night.

"It was great," said former CU player and assistant Nick Bahe, the Jays' radio color analyst. "It was perfect."

"I thought the crowd response was great," said Jays assistant Darian DeVries, a holdover from Altman's staff here. "The way it should have been."

"It was what I expected," said Creighton Athletic Director Bruce Rasmussen. "We have an intelligent crowd. People knew this was the time to properly thank Dana for all that he'd done here."

It was perfect. And the response provided the classy ending that this story was missing a year ago, when Altman left without saying goodbye, or anything, even to some of his closest friends.

He had returned last summer to speak to the players and friends he had left behind. But Altman used this trip to get personal again. As the Jays stretched and warmed up, Altman walked out to greet some of his former players.

So all that was left was to meet and greet the 12,000 or so folks Altman lured into buying Creighton season tickets years ago.

"I didn't know what to expect," Altman said. "People were great. They were great to us for 16 years here. It was a great atmosphere."

But now the Jays have to hit the road, and do it on the Matisse painting that is the Oregon basketball floor. Let's hope they don't get lost in the woods at midcourt at Matthew Knight Arena.

The Jays know their way around the Qwest Center. And they played with endless energy. Not that they were lacking incentive.

"It was definitely a little weird, seeing him on the other bench," said Antoine Young.

Weird?

"He was calling out plays that I knew from last year," Young said. "I knew what they were running because I ran it here."

Did it help?

"It didn't hurt," Young said.

Young and his teammates gave their former coach some flashbacks — and some moments he hadn't seen in a while.

Gregory Echenique (15 points, nine rebounds, four blocks), the transfer from Rutgers who was recruited originally by Altman for CU, showed the coach what he missed this year. Young, Josh Jones (11 points) and Kenny Lawson all played like they were trying to impress the old guy. Even Kaleb Korver hit a 3-pointer right in front of Altman.

The one guy Altman didn't recognize was the guy he'll study on film on the trip home: Doug McDermott, who led CU with 21 points and was flashing his multiple skills around the rim with both hands.

It was a terrific game, played at a breathless, racehorse pace at times. Altman's new team looked quicker, but his former team found more energy at all the right times.

Wonder why.

"It wasn't for him," Young said. "We really were trying to treat it like another game. We're trying to win. We're trying to win the CBI."

Do they make banners for beating your old coach?

Oregon basketball coach Dana Altman congratulates one of his former players, Josh Jones, on Creighton's win.

APRIL 19, 2011 • OMAHA STORM CHASERS

Werner's a Winner for Storm Chasers

IF YOU STILL don't understand why the Omaha Storm Chasers couldn't play ball downtown, take a drive out to Werner Park.

It becomes obvious as soon as you walk through the gate. The activity. The energy. The noise (a little loud; turn down the volume, please). Everywhere you look, there's stuff.

And by that I mean a merry-go-round (always busy), pickup basketball court (always full), wiffle ball field, playground and bouncy house. The bar in center field, when it gets over 50 degrees, will be a pen for social animals, à la the Qwest Center end zone for Creighton games.

Then there are the face painters. Long line. Forget law school. My girls are going to learn how to paint faces. Everywhere you go these days, there are face painters. Must be a nice racket.

It goes on and on. It's day care with a double-header. A three-ring circus with a baseball game. And the Chasers couldn't do most of it — including pocket the lion's share of the money from those long lines at all the concession stands — at TD Ameritrade Park.

When I met with Sarpy County officials a couple of years ago about this idea, I admired their vision but said there was no way they'd ever pull this off. They had to be proud on opening night. They did this right.

Werner Park is the new home for the Omaha Storm Chasers, the AAA team of the Kansas City Royals.

An Atmosphere That Can Warm the Heart, if Not the Toes

IT WAS AMAZING. It was strange. It was history. It was very cool. Make that very cold.

Sixty-four years from now, when the good folks of Omaha are debating whether to tear down the old ballpark and build a sports bio-dome, historians may look back at a tape of opening night at TD Ameritrade and wonder what was up with all of the empty seats.

It was cold, man.

You get only one chance to witness history. That explains why an estimated 18,000 fans — not the 22,197 announced number of tickets sold — showed up for the inaugural baseball game at Omaha's new downtown baseball gem.

If it hadn't been opening night, there would have been a lot fewer folks braving the temperatures in the 30s. And nobody would have blamed them.

So it wasn't a Norman Rockwell kind of opening night, with the sun shining and 24,000 fans wrapped tight around the new park in a glistening ribbon of blue and red.

It was a TD Ameritrade kind of opening night, which meant a good chunk of the crowd spent the evening in the concourse, where they could circulate the blood in their legs and watch the action at the same time.

By the late innings on the celebrated night, our big-league park looked like an Orioles-A's crowd had broken out.

The weather put a bit of a damper on opening night. Then again, it's April in Omaha.

That's why you build a concourse the size of a four-lane highway. That's why you have a club level, and why you plop down club level money, for a club level kind of night. Pass the Grey Poupon. Hotter the better.

Mother Nature could change the evening. But she couldn't spoil it.

It was a historic night. Great night. A night to remember, even for Creighton, which fell to Nebraska 2-1.

The Jays might have had some jitters in their new home. The vaunted CU defense had three errors.

The Huskers won the first game at Ameritrade Park on the back, or arm, of a Nebraska kid. Logan Ehlers, the freshman from Nebraska City, entered the game in the fourth and held CU to two hits in 5 1/3 innings. If Ehlers continues on a track to the major leagues one day, then Ameritrade Park will have that going for it. Which is nice.

The game between rivals was a mere sideshow.

The real star of the show was the gorgeous new park.

Down in the Nebraska dugout, head coach Mike Anderson looked around in awe at the fine-cut lawn and the navy blue seats.

"I love it," Anderson said. "The fans are right on top of you. It's going to be great for the fans. It has a great feel to it."

In the Creighton dugout, Dennis Poppe, the NCAA official in charge of the College World Series, was a kid in college baseball's biggest and newest candy store. Poppe was trying to imagine what this will be like in June, when it's warmer, when the world will be watching our new stage.

"It's very impressive," Poppe said. "What Rosenblatt did for Omaha, providing an icon, an 'I've got to go there' feeling, this stadium will do the same thing. It's a 2011 version."

One of the unique, and surreal, things about this evening was the backdrop. No more Desert Dome. No more I-80.

Hello, Kerrey Bridge. Hello, Qwest Center. Hello, downtown Omaha.

Oh, what a view. Especially at night. When the lights go up, TD Ameritrade Park is the place to be. Coors Field in Denver has great views. But there can't be many in baseball like this one.

On a cold night to remember, the thought was enough to warm your heart, legs and other extremities.

APRIL 20, 2011 • NEBRASKA/CREIGHTON BASEBALL

Bundled-up Creighton and Nebraska fans face the flag beyond center field for the national anthem at the inaugural game at TD Ameritrade Park.

JUNE 18, 2011 • COLLEGE WORLD SERIES

We Have a Lot of Good Years Ahead of Us

IT'S OPENING DAY of the 2051 College World Series. And two guys in the bleachers are talking about the story of the week.

"Can you believe that knucklehead mayor?" Joe asked.

"You mean the moron who wants to build a new ballpark?" Sam replied.

"Talk about spitting on tradition," Joe said. "He's going to ruin the event. I mean, he's talking about building a dome, with a movie theater, three restaurants and a shopping mall inside."

"Go figure," Sam said. "You remember the days when you just went to the ballpark to occasionally watch the game, walk around the concourse and hit a bar across the street afterward?"

"It's sad," Joe said. "They don't make ballparks like these anymore, with the walk-around concourses. And this is one of the last stadiums of its kind, without a roof. Say goodbye to the sun. What will you miss the most?"

"I'll miss parking downtown and walking up 12th Street," Sam said. "I don't know how many times I walked up that street with my dad, past all of the vendors, and looked up at that scoreboard with the 'Home of the College World Series' staring at you. It was like Main Street, CWS. Just magical."

"I'll miss that Zesto across the street," Joe said. "My dad told me about how they used to have to stand in line for a shake. Now you can call them up and they'll deliver to your seat in the stadium. I bet that they won't have that at the new dome."

"How about the sushi stand in right field?" Sam said. "It doesn't get any more old-fashioned than that."

"Or standing outside the team entrance on 13th Street, watching the players get off the bus and go through the door and down the tunnel," Joe said. "I have no idea where they went, but it was always cool watching them."

"I'll miss Diesing Plaza," Sam said. "That's the coolest entrance to a stadium in baseball, outside the right-field corner, with the 'Road to Omaha' statue there. It's where everyone hangs out, meets friends and family, takes photos with the skyline in the background."

JUNE 18, 2011 • COLLEGE WORLD SERIES

"You gotta love autograph day," Joe said. "I don't mind paying the $100 for a team autograph. The kids might be getting paid now, but they can always use the extra cash."

"Bet they won't have a kids' zone at the new dome," Sam said. "My dad always took me there. Remember they had a deal where you could throw to a former CWS star? I struck out some guy named Will Bolt. He threw the bat at me."

"I hope they have a major league corner, where the former big leaguers who played in the College World Series show up and sign autographs," Joe said. "I'll never forget meeting Taylor Jungmann. Great guy. He played for Texas, back before they became an independent and tried to start their own NCAA."

"What are they going to do with the College World Series Hall of Fame?" Joe asked. "They just built that 35 years ago. It attracts visitors year-round. You can't just move that, you know."

"Right," Sam said. "Or the Stadium View card shop. You can walk in there anytime and get a BBQ sandwich and a beer. For free."

"Is that where you bought that poster of Rosenblatt Stadium?" Joe asked.

"Yeah," Sam said. "Hard to believe that they actually played baseball in that place, isn't it? My kid's high school field is nicer."

"Look, they better have tailgating at this new dome," Joe said. "And room for my recliner and 80-inch full-definition TV."

"I just hope they have the portable bars and buffet lines set up in the parking lot, like they do now," Sam said. "Can you imagine tailgating without those?"

"And where do they expect us to play sand volleyball on the way back to our car, like we do now at the New Old Mattress Factory?" Joe asked.

"I don't know, but by the sounds of the new place, I won't be seeing my kids very much," Sam said. "Besides a movie theater, they're going to have a video arcade, batting cages and a separate baseball diamond, so the kids can play ball during the CWS. In fact, they're going to have a kids' tournament while the CWS is going on."

"Where are they going to put this amazing, wonderful new tribute to technology and corporate greed?" Joe asked.

"Down in South O, up on 13th Street, across from the zoo," Sam said.

"What a terrible idea," Joe said. "Who would ever go to a game there?"

TOM'S TAKE

REFLECTIONS ON

Time Is Right for Jays to Shine Downtown

CALL IT RENAISSANCE Row. D.J. Sokol Arena. Morrison Stadium. TD Ameritrade Park. The Qwest Center. They loom in north downtown Omaha like a skyline, on the Boulevard of Big Dreams.

Take football stadiums out of the equation. Does anyone in college sports have a more impressive lineup of home fields and courts than Creighton University?

Sokol Arena is lifting CU women's hoops and volleyball. Morrison Stadium and the Qwest Center have transformed Jays soccer and basketball. Put them on the map, locally and nationally.

Now it's Ed Servais' turn. Can Creighton baseball become a national player in its new digs? Or is 24,000-seat TD Ameritrade Park too big for its white and blue britches?

Here's what we know about TD Ameritrade Park: It doesn't have a ceiling. Now, neither does CU baseball. The future looks as big as the outfield and as wide as those concourses.

Are they paying attention at Haymarket Park? Creighton baseball has been the little brother around here. Don't look now, but little bro is about to hit a growth spurt. Is there any reason Creighton can't become Nebraska's equal — or better — in baseball?

The potential is there. The gap between the programs could close in a hurry. Creighton now has the best baseball facility in the state. Nebraska, meanwhile, is heading to the irrelevant world of Big Ten baseball. The Huskers could brag to the state's top talent that they played in the superior baseball league. Not anymore.

You can make the argument that the Valley is as good as, if not better than the Big Ten in baseball. Since the Big Ten's last College World Series appearance (Michigan, 1984), the Valley has had four schools make the CWS field: Wichita State, Creighton, Indiana State and Missouri State.

I don't want to bore you with Valley/Big Ten comparisons. But it's a push. Beginning next year, Creighton and Nebraska will have the same chance to make an NCAA regional: win your league or league tournament.

It's an interesting question: When Creighton and Nebraska go head-to-head for the top players in the future, will the Jays have the edge, playing in a facility that has the look and feel of a major league park?

Only if they can take advantage of their new situation. That's coach Ed Servais' department. He has a clear vision of Creighton baseball as a cousin to Creighton basketball, or even Gonzaga basketball. Maybe the Wichita State baseball of old, a program that carried itself as a CWS program in a mid-major league, with big-time facilities and schedule.

It's a vision that includes Creighton as a dominant Midwest program. A mid-major that, in this day of Oregon State and Fresno State, can make and win the CWS.

"I'd like to see us become a program like that," Servais said. "A program that plays at the highest levels, that plays on TV, that makes (recruits) take notice."

Step one will be to upgrade the schedule. With the home of the CWS as bait, he promises to lure some big fish to Omaha for non-conference games.

The Jays now practice every day at the home of the CWS. They dress every day in what amounts to a big-league clubhouse. If that doesn't open new doors for Creighton baseball, nothing will.

D.J. Sokol Arena is home to Creighton volleyball and women's basketball.

— APRIL 24, 2011

THE CHANGING SPORTS LANDSCAPE   2011

Osborne Building Strong Legacy as Athletic Director

DON'T ORDER THE rocking chair. Don't pick out a fishing boat. Tom Osborne isn't ready. He doesn't have time to retire.

There's a Memorial Stadium expansion project. Devaney Center renovation. New basketball practice facility going up. And a Haymarket arena that needs to jump from drawing board to shovel and dirt.

Meanwhile, he just extended and sweetened the contract of men's basketball coach Doc Sadler through 2016.

Last, but not least, he bumped up football coach Bo Pelini to $2.78 million per year, and added a year, through 2015, when the contract will pay Pelini $3.1 million. And yet, all of this activity, particularly the last two salary increases, raises a good question about Osborne.

Is the patriarch of Nebraska athletics getting his things in order so he can ride off into the sunset sooner than later?

Right now, all I see is a white Tahoe, not a horse. And Osborne's Tahoe is parked outside the Osborne Complex, not headed for a retirement house on Lake McConaughy.

"I suppose if you're a person in leadership, you don't want your successor worse off than you are," said Osborne, 74. "But I don't have a drop-dead date. No timetable. I don't have a contract. I work entirely at the chancellor's pleasure.

"I don't want to be around until I'm 85 or 90. That's always been a big concern for me, throughout my career, that you stay longer than you should. I'll know when it's time. Right now, we have some things in the works that I would like to see through."

That would be the hoops practice facility (set to open later this year), east Memorial Stadium project (2013), basketball arena (2013) and Devaney renovation (2014). Using that as a guide, it's easy to see Osborne on the job through at least 2013.

There's no hurry. Osborne is quietly and methodically — how else would he do it? — building an impressive résumé as A.D., including that little move to the Big Ten Conference.

In fact, with a little help from Pelini, Osborne could one day leave NU with a legacy as athletic director that would rival his legacy as football coach. Don't worry. That doesn't mean two statues.

It's apples and oranges. Osborne's coaching legacy was built over 25 years. It's made up of winning big and winning consistently and doing things the right way. His impact as A.D. has been more of a whirlwind, by comparison. But it's full of substance.

But his legacy needs some help from Pelini. If Bo can produce a Big Ten title, Rose Bowl and/or national championship, then Osborne's golden touch will have extended to the A.D.'s desk. If not, the legacy will be good, but will be missing the thing Husker fans crave: a return to football prominence.

Either way, he's done more than anyone — including him — could have imagined that Tuesday in October 2007, when most of us thought that he was taking over to calm the waters and hire a new football coach before heading back to the fishing boat.

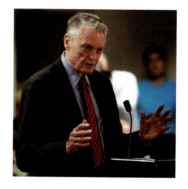

> "I'll know when it's time (to retire). Right now, we have some things in the works that I would like to see through."
>
> — TOM OSBORNE, NEBRASKA ATHLETIC DIRECTOR

A lot of people thought that Osborne would be lost at a time when athletic directors are schmoozers and salesmen, guys with their hands out. But the old conservative coach has been raising and spending money like another local icon. Guy named Warren Buffett.

"He has two things that every athletic director wants — credibility and trust," said Trev Alberts, UNO's A.D. "When you have those two things, a lot of doors can open for you."

In his second career, as A.D., Osborne has had the charge of starting something up, bringing Nebraska football back to life. Unlike his first career, Osborne has no direct control over that. But clearly it's on the right track.

Osborne has built a path to the future. He deserves a chance to enjoy the ride.

— MAY 1, 2011

SHATEL
TOM'S TAKE ON 20 UNFORGETTABLE YEARS OF SPORTS
BY TOM SHATEL

EDITOR
Dan Sullivan

DESIGNER
Christine Zueck

ASSISTANT EDITORS
Rich Mills
Frank Hassler

CONTRIBUTING EDITORS
Pam Richter
Pam Thomas
Bob Glissmann
Jim Anderson

PHOTO IMAGING
Jolene McHugh

RESEARCHERS
Jeanne Hauser
Michelle Gullett
Sheritha Jones

PRINT AND PRODUCTION COORDINATORS
Pat "Murphy" Benoit
Wayne Harty

SPORTS EDITOR
Thad Livingston

DIRECTOR OF PHOTOGRAPHY
Jeff Bundy

DIRECTOR OF MARKETING
Rich Warren

South Carolina celebrates its 2010 national title at the final College World Series at Rosenblatt Stadium.

INDEX

Alberts, Trev 21, 28, 268, 269, 283, 286, 287
Alcindor, Lew 59
Allen, Francis 11, 18
Allen, Forrest "Phog" 148
Altman, Dana 41, 46, 62, 76, 94, 129, 132, 178, 189, 206, 240, 241, 247, 248, 270, 288
Anderson, Gary 210, 249
Anderson, Mick 30
Anderson, Mike 290
Anderson, Ryan 230
Anderson, Sydney 257
Aspegren, Kelly 52

Badgett, Terrance 31
Baer, Ted 15, 159
Bailey, Bryan 82
Barnes, Nelson 110
Baum, Jay 111
Beck, Tim 285
Behrns, Pat 71, 121, 247, 286
Bencurik, Ryan 105
Benes, Alan 29
Bennett, Byron 4
Benning, Damon 88, 96, 199
Berringer, Brook 40, 53, 54, 82, 143
Bertman, Skip 84, 242
Bevilacqua, Lee "Doc" 113
Blais, Dean 280, 282
Blake, Lindsay 251
Bolowich, Elmar 282
Boozer, Bob 12
Bowden, Bobby 42
Bowden, DeAnthony 196
Brand, Myles 258
Brehaut, Jeff 86
Brown, Chris 167
Brown, Derek 9
Brown, Mike 140
Bryant, Don 111
Buchanan, Philip 174
Buffett, Warren 13, 249
Buford, Rodney 94, 129, 132
Burrow, Jamie 167
Bush, George W. 162
Byrne, Bill 48, 56, 68, 170

Calahan, Tom 242
Callahan, Bill 198, 203, 204, 205, 219, 221, 238, 243, 247
Carter, Justin 263
Chalmers, James 105
Chalmers, Mario 250
Chamberlain, Joba 216, 225, 247
Chandler, Derrick 3, 23, 28, 31
Childress, Rob 150
Christensen, John 268, 269
Chubick, Bruce 23, 31
Cipriano, Joe 2
Clanton, Jon 146
Claussen, Connie 94
Collier, Barry 186, 201, 211, 224
Cook, John 184, 220, 224, 232, 247
Costner, Kevin 66, 261
Crandell, Kenya 209
Crouch, Eric 165, 166, 168, 174
Crudup, Jevon 23
Cuevas, Jesse 95

Dahm, Jack 59
Daub, Hal 74
Davis, Tristan 238
Davis, Wes 100
Davison, Matt 106
Dedeaux, Rod 225
Delaney, Matt 86
Delaney, Jim 275, 282
Denney, Mike 212, 283, 286
Dent, Bucky 173
Deren, Brody 178
Detmer, Koy 21
Devaney, Bob 9, 11, 24, 25, 26, 98, 99, 143
Diesing, Jack Jr. 258
Dodds, DeLoss 281
Dotzler, Josh 261
Duncan, Donnie 10, 56, 281

Echo-Hawk, Tobin 64
Ellis, Dan 159
Elmer, Melissa 220
Elworth, Jim 251
Emfinger, Max 12
Enenbach, Jon 177
Erickson, Bret 76
Erickson, Dennis 8
Erstad, Darin 65

Ferentz, Kirk 261
Ferguson, Robert 277
Flynn, Kelly 270
Fraser, Ron 16
Frazier, Tommie 14, 20, 37, 43, 55, 73, 78, 143, 199
Frost, Scott 12, 88, 89, 96, 102, 107, 110, 115, 143
Fry, Hayden 123
Fuente, Justin 93

Gabbert, Blaine 267
Ganz, Joe 248, 262
Garner, Bernard 80
Garrido, Augie 181, 199
Gibbs, Gary 5
Gibson, Bob 118, 128
Gill, Turner 3, 168, 208
Gordon, Alex 215
Gorman, Bill 29
Graham, Wayne 191
Grear, Ron 15
Green, Ahman 51
Greinke, Zack 199
Griffin, Kelsey 273
Griffin, Maggie 220
Griffin, Marcus 229
Gunderson, Kevin 228
Gutierrez, Rick 47
Gutschewski, Scott 202

Hansen, Marc 19
Harvey, Ken 133
Hastings, Mike 172
Henderson, John 153
Hendry, Jim 7, 95
Henery, Alex 256
Herbster, David 209
Herman, Mike 251
Herold, Bob 210
Heyns, Penny 97
Hicks, Jarrett 204
Higdon, Ron 209
Higdon, Sandy 209
Hoggan, Jeff 149
Hoiberg, Fred 59
Hopper, Matt 187
Houghtelling, Christina 220
House, Larry 189
Huelshoist, Jerry 15

Idelman, Steve 32, 39

Jackson, Keith 225
James, Peaches 190
Jaworski, Tom 218
Jenkins, MarTay 87
Jeter, Lance 283
Johnson, Christy 72
Johnson, Donnie 144
Johnson, Jamar 45
Johnson, Trevor 192
Jones, Calvin 36
Jones, Corby 107
Jones, Donta 37
Jones, Josh 288

Kelsay, Chad 122
Kemp, Mike 104, 149, 158, 187
Kerns, Bud 15
Kiffin, Monte 186
Knight, Bob 176
Kofoed, Bart 32
Komine, Shane 150
Korver, Kyle 160, 188, 237
Kotsay, Mark 67
Koufax, Sandy 135
Krohn, Bob 17
Kropp, Tom 35
Kubik, Nicole 128

Landry, Leon 264
Lasorda, Tommy 59
Leach, Mike 204
Leahy, Don 87, 92, 104
Lee, Don 34
Leise, Bob 161
Leise, Jeff 161
Lewis, Yale 180
Lieberman-Cline, Nancy 49
Lil' Red, 113, 143
Locker, Jake 271
Lovelady, Greg 171
Lue, Tyronn 58, 95, 116

Mackovic, John 90
Makovicka, Jeff 53
Makovicka, Joel 112, 125
Mancuso, Bob 111
Maric, Aleks 236
Markowski, Andy 116, 131
Martin, Mike 134
Martinez, Taylor 278
McBride, Charlie 20, 37, 76, 88, 128, 146
McCant, Keithen 9
McCarney, Dan 172
McCarthy, Mick 251
McCartney, Bill 2, 4, 12, 29, 57
McConnell, Nils 251
McDermott, Doug 283
McDermott, Greg 274
McDill, Cori 130
McDonald, Darnell 122
McGuire, Al 2
McKenna, Kevin 113, 198
McKinney, Tyler 198
Meendering, Nancy 6
Mendoza, Russell 112
Miller, Jim 251
Minor, Damon 47
Mitchell, Johnny 5
Moore, Lindsey 272
Moore, Mikki 81
Moore, Tom 41
Moran, Mike 18, 19, 253
Morgan, P.J. 27
Morris, Warren 84, 85

Morrissey, Dan 222
Motz, Jimmy 213
Navratilova, Martina 13
Nee, Danny 23, 28, 31, 44, 59, 63, 80, 116, 148
Neumann, Tim 77
Newcombe, Bobby 155
Nunn, Terrence 229

O'Hanlon, Matt 266
Orr, Johnny 40
Osborne, Nancy 58, 108
Osborne, Tom iii, 8, 9, 10, 11, 12, 14, 26, 28, 42, 54, 58, 61, 68, 69, 88, 94, 102, 106, 108, 109, 110, 114, 136, 137, 143, 200, 234, 236, 244, 247, 275, 295

Parrella, John 21
Paul, Niles 265
Pavan, Sarah 237
Payne, Jack 33
Pederson, Steve 185, 194, 195, 198, 200, 237, 239, 243, 247
Pelini, Bo 183, 187, 192, 193, 247, 249, 254, 279, 285
Perlman, Harvey 275
Peter, Christian 41
Peter, Jason 93
Petersen, Darin 48
Pettit, Terry 6, 52, 70, 72, 141, 144, 173
Phelps, Michael 252
Phillips, Lawrence 55, 68, 69, 143
Piatkowski, Eric 3, 31, 44
Pierce, Jack 12
Pinkel, Gary 271
Pivovar, Greg 224
Pope, Orlando 236
Poppe, Dennis 27, 33, 156, 290
Prends, Alex 171

Rachels, Wes 117
Raiola, Dominic 152
Rasmussen, Bruce 113, 157, 282
Reed, Ed 174
Rehberg, Matt 2
Revelle, Rhonda 64
Riley, Jim 58
Rodgers, Johnny 145, 255
Rosenblatt, Steve 34
Ross, Cory 193, 221
Ruud, Barrett 173
Ryan, Katie 209

Sadler, Doc 230, 270, 284
Sanderford, Paul 130
Sanders, John 48
Sayers, Gale 227
Schlesinger, Cory 60
Schuchart, Mike 145
Schwartz, Brooke 130
Schwartz, Rachel 257
Sears, Ryan 113, 147, 158
Seaton, Tim 48
Servais, Ed 237, 294
Shanle, Scott 167
Shatel, Annamarie Jean 245
Shatel, Jennifer Phillip 119
Shatel, Katherine Paige 214
Shatel, Sarah Suzanne 169

Shires, Rose 91
Shriver, Pam 13
Sieckmann, Tom 17
Simon, Bret 127
Skogland, Mike 105
Smith, Chris 101
Smith, Kathleen 251
Snyder, Bill 120, 122, 193
Solich, Frank 108, 109, 125, 138, 143, 145, 168, 193, 194, 195
Spanheimer, Laura 207
Spanier, Graham 26, 56, 59
Spencer, Jack 15
Stai, Brenden 41
Stark, Jack 88
Stein, Alan 248
Stewart, Ed 53
Stewart, Kordell 41
Stewart, Norm 128
Suh, Ndamukong 260, 265, 267
Sutton, Eddie 112

Tagge, Jerry 93
Taylor, Aaron 111
Taylor, Terrell 179
Taylor, Zac 210, 231
Tenopir, Milt 88
Thater, Stephanie 13
Thibault, Mike 32
Thies, Doug 251
Thomas, Benard 205
Thompson, Dean 49
Thompson, Ed 121
Thompson, Tolly 77
Tolliver, Anthony 240
Torres, Johnny 103
Tubbs, Billy 38

Van Horn, Dave 112, 129, 133, 144, 158, 162
Van Horn, Karen 133
Varnes, Blair 134
Vermeer, Bob 164
Vermeer, Ryan 164
Vigness, Brent 64
Vitale, Dick 31
Vlieger, Brandt 144
Volk, Dave 165
Vosik, Andy 48

Wald, Tom 80
Walden, Jim 40
Walker, Ben 76, 158
Warming, Bob 22, 187
Washington, Fabian 204
Watts, Dane 230
Weber, Bruce 189
West, Matt 147
West, Mike 101
Weston, Allison 70
Wiegert, Erik 5
Wiegert, Zach 54
Wiggins, Shevin 106
Williams, Jamel 79
Wistrom, Grant 90, 95, 110
Woodhead, Danny 247
Woolridge, Andre 77
Wright, Jim 27
Wuerffel, Danny 79

Yori, Connie 59, 172, 186, 236, 270, 272
Yori, Mary 59, 64
Young, Dan 182

Zambri, Chris 151
Zanon, Greg 187

2011 INSIGHT I've enjoyed my relationship with Tom Osborne over the years. It has certainly never been dull. The first time we met I was sitting in a hot tub in the Manhattan, Kan., Holidome, and he stopped to argue about something I'd written. He would call me at home (before cellphones) when he had something to say or correct. He also announced my engagement to the world at the press conference the day before he coached his last game. He has an understated, yet pointed, sense of humor. That came out again in the late 1990s after a Nebraska home game. Osborne figured it was his turn to second-guess me. He was walking through the press box to do his postgame radio show. I felt someone stop and look over my shoulder as I was writing. It was Osborne, who said, "You misspelled a word." Touché. Osborne remembered doing that and agreed to re-enact the scene for this book. It's now one of my all-time favorite photos.

P.S.

Back when it seemed as if we covered the Orange Bowl every year, we made a lot of friends in South Florida. One of my favorites was "Andy" Massimino, one of the OB media chiefs and a high school vice principal in Miami. Andy used to check us in at the media room every year and, for a reason that escaped us, had his name in quotes. From left, "Lee" Barfknecht, "Eric" Olson and "Tom" pose with our main Orange Bowl guy.

Long, long ago, in a place far, far away — OK, Dallas in 1990 — the press box at Texas Stadium was patrolled by Randy Galloway, the legendary columnist and character then at the Dallas Morning News. Of course, he had a few opinions, which he would share at any given moment. Some of those moments happened when Randy decided that Cowboys coach Jimmy Johnson had made a bone-headed call. Running play on third-and-10. Reverse that went for a big loss. At that moment, Galloway would yell out, "OK, give me the headset," and while he wouldn't get the phone down to the sideline, he would get a huge laugh in the press box. "Give me the headset," a weekly column that ran in The World-Herald from 2002 to 2005, was dedicated to Galloway and all the other Galloways in the stands yelling for a headset during Nebraska games.

I went back to school in 2008, in the same way that Rodney Dangerfield once did. The class was called "Football 202," taught by Professor Bo Pelini. It was a way for Nebraska football to raise some money and offer the serious football fans a front-row look into the program. The best way to describe it would be to ask one question: Would you pay $249 to spend the day with Pelini and his staff in their football cave? A total of 132 said "yes."

A note from University of Nebraska-Lincoln Chancellor Harvey Perlman, acknowledging "the joys of girls' sports."

Dear Tom,
Congratulations on your new baby girl, but more importantly, on your recognition of the joys of girls sports. As a father of two daughters, let me warn you there is nothing colder than a girls soccer match in November!
Harvey

298 • 20 YEARS WITH TOM SHATEL

PHOTOGRAPHERS INDEX

Bob Bailie: 187

Bill Batson: 13, 53, 64, 121, 130, 141, 149, 163, 166, 225

Jeff Beiermann: 2, 13, 47, 50, 58, 71, 72, 78, 87, 90, 95, 110, 113, 115, 127, 130, 137, 138, 139, 140, 142, 144, 145, 147, 159, 164, 173, 174, 175, 179, 181, 189, 191, 198, 199, 201, 209, 210, 211, 213, 218, 219, 222, 225, 231, 235, 237, 248, 249, 261, 264, 270, 272, 273, 274, 283

Jeff Bundy: 3, 5, 7, 9, 15, 16, 23, 29, 32, 48, 54, 55, 59, 63, 66, 73, 82, 85, 86, 101, 102, 117, 120, 122, 128, 132, 145, 148, 150, 158, 159, 162, 165, 167, 168, 171, 179, 185, 188, 192, 193, 198, 208, 237, 242, 261

James R. Burnett: cover, iii, iv, 8, 126, 135, 190, 197, 206, 207, 216, 237, 244, 284, 297, 298

Jeffrey Z. Carney: 6, 28, 76, 77, 80, 81, 89, 93, 95, 96, 100, 106, 108, 114, 123, 128, 131, 144, 146, 152, 187, 225

Craig Chandler: 83, 229

Kiley Cruse: 2, 92, 103, 107, 116, 125, 145, 155, 158, 173, 187, 194

Mark Davis: 33, 277, 282, 283

DLR Group of Omaha: 156

Rebecca S. Gratz: front cover, ii, 58, 199, 202, 204, 217, 221, 225, 228, 230, 236, 240, 248, 252, 260, 261, 265, 270, 271, 272, 273, 288, 289, 295, 296, 299

Laura Inns: 160, 172, 173, 176, 183, 190, 196, 198, 226, 236, 251, 255, 269

Richard Janda: 49, 51, 59, 67, 74

Phil Johnson: 12, 18, 20, 22, 25, 27, 34, 36, 40, 59, 79, 94, 105, 113, 124, 158, 172, 178, 180, 211, 234

Chris Machian: iv, 280, 292

Yano Melingagio: 24

Matt Miller: cover, 10, 52, 182, 184, 186, 187, 200, 203, 205, 215, 220, 224, 233, 236, 238, 243, 249, 250, 257, 261, 267, 279, 281

Nobuko Oyabu: iv, 91, 145, 153, 157, 172, 177

Robert Paskach: 4, 13, 14, 17, 39, 41, 77, 98

Ed Rath: 62

Jill Sagers: 94

Alyssa Schukar: i, 239, 256, 262, 263, 300, back cover

Kent Sievers: iv, 59, 151, 154, 161, 212, 223, 241, 243, 246, 247, 249, 254, 258, 259, 260, 266, 271, 275, 276, 278, 282, 283, 285, 286, 287, 291, 294, 298

Rudy Smith: 37, 41, 95, 97, 111, 118, 127, 129, 130, 134, 170, 224, 227

Sandy Summers: 113

Christine Thompson: 95, 133

Jannet Walsh: 45

Reprints of all Omaha World-Herald photos are available from the OWHstore for a fee. Call 402-444-1014 to place an order or go to owhstore.com.